D0519757

READING HISTORY

GENERAL EDITOR
Michael Biddiss
Professor of History, University of Reading

Reformation England 1480–1642

PETER MARSHALL

Senior Lecturer in History,
University of Warwick

A Member of the Hodder Headline Group
London
Distributed in the United States of America by
Oxford University Press Inc., New York

For Andrew and Margaret

First published in Great Britain in 2003 by
Arnold, a member of the Hodder Headline Group,
338 Euston Road, London NW1 3BH

http://www.arnoldpublishers.com

Distributed in the United States of America by
Oxford University Press Inc.
198 Madison Avenue, New York, NY10016

© 2003 Peter Marshall

All rights reserved. No part of this publication may be reproduced or transmitted in any form or by any means, electronically or mechanically, including photocopying, recording or any information storage or retrieval system, without either prior permission in writing from the publisher or a licence permitting restricted copying. In the United Kingdom such licences are issued by the Copyright Licensing Agency: 90 Tottenham Court Road, London W1T 4LP.

The advice and information in this book are believed to be true and accurate at the date of going to press, but neither the author nor the publisher can accept any legal responsibility or liability for any errors or omissions.

British Library Cataloguing in Publication Data
A catalogue record for this book is available from the British Library

Library of Congress Cataloging-in-Publication Data
A catalog record for this book is available from the Library of Congress

ISBN 0 340 70623 6 (hb)
ISBN 0 340 70624 4 (pb)

1 2 3 4 5 6 7 8 9 10

Typeset in 10/12 Sabon by Phoenix Photosetting, Chatham, Kent
Printed and bound in Great Britain by MPG Books Ltd, Bodmin, Cornwall

What do you think about this book? Or any other Arnold title?
Please send your comments to feedback.arnold@hodder.co.uk

Contents

General Editor's Preface

The aim of this series is to provide for students, especially at undergraduate level, a number of volumes devoted to major historical issues. Each of the selected topics is of such importance and complexity as to have produced the kind of scholarly controversy which not only sharpens our understanding of the particular problem in hand but also illuminates more generally the nature of history as a developing discipline. The authors have certainly been asked to examine the present state of knowledge and debate in their chosen fields, and to outline and justify their own current interpretations. But they have also been set two other important objectives. One has been that of quite explicitly alerting readers to the nature, range and variety of the primary sources most germane to their topics, and to the kind of difficulties (about, say, the completeness, authenticity or reliability of such materials) which the scholar then faces in using them as evidence. The second task has been to indicate how and why, even before our own time, the course of the particular scholarly controversy at issue actually developed in the way that it did – through, for example, enlargements in the scale of the available primary sources, or changes in historical philosophy or technique, or alterations in the social and political environment within which the debaters have been structuring their questions and devising their answers. Each author in the series has been left to determine the specific framework by means of which such aims might best be fulfilled within any single volume. However, all of us involved in 'Reading History' are united in our hope that the resulting books will be widely welcomed as up-to-date accounts worthy of recommendation to students who need not only reliable introductory guides to the subjects chosen but also texts that will help to enhance their more general appreciation of the contribution which historical scholarship and debate can make towards the strengthening of a critical and sceptical habit of mind.

MICHAEL BIDDISS
Professor of History
University of Reading

Acknowledgements

All history books are collaborative projects. In addition to the many scholars whose work I have drawn on in the course of writing this one, I would particularly like to thank a number of friends and colleagues who have read and commented on drafts of chapters, to my inestimable benefit: Bernard Capp, Eric Carlson, Will Coster, Andrew Foster, Beat Kümin, Alec Ryrie, Alexandra Walsham and Bill Wizeman SJ. I am also grateful to successive generations of Warwick undergraduate and masters students who have listened to me talk about the English Reformation, and whose responses have sharpened up my act. I am indebted to Christopher Wheeler for encouraging me to undertake this book, and to Lesley Riddle for patiently urging me to complete it. Finally, I must thank Bella, Mimi, Kit, and especially Ali, for putting up with my grumpiness and making life bearable as I struggled to the finish.

PM
University of Warwick

Author's Preface

This book aims to provide students and their teachers with a new introduction to the event (more properly, the process) that we call the English Reformation. There is a clear need for such a volume in light of the vast quantity of published research the topic has generated over the last twenty years or so, much of which remains inside professional journals and expensive monographs, and fairly inaccessible to non-specialists. The continued academic interest reflects the importance of the theme. The Reformation has been called 'a watershed without parallel in the entirety of English religious history'.[1] It has a claim to be considered one of the most significant transforming episodes in English history of any kind. England's political and constitutional development, its relations with the rest of Europe, its cultural and artistic life, the development of the English language itself, were all set on new and momentous courses as a result of the decision to break away from the structures and traditions of medieval Catholic Christendom. Interpretations of the English Reformation have always been contentious. From the sixteenth century onwards, Catholic and Protestant writers have clashed about the motives of reformers, and about whether their policies were beneficial or harmful to the nation. A confessional edge to the debates has persisted through to modern times, reflecting the extent to which interpretations of the Reformation touch upon essential questions of identity. Through the nineteenth, and much of the twentieth century, it was natural to think of the Reformation as a foundation stone of England's destiny as pillar of a forward-looking nation state, and later a world empire. The forces of liberalism and modernization were released by the twin overthrow of foreign (papal) jurisdiction and backward medieval belief. It may be no accident that the greater self-doubt besetting Britain in the 1970s coincided with the beginning of a wave of 'revisionist' scholarship, which reinterpreted the Reformation as a hard-fought contest with no obvious long-term causes and no preordained outcome. A revisionist emphasis on the vitality of the pre-Reformation Church, and on the unpopular and politically driven

[1] Patrick Collinson, 'With a Small "r"' (review of Christopher Haigh's *English Reformations*), *Times Literary Supplement* (Oct. 22, 1993), 14.

character of much of the process of reform, was achieving establishment status by the mid-1990s. But revisionism has been both accompanied and succeeded by a rising tide of 'post-revisionist' scholarship, showing some of that affinity for accentuating ambiguity and paradox which is characteristic of our contemporary 'post-modern' culture. The Reformation, post-revisionists tend to argue, should be read as a success story, but precisely because it was not as destructive or alien as the revisionists suppose: deep underlying continuities link the religious cultures of 'Catholic' and 'Protestant' England.

The pattern therefore seems to be one of interpretative 'orthodoxies', which prevail for a time before being questioned, overthrown and replaced. But the reality is much less neat and pre-packaged. 'Post-revisionist' works sometimes predate 'revisionist' ones; individual historians change their views over time, or apply revisionist perspectives to some periods and issues, post-revisionist ones to others; revisionists and post-revisionists argue among themselves; many books, articles and their authors (thankfully) defy convenient historiographical labelling. Shifting interpretations of the English Reformation have been accompanied at every stage by changes in the sorts of questions historians ask and the types of sources they consult. In the later twentieth century, the focus of interest broadened out from the archival records of the centre (Acts of Parliament, royal proclamations) to those of the localities (Church court records, churchwardens' accounts, wills), as historians recognized that religious change was not simply something decided upon and imposed by the government, but a process that had to be mediated and negotiated, welcomed or resisted, in a host of local communities. Interest in the Reformation as an agent of long-term social and cultural change has led to a further enlargement of the source-base. Scholars now look to a wider variety of printed and literary sources – news pamphlets, ballads, poetry and plays – as well as to the more overtly religious material in prayer books, sermon collections and guides to conduct. There is greater attention to a range of visual sources: surviving artefacts and buildings; paintings and woodcut illustrations in books; fonts, windows and monuments in churches. Once the Reformation was the virtual sole property of political and ecclesiastical historians. Now they have to share it with colleagues whose expertise lies in social and cultural history, with art historians, gender historians and literary scholars.

One response to the explosion of themes, sources and methodologies in recent scholarship would be to give up the idea that there is any kind of 'story' which can meaningfully be told, to abandon the tradition of chronological narrative and adopt a purely thematic approach. The temptation has been resisted in this book: readers will notice that all the chapter titles contain dates, which (though they meander slightly) are intended to convey something important, a broad sense of how the religious condition of England changed over time. There are certainly sections (and even chapters) which are principally thematic, though they have been arranged to follow a kind of chronological logic, if not always a strict chronological order. The aim throughout has been to intertwine narrative with analysis, to combine descriptions of what happened with explanations of how it happened and what it meant. In fact, however, the distinction often drawn between narrative and analysis is a rather false one. The selection of which 'facts' to report is itself an analytical exercise; any 'narrative' of the English Reformation supplies of its very nature (even if only implicitly) both a definition and an interpretation of what that process or event is supposed to be. In a book of this sort, an introduction to the English Reformation as a historical construction, the selection of meaningful events is largely determined by what previous scholars have thought to be significant, though my own assumptions (explicit and implicit) are undoubtedly present in the way the story has been shaped.

This book is structured in a way intended to maximize its usefulness to those taking or teaching courses dealing with the English Reformation, and those interested in scholarly approaches to late medieval and early modern religion more generally. Each chapter is constructed around a topic or issue which has generated academic controversy, and on which there is a developed and often complex secondary literature. Within each chapter, an introductory overview explains the significance of the topic, three or four subsections sharpen the focus on particular aspects and debates, and an appended brief 'summation' attempts to bring out some key conclusions and place them in a broader context. Overly technical vocabulary has been kept to a minimum, and unfamiliar terms are explained on their first occurrence. I hope that this structure and approach will provide meaningful assistance to students in their preparation for seminars, essays and exam revision. But the aim has not been to produce a study guide or a series of loosely connected essays. Taken together, the chapters in this book are intended to comprise a fairly comprehensive and comprehensible account of the English Reformation as a whole. While it seeks to give everyone their due, and to review the debates in a fair and dispassionate manner, I have not adopted a line of deliberate neutrality. In evaluating the controversies, I offer my own verdicts on which are the most fruitful lines of enquiry, and on the judgements, methodologies and sources of evidence, which most coherently give shape to an understanding of what the English Reformation was about. If readers are able to detect quirks, biases or inconsistencies in any aspects of the presentation, I will feel pleased that the book is succeeding in a primary aim: that of encouraging a critical and discriminatory reading of the secondary sources by students, who too often feel left at the mercy of persuasive 'experts'.

A couple of guiding assumptions require further preliminary remarks. One is the scope of the book's chronology. Any survey containing a significant narrative element has of course to begin and end somewhere, but why 1480 to 1642? The question of the units of study that historians choose for themselves ('periodization') neatly illustrates the point about the inseparability of narrative and interpretation. Older accounts which saw the English Reformation as fundamentally a political transaction, an 'act of state', required a relatively short time-span to incorporate the significant actions, a bare quarter century from Henry VIII's repudiation of the authority of the Pope in the early 1530s to Elizabeth I's parliamentary 'Settlement' of religion in 1559.[2] But if 'the Reformation' is defined as the period during which the religious culture of the nation changed from profoundly Catholic to emphatically Protestant, and the process by which that transformation came about, then a compact sixteenth-century time-frame simply will not do. Increasingly, the attention of historians is turning to the social and cultural aspects of religious change, the full effects of which took decades, if not generations, to become apparent. Over the last few years the concept of a 'long Reformation' has become widely accepted among historians, though this insight has yet made fairly little impact on the materials readily available to students. There is, however, no consensus about where precisely the bookends should be set, with more adventurous scholars proposing the Restoration (1660), the Glorious Revolution (1688) or even the early nineteenth century as terminal dates.[3] Arguably, the usefulness of 'the Reformation' as a concept for focussing historical understanding starts to decrease when it is stretched too far. At the same time, however, decisions about when to close the book inevitably help to predetermine conclusions about the 'success', the transformative potential of the Reformation process. An account which terminates in, say, 1570 is likely to offer very different assessments of the quality of the parish clergy or the popular response to Protestantism, than one that runs to 1600 or 1625.

The choice here of a slightly extended century and a half from the later fifteenth to the early to mid-seventeenth century is determined partly by pragmatic considerations, to allow the inclusion of as much as possible of the most relevant recent scholarship. But it is also intended to signal that the Reformation makes most sense when it is recognized to be the product of overlapping and interweaving cultural and political processes – both an 'act of state' (or series of acts of state) and a sequence of religious and social transformations. The opening date of 1480 is a somewhat arbitrary one, allowing a more leisurely discussion of the state of the Church and religion in pre-Reformation England than is possible in accounts that pitch in around 1529 (while avoiding the suggestion that there is anything particularly significant about the date 1500). It does, however, coincide with a marked rise in the persecution of Lollard heretics, which some (though by no means all) historians see as a significant precondition for the early reception of Protestant teaching. Protestant teaching was still working a transformative effect on the cultural life of the nation through the early decades of the

2 The 'act of state' tag was first applied by F.M. Powicke, *The Reformation in England* (London, 1941), p. 1.

3 See the essays in Nicholas Tyacke, ed., *England's Long Reformation 1500–1800* (London, 1998).

seventeenth century, but the terminus of this book, 1642, is also a 'hard' political date, the year England erupted into fratricidal armed conflict. Concluding a book on the English Reformation with the outbreak of the English Civil War might seem like an act of historiographical trespass, but if so there are good reasons for committing it. Many of those who took part (on both sides) in the war felt that they were fighting for religion, to preserve or to push forward a particular vision of what the English Reformation was. After the wars, the religious landscape was forever changed, with a reluctant acceptance of religious pluralism, and the consolidation of three broad blocs within English Christianity: Anglicanism, nonconformist Protestantism and Roman Catholicism. The seeds of this triple flowering were planted in the Reformation period, though the resultant florescence was one that few before 1642 would have wished to see.

Alongside the dates in this book's title is a geographical assertion – is Reformation *England* a defensible object of study? Developments in England were part of a broader phenomenon of Reformation and Counter-Reformation in Europe as a whole, and also interacted with events in other parts of the British Isles. An overly national focus might be misleading in another way too, tending to smooth out the wrinkles in a Reformation that came to every English diocese, county, town and parish in a slightly different way and with slightly different results. A historiographical survey has perforce to follow its quarry, and there is no doubt that as a historical construct 'Reformation England' has long existed.[4] I have attempted, however, to remain attuned to issues of local and regional particularity in the reception of the Reformation. Wherever possible I attempt also to recover contemporaries' own perceptions of witnessing or participating in a drama of wider than national, indeed of cosmic dimensions.

4 Wales is touched on briefly in some of the following chapters, though linguistic and other issues require the Welsh Reformation to produce its own historians. See in particular Glanmor Williams, *Wales and the Reformation* (Cardiff, 1997).

1

Catholic England 1480–1530

Overview

In 1480, and for the next 50 years, England was Catholic England, an expression that now sounds like an oxymoron, or a place in a whimsical alternative universe. It was moreover, according to recent revisionist scholarship, a wholeheartedly Catholic England, a showcase of ecclesiastical vigour and orthodox piety. Just as Russia was the last place Marxist theorists expected to undergo revolution in the early twentieth century, so early sixteenth-century England seemed unfertile ground for a successful revolt against the Church. Since at least the mid-1970s, historians have regularly observed that the Tudor monarchs were on notably good terms with the papacy; that the English Church was almost uniquely fortunate in western Europe with the quality and commitment of its bishops and clergy; and that English lay (non-clerical) people participated with enthusiasm in ceremonies and sacraments, and poured considerable resources into their parish churches. In short, English religion was in remarkably good shape, though there is a degree of anachronism in phrasing the thought in this way. In the later Middle Ages, 'religion' did not enjoy the modern meaning of a self-contained system of belief and worship (the word itself usually referred to what went on in monasteries). Rather, 'religion' was so woven into every aspect of cultural, political, even economic life, that it could not easily be conceived of as something separate. In a real sense, 'the Church was society'.[1] This does not necessarily imply that pre-Reformation England was an inspiring 'age of faith', in which all were pious or devout, but it does mean that, unlike modern Christians, late medieval Catholics had no opportunity to opt out – their lives were shaped by a fundamentally religious culture.

Over the course of the sixteenth century, however, the religious culture of Catholic England was transformed into something else. Why and how this came about constitutes the core subject of this book, but a necessary first

[1] Robert Swanson, *Church and Society in Late Medieval England* (Oxford, 1989), p. vii.

step is to survey the religious regime that prevailed before that transformation was openly underway. The very concept of 'pre-Reformation' religion sometimes troubles historians of the later Middle Ages. The term smacks of hindsight, of a sidelong approach to a period and set of themes which demand treatment on their own terms.[2] There is a danger that scholars and students whose primary interest is the Reformation will be tempted to regard the decades, or even the century before the break with Rome as an unchanging constant, a kind of land before time.[3] Yet an account of England's religious revolution has to begin somewhere, and starting the narrative abruptly in the mid-1520s risks the misleading impression that the Reformation was shaped solely by fortuitous political developments, or was simply imported wholesale from the continent. Attention to the pre-Reformation context inevitably involves selectivity in the treatment of evidence and themes. The opening chapters of A.G. Dickens's classic *The English Reformation*, for example, highlight the importance of Lollardy, the limitations of 'conventional religion', and the institutional failings of the clergy and religious houses. By contrast, Eamon Duffy's powerful evocation of 'traditional religion' is focussed almost exclusively on parish religion and lay piety, with little to say about the Church as an institution, or about heterodoxy and dissent.[4]

In this chapter, the importance of religion (in the approximate modern sense) for the life of late fifteenth- and early sixteenth-century England will be examined under four thematic headings. The first of these looks at the religious outlook and experiences of lay people, and the role that the Church played in the life of local communities. The second highlights perceived institutional problems of the Church, and the state of the clergy. A third section explores the significance of unorthodox religious beliefs, and of the Church's response to them, and the fourth attempts to evaluate the balance of conflict and co-operation in relations between the institutions of the Church and the English Crown. The intention is not to sift the evidence for signs of impending Reformation. Revisionists have rightly warned against the assumption that because the Reformation happened it must have been necessary or inevitable.[5] On the other hand, revisionists themselves are

2 Clive Burgess, '"A Fond Thing Vainly Invented": an Essay on Purgatory and Pious Motive in Later Medieval England', in Susan Wright, ed., *Parish, Church and People* (London, 1988), p. 69; Christine Carpenter, 'The Religion of the Gentry of Fifteenth-Century England', in Daniel Williams, ed., *England in the Fifteenth Century* (Woodbridge, 1987), p. 72.

3 David Aers, 'Altars of Power: Reflections on Eamon Duffy's *The Stripping of the Altars*', *Literature and History*, 3rd ser., 3 (1994), 100.

4 A.G. Dickens, *The English Reformation* (2nd ed., London, 1989), chs. 2–4; Eamon Duffy, *The Stripping of the Altars: Traditional Religion in England 1400–1580* (New Haven and London, 1992), part 1.

5 Christopher Haigh, 'Introduction' in id., ed., *The English Reformation Revised* (Cambridge, 1987), p. 3.

sometimes half-jokingly accused of proving that the Reformation didn't happen, or at least of reducing it to an externally imposed 'act of state' which struck the world of late medieval Catholicism like a meteor from outer space. The way forward is surely to acknowledge that the religious changes of the mid-sixteenth century and the ways in which people would respond to them, were shaped and conditioned by what had gone before; that in its first phases the historical process which would in time become known as 'the Reformation' was an aspect of late medieval religious life, rather than something entirely external to it.

1.1 Faith and Community

In late fifteenth- and early sixteenth-century England (and for long afterwards), the place where faith met community was the parish. Parishes were the basic administrative units of the English Church (there were somewhat over 9,000 of them in early Tudor England), but they were also much more than this, and a great deal of recent research has focussed on parishes and parish records as a route to understanding the religious culture of ordinary lay people in the decades before the Reformation.[6] Everyone was supposed to be a parishioner somewhere; the place where they would get married and have their children baptized in the parish church, and in due course be buried in its churchyard. In between, they would attend parish services (appearance at Sunday mass was required by ecclesiastical law), and pay tithes (a 10 per cent tax on all agricultural produce and income) to the priest. There was no such thing as a typical parish. In towns like London, Norwich or York they might be tiny, jostling together in the shadow of cathedrals or friary churches (London had no fewer than 107 parish churches within the walls, and another ten in the suburbs). Since the creation of new parishes had effectively stopped by around 1300, towns which had grown after this date were less well provided for, and typically had but a single parish church. Rural parishes in southern and midland England were often compact; in the less intensively settled north, they could be geographically vast, and include numerous small settlements with their own 'dependent' chapels, subordinate to a distant parish church. All parishes, however, had certain features in common, especially the fact that financial responsibility for the upkeep of the church, and provision of much

6 Wright, *Parish*; Robert Whiting, *The Blind Devotion of the People: Popular Religion and the English Reformation* (Cambridge, 1989); Duffy, *Stripping*; Beat Kümin, *The Shaping of a Community: The Rise and Reformation of the English Parish c. 1400–1560* (Aldershot, 1996); Katherine French, Gary Gibbs and Beat Kümin, eds., *The Parish in English Life 1400–1600* (Manchester, 1997); Katherine French, *The People of the Parish: Community Life in a Late Medieval English Diocese* (Philadelphia, 2001).

of its equipment, was in the hands of elected lay representatives called churchwardens. Crucially for us, churchwardens kept accounts, over 200 sets of which survive for pre-Reformation England, an archive unparalleled elsewhere in Europe.[7] These show that huge amounts of money were being poured into parish churches. Supplementing the accounts with surviving physical evidence, it is possible to calculate that two-thirds of all English parish churches may have had major refurbishment in the fifteenth and early sixteenth centuries, much of it going beyond necessary repairs to include items of status and beauty. An example is the lavish new spire, for which the churchwardens of Louth (Lincolnshire) were able to raise the astronomical sum of £305 between 1501 and 1515. To revisionist historians like Jack Scarisbrick or Christopher Haigh, such costly activity clearly indicates 'that local communities took great pride in their churches.'[8] They also took pride in what went on inside them. Parishes by law had to pay for the necessary equipment for worship – service books, vestments, bells, altar cloths, banners and processional crosses – over thirty separate items. But accounts and some surviving parish inventories show parishes often going beyond the requirements, enhancing the experience of liturgy (the public prayer of the Church) through the provision of elaborate polyphonic music or the purchase of extra clerical vestments – in 1527 there were 20 sets rather than the obligatory one in the parish of Long Melford (Suffolk).[9]

Historians have taken a particular interest in what the accounts tell us about how the money for such projects was raised. In some places the wardens drew on rental income from parish properties, or imposed local levies, but elsewhere (and particularly in the countryside) we can observe a variety of enjoyable fund-raising activities taking place, activities which in themselves helped create a sense of community. These included church ales (the equivalent of the modern church fête, but much less decorous), parish plays (often based on the exploits of Robin Hood), Hock-tide celebrations after Easter (involving the symbolic kidnap and ransoming of young men by young women, and vice versa), May Day and summer games, and the mysterious form of Christmas collecting known as 'hoggling'. As Ronald Hutton has demonstrated, the Church and the structure of its 'ritual year' provided the basis of a popular festive culture in countless parishes, a 'Merry England' which was reaching its most developed form in the century

[7] Beat Kümin, 'The English Parish in a European Perspective', in French, Gibbs and Kümin, *Parish*, p. 26.

[8] J.J. Scarisbrick, *The Reformation and the English People* (Oxford, 1984), pp. 12–14; Christopher Haigh, *English Reformations: Religion, Politics, and Society under the Tudors* (Oxford, 1993), pp. 34–5.

[9] Beat Kümin, 'Masses, Morris and Metrical Psalms: Music in the English Parish c. 1400–1600', in Fiona Kisby, ed., *Music and Musicians in Urban Communities* (Cambridge, 2001); Peter Marshall, *The Catholic Priesthood and the English Reformation* (Oxford, 1994), p. 201.

before the Reformation.[10] The impression of lay people enthusiastically committed to the Church is further supported by the evidence of wills. These survive in their thousands for the early sixteenth century, and show that gifts of money and valuable objects to the Church (usually the testator's own parish church) were almost universal. Another symptom is the proliferation of parish guilds or fraternities, literally brotherhoods (though women could be members in their own right). These voluntary associations of lay people were dedicated to a saint or Christ-centred devotion (Our Lady's Guild, St Michael's Guild, Corpus Christi Guild) and had a mixture of religious and social obligations, holding an annual feast on the patron saint's day, maintaining lights before his or her image in church, ensuring decent burial for guild members and saying prayers for them. Most parishes seem to have had at least one fraternity, and they proliferated in towns: London had over 150 of them in the century before the Reformation and even somewhere like Great Yarmouth boasted at least 19.[11]

None of this is to say much about religion per se, about people's beliefs and patterns of piety. Late medieval religion was profoundly sacramental, that is, it held that God's cleansing power (his 'grace') became available to people by being channelled through particular ritual actions and forms of words, through special material objects and sacred places. There were seven official sacraments (baptism, confirmation, marriage, the ordination of priests, the anointing of the sick and dying, penance, the eucharist). The first five of these were essentially 'rites of passage', performed once to sanctify particular moments in an individual's life cycle. The other two, penance (the confessing of one's sins to a priest) and the eucharist (the ritual re-enactment of Christ's Last Supper in the ceremony known as the mass), were endlessly repeated, serving continually to renew grace in the penitent sinner. The mass had a special place in the contemporary religious imagination. Here, uniquely, Christ became physically present among his people. Mass was said in Latin by a priest standing with his back to the congregation at a high altar situated at the far east end of the church (the chancel). He was separated from the lay people in the body (the nave) of the church by an elaborately carved semi-solid 'rood screen' (so-called because of the great crucifix or rood which surmounted it). When the priest repeated Jesus's words, 'This is my Body... This is my Blood', the 'elements' used in the ritual ceased to be bread and wine and became the real body and blood of Christ, a daily miracle which the theologians referred to as transubstantiation. Lay people received the body of Christ in the form of a fine wheaten

10 Ronald Hutton, *The Rise and Fall of Merry England: The Ritual Year 1400–1700* (Oxford, 1994).

11 Scarisbrick, *Reformation*, ch. 2; Duffy, *Stripping*, pp. 141–54; Caroline Barron, 'The Parish Fraternities of Medieval London', in id. and Christopher Harper-Bill, eds., *The Church in Pre-Reformation Society* (Woodbridge, 1985).

disc or 'host', but this communion was for most people infrequent, taking place usually once a year at Easter time.[12] For the rest of the year there was greater emphasis on seeing the sacrament – at the moment of consecration when the priest elevated the host above his head, bells would be rung, candles lit and (according to later Protestant accounts at least) people would jostle with each other for the privilege of 'seeing their Maker'. Popular belief held that people would not go blind or die suddenly on a day when they had gazed upon God.[13] The mass was not just an occasion for intense individual devotion, but also for the expression and restoration of social harmony. No one 'out of charity' with their neighbours was to be admitted to receive communion. The custom of annual confession in the week before Easter was designed to impel people to make amends to those they had wronged, as well as to clear their consciences before God. During the mass an engraved plate known as a pax (literally, peace) was passed round for the worshippers to kiss as a sign of being at peace with each other. The consecrated host was itself the most powerful symbol of unity (an idealized microcosm of the totality of Christian believers, who, according to St Paul, constituted 'one body in Christ'). On Corpus Christi, the special summer feast day of the body of Christ, the host was carried in elaborate procession through the streets of Bristol, Coventry, York and other places, a means of demonstrating, and of restoring, the social unity of towns all too given to faction and internal conflict.[14]

The mass was also valued as the most effective way of helping the souls of the dead. Central to medieval Catholicism was the belief in purgatory, a third place in the afterlife, where the souls of those not wicked enough to deserve the eternal pains of hell, but not good enough to merit immediate entry into heaven (i.e. the vast majority of Christians), would be purged in painful fires until they had worked off the debt 'due' for sins committed in this life.[15] Theologians taught that all faithful Christians in this world and the next were part of a single 'communion of saints' – a Church Militant (on earth), Church Suffering (in purgatory) and Church Triumphant (in heaven) – and that the prayers of one party could benefit the others. A great deal of

[12] They received the bread but not the wine (communion 'in one kind') – a source of annoyance to later reformers.

[13] Miri Rubin, *Corpus Christi: The Eucharist in Late Medieval Culture* (Cambridge, 1991), pp. 55–63; Duffy, *Stripping*, ch. 3; Marshall, *Priesthood*, pp. 41–3, 83.

[14] John Bossy, 'The Mass as a Social Institution, 1200–1700', *Past and Present*, 100 (1983); Mervyn James, 'Ritual, Drama and the Social Body in the Late Medieval English Town', *Past and Present*, 98 (1983); Rubin, *Corpus Christi*, pp. 243–71.

[15] The actual forgiveness of sin was achieved by sacramental confession, but this still left a penalty or 'satisfaction' to be made, which penances imposed by the confessor were unlikely to cover in full. For a helpful summary of the theology, see Euan Cameron, *The European Reformation* (Oxford, 1991), pp. 79–83.

both the official theology and liturgy of the Church, and of popular religious practice, was based around this principle, and considerable effort went into securing the intercession of the living for the dead: at least two-thirds of all pre-Reformation will-makers explicitly requested prayers or masses to be said for them (and others may simply have taken such provision for granted, or made detailed arrangements while still in good health). These ranged (depending on the testator's means) from the establishment of a chantry, an institution where a priest would be employed to say daily masses, either in perpetuity or for a set number of years, at a particular altar or chapel, to an 'obit', a single annual commemoration on the anniversary of the death. The more humble might invoke the prayers of their neighbours through securing inclusion on the 'bede-roll', a list of all who had made gifts to the parish, read annually in church. The desire for intercession was also a prime motive for joining fraternities, which have been described as 'communal chantries'.[16] To historians of a previous generation it seemed clear that all this provision was motivated by fear, the fear of languishing for hundreds of years in the pains of purgatory, if prayers and intercessions were not ceaselessly directed upwards.[17] Most recent accounts, however, have tended to be more optimistic, noting the rarity of 'panic' clauses in wills (thousands of masses to be said by thousands of priests, as soon as possible), and also emphasizing the ways in which bequests for the dead were designed to improve the lot of the living. Chantry priests often helped with the round of services in the parish, or kept schools. Objects like chalices or vestments, inscribed with the donor's name, were given to churches both to solicit prayers and to enhance the splendour of liturgy. The poor benefited from the frequent distributions of bread and small money doles at funerals (their prayers were believed to be particularly pleasing to God).[18]

The centrality of purgatory underlines the extent to which late medieval religion involved a series of exchanges between the visible world and the invisible one. This appears clearly in the public veneration accorded to saints, the 'very special dead' who lived with Christ in heaven, and were thus able to intercede powerfully with him for the needs of supplicants on earth.[19] The saints were ubiquitous in England in the decades around 1500: carved and gilded images of them, flanked by rows of votive candles, stood

[16] Barron, 'Fraternities', p. 23.

[17] K.L. Wood-Legh, *Perpetual Chantries in Britain* (Cambridge, 1965), p. 313; Alan Kreider, *English Chantries: The Road to Dissolution* (Cambridge, MA, 1979), pp. 41, 93; Dickens, *Reformation*, pp. 29–30.

[18] Duffy, *Stripping*, pp. 341–66; Peter Marshall, *Beliefs and the Dead in Reformation England* (Oxford, 2002), pp. 18–33. The social utility of intercession is the theme of many articles by Clive Burgess. See in particular his '"Fond Thing Vainly Invented"'.

[19] A phrase of Peter Brown, *The Cult of the Saints: Its Rise and Function in Latin Christianity* (Chicago, 1981), ch. 4.

in every parish church, and two-dimensional representations were painted on walls, rood-screens and stained-glass windows. Christ's mother, the Virgin Mary ('Our Lady') was the focus of the most intense and universally diffused cult, but the number of venerated saints was legion, from those, like Peter, James, John or Mary Magdalene, with impeccable biblical references, to those (often supposed early martyrs) whose popularity rested on the colourful, not to say fanciful stories in the popular sermon collection known as *The Golden Legend*. There were also saints whose appeal was primarily regional or local: Yorkshire parishes might venerate St Robert of Knaresborough; Devon ones, St Sidwell of Exeter or St Urith of Chittelhampton.[20] The saints were not so much what they were to become in modern Catholicism – models of devout living to be emulated – as powerful supernatural beings, dispensers of visions and healing miracles, often with recognized specialisms: St Apollonia for toothache, St Loy for diseases of horses.[21] The power of the saints was channelled through their traces in the physical world, images and relics, sometimes housed in special shrines, to which the devout, the curious, or the desperate might travel on pilgrimage. Within England, the most popular shrines were those of Our Lady at Walsingham and of the martyred archbishop St Thomas Becket at Canterbury. The more adventurous might journey abroad, to the Shrine of St James at Santiago de Compostela, or to Rome or Jerusalem. It has been plausibly suggested that in the later Middle Ages an earlier obsession with the physical relics of saints was giving way to a greater interest in miracle-working images, though some relics retained their potency. Walsingham housed a portion of the Virgin's milk in addition to the famous statue there, and as late as the 1530s 'flocks' of pilgrims were reported trooping to view the relic of Christ's blood at the monastery of Hailes in Gloucestershire.[22] Theologians regarded images as didactic aids to devotion, 'lay men's books', but the distinction between the represented and the representation may have been more blurred in the minds of ordinary people, who spoke about 'Our Lady of Walsingham', 'Our Lady of Ipswich', almost as if they were separate persons.[23] There was without doubt a strong desire for the emotional, the tangible and visible in religion. This was reflected not just in the cult of

[20] Jonathan Hughes, *Pastors and Visionaries: Religion and Secular Life in Late Medieval Yorkshire* (Woodbridge, 1988), pp. 326–7; Eamon Duffy, *The Voices of Morebath: Reformation and Rebellion in an English Village* (New Haven and London, 2001), pp. 73–4.

[21] Duffy, *Stripping*, ch. 5; French, *People of the Parish*, pp. 194–207.

[22] Ronald Finucane, *Miracles and Pilgrims: Popular Beliefs in Medieval England* (London, 1977), ch. 11; André Vauchez, *Sainthood in the Later Middle Ages*, tr. J. Birrell (Cambridge, 1997), pp. 444–53; Hugh Latimer, *Sermons and Remains*, ed. G.E. Corrie (Cambridge, 1845), p. 364.

[23] Margaret Aston, *England's Iconoclasts: Laws Against Images* (Oxford, 1988), pp. 31–4.

the saints, but also in a strong devotional concern with the humanity of Christ, and an emotive and imaginative emphasis in prayers and imagery on his passion and crucifixion.[24]

The revisionist scholarship of the past two decades has made a powerful case for a vibrant, popular religious culture in the parishes, with little sign of disenchantment from the Church and its teachings. Clearly, late medieval parishioners 'were not waiting for the Reformation.'[25] But this does not necessarily mean that pre-Reformation religious life was immune from stresses and tensions. Some historians have argued that because fraternities were separate, voluntary organizations with membership fees and sets of rules, they created a degree of social distinction in religious practice. They might also imply some dissatisfaction with the limitations of what the parish could provide, particularly where fraternities drew their members from across parish boundaries.[26] Duffy, Kümin and others have rejected the notion of parish and guilds as rivals, pointing out that many of the latter existed to support parish activities (maintaining the church fabric, keeping lights burning before images in the parish church) and that fraternity chaplains frequently helped out with the parochial 'cure of souls' by hearing confession and saying mass.[27] Nonetheless, it is interesting to note that the parishes in London with active fraternities in Henry VII's reign were the same ones which a hundred years later funded the most lectureships for Puritan preachers[28] (see Section 6.1). This is not to say that fraternities were sponsors of early Protestantism. Their activities, such as arranging masses for souls in purgatory, were entirely orthodox. But there does seem to be here a continuity of the impulse towards active lay participation in religion, one that the official structures could not entirely contain.

Churchwardens' accounts have little to say about the social elite of the landed gentry, who tended not to play a hands-on role in the day-to-day running of parishes. The case has been made for an increasing gap opening up between the religious outlook of the gentry and that of their social inferiors – between what we can call with crude shorthand 'elite' and 'popular' religion. Could such a gap have been widened by the advent of printing (the first book was printed in England in 1477), accompanied by the slow but steady spread of literacy among the laity? The illiterate mass of

[24] Duffy, *Stripping*, pp. 234–56.

[25] French, *People of the Parish*, p. 208.

[26] John Bossy, *Christianity in the West 1400–1700* (Oxford, 1985), pp. 57–63; Gervase Rosser, 'Communities of Parish and Guild in the Late Middle Ages', in Wright, *Parish*; id., 'Parochial Conformity and Voluntary Religion in Late-Medieval England', *Transactions of the Royal Historical Society*, 6th ser., 1 (1991).

[27] Duffy, *Stripping*, pp. 141–54; Kümin, *Shaping*, pp. 148–59. But see the more equivocal conclusion of Ken Farnhill, *Guilds and the Parish Community in Late Medieval East Anglia c. 1470–1550* (York, 2001), pp. 166–71.

[28] Barron, 'Fraternties', p. 34.

the people experienced religion through the eye, through the spectacle of rituals and processions, and the imagery of statues and wall paintings. The literate could reflect on the inner meaning of religious texts. According to an influential book by Keith Thomas, the late medieval masses were scarcely Christianized in a meaningful sense. Their religion effectively took the form of protective magic – ceremonies to ward off crop failure or plague. There was little common ground with educated book-owners, clerical or lay.[29] Colin Richmond has pointed to evidence that the gentry in this period were increasingly establishing private chapels in their own houses, and in church were using their own private pews where they read books of devotion during the services. The gentry, he suggests, were withdrawing from a shared religious mentality into a private sphere of their own. Moreover, they were beginning to look down on popular religion with its shrines, pilgrimages and miracles, and thus became prepared to collude in its destruction when the Reformation came.[30] George Bernard has made similar suggestions: though practices like pilgrimage were undoubtedly popular, they were also intrinsically vulnerable to criticism and the large collections of (frankly rather suspect) relics housed in numerous English monasteries 'invited satire and incredulity'.[31] This was certainly the response of one famous visitor to England, the humanist scholar Erasmus, who in 1512–14 attended the shrines at Canterbury and Walsingham, and wrote up a caustic account of what seemed to him the corrupt and superstitious practices there.[32]

There is a danger in taking such interpretations too far. As Duffy has demonstrated, there was no hard-and-fast divide between the worlds of the literate and the illiterate. For example, the many thousands of printed lay prayer books, known as 'Primers' or Book of Hours, circulating in pre-Reformation England contained religious pictures, which could be used for meditation in exactly the same way as statues in church. The manuscript collections of instructive texts known as 'commonplace books', kept by some gentry, merchants and more educated parishioners, suggest an easy intermingling of 'elite' and 'popular' motifs – prayers and summaries of

[29] Keith Thomas, *Religion and the Decline of Magic: Studies in Popular Beliefs in Sixteenth- and Seventeenth-Century England* (London, 1971), ch. 2.

[30] Colin Richmond, 'Religion and the Fifteenth-Century English Gentleman', in R.B. Dobson, ed., *The Church, Politics and Patronage in the Fifteenth Century* (Gloucester, 1984); 'The English Gentry and Religion, c. 1500', in Christopher Harper-Bill, ed., *Religious Belief and Ecclesiastical Careers in Late Medieval England* (Woodbridge, 1991).

[31] George Bernard, 'Vitality and Vulnerability in the Late Medieval Church: Pilgrimage on the Eve of the Break with Rome', in John Watts, ed., *The End of the Middle Ages? England in the Fifteenth and Sixteenth Centuries* (Stroud, 1998).

[32] Erasmus, *The Colloquies*, ed. C.R. Thompson (Chicago and London, 1965), pp. 285–312.

official doctrine sit alongside zodiacal material and spells for conjuring angels onto the fingernail of a child. It seems, moreover, hard to argue that the printing press was in some way undermining traditional Catholicism when primers, lives of saints and service books comprised the largest part of the presses' output.[33] The diversity of late medieval religious practice, with its sacraments, relics, fraternities, festivities, pilgrimages and pious books, can plausibly be read as a sign of health and confidence. But the sheer variety also meant that there was little clarity and consensus about what was essential and what was peripheral in the practice of the faith – something to prove significant in Henry VIII's reign, when selected aspects of traditional Catholicism came under attack (see Section 2.3).

1.2 Reform and Stagnation

In general, modern revisionist writing has shown more interest in lay and parochial religion than in the institutional face of the late medieval Church, yet in the opening stages of the Reformation it would be the institutions – clergy, church courts and monasteries – which would first come under attack. Christopher Harper-Bill's contention that in any fair comparison with earlier and later periods, 'the institutions of the English church in the early sixteenth century do not appear to have been in urgent need of radical reform' is probably accurate.[34] Yet calls for reform, and indeed frequent bandying about of the word 'reformation', filled the air in these years.[35] In around 1511, John Colet, humanist dean of St Paul's, delivered a thunderous sermon to convocation (the Church's equivalent to the Houses of Parliament) blaming all the ills of the Church on the secular lifestyles and 'covetousness' of the clergy. He castigated their greed for tithes and promotions, and urged 'reformation of the Church's estate'.[36] A similar diagnosis was put forward in a treatise drafted by Henry VII's leading minister, Edmund Dudley, after he had fallen from favour at the start of Henry VIII's reign. Dudley urged the King to put an end to pluralism (the holding of more than one church living) and simony (the purchase of ecclesiastical office), and advocated the improvement of the clergy through greater education. There were a number of ironies here. Dudley had earlier shown no hesitation in securing ecclesiastical positions for various relatives and clients, and on Henry VII's behalf had received numerous payments from churchmen for confirmation in their

33 Duffy, *Stripping*, pp. 68–87, chs. 6–8.
34 Christopher Harper-Bill, *The Pre-Reformation Church in England 1400–1530* (London, 1989), p. 91.
35 Swanson, *Church*, pp. 312–14; Barry Collett, *A Long and Troubled Pilgrimage: The Correspondence of Marguerite D'Angoulême and Vittoria Colonna* (Princeton, 2000), p. 39.
36 J.H. Lupton, *Life of John Colet* (London, 1887), pp. 293–304.

offices. Colet himself was a pluralist (the strictures apparently did not apply to humanist scholars who needed the extra income to advance the cause of education).[37] The most notorious pluralist in early Tudor England was Cardinal Thomas Wolsey, a figure whom historians have usually thought to exemplify the abuses complained of in Colet's sermon.[38] Yet Wolsey owed all his promotions directly to the favour of Henry VIII, and can himself claim some credentials as a reformer, advocating schemes to increase the number of dioceses and tighten up the administration of canon law.[39] The aspiration for reform was almost universal in educated lay and clerical circles at the start of the sixteenth century (internationally, it was being sounded at the Fifth Lateran Council of 1512–17, which leading English churchmen attended). But at every level it confronted the reality of deeply vested interests. The jurisdiction of bishops was undercut by the exemption from their oversight of numerous parishes and religious corporations, and by the fact that they only controlled appointment to a minority of the spiritual promotions in their dioceses. Much ecclesiastical patronage was in the hands of lay people, who, from the King downwards, exercised it with a variety of spiritual and decidedly non-spiritual motives.

It is significant that Wolsey's most substantial reform initiative involved the closure of almost 30 small and decaying monasteries, and the redirection of the revenues to educational purposes (a grammar school in Ipswich and a new Oxford college). For the religious houses provide a case study in the complex blend of reform and stagnation to be found in the English Church in the immediate pre-Reformation decades. Conventional wisdom holds that the monasteries were 'in decline' in this period, both in terms of the numbers entering religious houses and in terms of the moral and spiritual standards being observed in them.[40] But it is extremely hard to generalize about this. Monastic numbers as a whole probably were down from an all-time high just before the Black Death, from which some communities never recovered. But others show the reverse trend: the Yorkshire monastery of Fountains, for example, more than doubled its numbers between 1494 and 1520 under the energetic abbot Marmaduke Huby.[41] The idea that

[37] Christopher Harper-Bill, 'Dean Colet's Convocation Sermon and the Pre-Reformation Church in England', in Peter Marshall, ed., *The Impact of the English Reformation 1500–1640* (London, 1997); Steven Gunn, 'Edmund Dudley and the Church', *Journal of Ecclesiastical History*, 51 (2000).

[38] In addition to the archbishopric of York, Wolsey held a succession of other dioceses, as well as the wealthy abbey of St Albans.

[39] Peter Gwyn, *The King's Cardinal: The Rise and Fall of Thomas Wolsey* (London, 1990), ch. 8.

[40] See, for example, G.R. Elton, *England Under the Tudors*, (3rd ed, London, 1991), pp. 105–6.

[41] John A.F. Thomson, *The Early Tudor Church and Society* (London, 1993), pp. 191–2.

monasteries were in a bad condition spiritually comes from the evidence of visitations (inspections) carried out by the bishops in the 'non-exempt' houses. From these it is easy to draw a picture of lukewarmness and slackness, with many complaints of poor attendance at services, ill-discipline, tyrannical or incompetent leadership by abbots and priors, and occasional sexual misdemeanours. There were a few real black spots, like St Albans in 1489–90, where the abbot was accused of robbing the shrine of St Alban to buy his office and of allowing his monks to resort to nunneries for immoral purposes.[42] But there is a need for caution in using the visitation evidence, which represents only a snapshot of a house at a particular time, and which aimed to find fault with the intention of putting it right. When the monastery at Welbeck (Nottinghamshire) was visited in 1478, it was found to have been ruined by the abbot's diversion of revenues to support his illegitimate children. But by 1491, under a replacement head, the house was thriving.[43]

In any case, there is evidence to set alongside the visitation reports suggesting a more positive picture. A vigorous building programme in many monasteries in the later fifteenth century paralleled that in the parish churches. The friars, who were based in towns, and whose vocation was to preaching and pastoral work among the laity, were attracting donations and requests for burial in their houses right up to the 1530s.[44] There was also the inspiring example set by a number of the newer, smaller orders – the Franciscan Observants (who came to England in the 1480s and had five houses) and the Bridgettines (who had a single house, Syon, near London), several of whose number (Richard Whitford, William Bonde) published devotional tracts in English for the edification of the laity. Strictest of all were the nine houses of Carthusians, whose inmates lived lives of austerity and solitary prayer. Significantly, it was these monks who provided the bulk of clerical opposition to Henry VIII's break with Rome in the 1530s (see Section 2.3). Before this cataclysm, they were patronized by royalty and nobility, and received a disproportionate share of the gifts that lay people made to religious houses in their wills.[45] Ironically, it was monks in closer day-to-day contact with the laity who seem to have inspired them less. The largest orders, the Benedictines and Augustinians, were major landowners and employers. They performed various social functions, acting as deposit houses for important documents and providing charity for the poor (though

42 David Knowles, *The Religious Orders in England III: The Tudor Age* (Cambridge, 1959), pp. 77–9.

43 Ibid., p. 43.

44 Richard Rex, 'The Friars in the English Reformation', in Peter Marshall and Alec Ryrie, eds., *The Beginnings of English Protestantism* (Cambridge, 2002), pp. 38–40.

45 Susan Brigden, *London and the Reformation* (Oxford, 1989), pp. 73–4.

historians disagree about how significant this was). Their abbots and priors entertained and hunted like other landowning gentry, and often did their duty as justices of the peace.[46] There is not much evidence that monasteries were actively disliked or undergoing any kind of fundamental crisis in the early sixteenth century.[47] They were simply taken for granted. But, with some exceptions, they may have been too closely integrated into lay society for their own good. The lack of much clear sense of identity, solidarity and purpose across the religious orders made it harder to mount a co-ordinated defence when Henry VIII turned on them in the 1530s.

For most people, however, regular contact with the clergy was not with monks, but with the 'secular' clergy in the parishes, an extremely large and diverse body.[48] Huge numbers of priests worked for wages with little job security, finding work where they could as fraternity chaplains, parish curates or temporary chantry priests. These were often scarcely better off than agricultural labourers, forming a kind of 'clerical proletariat', and frequently under the direct control of lay people. Above them were the rectors and vicars, themselves a highly diverse group, who were appointed by a patron (bishop, monastery or wealthy layman) to a parish 'living', and were entitled to collect the tithes.[49] It is thus difficult to generalize about the condition of the clergy and the nature of their relationship with the laity, though these are issues that have generated fierce debate. There is a long-standing view that that the privileges and abuses of the clergy produced widespread 'anticlericalism' among the pre-Reformation laity, and that this was a crucial element in the acceptance of the Reformation.[50] But revisionist historians like Haigh and Scarisbrick have suggested that the evidence for anticlericalism is something of an optical illusion, that there was no deep-seated dissatisfaction. Visitation evidence, it is argued, reveals comparatively few complaints about pastoral care, while surviving court records suggest that quarrels over tithes were rare. Conversely, levels of recruitment to the priesthood were at a record high in the first decades of the sixteenth century, something hard to

[46] Swanson, *Church*, pp. 82–6; Claire Cross, 'Monasticism and Society in the Diocese of York 1520–1540', *Transactions of the Royal Historical Society*, 5th ser., 38 (1988); N. Rushton, 'Monastic Charitable Provision in Tudor England', *Continuity and Change*, 16 (2001).

[47] Though see Sean Field, 'Devotion, Discontent, and the Henrician Reformation: The Evidence of the Robin Hood Stories', *Journal of British Studies*, 41 (2002), for the stereotypes of avaricious monks appearing in the Robin Hood ballads popular in the fifteenth and early sixteenth centuries.

[48] There may have been up to 40,000 priests in the parishes in the early sixteenth century: Haigh, *Reformations*, p. 5.

[49] Technically, a parish had a 'vicar' (literally, stand-in) where the parish had been granted to a religious house. This became corporate rector, receiving the greater part of the tithes.

[50] Dickens, *Reformation*, chs. 6, 13; 'The Shape of Anticlericalism and the English Reformation', in his *Late Monasticism and the Reformation* (London, 1994).

explain if the laity was overwhelmingly 'anticlerical'.[51] It is easy enough to find examples of priests who failed to say services properly, who were sexually immoral or grasping in demanding their tithes, though as with the monasteries, there is a temptation to give too much attention to the really juicy cases. It is worth noting that lay complaints against individual priests sometimes bemoaned that they did not 'do as other vicars and rectors' – the bad behaviour of a few did not necessarily reflect on the standing of the clergy as a whole. We should remember that people were taught to believe that there was no possibility of getting to heaven without the assistance of the priesthood – only they could say mass, hear confession and give the last rites to the dying. Much of what historians have termed 'anticlericalism' (a word unknown at the time) was probably prompted not by hatred of priests but by high expectations from them.[52] There is now a growing consensus that anticlericalism simply doesn't work as a straightforward 'cause' of the Reformation.[53] But it would be equally unwise simply to dismiss the significance of criticism of the clergy. In humanist circles it was common to sneer at the ignorance of rural clergy – 'a crop of oafish and boorish priests', as Colet's friend William Melton, chancellor of York Minster, called them in around 1510.[54] A literary tradition enjoyed by the educated laity, running from Chaucer in the fourteenth century to the playwright John Heywood in the early sixteenth, mercilessly satirized supposed instances of clerical greed and corruption. Criticism of this sort was certainly compatible with orthodox Catholic piety, but it also generated a repertoire of familiar 'anticlerical' themes and jokes, which the less orthodox would find useful in the future. The habit of looking critically at the institutions of the Church, the often frustrated aspiration for some kind of internal 'reformation', is certainly no indication that the system was on the verge of collapse. But it may have made it more difficult to mount a convincing defence of those institutions when a doctrinal attack on the Church began in the 1520s.

1.3 Heresy and Persecution

It is possible to argue that such a doctrinal attack on the Church was already under way in the late fifteenth century – what about the Lollards? These were real anticlericals, people reportedly saying such things as that they

[51] Scarisbrick, *Reformation*, pp. 45–8; Christopher Haigh, 'Anticlericalism and the English Reformation', in Haigh, *Reformation Revised*.

[52] Marshall, *Priesthood*, pp. 215–16 and *passim*.

[53] David Loades, 'Anticlericalism in the Church of England before 1558: an "Eating Canker"?', in Nigel Aston and Matthew Cragoe, eds., *Anticlericalism in Britain, c. 1500–1914* (Stroud, 2000).

[54] Peter Marshall, 'Mumpsimus and Sumpsimus: The Intellectual Origins of a Henrician *Bon Mot*', *Journal of Ecclesiastical History*, 52 (2001), 515–16.

would prefer to confess their sins to a tree than to a priest.[55] Lollards were in their origins disciples of the late fourteenth-century heretical Oxford theologian, John Wyclif, who attracted a radical following, including some high-ranking laymen, after teaching that the Church should have no property or secular power, that popes and priests should be obeyed only as far as their behaviour merited, and that the only source of religious authority was the Bible. Wyclif also condemned the doctrine of transubstantiation, and he attacked aspects of popular religion like pilgrimage and the veneration of images. The Church countered the threat with persecution. The death penalty was introduced for heresy in 1401, and the English translation of the scriptures undertaken by Wyclif's followers – the Wycliffite Bible – was banned in 1407. After Lollardy became associated with a revolt against Henry V in 1414, the upper classes got cold feet and withdrew their support. Thereafter Lollardy seemed to cease being a significant threat to the Church – persecution died off after the early decades of the fifteenth century, and the movement, it is usually argued, declined into a pattern of small dispersed pockets of disgruntled lower-class heretics, without much coherence in organization or beliefs.

But in the decade or so before the accession of Henry VII, something interesting seems to be happening – a marked increase in trials of Lollards which continued through the 1480s and 1490s, and reached a high point in 1511–12. The main areas affected were London, Kent, the Chilterns area of Buckinghamshire and Coventry. There is little or no sign of Lollardy in the north of England. It looks as though Lollardy was undergoing a genuine revival, with the bishops forced to react to a perceived threat. But some historians have been sceptical about this, suggesting that there may simply be better survival of records, or that increased political stability after the Wars of the Roses meant the bishops were not as preoccupied with political concerns as they had been in the 1450s and 60s, and could thus go looking for heretics. Richard Rex refers to the adoption of a 'zero tolerance' policy towards religious dissent after the arrival of the Tudors, while Robert Swanson has suggested that concerted heresy hunts were launched in 1511–12 as a way of demonstrating the importance and authority of the Church courts at a time when they were being criticized by common lawyers (see Section 1.4).[56] Survival or revival? It is not necessarily an either/or choice: the relative absence of persecution in the mid-fifteenth century may have allowed the consolidation and even expansion of Lollard groups.

From the historian's point of view, one happy result of the renewed persecution is that it supplies a considerable amount of information about how Lollard communities were structured, how Lollardy spread and what

[55] John A.F. Thomson, *The Later Lollards 1414–1520* (Oxford, 1965), p. 183.
[56] Richard Rex, *The Lollards* (Basingstoke, 2002), p. 113; Swanson, *Church*, pp. 345–7.

Lollards believed. Modern research has revised the traditional notion of early Tudor Lollards as invariably ignorant country-dwellers – in places like Coventry or Amersham in Buckinghamshire, Lollard suspects came from across the social scale. One of the accused in Coventry in 1511, for example, was a former MP and twice mayor of the town. London Lollards included leading figures in the prestigious trade guilds like the Goldsmiths' company.[57] More contentious is the question of whether a strain of Lollardy among the gentry had completely died out by the later fifteenth century. The fact remains that no landed gentleman was tried as a Lollard in Henry VII's reign, though it has been argued that this simply reveals 'the realities of gentry status', the bishops' reluctance to treat the powerful and well-connected in the same way as the lower orders.[58] The survival of splendidly produced volumes of Lollard sermons and bibles implies production and transmission in gentry households, and we cannot rule out the possibility that at the end of the fifteenth century some at least of the upper classes were starting to show a greater interest in unorthodox religious ideas. But the boundaries between orthodoxy and unorthodoxy are hazy here: ownership of English bibles among the educated elites might or might not imply heretical leanings. Among those known to have possessed them are the nuns of Syon Abbey and King Richard III, implausible candidates for Lollard affiliation.[59]

The question of what Lollards did that actually made them Lollards is an intriguing one. It is almost certainly wrong to think of Lollardy as a kind of 'counter-Church' or denomination; it does not seem to have had its own rituals or clergy. Indeed, Lollards do not in the main seem separated from the orthodox communities in which they lived. They took part in Catholic worship – accusations that they failed to go to confession or receive communion are rare. There are even cases of Lollard churchwardens.[60] The wills of known or suspected Lollards usually look the same as those of their orthodox neighbours. Of course, a justified fear of persecution might explain all this, but another possibility is that, for some, Lollardy was a kind of added spiritual dimension to parochial religious life. The one activity we know Lollards engaged in was to meet at each other's houses, where there were readings from the English Bible or other books. Lollardy displays few

[57] Andrew Hope, 'Lollardy: the Stone the Builders Rejected' in Peter Lake and Maria Dowling, eds., *Protestantism and the National Church in Sixteenth-Century England* (London, 1987); Derek Plumb, 'The Social and Economic Status of the Later Lollards', and 'A Gathered Church? Lollards and their Society', in Margaret Spufford, ed., *The World of Rural Dissenters 1520–1725* (Cambridge, 1995).

[58] Margaret Aston and Colin Richmond, 'Introduction', in id., eds., *Lollardy and the Gentry in the Later Middle Ages* (Stroud, 1997), p. 20. Rex, *Lollardy*, p. 103 counters that accusations of heresy would have been an obvious weapon in inter-gentry feuds.

[59] Swanson, *Church*, p. 343; Charles Ross, *Richard III* (London, 1981), pp. 128–9.

[60] Plumb, 'Status', pp. 106, 124–5.

of the characteristics of a modern evangelical sect. People were drawn in not so much by migrant teachers known to Lollard groups in different parts of the country (there seem to have been only a handful of these) but through their existing social and family networks – parents converted their children, husbands their wives, masters their apprentices. R.G. Davies has argued that personal connections were more important than formal beliefs in sustaining Lollardy, memorably remarking that 'if Wyclifism was *what* you knew, Lollardy was *who* you knew'.[61]

But what did Lollards actually believe? The confessions recorded at heresy trials suggest a wide variety of opinions, but also some recurrent themes: opposition to images, pilgrimage and prayer to saints; denial of the value of sacraments (especially confession and the mass); a stress on the importance of the Bible. From the trial evidence Lollardy can appear an essentially negative protest movement against the sacramental teaching of the Church, underpinned by rather grumpy common-sense rationalism – the priest could not make God in the mass, it was often said, for how can the house make the carpenter? But it is clear that Lollard trials give a rather skewed picture. No suspect was invited to offer a statement of his or her beliefs; rather the judges were interested in identifying where they had contradicted orthodox teaching, and getting them to retract their views or 'abjure'. The great majority of those arrested did so, and were in serious danger only if caught a second time: between 1485 and 1522 there were around 308 abjurations and 25 burnings.[62] Some historians have argued that the trial evidence creates a false impression of unity and consistency in Lollard beliefs; the concerns of the persecutors imposing systematic form on a mass of incoherent attitudes and diverse individuals.[63] Taken to the extreme, this argument can come close to suggesting that Lollardy never really existed – like witchcraft, it was a 'crime' created by its persecutors. But the alternative view, advanced most powerfully by Anne Hudson, argues that the judicial record presents a one-sided, unduly negative view of Lollard beliefs, which must be supplemented by the textual evidence of Lollard writings and especially the Wycliffite Bible. There are over 250 surviving manuscripts of the latter, more than for any other medieval work. Hudson sees a positive spirituality and underlying coherence in Lollard beliefs. For example, the opposition to images of saints was prompted by a sense of their social injustice – they took offerings away from the poor, the real images of Christ.[64] An argument against the idea of an intellectually

[61] R.G. Davies, 'Lollardy and Locality', *Transactions of the Royal Historical Society*, 6th ser., 1 (1991), 212.
[62] Thomson, *Later Lollards*, pp. 237–8.
[63] Ibid., p. 229; Robert Swanson, *Catholic England: Faith, Religion and Observance before the Reformation* (Manchester, 1993), pp. 35–8.
[64] Anne Hudson, *The Premature Reformation: Wycliffite Texts and Lollard History* (Oxford, 1988).

vibrant Lollard movement is that hardly any new Lollard works seem to have been written after about 1440, though old ones continued to be copied. There is in fact deadlock among historians about the significance of late medieval Lollardy. Revisionist writers stressing the popularity and vitality of the Church tend to marginalize it. Scarisbrick refers dismissively to Buckinghamshire's 'deep-rooted upland semi-paganism', which 'scarcely threatened the old order', while Rex complains of the 'disproportionate historiographical attention' lavished on the Lollards.[65] Such assessments are linked umbilically to an ongoing debate about the contribution Lollardy made to the Reformation from the late 1520s (see Section 2.1). But even if we think of Lollardy as a minority strand within, rather than as something outside the early Tudor Catholic Church, it adds to the picture of diversity and divergence in religious life, of a system sometimes struggling to accommodate different spiritualities and devotional practices.

1.4 Church and State

When full-scale Reformation came to England in the 1530s, however, its first and most conspicuous aspect was not the spiritual concerns of Lollardy, but the spectacle of a head-on crash between Church and State, and a fundamental reordering of their relationship. The King replaced the Pope as the supreme spiritual and administrative authority in the English Church, and the Church's independent system of law – canon law – was made subject to the authority of statute law, that made by the King in Parliament (see Section 2.2). Can any embryonic sign of these developments be detected in the decades before 1525? The answer must be an emphatic no, and yes. Certainly there was little indication that links with the Pope were to become so badly derailed in the not-so-distant future. Tudor–papal relations had got off onto a good foot, with Innocent VIII giving his blessing to Henry VII's usurpation of 1485.[66] Henry was able to reciprocate after 1494, when the papacy found itself directly challenged by French intervention in Italy. English foreign policy thereafter generally followed a pro-papal line, particularly since the early Tudors had no strategic interests in Italy, and was naturally interested in checking the ambitions of France. In return for political support, royal candidates were appointed to English, Welsh and Irish bishoprics, and the Crown was permitted to exact heavy taxation from the clergy. Despite what Reformation propaganda would later say about the financial burdens imposed by Rome, Henry VII and Henry VIII squeezed out of the English Church over two and a half times the sum that the popes

65 Scarisbrick, *Reformation*, pp. 6, 46; Rex, *Lollards*, p. 143.

66 C.S.L. Davies, 'Bishop John Morton, the Holy See, and the Accession of Henry VII', *English Historical Review*, 102 (1987).

did.[67] After the death of Henry VII's heir, Prince Arthur, in 1502, Julius II granted a request for Arthur's widow Catherine to be allowed to marry his brother, Prince Henry. It is of no small significance that Henry VIII seems to have expected as a matter of course that Julius's successor would be prepared to reverse this decision in the 1520s. Henry VII also hoped that the papacy would deliver him a propaganda coup by agreeing to declare as a saint Henry VI, the last of the Lancastrian line, from which the Tudors claimed descent. Canonization was a slow process, but a satisfactory final verdict would almost certainly have been achieved if Henry VIII's Reformation had not intervened to spoil it. Before this, however, Henry VIII had received his own propaganda boost from the Pope, in 1521 receiving the title 'Defender of the Faith' for his literary efforts against Martin Luther, something that at last put him on a par with the 'most Christian' kings of France, and his in-laws, the 'Catholic Kings' of Spain. In a variety of ways the spiritual authority of the Pope was useful to the English Crown, and was in consequence unchallenged by it.

Within England, however, the Pope's theoretical supremacy was diluted by a practical supremacy increasingly in the hands of the Crown, a creeping nationalization of the Church paralleled elsewhere in late medieval Europe. The early Tudor monarchs continued the pattern already established in the fifteenth century of appointing royal servants to bishoprics; effectively they used the resources of the Church to finance their bureaucracy. Some important state officials, like the Chancellor and the Lord Privy Seal, were invariably churchmen in this period.[68] The early Tudor bishops have enjoyed a good press from historians in recent years. Virtually all of them were graduates (and among them Wolsey sticks out both for his pluralism and for the irregularity of his personal life). The great majority, however, were trained in law (both canon and civil) rather than theology, appropriately enough for men who were primarily royal and ecclesiastical administrators. In itself, this did not make them bad bishops – several (including Wolsey) were benefactors of education, and most kept a conscientious eye on their dioceses, policing heresy and keeping discipline among clergy and laity through visitations and the Church courts. Many managed to be resident in their dioceses for long stretches of time, and those called away on royal business usually employed competent deputies.[69] But both the career patterns and the intellectual training of English bishops meant that they looked naturally to the Crown as the focus of their loyalty. It is entirely in character that the

67 Harper-Bill, *Pre-Reformation Church*, p. 18.

68 Swanson, *Church*, pp. 103–5; R.L. Storey, *The Reign of Henry VII* (London, 1968), p. 98.

69 Ibid., pp. 185–9; Thomson, *Tudor Church*, pp. 46–60; Stephen Thompson, 'The Bishop in his Diocese', in Brendan Bradshaw and Eamon Duffy, eds., *Humanism, Reform and the Reformation: The Career of Bishop John Fisher* (Cambridge, 1989), p. 250 (Appendix 3).

star theologian on Henry VII and Henry VIII's bench of bishops, John Fisher, was appointed to Rochester, the smallest and poorest of English dioceses; significant too that Fisher was the only one of the bishops openly to choose the side of pope rather than king when the episcopate was forced to make an uncomfortable choice in the 1530s.

Where the theory of a universal Church most often rubbed against the local control sought by the Crown was in the practice of the law, and the fact that two separate legal systems operated in England: the Church courts administered the canon law of the Church, while the common law exercised in the common law courts looked to the Crown as the ultimate source of jurisdiction. Most of the time the two systems operated without great tension, and with an agreed division of labour – the policing of moral offences and of heresy, for example clearly belonged to the Church. But there were regular complaints from common lawyers that the Church courts were stepping beyond their boundaries, for example, claiming jurisdiction over cases of unpaid petty debts on the grounds that these involved breach of a promise, a spiritual crime. Common lawyers counter-attacked by invoking the fourteenth-century statute of *praemunire* (literally, to protect). This was a law to prevent appeals over issues of appointments being made from royal courts to the papal court in Rome. But the loose wording of the statute allowed the interpretation that cases belonging to royal courts were not to be heard in any Church courts. In the early sixteenth century common lawyers' aggressive use of praemunire was starting to make serious inroads into the business of the ecclesiastical courts.[70] Yet the suggestion that Church courts were widely unpopular with the laity (a back-projection from charges of high-handedness and excessive fees made in the 'Reformation Parliament' in 1529–32) has been largely rejected by modern scholarship. In some areas, the Church courts offered a useful service (such as the opportunity to sue slanderers), and their policing of morals may have been approved of by 'respectable' lay society, worried that fornication would lead to bastard children becoming a charge on the parish.[71] A periodic source of tension, however, was the Church's long-standing insistence that clerics could be tried only in ecclesiastical courts, so-called benefit of clergy. The traditional test of whether a man actually was a cleric – the ability to read – meant that increasing numbers of laymen could claim the benefit of the lighter punishments the Church courts imposed. There was periodic 'moral panic' about this in the late fifteenth century, rather like modern tabloid stories about

[70] Swanson, *Church*, pp. 188–90; Gunn, 'Dudley', 514–15.

[71] Margaret Bowker, 'Some Archdeacons' Court Books and the Common's Supplication Against the Ordinaries', in D.A. Bullough and R.L. Storey, eds., *The Study of Medieval Records* (Oxford, 1971); Harper-Bill, *Pre-Reformation Church*, ch. 6; Thomson, *Tudor Church*, ch. 8. A more sceptical note is struck in Richard Wunderli, *London Church Courts and Society on the Eve of the Reformation* (Cambridge, MA, 1981).

repeat juvenile offenders who can't be touched by the courts. In 1489, the law was tightened to allow benefit of clergy to be claimed by laymen only once (murderers and thieves were to be branded on the thumb), and in 1512 there was a further attempt to restrict the privilege by specifying offences which were not covered by it, and exempting only those in the 'major orders' of subdeacon, deacon and priest.[72] Some churchmen, however, vigorously resisted all attempts to deny benefit of clergy to those in 'minor orders', and by the time the 1512 act came up for renewal in 1515, it had become embroiled with a notorious *cause célèbre*, the case of Richard Hunne.[73]

Hunne was a London merchant (and likely Lollard sympathizer) who in 1511 refused to pay the customary mortuary (death duty) to the local priest on the death of his infant son. Suit and counter-suit followed, with Hunne attempting to launch a praemunire action, and the diocesan authorities raising charges of heresy. When Hunne died in suspicious circumstances in the Bishop of London's prison in 1514, the bishop's chancellor, William Horsey, and the minor officials suspected of murdering him could not be brought to trial because of benefit of clergy, and lay feeling in London became inflamed. Matters were complicated further by a papal bull of 1514 reiterating the principle that laymen had no jurisdiction over clerics. This was appealed to in a sermon the following year by the Abbot of Winchcombe, Richard Kidderminster, who argued that any extension of the 1512 statute would be contrary to the law of God. He was opposed by the Warden of the London Franciscans (and court preacher), Henry Standish, who protested that the bull had not been formally received in England and that the 1512 act was socially desirable. When convocation threatened Standish with heresy proceedings, the royal judges declared that those concerned were guilty of praemunire. At this point Henry stepped in, and at a conference held at Baynard's Castle compromise was reached. The bill removing benefit from minor clerics was dropped, as were the praemunire charges and the heresy proceedings against Standish (a few years later Henry made him a bishop). Horsey was summoned before the royal court of King's Bench, but was allowed to plead innocence and be dismissed. The bishops' suggestion that the case be referred to the Pope was ignored.

Historians dispute the significance of the Hunne/Standish affair. Dickens hails it as 'a landmark in the development of Erastian and anticlerical opinion'; Scarisbrick dismisses it as an 'isolated clash'.[74] Despite the intensity of passions aroused on all sides, matters soon returned to normal, and the ecclesiastical and royal courts continued to exercise their comple-

[72] Thomson, *Tudor Church*, pp. 93–4.

[73] The best guide to this is J.D.M. Derrett, 'The Affairs of Richard Hunne and Friar Standish', in Thomas More, *The Apology*, ed. J.B. Trapp (New Haven and London, 1979).

[74] Dickens, *Reformation*, p. 113; Scarisbrick, *Reformation*, p. 47. 'Erastian' refers to the doctrine of lay control over the Church.

mentary jurisdictions without obvious strain. But in the course of the furore, some interesting things had been said. During the Baynard's Castle meeting, Henry told the assembled churchmen that 'we are kings of England, and kings of England in time past have never had any superior but God only.'[75] Although this sounds like the starting pistol for the Reformation, it has been argued that in making the remark Henry was not 'saying anything very new or anything very significant'.[76] Similar grandiose claims had been made on behalf of Richard II in the fourteenth century, and by other European monarchs. They expressed the widespread aspiration in later medieval Europe to conceive kingship in terms of Roman emperorship (an 'empire' was a completely independent sovereignty, while, under the feudal system, kings might owe fealty to other rulers). There are indications, however, that an interest in 'imperial kingship' was intensifying under the first Tudors. Henry VII had himself depicted on coins and elsewhere wearing an 'imperial' crown (a closed or arched type, rather than an open-topped circlet). More generally, Henry seems to have built on a fifteenth-century tradition of interpreting the coronation promise to defend the Church as a charter to exercise strong royal leadership over the Church. It is revealing that when Edmund Dudley made his plea for ecclesiastical reform in 1509, he evidently assumed that the initiative would come from the Crown.[77] Henry VIII went so far as to amend the coronation oath itself, limiting the promise to defend the rights and liberties of the Church to those 'not prejudicial to his jurisdiction and dignity royal'.[78] Though not to burst into full flower until the 1530s, when an Act of Parliament would unambiguously declare that 'this realm of England is an Empire', there is no doubt that the seed of imperial kingship was germinating much earlier in Henry's mind, and was linked there to the status of royal versus canon law.

The significance of all of this should not be pushed too far: there was no countdown to royal supremacy, and recent commentators have emphasized not only the good state of Anglo-papal relations in the early sixteenth century, but the generally peaceful pattern of coexistence and compromise that prevailed in practice between the two systems of jurisdiction.[79] That

[75] Gwyn, *King's Cardinal*, p. 51.

[76] Haigh, *Reformations*, p. 82.

[77] Anthony Goodman, 'Henry VII and Christian Renewal', *Studies in Church History*, 17 (1981); Gunn, 'Dudley', 510–11.

[78] Walter Ullman, 'This Realm of England is an Empire', *Journal of Ecclesiastical History*, 30 (1979), 183. Historians dispute whether the change was made in 1509, during the 1515 crisis, or in the later 1520s: Haigh, *Reformations*, p. 82 and n.; Pamela Tudor-Craig, 'Henry VIII and King David', in Daniel Williams, ed., *Early Tudor England* (Woodbridge, 1989), pp. 187–9.

[79] Harper-Bill, *Pre-Reformation Church*, pp. 22–3; Thomson, *Tudor Church*, pp. 79, 360; Swanson, *Church*, p. 190, though note also the latter's comment (pp. 184–5) that praemunire was 'a time-bomb ticking under the whole edifice of the spiritual courts'.

there was no necessary collision course between the interests of the English Crown and those of Rome is suggested by the career of Thomas Wolsey. Wolsey's extraordinary accumulation of promotions between 1514 and 1524 – archbishop, cardinal, temporary and then permanent legate *a latere* (i.e. a deputy exercising quasi-papal powers in England) – in practice facilitated centralized control of the English Church in the hands of his master, Henry VIII. But at every stage, the appropriate authorization was sought from and given by Popes Leo X and Clement VII, hoping in return for English diplomatic support.[80] There was a general commitment, on both a national and international level, to make the system of Church–State relations work. But over the course of the later 1520s and 1530s, it was to become clear just how much this depended on the ability of the English king to get his own way.

Summation

The revisionist scholarship of the last few decades has rescued late medieval Catholicism from the partisan caricature of earlier generations of Protestant and nationalist historians. We can now see that the institutions of the Church were not fundamentally 'corrupt', nor the religion of the people irredeemably 'superstitious'. There was no swelling tide of discontent against lordly bishops, grasping monks and tyrannical Church courts. But the demonstration that pre-Reformation religion was not like the caricature should be a starting-point of discussion, not its end. Certainly, there was nothing inevitable, or even likely, about the course events took after 1530, but across all of the areas we have surveyed it is possible to find reasons why England's traditional religious regimen may have been vulnerable in the face of the two novel developments of those years – an attack on the institutions of the Church, led by the Crown itself, and the simultaneous offer of a new style of religious devotion being made by early Protestant reformers.

Arguably, a great strength of the late medieval Church was its flexible and adaptable nature, its ability to 'accommodate a wide diversity of practices which brought satisfaction to people of many different levels of intellect and social status'.[81] There was in the early sixteenth century no shortage of enthusiastic devotion and committed lay piety, as the profusion of fraternities, chantries and religious books amply testifies. But not all of this energy was channelled directly through the 'official' sacramental structures of the Church. To the medievalist Peter Heath it has seemed that 'the very vitality of *parochial* lay piety' could represent 'spiritual aspirations not

80 Gwyn, *King's Cardinal*, pp. 33, 102, 265.
81 Harper-Bill, *Pre-Reformation Church*, p. 96.

always satisfied by the Orthodox Church or established clergy'.[82] Moreover, for some at least of those drawn towards an introspective piety, a piety in which meditation upon the Passion of Christ played a central role, the evangelical message of the first reformers, and their offer of untrammelled access to vernacular scripture, would strike a chord. (It would do so among the thoroughly orthodox, as well as those already inclined to Lollardy.) Meanwhile the desire to bring 'reformation' (in a non-doctrinal sense) to the personnel and institutions of the Church was widely articulated, by bishops, humanist churchmen, lay lawyers and politicians alike. Yet too often it was seen to flounder in a welter of competing interests and jurisdictions, in which those who advocated reform were as enmeshed as anybody else. The one authority with the wherewithal, and perhaps the will, to impose and direct reform was the English Crown. Its wearer had long been looked to as a 'rex Christianissimus', a most Christian king, with obligations to the welfare of the Church in his realm.[83]

Was early sixteenth-century England therefore in some sense 'ready' for Reformation? Caution is required here. Parallel developments can be discerned elsewhere in Europe (for example, the Spanish kingdoms) where there was no breach with the papacy and no, or only the most abortive, doctrinal rebellion. The appropriate geological metaphor is not that of the live volcano: a lava-bed of discontent hissing and bubbling with increasing vehemence before erupting with explosive and predictable force. We should think rather of a set of pre-existent fault-lines, which helped to determine the way the religious landscape would fracture when it was hit by an earthquake, which no one was particularly expecting to happen. The tremors and aftershocks would in due course bring down much of the edifice of traditional Catholicism described in this chapter. The epicentre was the conscience of the King.

82 Peter Heath, 'Between Reform and Reformation: The English Church in the Fourteenth and Fifteenth Centuries', *Journal of Ecclesiastical History*, 41 (1990), 678.

83 Swanson, *Church*, pp. 92–3.

2

Henry VIII's Reformation 1525–1547

Overview

Everybody knows, or used to know, that Henry VIII got rid of the Pope, dissolved the monasteries and had six wives. As a brief précis of the events of the reign which must have seemed most striking to contemporaries, this is hard to beat. But the meaning of all these developments remains contentious. The reformation of the English Church over which Henry VIII presided between 1530 and 1547 is perplexing, because it does not fit neatly into any of the boxes that would later be used to categorize religious positions in the sixteenth century. It was not Lutheran, Calvinist or even 'Anglican'. Henry consistently described himself as a Catholic, and expressed an abhorrence of 'heresy', but many of his contemporaries considered him a hypocrite for doing so. Modern assessments have differed not only over whether the policy Henry pursued is best described as 'Catholicism without the pope', but over whether there is any coherent policy of reform to be discerned in these years. Henry VIII's personal theology represents a moving target which scholars have found difficult to fix clearly in their sights. The sternest assessments have concluded that it came down in the end to 'a *melange* of incoherent prejudices', 'a ragbag of emotional preferences'.[1] Others have questioned whether what transpired through the 1530s and 40s was in any meaningful sense 'Henry VIII's reformation' at all, preferring to see a 'reformation' which was driven forward (and back) in ad hoc fashion by the triumphs and defeats of competing factions at the Court, and by the particular agendas of ministers such as Thomas Cromwell and Stephen Gardiner. Yet we should not concentrate exclusively on the motives of King and councillors. There was,

[1] Paul O'Grady, *Henry VIII and the Conforming Catholics* (Collegeville, MN, 1990), p. 10; Diarmaid MacCulloch, 'Henry VIII and the Reform of the Church', in Diarmaid MacCulloch, ed., *The Reign of Henry VIII* (London, 1995), p. 178.

in Christopher Haigh's useful terminology, 'reformation from below' as well as 'reformation from above'.[2]

This chapter explores the evolving shape of 'reformation' in Henry VIII's reign under three broad headings. First, it examines the movements for reform that from the mid-1520s could no longer be contained within the bounds of late medieval orthodoxy. It discusses their relative indebtedness to native and foreign influences, and the ways in which they came to discover points of mutual interest with the religious policies of Henry VIII and his advisors. Second, it surveys the development of 'Henrician' policies through the 1530s and 1540s, asking who was responsible for their formulation, and what kind of Reformation they collectively comprised. Lastly, it considers the impact of the Henrician reforms on the religious culture of the people, and addresses the vexed question of how changes, which appear to have been often unexpected and unwelcome, were nonetheless successfully imposed.

2.1 *Reformation without the King*

It is conventional wisdom that the Reformation in England began with Henry VIII's divorce from Catherine of Aragon. It did not. In the years when Henry was still the Pope's loyal 'defender of the faith', small but increasing numbers of English men and women had begun working for a transformation of the Church. They can hardly be called 'Protestants', a term scarcely used in England before the reign of Edward VI, and which implies battle lines more clearly drawn than they actually were. Nor were all 'Lutherans' in the strict sense: English reformers in the 1520s drew on the ideas of a range of continental reformers. Many would have described themselves as Catholics, but they had moved decisively away from the priorities of late medieval Catholicism. There is a growing consensus that 'evangelical' is the best label for members of this loose and varied movement, united by an emphasis on the transformative power of 'the Word of God'.[3] Opponents referred to them disparagingly as proponents of 'new learning'[4], though some of their ideas had long been aired in Lollard circles. What was new was the conviction that Christ's sacrifice on the cross had removed the necessity to perform 'good works' in order to attain salvation. 'Justification' in the eyes of God came through faith alone, formed by reading and hearing

[2] Christopher Haigh, 'The Recent Historiography of the English Reformation', in id., ed., *The English Reformation Revised* (Cambridge, 1987), pp. 19–21.

[3] MacCulloch, 'Henry VIII', pp. 168–9; Peter Marshall and Alec Ryrie, 'Introduction', in id., eds., *The Beginnings of English Protestantism* (Cambridge, 2002).

[4] Richard Rex, 'The New Learning', *Journal of Ecclesiastical History*, 44 (1993), who points out the anachronism of using the term as a synonym for humanism.

the scriptures. Monasteries, chantries, masses, vows, pilgrimage, veneration of saints, confession to priests – the Church's elaborate mechanisms for sanctifying humans in this world, and aiding their souls in the next – were either a distraction, or, more likely, a damnable delusion.[5]

The English bishops were on the ball when it came to heresy (they had mounted a concerted drive against Lollardy in 1511–12), and the threat of Lutheranism was taken seriously. In 1521 Wolsey commissioned university theologians to write books against Luther, an inspiring lead here being set by the King himself with his *Assertio Septem Sacramentorum* ('Defence of the Seven Sacraments'). Luther's works were publicly burned at the London pulpit of Paul's Cross in May 1521 and again in 1526, Bishop John Fisher preaching on both occasions. Books not heretics were incinerated in these years. Wolsey and Archbishop Warham of Canterbury took the view that those seduced by the ideas of Luther, at this stage mainly educated clergy, were wayward sons who could be privately persuaded to recognize the error of their ways.[6] Things changed with the replacement of Wolsey as chancellor by Thomas More in October 1529; the latter was horrified by the continuing spread of heresy and determined to take whatever measures were necessary. An importer of heretical books was burned in Kent in February 1530, though a much greater stir was created by the execution of the Cambridge scholar Thomas Bilney at Norwich in August 1531.

The fate of Bilney reminds us that the history of the evangelical 'movement' is the sum history of individuals – stories that should be told with sympathy though without hagiographical gloss. Bilney's conversion followed a pattern which seems close to that of Martin Luther himself. He found no peace of mind in endless fasting, pardons and masses, but achieved 'marvellous comfort and quietness' reading Erasmus's Greek New Testament and discovering in St Paul's letters that 'Christ Jesus came into the world to save sinners; of whom I am chief'. Determined to condemn dependence upon 'works of man's righteousness', he set off on a preaching tour of East Anglia in 1525, attacking the veneration of images.[7] Further inflammatory preaching led to a heresy trial in November 1527 where Bilney was prevailed upon to abjure, a notable propaganda victory for the authorities. But filled with remorse, he decided in 1531 he must go 'up to Jerusalem', resumed his public preaching against images and saints-cults and sealed his fate. His death caused widespread unease, for it was not clear to all that his criticism of abuses in popular religion actually constituted

[5] Throughout Henry's reign, however, many evangelicals retained (as Luther did) a belief in Christ's real presence in the sacrament: Alec Ryrie, 'The Strange Death of Lutheran England', *Journal of Ecclesiastical History*, 53 (2002).

[6] Craig D'Alton, 'The Suppression of Heresy in Early Henrician England', University of Melbourne PhD thesis (1999).

[7] Peter Marshall, 'Evangelical Conversion in the Reign of Henry VIII', in Marshall and Ryrie, *Beginnings*, pp. 16–17.

heresy. The same could be said of Robert Barnes, an Augustinian friar who did public penance at Wolsey's book burning of 1526. Under the influence of Bilney, Barnes launched a pulpit broadside against ecclesiastical abuses and Wolsey's misuse of power in Cambridge on Christmas Eve 1525. He may not yet have been a fully-fledged Lutheran, but he was soon to become one.[8]

If any individual represents the channel between extreme Erasmian criticism and full-blown theological dissent, it was William Tyndale. A Gloucestershire priest, and tutor in a gentry household, Tyndale had become exasperated with the ignorance of local clergy, and, like Bilney, inspired by Erasmus's New Testament (and Luther's German one of 1522). His ambition was to produce an English version, and in 1523 went to Bishop Cuthbert Tunstall of London seeking patronage. The approach is significant – hopes of reform from humanist bishops were not closed at this stage. But Tyndale was rebuffed and acquired instead the financial backing of a wealthy London draper, Humphrey Monmouth. Printing of the New Testament began at Cologne in 1525 and was completed at Worms in 1526. Thereafter copies of the work (of which there were new editions in 1534 and 1535) flooded into England, despite the authorities' attempts to keep them out.[9] Tyndale's New Testament was no plain and unadulterated 'Word of God'. 'Glosses' (or marginal notes) with a distinctly Lutheran spin guided the reader's interpretation, and some of the English translations were intentionally provocative ones. The Greek terms which were conventionally rendered in English as 'do penance', 'Church' and 'priest', were given as 'repent', 'congregation' and 'elder', translations with obvious implications for teachings about confession and the authority of the priesthood. Concerns about Lollardy meant that England, uniquely in western Europe, had no authorized vernacular scripture. The English bishops now paid the price for that pusillanimity as Tyndale's version fed a long-frustrated demand. From exile in Antwerp, Tyndale supplemented his translations with overtly polemical works. His *Practice of Prelates* (1530) castigated the papacy and the English bishops; *Obedience of a Christian Man* (1528) argued the clergy had usurped authority properly belonging to secular princes, with side-swipes at confession, worshipping of saints and purgatory.

Tyndale's readers included Simon Fish, a young common lawyer who, from Antwerp in 1528, published a short satirical tract which page for page proved as influential as any other text of the early English Reformation. *A Supplication for the Beggars* was supposedly a petition to the King from poor beggars, complaining violently against those 'sturdy beggars', the clergy. Its

[8] Carl Trueman, *Luther's Legacy: Salvation and the English Reformers 1525–1556* (Oxford, 1994), pp. 49–51.

[9] David Daniell, *William Tyndale: a Biography* (New Haven and London, 1994).

central contention was an explosive one: purgatory was 'a thing invented by the covetousness of the spiritualty', a means of siphoning the King's and the country's wealth into the hands of the Church. Fish's pamphlet provoked a disproportionately long refutation in Thomas More's *Supplication of Souls*, but this in turn prompted a work even more damaging to the Catholic cause, a *Disputation of Purgatory* by John Frith, a junior canon of Wolsey's Cardinal College, and another addition to the Tyndale circle in Antwerp. Frith's book supplemented the anticlerical jibes of Fish with learned and incisive scriptural argument, and his *Disputation* was a formative text for the first generation of English evangelicals. Frith also wrote on the eucharist, going further than Luther in his rejection of the real presence. His potential to become the towering figure of English evangelical theology ended in July 1533, when aged barely 30 he went to the stake at Smithfield.[10]

Such individual stories help to identify the various soil-types in which the evangelical plant took root and the possibilities for cross-fertilization between them. The importance of London, England's only major city, looms large. Luther's tracts first entered England via the German merchant community based at the Steelyard and its contacts with the local merchant elite. Some of these, like Tyndale's patron, Humphrey Monmouth, were already Lollard sympathizers. London was the base of operations for the shadowy 'Christian brethren', a group of merchants who arranged the importation and distribution of heretical works, though historians disagree over whether this was an organized secret society or simply a generic term for evangelical sympathizers.[11] In addition to an affluent and literate lay elite, London possessed the Inns of Court where common lawyers received their training, universities in all but name. Common lawyers were not genetically programmed to be heretics or anticlericals (Thomas More was one), but there was a tendency for them to resent the jurisdictional claims of the Church. Fish was one of a number of key names of the early Reformation to enter the Inns in the early 1520s.[12] Youth, it has been argued, was an important factor in the early reception of the Reformation, in its origins a religion of novelty and protest. The young law students at the Inns moved in a city with a markedly youthful immigrant population, and many young people may not have had time to become firmly attached to the faith of their fathers. Frith's opponents mocked him as 'young father Frith'.[13] We should

[10] Peter Marshall, *Beliefs and the Dead in Reformation England* (Oxford, 2002), pp. 48–51.

[11] A.G. Dickens, *The English Reformation* (2nd ed., London, 1989), pp. 93–4; John F. Davis, *Heresy and Reformation in the South East of England 1520–1559* (London, 1983), pp. 27–8. For scepticism, see Anne Hudson, *The Premature Reformation: Wycliffte Texts and Lollard History* (Oxford, 1988), pp. 482–3.

[12] Susan Brigden, *London and the Reformation* (Oxford, 1989), p. 116.

[13] Susan Brigden, 'Youth and the English Reformation', in Peter Marshall, ed., *The Impact of the English Reformation 1500–1640* (London, 1997), p. 58 and *passim*.

note, though, that evangelicals did not boast of their own youthfulness (like novelty, regarded in the sixteenth century in a negative light). Martin Luther was a middle-aged convert to the gospel, as, in England, were Tyndale, Latimer and Cranmer.

If youth and education meant a greater openness to new ideas, then it is unsurprising that the universities have long been identified as the most fertile ground for reform. A sense of proportion is required here. Most Oxford and Cambridge scholars remained orthodox in this early period; indeed many were actively engaged in writing and preaching against Lutheran heresy.[14] Nor should it be assumed that 'humanism' was the high road to Protestantism. It is true that Bilney discovered in Erasmus's New Testament something remarkably akin to Luther's notion of justification by faith, but the ethos of humanist scholarship was too widely diffused for humanists to comprise a distinct 'party', and many humanist scholars remained loyal to the Church.[15] It may also be that the traditional emphasis on Cambridge as birthplace of the English Reformation requires modification. Recent scholarship has warned us against reading too much into a single unspecific reference in John Foxe's later *Book of Martyrs* to a group of scholars meeting to discuss theology at the White Horse Tavern, a hostelry which became known as 'Germany' because of the radical views espoused there.[16] Nearly every major name of the early Reformation has been associated with the White Horse, but discussions there were probably limited to a small circle of the associates of Barnes and Bilney. The conditions of college life, however, provided opportunities for powerful and enduring personal influences. Several reformers later attributed their conversion to Barnes or Bilney at Cambridge at this time. These included Hugh Latimer who in his turn was credited with bringing many to the gospel.[17] The universities were not insulated, either from each other or from the world outside. A clutch of Oxford 'Lutherans' were discovered in Wolsey's new foundation of Cardinal College in 1528, some of whom (like Frith) were Cambridge imports. Christopher Haigh has argued that these circles in Oxford and Cambridge were not fully formed Protestant cells, that 'fervent biblical piety rather than... specifically Lutheran ideas' animated many of the participants.[18] The point has validity, though we should bear in mind that 'heresy' is what the Church authorities say it is. By the end of the 1520s

14 Richard Rex, 'The English Campaign against Luther in the 1520s', *Transactions of the Royal Historical Society*, 5th ser., 39 (1989).

15 Id., 'Humanism', in Andrew Pettegree, ed., *The Reformation World* (London, 2000).

16 Diarmaid MacCulloch, *Thomas Cranmer: A Life* (New Haven and London, 1996), pp. 25–6; Rex, *Henry VIII*, pp. 40–1.

17 Marshall, 'Conversion', pp. 35–6.

18 Christopher Haigh, *English Reformations: Religion, Politics, and Society under the Tudors* (Oxford, 1993), pp. 58, 61.

the bishops were deeply alarmed by what young (and not-so-young) scholars were getting up to in the colleges, and by its potential to spill out and infect the wider community.

Interest in evangelical ideas was not limited to the 'golden triangle' of London and the universities. The most famous provincial heretic of these years is the gentleman William Tracy (like Tyndale, a Gloucestershire man). Tracy achieved the unusual distinction of being punished for heresy after his death in October 1530, his corpse exhumed and burned by the chancellor of Worcester diocese. The trigger was Tracy's will, which began with an unambiguous assertion of belief in justification by faith and went on to 'bestow no part of my goods for that intent, that any man should say or do to help my soul'.[19] Copies of the will were almost immediately circulating in manuscript in London, and a couple of years later it was printed in Antwerp with commentaries by Frith and Tyndale, becoming in due course a model for other Protestant testators to follow.[20] Tracy's conversion suggests the potential of evangelicalism to reach beyond the circles of university intellectuals and capture the imagination of the landed social elite, an ominous development from the authorities' point of view.

Attention to the geographical patterns of early evangelical growth begs an important question about origins, for at first glance it appears that 'Lutheran' heretics are often found in places with a known Lollard presence in preceding decades: London, Bristol and Gloucestershire, parts of Essex, Kent and East Anglia. Views on the contribution of Lollardy to the development of the English Reformation represent round two of the debate over whether the Lollards were a spent force or a swelling tide in the pre-Reformation Church. In an early work, Dickens urged Reformation historians to pay more attention to 'a diffused but inveterate Lollardy revivified by contact with continental Protestantism'.[21] Subsequently, J.F. Davis went further, arguing that rather than merely providing a seed-bed from which the Reformation could grow, the ideas of early evangelicals like Thomas Garrett, Thomas Arthur and Thomas Bilney were essentially Lollard in character and content.[22] By contrast, revisionist scholars like Haigh, Scarisbrick and Rex regard Lollardy as too weak, incoherent and fragmented to play any role in the Reformation other than to be overtaken by it, the latter going so far as to say 'it was Lollardy, not Catholicism, that was morally bankrupt, intellectually empty, and in a state of terminal decay on the eve of the Reformation.'[23]

[19] William Tyndale, *An Answer to Sir Thomas More's Dialogue*, ed. Henry Walter, (Cambridge, 1850), p. 272.

[20] John Craig and Caroline Litzenberger, 'Wills as Religious Propaganda: the Testament of William Tracy', *Journal of Ecclesiastical History*, 44 (1993), 424–5.

[21] A.G. Dickens, *Lollards and Protestants in the Diocese of York* (Oxford, 1959), p. 243.

[22] Davis, *Heresy and Reformation*; id., 'Lollardy and the Reformation', in Marshall, *Impact*.

[23] Richard Rex, *The Lollards* (Basingstoke, 2002), p. 132.

Controversy over the extent of overlap between Lollardy and Protestantism goes back to the sixteenth century itself. From the early 1530s, old Lollard texts were being printed abroad in evangelical editions in order 'to muster precedent and example'.[24] As the label 'new learning' suggests, sixteenth-century Protestants were intensely vulnerable to the accusation of 'novelty'. 'Where was your Church before Luther?' To later propagandists like Foxe, the Lollards provided an answer, a link in the chain of the 'true Church' that had always resisted the corruption of Rome. Yet Foxe was not above occasionally doctoring his account of Lollard trials to omit utterances which did not chime with later Protestant orthodoxy.[25] Doctrinal similarities between Lollardy and evangelicalism are immediate and striking: dislike of images, pilgrimage and the cult of the saints; rejection of the sacramental powers of the priesthood; most of all, a stress on the importance of vernacular scripture. But Lollards had not found their way to the central theological insight of Luther and his English disciples: that people are 'justified' solely through their faith in Christ. In its own way, Lollardy was as much a 'good works' religion as late medieval Catholicism.

Continuity or discontinuity? The geographical evidence is suggestive but inconclusive.[26] The most fruitful approach is to establish continuities of personnel, to demonstrate that individual Lollards were receptive to the message of new evangelism and contributed to its transmission. Though evidence is patchy, there are a few cases where such connections can be established. The Amersham Lollard Thomas Harding was under suspicion in 1506, and again in 1522. Ten years later he was discovered in possession of books by Tyndale and a copy of Tyndale's New Testament. At his trial he demonstrated an awareness of justification by faith alongside more traditional Lollard views.[27] In 1527, John Tyball and Thomas Hilles, Lollards from Steeple Bumptsead in Essex, journeyed to London to buy a Tyndale testament from Robert Barnes, then under house arrest in the priory of the Augustinian friars. The case points to a network of links between the new heresy and the old: these rural Lollards knew exactly where to come. But there is a twist in the tale. Tyball and Hilles brought with them their precious manuscript gospels and epistles, which Barnes 'did little regard, and made a twit of it, and said "a point for them, for they be not to be regarded toward the new printed Testament in English"'.[28] This was no meeting of

24 Margaret Aston, *Lollards and Reformers: Images and Literacy in Late Medieval Religion* (London, 1984), p. 224.

25 John A.F. Thomson, 'John Foxe and some Sources for Lollard History', *Studies in Church History* 2 (1965), pp. 252–7.

26 See Rex, *Lollards*, pp. 119–31 for the argument that continuity arguments are plausible only when established at the most local level, and not based on broad correlations of counties or dioceses.

27 Hudson, *Premature Reformation*, pp. 505–7.

28 A.G. Dickens and Dorothy Carr, eds., *The Reformation in England to the Accession of Elizabeth I* (London, 1967), p. 35.

equals; the Lutheran friar clearly felt he had little to learn from the long-secret witness of the Wycliffite tradition.

There are powerful arguments for playing down the contribution of Lollardy. No first-rank reformer of Barnes's generation seems to have had a Lollard background; indeed leading evangelicals often stressed the depth of their commitment to traditional Catholicism in the years before their conversion. A striking number, like Barnes himself, emerged from the ranks of the friars – popular preachers who for a century and more had been in the forefront of combating Lollardy.[29] Yet it would be premature to close the book on the question, not least because despite the categorizations of historians it is often hard to say for certain if someone was a Lollard, a Lutheran or something else. Bilney is a case in point. The content of his preaching – condemnation of vows, prayer to saints and images – reflected Lollard priorities, and the Lollard evangelist John Hacker was reported as saying he would walk 20 miles to hear Bilney preach. But Bilney's humanist background, and his Luther-like view of justification, makes him seem an unlikely Lollard. It has been argued that since the Church courts were long accustomed to catching Lollards, the questions put to suspects might have given a deceptively Lollard tinge to 'new' heretics.[30] But given the overlap of Lollard and evangelical beliefs it is equally possible that some heretics tried throughout Henry VIII's reign and beyond may be Lollard survivors rather than recent converts. To the base-line question of whether Lollardy predisposed some English people to receive the evangelical message, the answer is undoubtedly that it did, though a longstanding dislike of heresy may have predisposed many other people against the new doctrines. It is also fair to point out that reforming ideas were able to spread rapidly in European societies (France, Germany, The Netherlands), which had no recent tradition of popular unorthodoxy. Still more difficult to assess is the extent to which Lollardy shaped or influenced the directions in which English Protestantism was to develop. Diarmaid MacCulloch has pointed out that three of its most dominant characteristics in later decades – its interest in Old Testament law, its detestation of images and its 'Swiss' (rather than Lutheran) understanding of Christ's presence (or rather absence) in the eucharist – all have a Lollard look about them.[31] This, however, was not an influence openly acknowledged. While debates about Lollardy and the Reformation will continue, it is clear that the prospects of the evangelical message depended primarily on its ability to appeal to those whose religious outlook was formed within the Christ-centred piety of orthodox Catholicism.

[29] Marshall, 'Conversion', pp. 30–2; Richard Rex, 'The Friars in the English Reformation', in Marshall and Ryrie, *Beginnings*.

[30] Rex, *Henry VIII*, pp. 137–8.

[31] Diarmaid MacCulloch, 'England', in Andrew Pettegree, ed., *The Early Reformation in Europe* (Cambridge, 1992), pp. 172–3. See also Ryrie, 'Lutheran England', 80–1.

Revisionist historians emphasize the distinctly limited achievements of early English evangelicals. In 1530, the old devotional order was still 'a Church unchallenged'.[32] Everywhere in England (even at the University of Cambridge) evangelicals were a small minority, and across large swathes of the country they were as rare as daffodils in December. Could the evangelical movement have succeeded without the change in the political climate that was about to take place? Across Western Europe, the Reformation succeeded where state power supported it, and failed where the resources of government were powerfully marshalled against it.[33] But this does not mean we should see the early evangelical movement as a historiographical dead-end, and regard the reformation in Henry VIII's reign as a straightforward 'act of state'. Reformation 'from above' and 'from below' are not alternative explanations, but interlocking pieces of a complex jigsaw. We should note several characteristics of the evangelical movement at the turn of the 1530s. In the first place, it was not noticeably in retreat. Neither the blandishments of Wolsey nor the punishments of More had succeeded in stemming the flow of converts. In Tyndale's New Testament it had a not-so-secret weapon which was meeting the frustrated aspirations of at least a section of the literate laity. Importantly, converts were being made in places from which Lollardy had either retreated or failed to make any impact: the universities, the Inns of Court, the orders of friars. The 'new learning' was a minority faith with a limited geographical diffusion. But in early Tudor England, not all persons or places were of equal weight: early evangelical converts were often people of influence in positions of importance. Lastly, and most crucially, in their hostility to the pretensions of the clergy, their insinuation that purgatory was a fraud enabling the Church to amass wealth and lands, their insistence that popes were scheming foreign rulers intent on the subversion of the State, the evangelicals were saying some things that the King himself was soon to find seductively persuasive.

2.2 *Catholicism without the Pope?*

The early English Reformation acquired its distinctive character from the convergence of a spiritual reform movement with the dynastic and political requirements of the English Crown. But it did not seem necessary or inevitable to most contemporaries that any such convergence should take place. When Henry broke with Rome, and declared himself to be Supreme Head of the Church of England, many saw a merely jurisdictional change, which would not affect the firm Catholic faith of the King and the great

[32] Haigh, *Reformations*, part I.

[33] Though there are exceptions (Ireland, Scotland, the Netherlands) to this usually reliable rule.

mass of his subjects. Others, probably a minority, held that to repudiate the Holy Father was itself a heretical act.

There is no doubt that the Reformation in England would have taken a very different course, and may even have been strangled at birth, had it not been for what contemporaries called 'the King's great matter', his determination to secure a divorce (technically, an annulment) from his wife Catherine of Aragon. It is usual to suppose that anxieties about the succession played a vital role in Henry's thinking, and this may well have been so. By 1525 Catherine was 40 years old (six years her husband's senior), and though she had given birth to six children, only the Princess Mary, born in 1516, had survived more than a few days. There were unlikely to be more children, and the sole precedent for female rule (the twelfth-century civil war precipitated by the accession of Henry I's daughter, Matilda) was not an encouraging one. The Tudor dynasty was almost certainly less secure in Henry's mind than it seems to us in retrospect. His father's usurpation of the throne, founded on a distinctly tenuous dynastic claim, was within living memory, and there were still Yorkist princes to pose as plausible alternative candidates. Henry had a stroke of luck in 1525 when the last of Richard III's nephews, Richard de la Pole, was killed fighting for the French in Italy, but the investiture the same year of the King's illegitimate son Henry Fitzroy with the royal title Duke of Richmond suggests the succession was very much on his mind. There was, however, no precedent for the accession of a royal bastard: remarriage and the production of a legitimate male heir must have seemed by far the best option.

Henry's determination to pursue this path was more than cynical political expediency; he had become convinced in his conscience that marriage to Catherine was sinful in the eyes of God. Henry, a highly educated renaissance prince, knew his Bible, and two passages in the Book of Leviticus warned that if a man took his brother's wife 'it was an unclean thing' and (ominously) 'they shall be childless'. Catherine *had* been his brother's wife, briefly married to Henry VII's heir Prince Arthur (d. 1502). Under canon law this created an obstacle to the marriage with Henry that his father desired to maintain the alliance with Catherine's parents, Ferdinand and Isabella of Castile and Aragon. Pope Julius II provided the requisite dispensation, and the marriage took place shortly after Henry's accession in 1509. But Henry's growing preoccupation with his 'childless' state in the later 1520s (Mary didn't count) persuaded him the dispensation should never have been granted, and the central aim of the 'divorce campaign' gathering momentum from 1526 was to persuade the current Pope Clement VII to pronounce the marriage invalid on the technical grounds of consanguinity (close kin-relationship). A king trying to repudiate his wife was a major political event, but the attempt to put pressure on the papacy for this purpose was within a contemporary frame of expectation. Nonetheless, the fact that Henry and his advisors stuck firmly to their guns on the argument from Leviticus meant that a profoundly theological principle – the primacy of the clear word of scripture over the dispensing authority of the Pope – was from the outset at the heart of royal policy-making.

There was another factor in all this, of course, and another important link to the outlook of evangelical reform. Henry did not want to remarry in the abstract. He wanted to marry Anne Boleyn, a lady-in-waiting of Catherine's he had become increasingly obsessed with since about 1525–6. Modern scholarship has persuasively asserted that Anne was not a passive catalyst of the Henrician Reformation, but an important player in her own right. Brought up at the French Court where she had acquired an evangelical interest in scripture, Anne was to prove a powerful patron of English reformers.[34] There is no firm foundation for the story that she passed to Henry a copy of Fish's *Supplication for the Beggars*, but she does seem to have given him a copy of Tyndale's *Obedience of a Christian Man* (or at least pointed out some choice passages concerning royal dignity and papal misdemeanour). Henry is supposed to have announced 'this is the book for me and all kings to read'.[35] Anne was feeding the King's mind, but keeping his hands off her body. Her determination not to become a royal mistress and to hold out for the prize of being queen was an important element pushing forward the divorce campaign.

While it would have been embarrassing for Clement VII to overturn the ruling of his predecessor, he would probably have been prepared to do it, to maintain the papacy's usually good relationship with the English Crown, and in recognition of Henry's frankly reasonable concerns about dynastic stability. But political circumstances in Italy, which had long played to the English Crown's advantage in relations with the papacy, now worked against it. Clement was caught in the crossfire between the French King Francis I and the Habsburg Emperor, Charles V, as they struggled for control of northern Italy. Charles was determined that Henry should not repudiate Catherine, his aunt. While the Pope played for time, only in 1529 granting a commission for Wolsey and fellow-legate Cardinal Campeggio to begin divorce proceedings in England, the reality was that the progress of Henry's suit depended upon the success of French arms. When Francis's army was routed at Landriano in June 1529, Clement revoked the divorce case to Rome, and effectively ended the chances of a successful outcome for Henry (as well as the career of Wolsey, who was stripped of the chancellorship in October, and died in disgrace the following year). A radicalization of policy followed, designed first to bully Clement into granting the divorce, and when that failed, to settle the matter unilaterally in England. Henry's Royal Supremacy, it is fair to say, was in great measure the product of his failure to secure the divorce in any other way.

34 Maria Dowling, 'Anne Boleyn and Reform', *Journal of Ecclesiastical History*, 35 (1984); Eric Ives, 'Anne Boleyn and the Early Reformation in England', *Historical Journal*, 37 (1994). For an opposing view, see George Bernard, 'Anne Boleyn's Religion', *Historical Journal*, 36 (1993).

35 Eric Ives, *Anne Boleyn* (Oxford, 1985), p. 163.

But the Royal Supremacy was not an idea thought up on the back of an envelope. As we saw in Section 1.4, notions of 'imperial kingship' had been on the Crown's mind for some time, and were focussed by the occasional spats over the respective scope of secular and canon law. The hostility of common lawyers to the jurisdictional claims of the Church was allowed free rein in the Parliament of 1529, when 'anticlerical' bills were passed regulating mortuary and probate fees, and restricting pluralism.[36] There was growing interest in the ideas of the common law theorist Christopher St German, whose textbook *Doctor and Student* (revised in 1530 and 31) attacked benefit of clergy and heresy laws, arguing that canon law should be confined to entirely spiritual matters, like the form of sacraments. Legal arguments against the jurisdictional independence of the Church were to be complemented by theological and historical ones. In 1530, Henry approved a suggestion by the Boleyn chaplain, Thomas Cranmer, that university canonists and theologians be consulted for their opinions on the divorce (the foreign universities generally found against Henry's case, except in France where royal policy was favourable, and Henry provided generous bribes). At the same time, a royal 'policy-unit' was established to examine what bearing scripture, history and the Church fathers had on the settlement of the King's divorce. Cranmer, Edward Foxe and Edward Lee (all soon to be bishops), along with the Italian friar Nicholas de Burgo, produced in September 1530 a document known as the *Collectanea satis copiosa* (the 'sufficiently big collection'). This purported to show that since Anglo-Saxon times English kings had enjoyed spiritual supremacy in their dominions, and possessed by right a theocratic (sacred or priestly) kingship like that exercised by the later Roman emperors. Henry could thus legitimately call on any English bishop to announce his divorce.[37]

By the end of 1530, Henry had sufficient theoretical justification to break with the papacy and assert ecclesiastical independence. In fact, it took another three years for these steps to be irrevocably taken, the complex political manoeuvrings of the interim period in part a reflection of conflicting groupings around the King. Catherine's supporters at the court were fighting a rearguard action, while the Boleyns and their allies were pressing for a radical unilateral solution, and a powerful noble faction around the Dukes of Norfolk and Suffolk still hoped the Pope could be strong-armed into granting the King's request. In 1531, the entire English clergy were (somewhat bizarrely) charged with praemunire for illegally exercising jurisdiction through the Church courts. A 'Pardon of the Clergy' was offered in return for a fine of £100,000 and recognition of Henry as 'Supreme Head of the Church' (somewhat undermined by the insertion, at Bishop Fisher's

[36] Stanford Lehmberg, *The Reformation Parliament 1529–1536* (Cambridge, 1970), pp. 81–102. Probate refers to the verification of wills by Church courts.

[37] Virginia Murphy, 'The Literature and Propaganda of Henry VIII's First Divorce', in MacCulloch, *Henry VIII*, pp. 146–8.

instigation, of the qualifying phrase 'as far as the law of God allows'). In 1532, the House of Commons issued a 'Supplication against the Ordinaries', a compendium of grievances (many of them objectively unfair) against the practices and procedures of the Church courts. Miscalculating the extent to which the Supplication reflected official thinking, the bishops produced a defensive reply, which infuriated Henry (and probably cost Stephen Gardiner, who had penned the document, promotion to Canterbury when it became vacant later that year). The King now demanded a 'Submission of the Clergy', under which the bishops surrendered their independent right to make canon law – a crucial shift in the balance of power between Church and State. With the clerical estate at home subdued, the guns were turned on the papacy itself. In March 1533 the Act in Restraint of Appeals provided the first definite rejection of papal authority with its emphatic statement (drawing on the pseudo-history of the *Collectanea*) that 'divers sundry old authentic histories and chronicles' proved 'this realm of England is an Empire'. The King's first marriage was formally annulled in May 1533, and in June Anne Boleyn was crowned Queen (her delivery in September of a daughter, the future Queen Elizabeth, was a big disappointment). The antipapal revolution was completed in 1534 by an Act declaring it no longer heresy to deny the Pope's power, a Supremacy Act confirming the King's new title, and a Succession Act confirming the Boleyn marriage and vesting succession in its offspring. (Parliament, it should be noted, did not *make* Henry Supreme Head of the Church, but publicly declared the title, which had always been his by divine will.)

By 1534, through a combination of accident and design, Henry VIII had established an ecclesiastical system unique in Europe, a royal supremacy which empowered the King to control all aspects of the Church's administration, and to define its doctrine. It was not obvious that the faith of the English Church would be materially affected; the Dispensations Act of 1534 insisted that Henry had no intention 'to decline or vary from the congregation of Christ's Church in any things concerning the very articles of the Catholic faith'.[38] Martin Luther was singularly unimpressed, and there was disquiet too among some English evangelicals, including Tyndale, who felt that 'headship' of the Church was an honour belonging to Christ alone. By contrast, many orthodox Catholics, including the talented and ambitious bishop of Winchester, Stephen Gardiner, were wholehearted supporters of the supremacy. One who was not was the erstwhile chancellor, Thomas More. Ironically, More had never been an ardent papalist, but he was convinced that breaking communion with the universal Church would encourage deviation in doctrine, that schism would lead to heresy. Events

[38] Henry Gee and William Hardy, eds., *Documents Illustrative of English Church History* (London, 1896), p. 225.

would prove More right and Gardiner wrong. Despite Henry's demurs, the royal supremacy displayed from the outset its potential to alter the faith of the nation.

In the first place, the divorce campaign transformed the outlook for English evangelicals. The energies of the university scholars who had written against Luther in the early 1520s were increasingly diverted into finding arguments for the divorce, leaving Thomas More, by the early 1530s, as a solitary voice engaged in polemic with the English evangelicals Tyndale, Barnes and Frith. More's resignation as chancellor in 1532 was an important moment. The new chancellor, Thomas Audley, released heretics from prison, and the persecution, which had intensified under More, effectively came to an end. Previously suspect figures, such as Barnes or Hugh Latimer, began to receive signs of royal favour, and a number of evangelical sympathizers came to occupy positions of real political importance. Among these a key figure was Thomas Cromwell, a lawyer and former servant of Wolsey who had proved useful in managing business in the Reformation Parliament. Appointed king's secretary, and Lord Privy Seal, Cromwell was elevated further in January 1535 to the new post of 'Vicegerent in Spirituals', which gave him delegated authority to exercise the Supremacy (outranking all the bishops). Cromwell has been a controversial figure in early Tudor historiography, not least because of the sometimes exaggerated claims made on his behalf by G.R. Elton, who regarded him as the mastermind behind the parliamentary formulation of 'imperial' sovereignty, as well as the principal architect of a broader 'Tudor revolution in government'. The latter concept has been comprehensively repudiated by more recent scholarship and John Guy has demonstrated convincingly that the ideology of the 1533 Appeals Act drew on older ideas as well as a broader range of royal advisors.[39] Nonetheless, Cromwell was an undeniably key figure in the formation of religious policy after 1535, and a recent attempt to portray him as the cipher-like functionary of an all-domineering king takes revisionism too far.[40] While Elton's Cromwell was an essentially secular figure, most recent assessments stress his genuine commitment to the cause of 'the gospel', and the damage suffered to that cause by his execution in 1540.[41]

An equally, in the longer term perhaps yet more important promotion was that of Thomas Cranmer, the surprise candidate for the See of

39 For the critique of Elton, see the essays in Christopher Coleman and David Starkey, eds., *Revolution Reasessed: Revisions in the History of Tudor Government and Administration* (Oxford, 1986); John Guy, 'Thomas Cromwell and the Intellectual Origins of the Henrician Revolution', in id., ed., *The Tudor Monarchy* (London, 1997).

40 George Bernard, 'Elton's Cromwell', *History*, 83 (1998).

41 See particularly Susan Brigden, 'Thomas Cromwell and the "Brethren"', in Claire Cross, David Loades and J.J. Scarisbrick, eds., *Law and Government under the Tudors* (Cambridge, 1998).

Canterbury in 1532 after the death of Archbishop Warham. Cranmer had held no position higher than archdeacon, but had proved his intellectual worth in the divorce campaign, and enjoyed the patronage of the ascendant Boleyns. His appointment meant that for the next 20 years a cautious but committed advocate of evangelical reform was positioned at the heart of English government.[42] Anne Boleyn's influence was more fleeting, but until her fall from grace in 1536, she was another powerful friend of reform, securing bishoprics for Hugh Latimer (Worcester) and Nicholas Shaxton (Salisbury). Other promotions to the episcopal bench in these years (William Barlow to St Davids, Edward Foxe to Hereford, Thomas Goodricke to Ely, John Hilsey to Rochester) provided Cranmer with a counterweight to the influence of conservative bishops such as Gardiner, Tunstall (now at Durham), and his replacement at London, John Stokesley.

The point is not that Henry necessarily approved of such men's beliefs, but that he needed their energy and talents. Throughout the 1530s, Henry saw the main danger to his Church coming not from heretics, but from 'papists', opponents of Royal Supremacy, open or covert. Reformers were keen to participate in the propaganda campaign against the Pope, though in the main they were less bothered about papal usurpation of Henry's supposed rights than about the papacy's unscriptural and perverted doctrine. They were particularly active at the important open-air pulpit of Paul's Cross, where Cromwell took control of the preaching rota away from the unreliable Stokesley and entrusted it to Hilsey of Rochester. Preachers there and elsewhere took the opportunity to attack images, prayer to saints and purgatory in terms which were still technically heretical, but often tolerated in practice. Conservative preachers counter-attacked, but frequently found themselves facing the sharp end of official disapproval. In an attempt to damp down controversy, an order was issued in June 1534, that for a year no one was to preach for or against purgatory, saint worship, clerical marriage, justification by faith, pilgrimage and miracles.[43] At a stroke long-cherished orthodoxies had been reduced to the status of contentious opinions.

With this wind behind them, the evangelical party made significant gains in the 1530s. A notable early success was the Ten Articles of 1536, the Henrician Church's first official statement. Interpretation of this document (the outcome of a closely argued contest between evangelical and conservative bishops) has divided modern commentators. Richard Rex regards the articles as largely orthodox; Christopher Haigh and A.G. Dickens (in agreement for once) as displaying Lutheran influence.[44] Only three of the seven

42 MacCulloch's *Cranmer* supercedes all previous accounts.

43 Thomas Cranmer, *Miscellaneous Writings*, ed. J.E. Cox (Cambridge, 1846), pp. 460–1.

44 Rex, *Henry VIII*, pp. 145–7; Haigh, *Reformations*, pp. 128–30; Dickens, *Reformation*, p. 200.

sacraments were discussed (baptism, eucharist, penance – on the grounds that these were instituted by Christ in scripture). There was a toned-down version of justification by faith and criticism of abuses connected with saints and their images. The treatment of purgatory represented another departure from tradition. Prayer for the dead was allowed, but their location and condition was 'uncertain to us by Scripture'. The same kind of watered-down Lutheranism was apparent in the fuller *Bishops' Book* of 1537, and the attack on 'abuse' of images was echoed in Injunctions issued by Cromwell to the parish clergy in 1536 and 1538 (see Section 2.3).

The most dramatic evangelical successes of the 1530s form a matched pair of constructive and destructive alterations to the fabric of English religious life. The positive achievement was persuading Henry (in the Injunctions of 1538) to sanction the order for an English Bible in all parish churches. To evangelicals, letting the 'Word of God' go free to reach the people in their own language was fulfilment of a long-delayed ambition. Henry's motives in agreeing to it are harder to fathom. The King was certainly drawn to some aspects of an 'Erasmian' reform programme, though Richard Rex's suggestion that Henry believed 'reading the bible would inculcate the supremacy and foster obedience' may be nearest the mark (the official 'Great Bible' of 1539 was adorned with a Holbein frontispiece showing Henry seated in majesty, handing out bibles to grateful, and hierarchically ranked subjects). The bibles which found their way into churches after 1538, were, however, essentially evangelical texts, with Tyndale's work of translation at their core.

If the provision of vernacular scripture opened a new chapter in English religious culture, equally significant was the closing of an old one: the dissolution between 1536 and 1540 of some 800 religious houses and the ending of monastic life in England and Wales for nearly three centuries. The dissolution of the monasteries is a curiously neglected theme, the last major study published nearly half a century ago.[45] But alongside its intrinsic importance it focusses in microcosm many of the broader questions relating to the character of the Henrician Reformation. Was the direction of policy Henry's own, or steered by more radical advisers? Was it coherently planned, or an ad hoc response to events? Why, given the centrality of religious houses to the religious and social life of the nation, was the policy so broadly accepted?

The dissolution was a two-stage affair: the smaller monasteries were closed by statute in 1536, the larger houses 'persuaded' to surrender to the Crown between 1537 and 1540. It was from the outset a demonstration of the Royal Supremacy in action. Using his powers as vice-gerent, Cromwell arranged a royal visitation of all monasteries over the autumn and winter of

[45] David Knowles, *The Religious Orders in England III: The Tudor Age* (Cambridge, 1959).

1535–6 (including those traditionally exempt from the oversight of their diocesan bishop). The visitors were handpicked by Cromwell, and the reports they compiled painted a highly negative picture, harking principally on two themes: the sexual corruption of the monks and 'superstition', by which was meant the possession of suspect relics. It has been usual to regard the visitation and the *Compendium compertorum* (collection of complaints) it produced as a sham, intended from the outset to justify action against the monasteries with exaggerated and inaccurate findings. Undoubtedly, the visitors were looking to find fault, though some recent research suggests that they may have been more scrupulous in their methods than previously assumed, and some monasteries, such as Durham, actually received favourable reports.[46] Their activities nonetheless beg an important question: was there from the outset a blueprint for complete or partial dissolution in Cromwell's (and the King's?) mind?

It is impossible to pronounce definitively on this. One possibility is that the dissolution policy gradually took shape during the visitation itself, as Cromwell came to see the uses to which the reports could be put.[47] But it is likely that some kind of action was envisaged from the start. As Richard Hoyle has shown, various schemes for at least partial disendowment of the monasteries were being discussed in Parliament from 1529 onwards.[48] In March/April 1536 an Act was passed dissolving all monasteries with an annual income of less than £200. It highlighted the 'manifest sin, vicious, carnal, and abominable living' taking place in the small abbeys, and there is evidence that MPs were shown the shocking findings of the visitors. The Act was thus presented as a necessary reform, not an attack on monasticism itself, and inmates from dissolved monasteries were given the option of transferring to larger houses of the same order.[49] There are good reasons for suspecting government insincerity. Smaller houses may often have had lower standards of discipline, though the visitors' *Compendium* had in fact found all the same vices in the larger monasteries. In any case, only 243 of the 419 houses assessed at £200 were actually closed. The others were exempted, either by making payments to the King, or because (particularly in the north) so many monks and nuns wished to transfer that room could not be found in the larger monasteries. Most likely the emphasis on reform was necessary to get the Act through Parliament, particularly the Lords, where abbots of the larger monasteries sat. Rationalization of monasticism along 'Erasmian' lines was a widely acceptable ideal, which echoed Wolsey's policies of the 1520s. If, however, the intention at this stage was to

[46] See Anthony Shaw's forthcoming University of Warwick PhD thesis.
[47] Rex, *Henry VIII*, pp. 60–1.
[48] Richard Hoyle, 'The Origins of the Dissolution of the Monasteries', *Historical Journal*, 38 (1995).
[49] Gee and Hardy, *Documents*, pp. 257–68.

implement a complete dissolution, the 1536 Act prepared the ground poorly, allowing the transfer of inmates, and praising the larger monasteries where 'thanks be to God, religion is right well kept and observed.'

Nonetheless, by 1540 all of them had gone. A second dissolution Act was passed in 1539, though this served principally to legitimize a process already essentially complete, the individual 'voluntary' surrender of houses to the King. Important here was the involvement of monasteries in the northern rebellion of 1536 (see Section 2.3). Six abbots and priors were executed, and their houses seized (with questionable legality) by the Crown. The abbot of Furness (Lancashire) sought to avoid the same fate in 1537 by surrendering his monastery, setting a pattern repeated nationwide as commissioners were despatched with authority to force similar surrenders. Perhaps the monks helped to bring the final decision upon themselves. When the trickle of voluntary surrenders began, many abbots assumed the end was near, and tried to make friends locally by granting pensions and letting out estates cheaply on long leases. Cromwell's circular letter of spring 1538 ordering this to stop and swearing that no general dissolution was intended probably marks the point at which that very policy had been resolved upon. It is unlikely that anyone was convinced by the fiction of 'voluntary' surrenders. But as in 1536 the government was obliged to assuage opinion in Parliament by associating its actions with constructive religious reform. An Act was passed in 1539 granting Henry authority to found new bishoprics, cathedrals and collegiate churches (something for which he did not need statutory authority). But the idea that monastic wealth might be reassigned to other religious and charitable uses was one the government was keen to encourage. In the event, this happened on a very limited scale: the only substantial redirection of funds was the founding of six new dioceses with monastic churches and estates: Bristol, Chester, Gloucester, Oxford, Peterborough and Westminster.

This account of the dissolution suggests short-term, pragmatic responses rather than a master plan. The impression is reinforced if one accepts the conventional wisdom that money motives were paramount throughout. Among recent assessments, Haigh in particular emphasizes financial crisis management, driven by developments in foreign policy and the need to pay for defences. In 1535–6 Henry was diplomatically isolated; the Pope had prepared a bull declaring his deposition, and Charles V was riding high after victories in North Africa. In the early months of 1538 the situation was yet more threatening: Charles V and Francis I had uncharacteristically declared a truce, and Paul III (employing the renegade Englishman Reginald Pole as his legate) was encouraging them to join forces in a 'crusade' against schismatic England.[50] Yet one might ask why this aspect of Church wealth (as opposed to episcopal lands or the treasures of parish churches) was particularly vulnerable, and whether, if there had been no invasion scare in

[50] Haigh, *Reformations*, pp. 130–1.

1538–9, the greater monasteries could have survived the demands of Henry's renewed military campaigns in France and Scotland in the early 1540s? Ideological motivation has been somewhat underplayed in accounts of the policy towards religious houses. It did not escape the King's notice that much of what opposition there was to the declaration of the royal supremacy came from within the religious orders, whose international links made them particularly suspect in Henry's eyes. (One order, the Franciscan Observants, had been suppressed completely before 1536.) The association of monasticism with treason was reinforced by the Pilgrimage of Grace, the King declaring to Norfolk in February 1537 that 'all these troubles have ensued by the solicitation and traitorous conspiracies of the monks'.[51] Ideology certainly motivated the evangelicals among Henry's advisers. Cranmer, Latimer and Cromwell regarded monasticism as a fraud, its vows arrogant and hypocritical. Monasteries also underpinned belief in the false doctrine of purgatory, Latimer seeking to persuade Henry in 1536 that as 'the founding of monasteries argued purgatory to be, so the putting of them down argueth it not to be'.[52] Most particularly, as the sites of most relics and shrines, monasteries encouraged 'superstition' and 'idolatry' among the laity. The campaign against the greater monasteries was heralded at the start of 1538 by the exposure of 'fraudulent' relics and images at Paul's Cross in London – the specimen of Christ's blood venerated at Hailes was declared to be the blood of a duck.[53]

Such reflections inevitably raise questions about the ownership of the dissolution policy. Were Cromwell and his allies pushing Henry further than he would otherwise have chosen to go? This seems on balance unlikely. 'Superstition' was a justification for attacking religious houses that evangelicals and 'Erasmians' could agree upon, and its eradication flattered the King's self-perception as a Catholic reformer of religious 'abuses'. Henry never expressed regrets about his destruction of monasticism, and the reformers had a notable lack of success in moving him on other issues about which they felt passionately (such as the abolition of the mass). While a truncated monasticism, cut off from the papacy and its brothers and sisters abroad, might conceivably have survived under the Royal Supremacy, circumstances combined to make this unlikely. The dissolution of the monasteries probably deserves its traditional status (underplayed in recent accounts) as the most significant achievement of the 'official' Henrician Reformation. It also reveals more clearly than any other process the dynamics that energized that Reformation: the ability of evangelical reformers to harmonize their aims and rhetoric with the outlook of

51 J.W. Clay, ed., *Yorkshire Monastic Suppression Papers*, Yorkshire Archaeological Record Series, 48 (1912), p. 34.

52 Marshall, *Beliefs*, p. 82.

53 Peter Marshall, 'The Rood of Boxley, the Blood of Hailes and the Defence of the Henrician Church', *Journal of Ecclesiastical History*, 46 (1995), 689–96.

Erasmian humanism, and to strike a chord with the prejudices of a generally conservative king.

This may be to make things sound too neat and pre-packaged. For the progress of the Henrician Reformation after 1538 was anything but smooth and predictable. Even at the high point of evangelical success in the 1530s, Henry had not dispensed with the services of conservative Catholic counsellors such as Norfolk, Gardiner and Tunstall, men determined to block the Cranmer–Cromwell agenda, and to persuade the King that the evangelicals were promoting not reform, but heresy. Many of Henry's natural instincts were in tune with theirs, and the twin scares of rebellion in the north in 1536 and threatened Franco-Imperial invasion in 1538 made the King anxious to demonstrate his credentials for Catholic 'orthodoxy', at home and abroad. It is an exaggeration to claim that in November 1538 'Henry VIII stopped the Reformation dead'[54], but a conservative reaction certainly seemed to be underway, with a proclamation defending traditional ceremonies, and the trial of the sacramentarian heretic, John Lambert, over which Henry himself pompously presided clad in the white of theological purity.[55] In 1539 the King allowed the passing of the Act of Six Articles (engineered by Tunstall and Norfolk) which reaffirmed the value of a string of evangelical bugbears: confession, transubstantiation, vows, private masses, communion in one kind only and clerical celibacy. A yet greater triumph for the conservatives followed in 1540: the arrest and execution for treason and heresy of their most formidable opponent, Thomas Cromwell. After the death of Jane Seymour, Cromwell had pressed the case for a marriage to the daughter of the Duke of Cleves, an Erasmian Catholic allied to the German Lutheran princes. By the time the marriage took place in 1540 Henry regarded the alliance with Lutheran heretics as embarrassing and unnecessary, and he found his new bride distinctly unappealing. In these propitious circumstances, Cromwell's enemies were able to produce evidence that he had protected sacramentarian heretics in the garrison town of Calais, and the minister went to the block in July 1540. A week later three leading evangelicals (including Robert Barnes) were burned for heresy, though in a bizarrely distasteful display of even-handedness three papist partisans of Catherine of Aragon were hanged for treason at the same time. The conservatives suffered their own conjugal embarrassment when the fifth royal wife, Norfolk's niece Catherine Howard, was executed for adultery in 1542. But the following year saw further gains. A *King's Book* replaced the 1537 *Bishops' Book* (the titles reflecting the fact that Henry had never lent his formal authority to the latter). Transubstantiation was reasserted and justification by faith decisively rejected. At the same time Gardiner and his allies were pressing Henry to withdraw the English Bible, which they argued

[54] Haigh, *Reformations*, p. 152.
[55] 'Sacramentarians' denied the real presence of Christ in the eucharist.

(with some justification) was encouraging religious dissension. Henry took the point to the extent that an 'Act for the Advancement of True Religion' excluded members of the lower orders and all women below the level of the gentry from reading scripture, a cruel blow for the reformers.

It is tempting to view Henry VIII's reformation as a game of two halves: a radical 1530s and a reactionary 1540s. But the extent of the conservative triumph after the fall of Cromwell should not be exaggerated. Monasteries and shrines were not restored and, despite the restrictions, the Bible was not removed from parish churches. Even conservative successes were sometimes qualified ones. The Six Articles upheld the concept of transubstantiation, but (contrary to Norfolk's original intentions) avoided using the word itself. They also described confession to a priest as 'expedient and necessary to be retained', rather than something commanded by the law of God, Henry lambasting Bishop Tunstall for daring to remonstrate with him over the matter. The *King's Book* was reactionary on the mass, but radical on purgatory, banning the use of the word and advocating prayer for the dead in only the most generalized sense.[56] Moreover, just as the conservatives had retained some royal favour in the 1530s, they were not able to completely oust their opponents in the succeeding decade. In 1543 a determined effort was made to engineer the fall of Cranmer, conservative clergy in his own diocese of Canterbury compiling a dossier of heretical activities that had been allowed to go unchecked there. But this 'Prebendaries' Plot' misfired when Henry decided to stand by his archbishop, informing him jokily, 'I now know who is the greatest heretic in Kent'.[57] A subsequent attempt to bring down Henry's last wife, Catherine Parr, and other Court ladies by implicating them with heretical circles in London, similarly came to nought in 1546. The conservatives were hampered by the unpredictability of the King, but also by their own vulnerability to smears of papalist treason, the mirror image of the heresy with which they sought to tar their opponents. In 1544 Gardiner's own nephew, Germaine, was executed for supporting the Pope (though Gardiner himself was able to evade Cromwell's fate). Crucially, reformers remained well established at the Court, and enjoyed an immediate access to Henry, which would prove crucial in the intensified faction fighting which preceded the King's death (see Section 3.1).

The twists and turns of religious policy over the last dozen years of Henry's reign have produced widely divergent assessments of how those policies were formulated. One influential interpretation holds that the competition of court factions was the motor of politics, that the King was steered one way and then another depending on who captured his 'ear' at

[56] Glyn Redworth, 'A Study in the Formulation of Policy: The Genesis and Evolution of the Act of Six Articles', *Journal of Ecclesiastical History*, 37 (1986); Marshall, *Beliefs*, pp. 77–8.

[57] MacCulloch, *Cranmer*, p. 316.

any particular moment.[58] In contrast, George Bernard and others have argued that the King himself was the dominant figure in politics, and that far from being manipulated, he presided skilfully over the factional quarrels to achieve a coherent 'middle way' in religion.[59] Both approaches have convincing elements, but risk over-simplifying a complex situation if pushed too far. Religious developments under the Royal Supremacy responded to a number of contrary pressures, Henry's need to crush opposition within the realm, but also not to antagonize Catholic opinion outside it. What is not in doubt is the crucial importance of the personality and prejudices of the King. Henry looks like a conservative Catholic, fiercely attached to the mass. But at the same time he was lukewarm about purgatory, and cheerfully sanctioned the destruction of monasteries and shrines. He was also anticlerical, deeply distrustful of clerical power and pretensions. Most of all, Henry believed in himself, and the Royal Supremacy he had become convinced was his birthright. Pamela Tudor-Craig and Richard Rex have persuasively suggested that Henry modelled himself on the kings of the Old Testament – rulers with a hot line to the Almighty and a divine mandate to reform abuses and preserve true religion.[60] Henry's own political testament was a speech to Parliament at Christmas 1545 in which he bemoaned a lack of unity, accusing some of being 'too stiff in their old mumpsimus' (old-fashioned Catholicism) and others of being 'too busy and curious in their new sumpsimus' (evangelical reforming). But this was not quite the moderate middle path it seemed: 'mumpsimus' was a well-known evangelical buzzword, used by reformers like Tyndale and Cranmer to sneer at a wide range of traditional values and devotions.[61] The King's 'Catholicism without the Pope' was a strange sort of Catholicism.

2.3 Compliance without Complaint?

As Henry himself came regretfully to realize, part of the price of his project to nationalize the English Church and refashion it in his own image was to enshrine religious division. In the end, the government was able to contain

[58] David Starkey, *The Reign of Henry VIII: Personalities and Politics* (London, 1985), chs. 6–7; Eric Ives, 'Henry VIII: the Political Perspective', in MacCulloch, *Henry VIII*, pp. 27–34.

[59] George Bernard, 'The Making of Religious Policy, 1533–1546: Henry VIII and the Search for the Middle Way', *Historical Journal*, 41(1998); Glyn Redworth, 'Whatever Happened to the English Reformation?', *History Today* (October, 1987).

[60] Tudor-Craig, 'Henry VIII and King David', pp. 189–98; Rex, *Henry VIII*, pp. 173–5.

[61] Peter Marshall, 'Mumpsimus and Sumpsimus: The Intellectual Origins of a Henrician *Bon Mot*', *Journal of Ecclesiastical History*, 52 (2001), 516–20.

and suppress the opposition to which its policies gave rise. But compliance was not something Henry and his advisers could take for granted; rather it was a political objective they had to work extremely hard to secure.

As the campaign for the divorce transmuted into an offensive against the papacy, the great majority of the nation's elite appeared firmly on side. But there were disconcerting ripples beneath the surface. In the Commons, antipapal legislation, including the appeals and supremacy Acts, did not pass without protest. One dissident MP, Sir George Throckmorton, was hauled in for a private interview with Henry in 1533. Orchestrating some of this activity behind the scenes was the most prominent opponent of the divorce among the secular elite, Thomas More, whose retirement from public affairs in 1532 was not as complete as he liked to pretend. More's clerical allies included the Bridgettine monk, Richard Reynolds, who threatened Throckmorton in confession with the loss of his soul if he did not stick to his guns.[62] Prominent members of other strict orders, the Franciscan Observants and the Carthusians, were also known to favour Queen Catherine and the Pope. Among the higher clergy, protest was muted after the 'Surrender' of 1532, though it is clear that a number of bishops, Tunstall of Durham, Richard Nix of Norwich, and particularly Fisher of Rochester, were deeply unhappy about the direction of events. At the time of his death in August 1532, Archbishop Warham may have been preparing to emulate his famous predecessor, Thomas Becket, and take a stand in defence of the liberties of the Church.

The claim to pass judgement on the King's great matter was by no means limited to a small circle of leading clerics and laymen. A surprisingly powerful voice was a young woman called Elizabeth Barton, the Nun (or Holy Maid) of Kent, a serving girl who had entered a convent in 1525 after a miraculous cure from illness, with a reputation as a visionary and worker of miracles. In the late 1520s she began to prophesy that Henry would not remain king for six months if he put aside Queen Catherine. Barton's revelations once seemed 'no more than a minor embarrassment to Henry and his servants.'[63] Yet historians are now inclined to regard her as perhaps the most dangerous of all Henry's early opponents.[64] Her prophetic powers won her a large popular following, as well as the patronage of Archbishop Warham and Bishop Fisher (Thomas More was more cautious). Moreover,

62 John Guy, *The Public Career of Sir Thomas More* (New Haven and London, 1980), pp. 207–12.

63 T.M. Parker, *The English Reformation to 1558* (Oxford, 1950), p. 82.

64 Richard Rex, 'The Execution of the Holy Maid of Kent', *Historical Research*, 44 (1991); Diane Watt, *Secretaries of God: Women Prophets in Late Medieval and Early Modern England* (Cambridge, 1997), ch. 3; Ethan Shagan, 'Print, Orality and Communications in the Maid of Kent Affair', *Journal of Ecclesiastical History*, 52 (2001).

her pronouncements against the divorce undoubtedly tapped a vein of popular sentiment. Thomas Cromwell's postbag in the mid-1530s included a stream of reports from all parts of the country of disloyal and seditious talk on the part of ordinary lay folk and priests. Typical was the outburst of a Suffolk woman in 1535: Anne Boleyn was a 'goggle-eyed whore', and she hoped she would never produce a living child.[65] The government could be in no doubt that the nation as a whole was far from unanimously cheering on the King's proceedings. Yet what mattered was as much the quality as the quantity of opposition. By 1533–4 those identified with hostility to the divorce and supremacy included the country's most internationally renowned humanist scholar, the most talented theologian on the bench of bishops, the most venerated popular prophetess in a generation, the most saintly and austere members of the religious orders. A.G. Dickens's grudging concession that Henry's actions provoked 'a certain measure of resistance from various minority-groups' hardly does justice to the severity of the threat as the government perceived it.[66]

The government's success in neutralizing much of the opposition came down to a combination of stick, carrot and fluke. Among instances of the latter, the timing of Warham's death was important, allowing the installation of the compliant Cranmer at a critical moment. If an Archbishop of Canterbury had been able to act as the focus for opposition in the mid-1530s things would have proved much harder. Among strategies consciously adopted, that of forcing die-hard opponents into the open was one of the most successful. The Succession Act passed in spring 1534 required all adult males to take an oath accepting the lawfulness of the Boleyn marriage (the spiritual authority of the Pope, though implicit, was not directly addressed, a shrewd move on the government's part). Among the laity, Thomas More was alone in declining to swear, as was John Fisher among the bishops, though several other clergy refused, particularly among the Carthusians. (In fact, the religious orders in general were identified as sources of dissent, and given a more comprehensive oath explicitly denying papal power.) The oath sought to make the nation as a whole into accomplices of the King, and this was combined with demonstrations of the consequences of refusal. On the day London citizens were summoned to swear, the dismembered body parts of Elizabeth Barton and her accomplices were fixed to the city gates. Barton had been arrested and denounced as a fraudster and a harlot at the end of 1533, and executed through the legal short cut of an act of attainder. Since she had spoken her mind openly, rather than plotted secretly, it had proved difficult to make a treason charge stick, a potential difficulty in dealing with opponents overcome in

[65] G.R. Elton, *Policy and Police: The Enforcement of the Reformation in the Age of Thomas Cromwell* (Cambridge, 1972), p. 137.
[66] Dickens, *English Reformation*, p. 145.

November 1534, when a new Treasons Act declared that treason could consist of mere talk as well deeds or writings. In April 1535, three Carthusian priors (including John Houghton of the prestigious London Charterhouse) were hanged, drawn, and quartered, and a further fifteen members of the order were executed or starved to death in prison over the next two years. To the horror of opinion across Europe, Fisher and More went to the block in June and July; the former openly proclaiming his adherence to the papacy, the latter's strategy of maintaining silence punctured by the perjured evidence of Richard Rich. They were not the last high-ranking victims to go to the block in the 1530s. In 1538, the family of Reginald Pole was purged during the so-called 'Exeter Conspiracy' (his mother, the 68-year old Countess of Salisbury was beheaded in 1541).

Did this, as some have thought, constitute a 'reign of terror'? G.R. Elton dedicated perhaps his most enduring work, *Policy and Police*, to disproving the claim. Elton's determination to demonstrate that Cromwell was in the right, and always acted in accordance with the rule of law, can try the reader's patience. But he was undoubtedly correct to insist that terror was targeted, not indiscriminate. High-profile dissidents, whose opposition represented a public rebuke to the King, went to the scaffold, but more obscure characters, whose disloyalty may have been released by drink, were often let off with a warning. Nonetheless, on Elton's own figures, a total of 329 persons were executed on treason charges between 1532 and 1540: the leniency of the regime could not be taken for granted.[67] The effect of executions in cowing the resistance cannot be quantified, but it must have been considerable. Bishop Tunstall was one who in early 1534 was faced with a straight choice between obedience and the Tower, and chose the path of circumspection.

Violence, real or threatened, was only one aspect of the campaign to secure acceptance of the Royal Supremacy. The 1530s witnessed a sustained and co-ordinated policy of public persuasion through the pulpit and the printing press. From 1533 all preachers were commanded to give regular sermons in support of the Supremacy and denouncing the Pope. A number of short accessible tracts drew on the resources of the *Collectanea* to make the case for royal headship. These included *The Articles devised by the whole consent of the king's most honourable council* (1533), which for the first time reclassified Clement as 'bishop of Rome', and a *Little Treatise against the muttering of papists in corners* (1534), which introduced the derogatory term 'papist' into common parlance. A more scholarly and international audience was catered for in Edward Foxe's *De Vera Differentia* ('Of the true difference', 1534), and Gardiner's *De Vera Obedientia* ('Of true obedience', 1535). The intention was to make the Pope into a non-person, an insignificant Italian bishop, whose very name was to be scored out of service books

[67] Elton, *Policy*, p. 387.

(priests who thought they could get away with merely pasting slips of paper over it were regularly reported to the authorities). It is difficult to judge the effectiveness of this propaganda, though a generation later, the Catholic exile William Allen was convinced that 'when they first began to touch and taunt the Pope in every sermon, in every play, in book and ballad', people who had not previously given him much thought started to think 'there lay some great ground of matter and weight of truth upon that point'.[68]

No amount of propaganda, however, was able to prevent a massive outbreak of popular unrest in the latter months of 1536, a series of linked rebellions, which engulfed Lincolnshire and the northern counties and became known as the Pilgrimage of Grace (though this title properly belongs to the rising in Yorkshire led by the lawyer Robert Aske). The scale and significance of these events is difficult to exaggerate. In Yorkshire alone some 40,000 men may have been up in arms, a force much larger than any the Crown could put into the field against it. Fortunately for Henry, it never came to the test of battle. For decades, historians have anguished about whether the causes of the Pilgrimage were 'secular' or 'religious', and whether it should be regarded as a genuinely popular movement, or the outcome of an anti-Cromwell conspiracy hatched at the Court.[69] The most persuasive recent assessments have reasserted the common-sense view that the people rose on their own account (encouraged by the rumour-mongering of the clergy), and that their concerns were essentially religious ones: the closure of the smaller monasteries, the royal injunctions which followed on the heels of the Ten Articles, and which publicized the ruling that all lesser holy days falling in harvest time were to be abolished, and all dedication feasts of churches to be observed on the first Sunday in October.[70] 'Religion' here need not necessarily mean the finer points of doctrine, or even an undue concern with the respective authority of pope and king. (The rebels' articles demanded a restoration of papal headship in matters of faith, though this seems to have been largely at the instigation of Aske.) But policies associated with Cromwell, which interfered with local customary ways, could easily be recognized as 'heresy', opposition to which supplied the umbrella under which a range of other grievances (such as excessive taxation) could be brought together. The rebels called themselves 'pilgrims' and marched behind the banner of the Five Wounds of Christ.

68 William Allen, *A Defence and Declaration of the Catholike Churchies Doctrine touching Purgatory* (Antwerp, 1565), fol. 235r.

69 Dickens, *Reformation*, p. 150 ('The roots of the movement were decidedly economic'); G.R. Elton, 'Politics and the Pilgrimage of Grace', in B. Malament, ed., *After the Reformation* (New Haven, 1980).

70 C.S.L. Davies, 'Religion and the Pilgrimage of Grace', in Anthony Fletcher and John Stevenson, eds., *Order and Disorder in Early Modern England* (Cambridge, 1985); Richard Hoyle, *The Pilgrimage of Grace and the Politics of the 1530s* (Oxford, 2001).

Rumours that parish churches were to be closed and their treasures seized (plausible in the light of what was happening to the monasteries) were particularly important. It is significant that in Lincolnshire the trouble began in Louth, in East Yorkshire at Beverley, and in Cumberland at Kendall: all had elegant parish churches in which the laity had invested heavily.

After the initial outbreak in Lincolnshire at the start of October, the rising spread to Yorkshire, and further outbreaks took place in Lancashire and the Lake counties. In most places the commons sought and received the leadership of the local gentry. The regional capital, York, was occupied on 16 October, and a week later Lord Darcy (a supporter of Catherine of Aragon) surrendered the royal castle at Pontefract with suspicious haste. The Duke of Norfolk, who might himself have been expected to sympathize with the pilgrims' aims, co-ordinated the loyalist response, and in the event saved the day for Henry, dissuading the King from precipitate action, and persuading the rebels to go home with a free pardon and a promise that a new parliament would address their grievances. A renewed outbreak of disorder in the East Riding in early 1537 gave Norfolk the excuse to impose martial law, and Aske, Darcy and other ringleaders were executed. Nonetheless, it had been touch-and-go for the Henrician Reformation. If Norfolk, or other powerful conservative magnates such as the earls of Derby and Shrewsbury, had wavered in their allegiance, Cromwell might have gone to the block four years early, and a wholesale reversal of policy ensued.

The scale of popular involvement in the Pilgrimage of Grace suggests a widespread unease about Henrician religious policies as they impacted at the parish level. Such anxieties have seemed unreal or exaggerated to a viewpoint which holds that 'real' Reformation did not hit English local communities until the reign of Edward VI, and which notes that the Latin mass, obligatory confession, and other traditional sacraments continued throughout the reign. Yet it is important not to forget that a determination to remodel the priorities of popular religion was a consistent thread of Henrician policy. A closer look at the Royal Injunctions of 1536 and 1538 is in order here. The 1536 Injunctions forbade preachers to extol the merits of images, relics and pilgrimages, and instructed the people not to place their trust in such things. The 1538 Injunctions went further in ordering that images 'abused' by pilgrimage or offerings were to be taken away. This implied not only the closure of the great national pilgrimage centres, but the removal of some of the most popular images from parish churches. No lights were henceforth to burn before images (except on the rood-loft and before the reserved sacrament). Sermons were to be preached against offering of money or candles to images and relics, or praying with rosary beads, as 'men's phantasies besides Scripture', things 'tending to idolatry'.[71] In

[71] W.H. Frere and W.M. Kennedy, eds., *Visitation Articles and Injunctions of the Period of the Reformation* (3 vols., London, 1910), ii. 37–8.

effect, this was a declaration of war on the cult of the saints, heartbeat of medieval popular religion. The pressure was scarcely reduced in the 'reactionary' 1540s. The ceremony of the 'boy bishop' on the feast of St Nicholas (when in ritual and festive 'inversion' a young boy would be clad in episcopal robes and preach a sermon) was banned by proclamation in 1541. In the same year Henry was on progress in the north of England, and appalled to find some shrines still standing there. He wrote to Cranmer ordering they be removed at once. Hostility to much traditional religious culture was a marked feature of Henry's 'Catholicism'. In the preface to the *King's Book* he congratulated himself on cleansing his realm from 'hypocrisy and superstition'.[72]

How did the laity react to these initiatives? In an important case study of image cults in the south-west of England, Robert Whiting has demonstrated (through an analysis of income and expenditure in churchwardens' accounts) that though traditional devotions were thriving up to the mid-1530s, the Injunctions had an immediate and drastic impact. Offerings to images virtually disappear from the accounts after 1536 (even before the 1538 Injunctions actually banned them), and after 1538 no new images are purchased.[73] Ronald Hutton's national survey of surviving accounts confirms the pattern: the 1538 order for the extinguishing of lights was rapidly complied with, and only one parish (St Nicholas, Bristol) put up a new image before the accession of Mary. This does not seem to reflect widespread enthusiasm for reform. The response to the one positive instruction of 1538 – the order to acquire an English Bible – was much less prompt. Most of the parishes began to comply only after a 1541 proclamation threatened defaulters with fines.[74] The suggestion that parochial reactions to the Henrician reforms were marked by passivity, and a rapid crumbling of traditional religious attitudes, has been challenged by Haigh, who argues that conventional parish religion continued to thrive through the 1540s. Church ales were held, Corpus Christi plays were performed at places like Sherborne in Dorset and Ashburton in Devon, and money previously spent on images was diverted to other traditionalist purchases like organs and vestments. The swift compliance with the order to extinguish lights was in fact a way of protecting images by giving the authorities no excuse to remove them, and such lights could be moved onto the rood-lofts where they retained in people's minds their association with a particular saint's image.[75]

72 *The King's Book 1543*, ed. T.A. Lacey (London, 1895), p. xi.
73 Robert Whiting, 'Abominable Idols: Images and Image-breaking under Henry VIII', *Journal of Ecclesiastical History*, 33 (1982).
74 Ronald Hutton, 'The Local Impact of the Tudor Reformations', in Marshall, *Impact*, pp. 144–6.
75 Haigh, *Reformations*, pp. 156–9.

If Whiting exaggerates the tendency of traditional religion to collapse like a house of cards[76], it may be that Haigh overestimates its resilience. The evidence from churchwardens' accounts can be supplemented by that from wills, and these reveal some significant patterns. Across most of the country, requests for masses and prayers for the testator's soul were running at roughly half the rate in the 1540s that they had in the 1520s, and bequests to fraternities show the same pattern of decline.[77] Both purgatory and the intercessory role of the saints (patrons of the fraternities) had been subjected to particular official hostility. Wills do not provide clear evidence for a widespread loss of 'belief' in these doctrines, but will-makers understandably hesitated about investing where the government might move in and confiscate the endowment, a concern sharpened by the dissolution of the monasteries, and by an Act of 1545 (unimplemented) which authorized Henry to dissolve any chantries or colleges to help meet the costs of the French war. As people prudently reduced their level of investment in intercession, however, could they sustain the same intensity of belief in a fiery purgatory? As images were removed or downgraded, could the saints retain the same emotional hold? Reformers well understood that there was a psychological effect in stripping away the externals of traditional religion. When monasteries were dissolved, the treasure of the shrines seized, or wonder-working images smashed up at Paul's Cross, the heavens did not open, and an army of avenging angels did not pour forth.[78]

Such reflections may help explain the results of popular compliance, but not the phenomenon itself. An early twentieth-century scholar, F.M. Powicke, remarked that 'the general acquiescence is surely one of the most mysterious things in our history'.[79] The perplexing issue of why in the end English people accepted a Reformation which most of them neither expected nor welcomed, has application to much of the sixteenth century, not just the reign of Henry VIIII. But it is appropriate to confront it here, in the Reformation's opening stages (see also Section 3.2). Part of the reason has already been suggested: the coercive power of the Tudor State, and its increasingly sophisticated propaganda apparatus. Nor should we underestimate the strength of instinctive obedience to the Crown: every instance of popular disaffection recorded in Elton's *Policy and Police* is also evidence of neighbours sufficiently scandalized by disloyal talk to report it to the

76 Particularly in his textbook, *Local Responses to the English Reformation* (Basingstoke, 1998).

77 Marshall, *Priesthood*, p. 51; Robert Whiting, '"For the Health of my Soul": Prayers for the Dead in the Tudor South-West', in Marshall, *Impact*, p. 126; Brigden, *London*, pp. 386, 389.

78 C. John Sommerville, *The Secularization of Early Modern England* (Oxford, 1992), pp. 61–2; Margaret Aston, 'Iconoclasm in England: Official and Clandestine', in Marshall, *Impact*, pp. 167–74.

79 F.M. Powicke, *The Reformation in England* (London, 1941), p. 7.

authorities. The habit of loyalty was particularly grounded in the social elites, clerical and lay. These did not merely experience royal policy, but collaborated with and implemented it. As royal or diocesan administrators, sheriffs or justices of the peace, they played an integral part in the governance of the realm, and drew status from the contribution they made. Moreover, as suggested in Section 1.1, it is possible that sections of the gentry, without experiencing evangelical conversion, were becoming emotionally disengaged from some features of popular religion, ready to countenance a reform along apparently 'Erasmian' lines. Thus at the height of the monastic dissolutions, the humanist Sir Thomas Elyot, a religious conservative and friend of Thomas More's, could write to Cromwell assuring him that no one detested as much as he did 'vain superstitions, superfluous ceremonies'.[80] Like many others, Elyot hoped to get a share of the spoils of the dissolution. As a result of Henry's profligate spending on war in the 1540s, two-thirds of the monastic lands were sold into the hands of the landed elites. Their acquisition did not make the beneficiaries into Protestants, but it implicated them firmly with the Crown's reform policies, and made them think twice about any suggestion of reverting to the world before 1533. The compliance of lower social groups, the parish clergy, yeomen who served as churchwardens, and mass of ordinary parishioners, is more mute and impenetrable. But these were people with limited choices in most aspects of their lives, for whom open defiance of authority was both an unnatural instinct and a grave personal risk. Many may not have liked the direction in which things were going, but they were in no position to guess the final destination. In this, their betters were no wiser. During his last years, Bishop Stokesley of London is reported to have exclaimed 'Oh! that I had holden still with my brother Fisher, and not left him, when time was'.[81] Yet Stokesley can hardly be blamed for failing to predict in the early 1530s that the breach with Rome would be permanent, and would lead to momentous alterations in religious life. From 1529 onwards, changes came incrementally, and did not always seem irreversible. At each stage, enough of the traditional and familiar was left to make life bearable for those who did not welcome change. In any discussion of acquiescence and compliance, however, it is as well to remember the Pilgrimage of Grace: in 1536 (and not for the last time) thousands of English people risked their lives in opposing the changes, and almost succeeded in reversing them.

Summation

The great medieval theologian Thomas Aquinas thought the nature of God could be grasped only by listing what he was *not*. It is tempting to feel the

[80] British Library, Cotton MS Cleo. E. iv. fo. 260r.
[81] J.J. Scarisbrick, *Henry VIII* (London, 1968), p. 327.

same way about the Henrician Reformation. It was not a Protestant Reformation, nor in any meaningful sense 'Catholicism without the Pope'. It was not straightforwardly an 'act of state', though even less did it exhibit the characteristics of a spontaneously popular movement. It was not even unambiguously Henry VIII's reformation, though neither did its control and direction belong to any one minister or group of advisors. Yet the subsequent development of English religion was substantially shaped by the events of the reign. Henry's crowning creation, the Royal Supremacy, was for good or ill the inescapable context for the possibilities of practising one's faith in England for a century to come. Aware of its double-edged nature, evangelicals had nonetheless tied their fortunes to it. They were to reap the benefits in the next reign, and pay the penalty in the one after.

It is possible to argue that the fundamental rhythms of religious life for most people were relatively undisturbed by Henry's reformation. The pope in Rome may have meant little to rural parishioners in Staffordshire or Sussex. Mass was still said in their churches, which retained their altars, rood-lofts and stained glass, and many of their statues. In the judgement of Henry's first modern biographer, A.F. Pollard, the King 'never wavered in his adhesion to the cardinal points of the Catholic faith'.[82] But this is to minimize the seismic nature of events. The breach with the papacy was as much as anything a break with the past – an overthrowing of the claims of tradition, custom and consensus reiterated in the eradication of religious houses which had stood for hundreds of years, and in the destruction of shrines (Our Lady of Walsingham, St Thomas of Canterbury) which had helped define the English people's sense of who they were. Whole areas of ancestral piety had been reclassified as worthless 'superstition'. It is revealing that when a 1538 royal proclamation reasserted rituals (such as venerating the cross on Good Friday) which evangelicals detested, it did so not because they were an essential expression of unchanging Catholic truth, but because the King happened to regard them as 'good and laudable ceremonies. . . which as yet be not abolished nor taken away'.[83] Expediency had become a touchstone of religious policy. Yet, equally significantly, the 'Word of God', which Henry had placed in every parish church, was increasingly appealed to as the supreme external test of what was permissible or proscribed. Where to strike the balance between pragmatism and principle was an issue that would divide Catholics and Protestants alike for the remainder of the century and beyond. For a king obsessed with unity and obedience, it is ironic that division was Henry's principal legacy.

[82] A.F. Pollard, *Henry VIII* (London, 1902), p. 310.

[83] P.L. Hughes and J.F. Larkin, eds., *Tudor Royal Proclamations* (3 vols., New Haven and London, 1964–9), i. 272.

3

Edwardian Revolution 1547–1553

Overview

Exiled on the continent in Queen Mary's reign, the evangelical Richard Morison made an imposing claim about reformation in his homeland under Edward VI: 'the greater change was never wrought in so short space in any country since the world was.'[1] The years 1547 to 1553 witnessed an unprecedentedly intense campaign to transform the character of Christian worship and belief, which fully justifies the label of revolution.[2] It was a revolution too in the more original sense of a complete rotation, an attempt to turn back to the purity of the Church of the apostles, and to strip away the accretion of centuries: the cult of the saints, purgatory, a warped theology of sacraments and the mass. The modern analogy is less with the overthrow of *ancien regimes* in 1789 and 1917 than with the 'cultural revolution' of 1960s China, in which central government worked in alliance with cadres of true believers to undermine unreliable elements in positions of authority, and radically reconstruct the outlook of the people as a whole.

Despite all this, Edward's reign has, until comparatively recently, been the neglected orphan of English Reformation studies. In part this was because a nationalist historiography found little to celebrate in what seemed a brief and confusing interlude between the Tudor glories of Henry and Elizabeth. In part also because the crusading Protestant zeal of Edwardian reformers has been something of an embarrassment to an Anglican tradition which came eventually to define itself as a moderate arbiter between the best aspects of Protestantism and Catholicism. Thus, in the late 1940s the Anglo-

[1] Diarmaid MacCulloch, *Tudor Church Militant: Edward VI and the Protestant Reformation* (London, 1999), p. 102.

[2] T.M. Parker, *The English Reformation to 1558* (Oxford, 1950), ch. 8, 'The Protestant Revolution'; Philip Hughes, *The Reformation in England*, (3 vols., London, 1950–4), ii. ch. 2 'The Revolutionary changes'.

Catholic historian Henry Maynard Smith could dismiss as 'absurd' the notion that Edward's reign did anything to determine the subsequent character of the Church of England. The period was 'theologically dominated by foreign refugees', whose outlook 'had no roots in the English soil'.[3] Yet the best recent work recognizes that what was done in 1547–53 set the agenda for reform for a century to come. The 'foreign' influence on the Edwardian Reformation now also seems less a brief distasteful dalliance, than an invitation to set developments in England more meaningfully in a broad European context.

Nonetheless, a consensus over the interpretation of religious developments in Edward's reign has failed to emerge. At one level, scholars are divided over whether to regard the Edwardian Reformation as (in the immortal categories of *1066 And All That*) a 'Good Thing' or a 'Bad Thing', whether to emphasize its ruthlessly unforgiving destruction of traditional religious culture, or its genuine idealism and aspirations for social justice.[4] The essential coherence of Edwardian religious policy has also invited contradictory assessments. Christopher Haigh, for example, has mocked the idea that there was 'a clockwork Reformation' in Edward's reign. Rather the progress of the Edwardian Reformation, like its Henrician parent, was characterized by 'spasmodic fits, uncertain starts, and threats of reversal'. Diarmaid MacCulloch, by contrast, can discern continuity and consistency, the determined working out of a calculated programme of reform.[5] If (as we saw in Section 2.2) Henry's reformation can appear as a meal of two contrasting courses, Edward's reign presents the same temptation in concentrated form. It has often been seen as a tale of two dukes: the King's uncle Edward Seymour (Somerset) who controlled the government until his fall in 1549, and John Dudley (Northumberland) who replaced him in the second half of the reign. An older historical tradition, which regarded the former as the liberal and tolerant 'good duke' of Somerset, and the latter as an unprincipled opportunist, has come under sustained and convincing criticism over the last 25 years.[6] But apparently marked contrasts in the style and pace

[3] Henry Maynard Smith, *Henry VIII and the Reformation* (London, 1948), p. 453.

[4] Eamon Duffy, *The Stripping of the Altars: Traditional Religion in England 1400–1580* (New Haven and London, 1992) takes the first tack; MacCulloch, *Church Militant* the second.

[5] Christopher Haigh, *English Reformations: Religion, Politics, and Society under the Tudors* (Oxford, 1993), pp. 168–9; MacCulloch, *Church Militant*, chs. 2–3.

[6] The interpretation in W.K. Jordan's *Edward VI: the Young King* (London, 1968) and *Edward VI: the Threshold of Power* (London, 1970) is attacked by Michael Bush, *The Government Policy of Protector Somerset* (London, 1975); Dale Hoak, 'Rehabilitating the Duke of Northumberland: Politics and Political Control, 1549–53', in Jennifer Loach and Robert Tittler, eds., *The Mid-Tudor Polity c. 1540–1560* (Basingstoke, 1980); David Loades, *John Dudley, Duke of Northumberland, 1504–1553* (Oxford, 1996).

of reformation between 1547–49 and 1550–53 still demand to be accounted for. And what of the young king himself? Moving away from the world in which policy was formulated to that in which its effects were felt, few scholars would now deny that the Edwardian Reformation exercised a drastic effect on the fabric and rituals of English parish religion. But whether traditional religious culture was resilient enough to bounce back from these blows is a matter of debate. The impact that 'reformation from below' was able to make once it enjoyed official blessing is another point at issue. G.R. Elton announced in 1977 that 'by 1553 England was almost certainly nearer to being a Protestant country than to anything else'.[7] Was he correct, and what sort of 'anything else' might we expect to find at this date?

The following discussion views the Edwardian revolution from three overlapping and equally essential perspectives. A first section examines the key figures and events in the making of religious policy: what sort of reformation was planned, by whom, and what were the circumstances propelling or constraining it? The second section considers the impact of Edwardian reform on religious life in the localities, and the ways in which clergy and laity adapted and responded to it. The final section evaluates the evidence for the growth of Protestant conviction in English society in these years, and considers whether a permanent and irreversible shift in the religious temper of the nation had been able to take place.

3.1 Reformers and their Priorities

If there is uncertainty whether the first phase of Reformation in England can legitimately be termed 'Henry VIII's Reformation', we might pause still longer before ascribing authorship of the events after 1547 to his son. Edward VI was barely nine years old when he acceded to the throne in January 1547. He died in July 1553, still a 'minor', three months short of his sixteenth birthday. The Royal Supremacy over the Church was thus exercised on the King's behalf throughout his short reign, and the circumstances in which his father bequeathed it to him are of crucial importance. The last years of Henry's reign supplied few indications of impending dramatic change. The conservative councillors, Gardiner, Norfolk, Thomas Wriothesley, were riding high in the 1540s, and heretics were again being consigned to the flames. But a regrouped Cromwellian faction was firmly entrenched at the court, and allied to it were the rising stars Seymour and Dudley, important figures in the prosecution of the war against Scotland. The evangelical theologian Thomas Cranmer still occupied the see of Canterbury, biding his time. As the King's health deteriorated through

[7] G.R. Elton, *Reform and Reformation: England 1508–1558* (London, 1977), p. 371.

1546, the rival factions looked towards the composition of the regency council to be established by Henry's will. At the beginning of December, disaster struck the conservatives. Norfolk's son, the wayward Earl of Surrey, was arrested for flaunting his family's royal blood, and his father was charged with 'misprision' (knowing about the treason). At the same time, Gardiner proved uncooperative over an exchange of lands with the King, a quarrel that the evangelicals exploited, even if they did not engineer it. On 13 December 1546, Henry made changes to his will: the names of Norfolk and Gardiner were struck from the list of councillors, delivering a majority to the Seymour faction. It is possible that the will was further tampered with after the King's death, allowing the regents to enrich themselves through the insertion of an 'unfulfilled gifts clause' alleging unwritten promises the King had made in his last weeks.[8] In February the councillors proceeded to appoint Somerset as 'Lord Protector' of the new king (something Henry had certainly not envisaged), and the dismantlement of the Henrician religious settlement began.

Perhaps what ensued therefore was Protestant Reformation by serendipity; the Edwardian polity was a decisively evangelical rather than a 'Henrician Catholic' one because of the chance outcome of factional manoeuvres and the precise timing of the old King's death.[9] But another interpretation is that Henry was already beginning to steer things in this direction. In August 1546 Henry made a bizarre off-the-cuff suggestion to a French ambassador, to change 'the mass in both the realms into a communion service'. Moreover, the tutors charged with the education of the young prince, Richard Cox, John Cheke and Roger Ascham, were clearly evangelical sympathizers.[10] The former may have been mere diplomatic posturing, and it is likely that the tutors were primarily chosen for their humanist credentials, rather than for beliefs which were not openly displayed until later. Yet in excluding Gardiner from the council, Henry is supposed to have remarked 'I myself could use him, and rule him to all manner of purposes... but so shall you never do'.[11] It is not intrinsically implausible that Henry in his last months sanctioned a lurch in a reforming direction in order to safeguard the royal supremacy from potential papists like Gardiner. An unwavering love of his royal ecclesiastical prerogative was the one unquestionably consistent aspect of Henry VIII's theology.

8 David Starkey, *The Reign of Henry VIII: Personalities and Politics* (London, 1985), pp. 159–65.

9 Haigh, *Reformations*, pp. 166–7.

10 J.J. Scarisbrick, *Henry VIII* (London, 1968), pp.472–4; Jordan, *Young King*, pp. 27–8, 41–2; Glyn Redworth, *In Defence of the Church Catholic: The Life of Stephen Gardiner* (Oxford, 1990), pp. 244–6.

11 John Foxe, *Acts and Monuments*, ed. S.R. Cattley and G. Townsend (8 vols., London, 1837–41), v. 692.

How Edward VI would have employed *his* royal prerogative, had he lived to adulthood, is one of the more intriguing 'what ifs' of the sixteenth century. Protestant reformers liked to identify Edward with Josiah, the godly boy king of the Old Testament, and a consistent tradition thereafter emphasized his precocious Protestant piety. Not all modern commentators have been convinced. Both W.K. Jordan and Jennifer Loach in their biographies of Edward made considerable use of the young King's personal 'chronicle', a document that shows infinitely more interest in military campaigns and tournaments than in the ongoing reform of the Church. Edward was pious enough, Loach concluded, but also 'a typical aristocratic youth of the sixteenth century'.[12] But the case for recognizing Edward as (in John Foxe's description) the 'godly imp' has been forcefully restated by MacCulloch. Edward's surviving school exercises suggest a fervent evangelical commitment, which became more evident as the reign progressed. His successive redrafting of the statutes of the Order of the Garter reveal a determination to excise all traces of papistry (including the traditional association with St George), and in 1551, aged thirteen, Edward personally intervened during the consecration of Bishop Hooper to strike out with his pen allusions to the saints from the oath of supremacy the bishop was about to swear. Edward was highly resistant to any concession allowing his Catholic half-sister Mary to hear mass, even when the Emperor Charles V was threatening war over the issue, and the desperate gamble at the end of the reign to exclude Mary and place Lady Jane Grey on the throne may well have been Edward's own brainchild rather than (as is usually assumed) Northumberland's.[13] Gardiner and other conservatives protested that there should be no deviation from Henry VIII's religious policies until the minority came to an end. But this was a temporary resistance strategy: 'there is no evidence that points to a change in policy in a more traditional direction had Edward lived.'[14] The conservative bishops were to be confronted in the most unforgiving way with the heretical potential of the royal supremacy they had helped to defend and sustain.

The preferences and prejudices of the King were no irrelevance in the formulation of religious policy, and were regarded with increasing seriousness as the moment of his majority approached – the most recent research has convincingly questioned the old assumption that Edward was an always sickly boy whom informed observers did not expect to live long.[15] Nevertheless, real political power throughout the reign lay in the hands of

12 Jordan, *Threshold*, pp. 532–5; Jennifer Loach, *Edward VI* (New Haven and London, 1999), pp. 53–4, 135, 157–8, 181.

13 MacCulloch, *Church Militant*, pp. 21–41.

14 Catharine Davies, *A Religion of the Word: The Defence of the Reformation in the Reign of Edward VI* (Manchester, 2002), p. 10.

15 Loach, *Edward VI*, pp. 159–62.

his elders, first Somerset, and then Northumberland. Somerset's policy in religion is endlessly epitomized as 'moderate' and 'tolerant' in the two-volume history of the reign by W.K. Jordan. In addition to a supposed concern for the poor manifested in opposition to enclosures, Somerset was a man who 'simply did not believe that force was a proper or a useful instrument in religious policy'. Only one conservative bishop (Bonner) was actually deprived during his rule, though Gardiner was also imprisoned for his obduracy.[16] In contrast, Michael Bush has argued that Somerset's interest in social reform was conventional and opportunistic, conditioned largely by a desire to finance an increasingly unsuccessful war in Scotland (with the aim of forcing the Scots to accept a marriage between Edward and the young Mary Queen of Scots). If Somerset did not create Catholic martyrs, it was because the conservative clergy largely kept their heads down. Where Jordan saw a kind of proto-Anglican, Bush more realistically identified a man of advanced Protestant views, but one severely constrained by the demands of his foreign policy. In order to ensure the neutrality of the Emperor in England's struggle with Scotland (and Scotland's ally, France), Somerset's reformation had to seem at least to be cautious and restrained. Thus Mary was allowed to continue to hear mass, and reform legislation of 1547 fastidiously observed that there was 'no condemning hereby the usage of any church out of the King's majesty's dominion.'[17] The argument has been refined by MacCulloch, who suggests that Somerset's regime deliberately sent out contradictory signals because it had simultaneously to appease incompatible aspirations: those of the Emperor, of conservative lay and clerical opinion at home, and of its own enthusiastic evangelical supporters. The resultant policy 'was not so much moderate as schizophrenic', but was still geared towards an eventual root and branch reform of the English Church.[18]

Certainly, the assertion that the reform programme of 1547–9 was a moderate one requires a very elastic definition of 'moderation', for in these few years the worship and theology of the English Church was transformed to a very great degree. Caution and calculation characterize the actions of the regime's first year. An official set of Homilies issued in July 1547 included (to Gardiner's chagrin) a clear assertion of justification by faith, though nothing was said for the moment about the nature of the eucharist. In August royal visitors were despatched across the country, armed with injunctions for parishes, which seemed on the surface to be a reissue of Cromwell's Injunctions of 1538. The added requirement to acquire a copy of Erasmus's *Paraphrases* of the gospels reinforces the impression of a middle-of-the-road approach. But the Injunctions continued to snip at the

16 Jordan, *Young King*, pp. 125–6, 128, 214.
17 Bush, *Protector Somerset*, ch. 5.
18 MacCulloch, *Church Miltant*, pp. 57, 61, 81.

fabric of local religion, banning parochial processions and the placing of lights on the rood-loft (where many had been moved in 1538). Where the earlier Injunctions had required the removal of 'abused' images, the 1547 set demanded their destruction, extending the definition of 'abuse' to include the use of incense. The visitors charged with enforcing the Injunctions were Protestant enthusiasts who interpreted their brief in a maximalist way, provoking arguments across the country as to whether particular images could be retained. At the end of 1547 all images were removed from London churches, and in February 1548 the council extended the order to the whole country. At the same time, traditional ceremonies which Henry VIII had allowed to remain – the use of ashes on Ash Wednesday, palms on Palm Sunday, and 'creeping to the cross' on Good Friday – were done away with.

In the meantime, the Parliament of November 1547 had swept away the Henrician treason and heresy legislation, including the Six Articles, more probably to clear the way for further reform and to indemnify the leaders of the regime from charges of heresy, than because of an anachronistic belief in 'toleration'. The lifting of restrictions on printing encouraged popular attacks on the mass, and an Act at the end of 1547 against 'irreverent talkers of the sacrament' looks as though the government was attempting to apply the brakes. But as with the policy towards images, ostensibly moderate and restrained language could act as a cover for forwarding a reform agenda. The act also provided for the laity to receive communion in two kinds (wine as well as bread), and for the administration of this the council produced in 1548 a vernacular 'order of communion' to be inserted into the Latin mass. For good measure this declared confession to a priest to be optional rather than compulsory. A more decisive move away from the devotional priorities of the old Catholic world came at the end of 1547 with the passing of a bill to dissolve all chantries, hospitals and fraternities and empower the government to seize all revenues devoted to intercessions for the dead. Commissioners subsequently oversaw the confiscation of the endowments of around 4,000 chantries, colleges and hospitals, and a probably much larger number of obits and parochial guilds.[19] Some commentators have seen the motivation behind the Chantries Act as an essentially 'secular' one, an impression reinforced by the surprising fact that Archbishop Cranmer voted against the fourth reading in the House of Lords.[20] The timing of the measure probably was conditioned by the financial demands of Somerset's war with Scotland, and some evangelicals (correctly) suspected a repeat performance of the monastic dissolution, with a failure to deliver on promises about the conversion of revenues to education and poor relief (the

19 Alan Kreider, *English Chantries: The Road to Dissolution* (Cambridge, MA, 1979), ch. 8.

20 Haigh, *Reformations*, p. 171; Diarmaid MacCulloch, *Thomas Cranmer: A Life* (New Haven and London, 1996), p. 377.

government made about £110,000 from the sale of chantry property). But the purported rationale for dissolution was an unambiguously ideological one: 'vain opinions of purgatory and masses satisfactory' had blinded people to an understanding of 'their very true and perfect salvation through the death of Jesus Christ'.[21] The theology of purgatory was being undermined in Henry VIII's reign; it was unthinkable that the chantries could have survived the evangelical regime of Edward VI.

The outlawing of requiem masses served further to spotlight the most pressing theological question of the reign, perhaps of the entire Reformation – the nature of the eucharist. Henry VIII had defended the mass, but Protestants loathed it as an 'idol'. In their view, transubstantiation encouraged the damnable worship of a piece of bread, and the Catholic teaching that the mass was a sacrifice, one in substance with Christ's sacrifice on the cross, seemed a blasphemous insinuation that Christ's redeeming work was insufficient. But the evangelical movement itself was badly divided over eucharistic theology. Luther, taking his cue from the words of scripture 'this is my body', held fast to a real and objective 'presence' of Christ in the bread and wine, against the teaching of Zwingli and other reformers that the words were to be understood symbolically. Cranmer had long been planning a reform of the liturgy, and by 1547 his thinking on the issue had gone beyond Luther's. But the strength of conservative feeling at home, and the sensitivity of Protestant divisions abroad, made the issue the theological equivalent of nitro-glycerine: it had to be handled with care.

The introduction of a reformed eucharistic service with the publication of a new 'Book of Common Prayer' in June 1549 followed the pattern established over the previous two years: the government responded to the agitation of zealots by imposing a solution considerably less 'moderate' than it appeared on the surface. There was an unprecedented surge of printing in 1548, much of it accounted for by short tracts virulently attacking and satirizing the mass. The regime made little effort to regulate this 'unofficial' pressure, and a couple of the tracts were the work of Somerset's chaplain, William Turner.[22] In advance of a change in the law, entirely vernacular services were being permitted at St Paul's and other London churches. The Act of Uniformity that imposed the new prayer book could thus speak of the need 'to stay innovations' and secure 'a uniform quiet and godly order'.[23] The 1549 communion service, then and subsequently, has been seen as a very conservative reform. The new rite largely kept the structure of the old service, and billed itself with unabashed woolliness as 'the supper of the Lord and the holy communion, commonly called the mass'. Yet decisive

21 Henry Gee and William Hardy, eds., *Documents Illustrative of English Church History* (London, 1896), p. 328.
22 Haigh, *Reformations*, p. 173; Davies, *Religion*, ch. 1.
23 Gee and Hardy, *Documents*, pp. 358–9.

changes were instituted. Cranmer pruned all the language suggesting the eucharist was a sacrifice, and he omitted the elevation of the host, the traditional symbolic declaration of the real presence. The very fact that the liturgy was now in English would have seemed to many a remarkable, if not shocking innovation. The prayer book was designed to make just enough concessions to the past to forestall forceful conservative protest, though in this its success was decidedly mixed. From his prison cell Gardiner announced that he could accept it as orthodox (perhaps a wrecking tactic designed to create divisions among the Protestants). But the book also precipitated serious popular unrest in the midlands and the south-west (see Section 3.2). Foreign friends of the regime (such as Martin Bucer and John Calvin) criticized the retention of features like old-fashioned clerical vestments, and a suggestion of prayers for the departed, but they were given assurances: such things were a concession to 'the infirmity of the present age', and were 'only to be retained for a time'.[24]

A wave of agrarian unrest swept across southern and midland England in the summer of 1549, coinciding with conservative revolts against religious innovations in Devon and Cornwall, Yorkshire and the south midlands. By seeming to provoke the unrest in the first place, and then prepare to appease the insurgents (at least those who had no complaint to make about the government's religious policies), Somerset lost the confidence of his fellow councillors, and was toppled in a coup led by Northumberland. There was widespread expectation, at home and abroad, that this would herald a regency of the Princess Mary and a reversal of the religious reforms. But having worked with conservatives like Wriothesley and the Earl of Arundel in order to oust Somerset, Northumberland turned on his erstwhile allies and excluded them from the council, embarking on an intensified programme of religious reform. In recent assessments, Northumberland has not exactly wrested the 'good duke' mantle from his rival, but he has at least stopped being the bad duke, and is given credit for administrative reforms and for ending the disastrously expensive war with France, as well as for his more collegiate approach to the business of government (unlike Somerset, Northumberland never assumed the title Lord Protector, remaining more modestly 'Lord President of the Council').[25] How genuine Northumberland was in his commitment to Protestant reform is a trickier question. He died on the scaffold formally a Catholic, having recanted his heretical views after the accession of Mary. During his period of power, some reformers suspected that Northumberland was a 'carnal gospeller', his commitment to the cause merely opportunistic. Yet from the 1530s Northumberland had been associated with evangelical circles, and had patronized advanced

[24] Henry Robinson, ed., *Original Letters relative to the English Reformation* (Cambridge, 2 vols., 1846–7), ii. 535.

[25] See works cited in note 6.

reformers like John Hooper. Whether his ideological attachment to it was deep or shallow, the pursuit of a Protestant policy made overwhelming political sense from Northumberland's perspective. He could expect nothing from a Marian regency, and his position depended increasingly on his ability to retain the confidence of the young King (unlike Somerset he had no claim by blood to a position in the King's counsels). Shifting diplomatic and financial circumstances also tipped the scales in the direction of more radical reform. Peace with France by the 1550 Treaty of Boulogne eased some of the necessity to appease Charles V (Mary came under increasingly intense pressure to give up the mass in the last years of the reign). In addition, the truly horrendous state of the royal finances (debts of £250,000 by the early 1550s) produced an irresistible temptation: to plunder the remaining wealth of the parishes and bishoprics in the name of simplified and purified worship and ministry. A final factor, which cleared the way for an intensification of the reform programme, was the weakening of the conservative resistance. Not only had armed rebellion against the Reformation been bloodily crushed in the autumn of 1549, but also a combination of retirement, death and deprivation produced a decisive shift in the balance of the episcopate. Bonner of London had lost his see in October 1549, and over the next couple of years Gardiner and half a dozen other traditionalists went the same way. The replacements, especially Ridley of London, Ponet of Winchester and Hooper of Gloucester, were enthusiasts for reform.

A royal circular to the bishops at the end of 1549 ordered the destruction of all Latin service books: there was to be no going back.[26] In March of 1550 a new Ordinal (the book with the form for consecrating priests and bishops) was issued which enunciated a new understanding of the clerical office. Medieval priests were ordained to 'offer sacrifice and celebrate mass'; this was changed to 'preach the word of god and minister the holy sacraments'. The most obvious symbols of a sacrificing priesthood were the stone altars to be found in all English churches. In May 1550 Ridley ordered the removal of altars in London diocese, and their replacement with wooden tables, and other reformers followed suit. In November the council extended the policy to the country as a whole. In this manner the way was being cleared, literally, for the introduction of a new communion service. Many reformers were uneasy about the studied ambiguity of the 1549 liturgy, the scope it allowed for belief in the real presence, and for conservative priests to celebrate the communion service in such a way as to 'counterfeit the mass'.

Its replacement, enforced by a second Act of Uniformity in 1552, closed the loopholes. The phrase 'commonly called the mass' was now dropped from the 'Lord's supper or holy communion', which was to be celebrated

26 MacCulloch, *Church Militant*, pp. 95–6.

not at an altar, but at a 'Lord's table' placed east–west in the church with the minister (clad only in a simple surplice) standing at the side. Ordinary bread rather than traditional wafers was to be used for the sacrament, and if any were left over then 'the curate shall have it to his own use' – there could be no clearer signal that here was no presence of Christ beyond the spiritual feeding of the communicant at the moment of reception. More generally the 1552 Prayer Book delivered a comprehensive repudiation of the efficacy of traditional rites and ceremonies: anointing with oil was removed from the services of baptism, ordination and visitation of the sick, and the burial service was rendered yet more austere than it had become in 1549. In all of this, the Church's official forms of worship 'broke radically with the remembered past'.[27]

Yet this 1552–3 high-water mark of Reformation was not reached without cross-currents and turbulence. As the pace of reform quickened after 1549, cracks in Protestant unity began to appear. At the centre of several of these was Northumberland's fiery protégé, John Hooper, who unlike most leaders of the Edwardian Church had enjoyed the ideological purity of continental exile during the dark days of Henrician reaction. On his appointment as Bishop of Gloucester in 1551, Hooper refused to be consecrated wearing the vestments, which were still required by the 1550 Ordinal. The row was symbolic of the divergent outlook of reformers like Cranmer and Ridley who believed such matters as the wearing of vestments to be *adiaphora* (a Greek term meaning 'things indifferent'), tolerable for the sake of order and unity, and fundamentalists like Hooper who held that whatever was not commanded by scripture was forbidden by scripture. In one form or another, this disagreement would dog the progress of the English Reformation for decades to come. Without political backing (and after a spell in prison) Hooper was made to back down, but when a second dispute blew up in 1552, the council's support for Cranmer was less evident. In November 1552 the Scots exile John Knox preached a sermon before the King arguing that the requirement in the new prayer book to receive communion kneeling amounted to nothing less than idolatry. Pressed by the council to amend the relevant rubric (instruction), Cranmer refused, and so the councillors on their own authority inserted the notorious 'black rubric' stating that kneeling implied no adoration of the bread and wine nor any 'real and essential presence' of Christ's natural body (it was black because the printers had run out of the red ink in which rubrics were customarily printed). Usually regarded as a defeat for Cranmer, the archbishop's most recent biographer has insisted the black rubric was in fact a victory over the zealots like Knox: kneeling remained, and the rubric perfectly expressed Cranmer's own eucharistic theology.[28] Yet the incident revealed how the

[27] Jordan, *Threshold*, p. 348.
[28] MacCulloch, *Cranmer*, pp. 525–8.

authority of the Edwardian episcopal establishment was vulnerable to outflanking manoeuvres by fiery reformers with an entrée to the court.

If Cranmer faced down his critics over the requirement to kneel, Northumberland was able to make life uncomfortable for the archbishop in other ways. Cranmer's long-cherished scheme for a radical overhaul of canon law was vetoed by the duke in 1553, who distrusted its implication of greater autonomy for the ecclesiastical courts (there was no thorough Protestant revision of the medieval canon law until 1604). Foot-dragging by the council also meant that a formal confession of faith for the English Church, the Forty-Two Articles, which Cranmer had presented in spring 1552, were not actually issued until June 1553, a few weeks before the reign and the experiment in Protestantism came to an abrupt end. By this point, even many of Northumberland's allies among the reformist clergy had come to distrust his motives. Redistribution of the Church's resources to support the godly ends of preaching and education would have commanded widespread support, but Northumberland's approach seemed more like naked expropriation, particularly his attitude towards the last great drainable reservoir of ecclesiastical wealth, the estates of the bishoprics. In March 1550 the newly founded bishopric of Westminster (one of the few gains from the dissolution of the monasteries) was suppressed, the Crown taking half the property. In 1551 the diocese of Worcester was collapsed into that of Gloucester, with the Crown again taking a substantial cut. Other bishops were forced to make disadvantageous exchanges of manors with the Crown and saw their income fall by as much as a third. Northumberland's most audacious plan was to carve up the mighty bishopric of Durham, after Tunstall had been arrested on highly dubious treason charges. There was to be a new bishopric of Newcastle, and a massive transfer of revenues to the Crown (no final action on this was taken before the King's death).[29] It was not difficult to provide a specious evangelical rationale for such moves. Reformed bishops should not be Wolsey-esque prelates; perhaps a reformed Church did not require an episcopate at all. Less easy to get at was the remaining wealth of the parish churches, though here too the argument could be advanced that churches putting on sober Protestant services had no need for stocks of elaborate vestments and precious chalices. Surveys of church goods (which had begun under Somerset) led to an order in March 1551 for the surrender of all remaining church 'plate', and confiscations began the following year. By this point many parishes had done the sensible thing and started to sell off their treasures (see Section 3.2)

The squabbles and squalid expropriations of the last years of the Edwardian Reformation illustrate the acute dilemmas of an evangelical,

[29] David Loades, 'Thomas Cranmer and John Dudley: An Uneasy Alliance, 1549–1553', in Paul Ayris and David Selwyn, eds., *Thomas Cranmer: Churchman and Scholar* (Woodbridge, 1993).

spiritual movement that suddenly found itself landed with the religious welfare of an entire nation and the stewardship of an elaborately institutional Church. Catharine Davies has persuasively argued that Protestants who had got used to thinking of themselves as a beleaguered godly minority experienced profound difficulties adjusting to being the religious establishment. Deeply distrustful both of the common people and of powerful 'carnal gospellers', the clerical reformers offered exhortation, but shrank from the kind of thorough-going institutional reform that the situation demanded: 'given the strong element of anticlericalism in Protestant propaganda, particularly the attacks on clerical venality and episcopal extravagance, the problem of adequately financing the ministry was not an easy one for Protestants to confront'.[30] At the same time, Edwardian Protestant leaders, and particularly Thomas Cranmer, were shackled by their unquestioning commitment to the institution of the Royal Supremacy. If, as Cranmer seems to have thought, the King could make and unmake priests and bishops, and the Church had no God-given right to independent jurisdiction or *dominium*, then there were few grounds for convincing protest should the Crown decide to disburden the Church of its assets.[31]

Betrayed hopes, cynical opportunism and missed opportunities are unmistakable features of the Edwardian Reformation, but they are hardly the whole story, or even the main chapter headings. If leading reformers disagreed about the pace and presentation of reforming initiatives, they were seldom divided about fundamental issues of theology, and they shared a determination to transform society through the liberating message of the gospel. An awareness of the magnitude of the task, and the reality of the papist threat, was a strong unifying bond. Political circumstances before and after 1549 created changes of pace and tone, but not of overall direction. A crucial continuity across the vicissitudes of the reign was, as MacCulloch has insisted, the central role played by Thomas Cranmer, principal architect of all the major reforms in worship and theology.[32] Cranmer was not a strikingly original systematic theologian, an English Luther or Calvin, but he was a determinedly thoughtful man of action, and a tireless facilitator, whose network of contacts extended far beyond the shores of Edward's kingdom. The 'foreign influence' which earlier historians were inclined to regard as an embarrassing black mark on the Edwardian Reformation cut both ways: it was in Edward's reign that England came to play a central role in the survival and development of the European

30 Davies, *Religion*, pp. 108, 127, 231–2; '"Poor Persecuted Flock" or "Commonwealth of Christians": Edwardian Protestant Concepts of the Church', in Peter Lake and Maria Dowling, eds., *Protestantism and the National Church in Sixteenth Century England* (London, 1987).

31 Loades, 'Cranmer and Dudley', p. 165; MacCulloch, *Cranmer*, pp. 278–9.

32 MacCulloch, *Church Militant*, p. 102.

Protestant movement. Charles V's decisive victory over the Protestant princes at the battle of Mühlberg in 1547, and his imposition in the following year of the highly restrictive Interim of Augsburg, led to a flood of religious refugees into England, the only front-rank European power to espouse the Protestant cause. The immigrants were catered for by a 'stranger church' established in London under the supervision of the exiled Polish reformer, Jan Laski. Allowed to perform its own ceremonies, and discipline its own members, this congregation constituted 'a radical Protestant community which by its very existence would serve as a constant spur to further reform in the English Church itself'.[33] Laski proved something of a thorn in the flesh for Cranmer, allying himself with Hooper over the vestments controversy. More congenial guests among the forty or so foreign divines who arrived in England in Edward's reign were the Italian evangelicals Bernardino Ochino and Peter Martyr Vermigli, and the leading German reformer Martin Bucer – the latter two were appointed to chairs of divinity at Oxford and Cambridge respectively. Had he been less alarmed by the prospect of sea travel, the foremost Lutheran theologian, Philip Melanchthon, might also have accepted Cranmer's invitation. These developments were indicative of a 'fervent Protestant internationalism' on the part of the Edwardian Church.[34] Only a couple of years before Edward's accession, the papacy had begun its fight-back against the forces of the Reformation by convoking the Council of Trent, and Cranmer's most cherished (but frustrated) wish was for a Protestant general council to meet in England and direct resistance to it. Cranmer was ambitious that England should help steer the European Protestant movement, but also anxious not to rock the boat. He held off producing the Forty-Two Articles until after the general council scheme had fallen through, and slowness in making definitive statements about the eucharist was due in part to a desire not to upset sensitive negotiations about this among the European reformers, which culminated in an agreed statement between Geneva and Zürich, the *Consensus Tigurinus* of May 1549. It was more than anything else an inability to agree about the eucharist that prevented the creation of a completely united Protestant front: the Lutherans held firmly to their belief in the real presence and rejected the definitions of the Swiss 'Reformed' party. Edwardian England aligned itself decisively with the Reformed camp: Lutheranism was only ever thereafter to be a marginal influence on the development of the English Reformation. It is often asserted that the Edwardian Reformation was a 'Calvinist' one, with the implication that it was more extreme than its Elizabethan successor. Ironically, it was only in Elizabeth's reign that most English divines began to consider Calvin the supreme theological arbiter. If there was a primary overseas influence on the

33 Andrew Pettegree, *Foreign Protestant Communities in Sixteenth-Century London* (Oxford, 1986), p. 35.

34 MacCulloch, *Church Militant*, p. 79.

Edwardian Church, it is likely to have been Heinrich Bullinger, Zwingli's successor at Zürich, who maintained regular correspondence with many English reformers, and whose works were widely translated. But it is unwise to look for a pre-prepared label – 'Calvinist', 'Zwinglian', or even 'Bullingerian' – to slap on the reforms of 1547–53. The Edwardian Revolution had its own momentum, and it was part of the mainstream, not a minor tributary.

3.2 Communities and their Responses

The question of which foreign Protestant intellectual most informed the thinking of Edwardian bishops was probably of little interest to the men and women in the parishes who experienced episcopal policy at the sharp end. If the furnishings of parish churches and the forms of parish worship were adjusted in Henry VIII's reign, in Edward's they were transformed. Eloquent testimony to this is found in the chronicle of Robert Parkyn, a conservative Yorkshire priest writing about the matters that most affected him and his parishioners: 41 lines on the course of events from 1532 to 1547; 363 lines on 1547–53.[35] The perception was shared by the churchwardens of Stanford in the Vale, Berkshire, referring in Mary's reign to 'the time of schism when this realm was divided from the Catholic Church'. Surprisingly, they did not mean 1534, but rather the 'second year of King Edward the Sixth', when 'all godly ceremonies and good uses were taken out of the Church within this realm'.[36] Recent post-revisionist scholarship, in seeking to account for the acceptance and ultimate success of the Reformation, has stressed its incremental character, its impact spread out over generations.[37] But there was little that was incremental about the concentrated dose of Reformation administered to local communities in 1547–53. The imperial ambassador, who was able to report home in 1548 that changes were neither radical nor irreversible, should have spoken to the churchwardens of Stanford.[38]

In the opening months of the reign, the Royal Injunctions, which Jordan (inevitably) termed 'careful and moderate', staked out the agenda for a radical overhaul of popular religion.[39] To the dismay of Robert Parkyn, they banned the parochial processions with which Sunday and feast-day masses

[35] A.G. Dickens, ed., 'Robert Parkyn's Narrative of the Reformation', in Dickens, *Reformation Studies* (London, 1982).

[36] Eamon Duffy, 'Cranmer and Popular Religion', in Ayris and Selwyn, *Cranmer*, p. 204.

[37] Christopher Marsh, *Popular Religion in Sixteenth-Century England*, (Basingstoke, 1998); Norman Jones, *The English Reformation: Religion and Cultural Adaption* (Oxford, 2002).

[38] Bush, *Protector Somerset*, p. 122.

[39] Jordan, *Young King*, p. 162.

began, something which, Eamon Duffy has argued, 'struck at the heart of one of the principal expressions of medieval communal religion'.[40] They also, as we have seen, led directly to the removal of all religious imagery, transforming the internal appearance of parish churches. The evidence of churchwardens' accounts suggests that parishes dutifully removed their statues and roods, and in due course whitewashed their muralled walls. The terse record of disbursements – 'Item, paid to Henry Boreg for takyng down the images... xiid' – cannot tell us how grudgingly they did so.[41] But in many places images were hidden away rather than sold or destroyed.[42]

In tandem with the requirement to remove images over the course of 1548, parishes had to face the implications of parliament's decision to dissolve the chantries. This involved not merely the redundancy of thousands of chantry priests, but the winding up of parish fraternities, the snuffing out of countless 'obit lamps' and the silencing of bede-rolls which had kept alive the memory of more humble parish benefactors. It brought home to the people a central doctrinal insight of Protestantism – that purgatory did not exist and the dead must not be prayed for – in the most stark and unavoidable way. This, perhaps, was the most traumatic and inordinate demand that the Reformation made on the psyche of the English nation, but we have frustratingly little evidence for how people actually felt about it. As we saw in Section 2.3, there is evidence of an overall decline of investment in intercession from Henrician wills, though the extent to which this directly reflects changes in belief remains uncertain. Examining the level of Edwardian intercessory bequests to get at popular attitudes towards purgatory is a fairly useless exercise. Testators could not leave money to institutions that had been abolished, and practices that had been declared illegal. Nonetheless, it is intriguing to note that as the percentage of wills requesting masses fell, that leaving bequests for alms rose markedly nationwide, and testators sometimes explicitly stated that legacies were to go to the poor if masses, prayers or obits would not stand with the law.[43] It was a long-standing social expectation that the poor would pray for the souls of benefactors. But the evidence here is ambiguous. Protestant teaching encouraged generosity to the poor as the godly alternative to offerings wasted on images and masses, and the conditions of the difficult middle years of the sixteenth century may have made the alleviation of poverty seem a more pressing social concern. Another possibility is that the discovery there was no such place as purgatory may have been experienced by many as a form of relief, bringing in the words of Alan Kreider, 'joyful release from

40 'Parkyn's Narrative', p. 295; Duffy, *Stripping*, p. 452.

41 Anthony Palmer, ed., *Tudor Churchwardens' Accounts* (Hertfordshire Record Society, 1985), p. 66 (parish of Baldock, 1548).

42 Haigh, *Reformations*, p. 170.

43 Peter Marshall, *Beliefs and the Dead in Reformation England* (Oxford, 2002), pp. 102–3.

an acutely existential dread'.[44] But the widespread (and long-term) tendency for parishioners to cling to vestiges of traditional funeral custom suggests that many found it difficult to make so clean a break with the past, where the needs of the dead were concerned.[45]

Communities, however, had to cope with the economic and social implications of the dissolution of the chantries, a process not simply imposed from outside, but one in which local people were often implicated. During the later part of Henry's reign, there had been an increasing number of private dissolutions to forestall government action. As the dissolution itself got under way, some patrons made efforts to resume the lands of their ancestors' foundations, and within a short time many of the elites, both urban and gentry, were purchasing chantry lands. There was also a fair amount of simple embezzlement of chantry property.[46] The impact of the dissolution in areas such as education and poor relief has been contentious. Jordan was concerned to minimize it, arguing that Edwardian 'commonwealth' preachers exaggerated the role of chantries in providing schools and almshouses, and that local commissioners were able to divert many revenues to 'socially useful' purposes.[47] Dickens provided a more balanced assessment, conceding that though the aims of the Crown were entirely predatory, energetic action by local communities led over the medium term to the refounding of many schools and hospitals.[48] The consequences for pastoral provision and parish finance were more serious. The fraternities had been major fund-raisers in many parishes, as well employers of chaplains. The majority of chantry priests were involved in helping out in parishes, saying masses and hearing confessions, especially in parts of the north where in large, scattered, moorland parishes, chantries often operated as de facto parish churches. A striking result of the dissolution was an overall huge loss of clerical manpower, not only because of vanished career opportunities, but because the release of so many former chantry priests (on top of ex-monks) on to the clerical job market discouraged ordinations to the extent that there was a real shortage of clergy for the best part of a generation. In one region, the East Riding of Yorkshire, there were 587 secular priests resident in the mid-1520s, and perhaps another 140 monks and friars. In 1552 there were 185 clergymen in all and fewer still in Elizabeth's reign.[49]

[44] Kreider, *Chantries*, p. 93; A.G. Dickens, *The English Reformation* (2nd ed., London, 1989), pp. 29–30; Marsh, *Popular Religion*, p. 66.

[45] Marshall, *Beliefs*, pp. 126–41.

[46] Kreider, *Chantries*, ch. 6; Ethan Shagan, *Popular Politics and the English Reformation* (Cambridge, 2003), ch. 7.

[47] Jordan, *Threshold*, pp. 188, 197, 239.

[48] Dickens, *Reformation*, pp. 230–42.

[49] Peter Marshall, *The Face of the Pastoral Ministry in the East Riding, 1525–1595* (York, 1995), pp. 3–4.

It was the clergy more than any other social group who felt the effects of the Edwardian revolution. They were to be no longer a sacramental priesthood, but a preaching ministry. Yet this was not a role for which they had been prepared. Bishop Hooper's Gloucester visitation of 1551, in which it emerged that over half the priests examined could not repeat the Ten Commandments, and a third could not find the Lord's Prayer in the Bible, has often been cited as shocking evidence of the deplorable ignorance of the late medieval parish clergy. But more probably it points to the limitations of a group who had never expected to have to ground their ministry on a familiarity with vernacular scripture.[50] The abolition of the mass must, in the short term at least, have lowered priestly status in the eyes of the laity, and a further blow to clerical authority was the removal of the requirement on lay people to confess their sins to them. A number of Edwardian reformers, though they detested the theology of confession, lamented a pastoral opportunity lost[51] (see Section 6.1). An opportunity gained by the clergy was the right to get married, enshrined in an Act of Parliament of 1549. To reformers, this constituted a necessary declaration that the priesthood possessed no special status over the laity, as well as a practical cure for the sexual transgressions to which the enforced celibacy of the clergy had given rise. Priests took advantage of the invitation in highly uneven numbers: nearly one third of the London parish clergy married in Edward's reign, and a quarter did so in Essex, Norfolk and Suffolk. The figure was only one in ten in Yorkshire, and less than one in twenty in Lancashire. Though it would be unwise to draw too close a correlation between the desire to wed and support for the Reformation, this nuptial geography probably does reflect an overall strength of attachment to traditional ways. In the north in particular, the cultural taboo against clerical marriage remained strong, and ministers' wives were liable to be vilified as 'priests' whores'.[52]

Public abuse of clerical wives is a reminder that lay responses to Edwardian religious policies were not invariably passive. Resentment exploded in the summer of 1549 with a major outbreak of rebellion in Devon and Cornwall, and serious disorders in Oxfordshire, Buckinghamshire and the North Riding of Yorkshire (where the dissolution of local chantries was the precipitating factor). The rising in the south-west has been nicknamed the 'Prayer Book Rebellion', though in fact the demands of the insurgents constituted a comprehensive repudiation of all

[50] Dickens, *Reformation*, pp. 272–3; David Newcombe, 'John Hooper's Visitation and Examination of the Clergy in the Diocese of Gloucester, 1551', in Beat Kümin, ed., *Reformations Old and New: Essays on the Socio-Economic Impact of Religious Change, c. 1470–1630* (Aldershot, 1996).

[51] Davies, *Religion*, p. 100.

[52] Peter Marshall, *The Catholic Priesthood and the English Reformation* (Oxford, 1994), pp. 163–73; Helen Parish, *Clerical Marriage and the English Reformation* (Aldershot, 2000), pp. 180–6.

the religious innovations of Edward's reign (and a substantial number of Henry's). Images were to be set up again; palms, ashes and holy water restored. Priests at every mass were to 'pray specially by name for the souls in purgatory', and the English Bible was to be removed for encouraging heresy. There was realism about a complete return to the world before the break with Rome. Henry's Six Articles were to be reinstated (an implicit echo of Gardiner's argument about change during a minority), and only half the monastic lands were to be restored, though this was enough to discourage all but a handful of local gentry from taking part in the rising. The articles contained no specific call for the restoration of the papal supremacy, though the demand for Cardinal Pole to be recalled 'and promoted to be first or second of the King's Counsel' was hardly imaginable in other circumstances. It was the new liturgy, however, which had clearly tipped the balance: the 1549 communion service did not seem a moderate and gradualist reform in the parishes of rural Devon. It was 'but like a Christmas game'; the Latin mass was the real thing. There should be communion in one kind only, the laity receiving at Easter, and the reserved sacrament was to be restored to its place above the altar.

The events of the rising were brief, but bloody. Trouble had been brewing in Cornwall for some time, with riots at Penryn in 1547 and Helston in 1548. The introduction of the prayer book in June 1549 sparked a larger outbreak around Bodmin, and a force soon marched to join up with rebels who had risen simultaneously in Devon. By the end of the month perhaps 7,000 were in arms under the banner of the Five Wounds, and had laid siege to Exeter. The government, distracted by the closer agrarian disturbances in East Anglia, at first underestimated the seriousness of what was happening and allowed the rising to spread. By late July, however, a force under Lords Russell and Grey arrived in the south-west (having crushed the Oxfordshire rising en route), and the rebels were routed in a series of engagements between August 4 and 16, ending with the slaughter of around 4,000 rebels at Sampford Courtenay in Devon, where two months earlier the parishioners had forced their priest to don 'his old popish attire' and say the Latin mass.

Historians of the Reformation have argued over whether the South-West Rebellion was a storm in a teacup or the pot boiling over. As in 1536, religion was not the only cause of discontent. Joyce Youings has established that Somerset's anti-enclosure policy (which involved a poll-tax on sheep) caused considerable disquiet in the sheep-rearing south-west, and taxation and high prices appear to have been grievances in sets of rebel articles which no longer survive.[53] The secular elements of the rising have been more emphatically asserted by Robert Whiting, who seeks to minimize its general

[53] Joyce Youings, 'The South-Western Rebellion of 1549', *Southern History*, 1 (1979).

significance and seriousness. Whiting argues that rebel numbers were relatively low, and that there were numerous examples of loyalist sentiment (the city of Exeter held out against the rebels).[54] It must, however, be conceded that a major religious rebellion in 1549 poses distinct problems for Whiting's overall thesis of rapid and complete popular compliance with the wishes of the government.[55] All early modern popular rebellions ignited in a complex alchemy of local, social and ideological causation. Yet we should hesitate before dismissing the South-West Rising as substantial evidence for the unpopularity of the Edwardian reforms. The main reason why resentment took a violently activist form here is probably less to do with the supposed cultural backwardness of Devon and Cornwall, than with the political structure of the region. The area was bereft of strong noble leadership after Henry VIII's purge of Cardinal Pole's relatives in 1538, the execution of the Marquis of Exeter and imprisonment of his heir. Elsewhere in the summer of 1549, potentially serious disorder was nipped in the bud by prompt and decisive aristocratic action (for example in Sussex by the Earl of Arundel).[56] Historians are sometimes too quick to draw conclusions from the 'surprising' absence of resistance to officially imposed Protestant reforms. Treason in arms was a drastic and irrevocable step to contemplate. In the unusual circumstances where it could take place (in 1549, as in 1536), it provides a window onto an otherwise hidden world of seething resentments.

Most local communities may not have liked the Edwardian reforms, but in the end they had to lump them. As the predatory intentions of Northumberland's government became clear, many parishes (about three-quarters in the sample of surviving churchwardens' accounts) began to sell off their mass-saying equipment and stores of church plate. The proceeds were usually deployed quickly on projects of local concern: repair of roads, bridges and church buildings, the construction of harbours and canals.[57] Such sales constitute a deeply ambiguous form of 'resistance'. There was an obvious determination the government would not get its hands on local resources, but also a recognition that the regime was going to get its way, and a preparedness to close the book on old customs. A poignant case study in the mentality of unwilling compliance is Eamon Duffy's account of the small moorland parish of Morebath (Devon). Despite its poverty, Morebath

54 Robert Whiting, *The Blind Devotion of the People: Popular Religion and the English Reformation* (Cambridge, 1989), pp. 34–8.

55 Elaborated in his *Local Responses to the English Reformation* (Basingstoke, 1998).

56 Youings, 'Rebellion', pp. 115–17; Barrett L. Beer, *Rebellion and Riot: Popular Disorder in England during the Reign of Edward VI* (Kent, OH, 1982), pp. 153–4.

57 Jordan, *Threshold*, pp. 392–4.

was possessed of a rich devotional life before the Reformation, its many images and lights supported by complex funding arrangements involving the communal custody of sheep belonging to the church. The parish accounts were painstakingly kept by the vicar, Christopher Trychay, like Robert Parkyn a conservative whose ministry spanned the reigns of the four last Tudors. Trychay's pet project was the raising of funds for a lavish set of black requiem vestments, and after twenty years of small donations the vestments were purchased in July 1547, just as liturgical reform was about to make them superfluous. The visitation of 1547 forced the sale of the church sheep, leading to a collapse in Morebath's finances, and further disposals of parish equipment. In 1549, five young men of the parish were despatched to join the rebel army outside Exeter, their expenses listed, with staggering audacity, in the churchwardens' accounts. But after this brief quixotic protest Morebath fell into line, removing its altars and rood-loft in 1551, and delivering a pathetic remnant of church goods to royal commissioners in 1552. In 1553 the accounts referred for the first time to the King as 'of the Church of England. . . the supreme head'.[58] Morebath, it would seem, was traumatized but tamed by the Edwardian Reformation, and its experience is unlikely to have been unusual. Across the nation, a cumulative result of the changes may have been to reduce the importance of the parish church as a focus of local identity. The evidence from Church courts points to a growing level of absenteeism from services in Edward's reign, and wills suggest a collapse in bequests to churches (in the north of England, from over two-thirds of testators to less than one) which exacerbated the problems of parochial finance.[59] One way that churchwardens, particularly in London, found of making ends meet was to sell old memorial brasses, an expedient that met with the approval of reformers who considered the requests for prayers they contained as 'superstitious' and their religious imagery as 'idolatrous'.[60] Such actions, along with the disposal of church ornaments inscribed with the names of benefactors, and the putting aside of the lists of the generous dead in parish bede-rolls, were breaks in the continuity from one generation to the next, little lapses into social amnesia. In taking them, parish officials were colluding, wittingly or otherwise with a fundamental aim of Edwardian iconoclasm, to impel the English people to cast off the embrace of the past, and forget the wicked ways of their forefathers. The 1547 Injunctions commanded the complete destruction of all shrines, and all imagery associated with miracles and pilgrimages 'so that there remain no memory of the same'.[61]

58 Eamon Duffy, *The Voices of Morebath: Reformation and Rebellion in an English Village* (New Haven and London, 2001), especially ch. 6.
59 MacCulloch, *Church Militant*, p. 106; Haigh, *Reformations*, pp. 181–2.
60 Marshall, *Beliefs*, pp. 104–8.
61 W.H. Frere and W.M. Kennedy, eds., *Visitation Articles and Injunctions of the Period of the Reformation*, (3 vols, London, 1910), ii. 126.

3.3 Protestants and their Testaments

By no means all English men and women felt like Robert Parkyn or Christopher Trychay, that the reforms emanating from the centre were a threat to be resisted, a crisis to be endured. The evangelical cause had continued to win adherents under conditions of sporadic persecution throughout Henry VIII's reign; its ability to do so was dramatically increased after 1547 when the threat of persecution was lifted and the resources of the State were thrown behind it. The Edwardian religious establishment was interested not just in coercion, but conversion, in spreading the liberating message of the gospel which would restore men and women fallen in sin and idolatry to a right relationship with their God. Charismatic Protestant preaching was a hallmark of the reign.[62] Licensed preachers like Thomas Lever, John Bradford, Mathew Parker, Rowland Taylor and Thomas Becon drew large crowds, at Pauls Cross in London and in the provinces. The most celebrated preacher of all was Hugh Latimer, who declined the invitation to return to a bishopric (he had resigned in 1539) to concentrate on the work of evangelism. Though historians no longer believe that such preachers constituted a distinct 'commonwealth party', their characteristic linking of the themes of the gospel to wider social criticism, and their moralistic appeals for economic justice, and reciprocal duties between rich and poor had the potential to strike a chord with people beyond the confines of bookish heresy.[63] Alongside preaching, the press too reached out to a wider audience; one recent study speaks of 'a revolution in English print culture' in Edward's reign. With the lifting of censorship, and with the technical assistance of immigrant Dutch printers, London's presses were producing more than twice as many editions annually in the early 1550s than they had done a decade earlier. Overwhelmingly these were Protestant works, ranging from translations of foreign divines, and theological works by leading English reformers, to racy polemical tracts and numerous editions of scripture.[64]

62 MacCulloch, *Church Militant*, p. 2 has protested that the word 'Protestant' was not in widespread use before Mary's reign, and that the gospellers of Edward's reign are best still referred to as 'evangelicals'. The point has validity, but confessional demarcations were already much clearer than they had been two decades earlier, and there are obvious continuities of priorities and personnel between Edwardian 'Protestantism' and its younger Marian and Elizabethan siblings.

63 The 'commonwealth party' is debunked by G.R. Elton, 'Reform and the "Commonwealth-Men" of Edward VI's Reign', in Peter Clark, Alan G.R. Smith and Nicholas Tyacke, eds., *The English Commonwealth 1547–1640* (Leicester, 1979), and (partially) rehabilitated by MacCulloch, *Church Militant*, pp. 122–6.

64 Andrew Pettegree, 'Printing and the Reformation: the English Exception', in Peter Marshall and Alec Ryrie, *The Beginnings of English Protestantism* (Cambridge, 2002).

What effect was all this evangelistic effort having on its intended audience? No serious scholar now proposes that most English people became Protestants in the reign of Edward VI, and neither does anyone suppose that a precise statistical breakdown of the religious allegiances of the English people can be meaningfully produced. But questions of the numerical scale and geographic extent of Protestant advance remain important ones in assessing the character and potential of the English Reformation at this crucial juncture. One well-established school of thought holds that over the course of Edward's reign Protestantism acquired a kind of critical momentum, that it became literally unstoppable (dooming in advance the attempt to stop it under Mary). This, as we have seen, was the view of G.R. Elton, and also of W.K. Jordan who claimed that Protestantism became 'deeply and inextricably rooted' in London, other urban centres, and the prosperous south-east, and that the gentry and merchant classes who held the ultimate resources of power in the State became 'predominantly and irreversibly Protestant'.[65] In a slightly more careful formulation, A.G. Dickens argued that by the accession of Elizabeth, Protestantism had 'attained a greater psychological vitality and cohesion in English society than had the cause of conservative Catholicism'.[66] Some revisionist writers by contrast have insisted on Protestantism's continuing small minority status: the Protestants could come out of the closet after Mary's death, 'but it had not been very crowded in there.'[67]

The debates are fuelled by conflicting assessments of the intrinsic attractiveness of both traditional religious culture and new evangelicalism, but also by the fragmentary nature of the evidence. The number of individuals who can be shown to have been committed Protestants in mid-Tudor England is relatively small, a problem ironically compounded for Edward's reign by the fact that persecution generates records in a way its absence does not. A 'Biographical Register of English Protestants' compiled by John Fines produced around 3,000 names for the whole period 1525–1558.[68] Historians of crime are accustomed to speak about the 'dark figure', the volume of actual offences that never made it to the courts, and here the dark figure must be considerable indeed. A maximalist approach like that of Dickens points to the probable loss of records, and the likelihood that very many Protestants kept their heads down in conditions of persecution under Henry and Mary. Revisionists counter that popular hatred of heresy implies

65 Jordan, *Young King*, p. 346 .

66 A.G. Dickens, 'The Early Expansion of Protestantism in England, 1520–1558', in Peter Marshall, ed., *The Impact of the English Reformation 1500–1640* (London, 1997), p. 107.

67 Haigh, *Reformations*, p. 201.

68 John Fines, *Biographical Register of Early English Protestants, c. 1525–1558* (2 vols., 1981–85).

a high 'detection rate'.[69] One possible way out of the blind alley of rival guesswork is to pay close attention to wills, the one source of evidence that survives in sufficient quantity (tens of thousands, covering most parts of the country) to allow the tracing of meaningful statistical patterns. The technique is to analyse will preambles (the opening statement of the will, bequeathing the soul to God). The idea is not a new one – it was pioneered by Dickens in the 1950s – and it remains highly controversial.[70] Before the 1530s, the great majority of preambles followed a similar form, entrusting the soul to God, Our Lady and 'the Holy Company of Heaven' (i.e. the saints). Subsequent divergences from this pattern are used to suggest the erosion of traditional religion and the advance of Protestantism. Usually, three broad categories of preamble are identified: 'Catholic', with invocations of the virgin and saints; 'Protestant', in which reference is made to hope of salvation solely through the merits of Christ's passion; and a third type in which the soul is bequeathed to God without further elaboration (historians have differed over whether this is best described as 'reformist', 'neutral' or 'ambiguous').[71] Virtually all recent local studies of the Reformation have employed this approach in some way or other, and in general the findings agree. The traditional form is predominant everywhere up until the mid-1540s, and then goes into a far from uniform decline (in Edward's reign it is found in only 5 per cent of Kentish wills, but 58 per cent of those from Northamptonshire). In most areas the ground is taken up by 'neutral' rather than overtly Protestant formulae. Edwardian London was unique in having 32 per cent of wills with Protestant preambles; even in Kent the figure was only 7 per cent. The overall message seems evident: a marked decline of traditional belief, combined with steady (and in some places impressive) Protestant advance.

Of course, matters are not quite so straightforward; it would be delusional to regard statistics derived from wills as a kind of MORI poll of popular religious belief. Will-makers were a distinctly unrepresentative sample of the population, older, wealthier and overwhelmingly more male than the average subject of King Edward. Moreover, preambles cannot be taken at face value as testaments of personal belief. Wills, almost invariably dictated from the deathbed, were generally written by parish clergy or by

[69] Dickens, *Reformation*, pp. 330–1; Haigh, *Reformations*, pp. 198–9.

[70] A.G. Dickens, *Lollards and Protestants in the Diocese of York*, (Oxford, 1959), pp. 171–2, 215–21. Scepticism about the method is expressed by J.D. Alsop, 'Religious Preambles in Early Modern English Wills as Formulae', *Journal of Ecclesiastical History*, 40 (1989); Alec Ryrie, 'Counting Sheep, Counting Shepherds: the Problem of Allegiance in the English Reformation', in Marshall and Ryrie, *Beginnings*, pp. 85–7.

[71] The most sophisticated analysis of categories is that of Caroline Litzenberger, 'Local Responses to Changes in Religious Policy Based on the Evidence from Gloucestershire Wills', *Continuity and Change*, 8 (1993).

professional scribes, who in many cases probably suggested an appropriate formula (some of these have been shown to come from contemporary printed 'precedent books'). It is not difficult to find wills where a stridently Protestant preamble is followed by a request for masses, or of villages where over a period of years all the wills have identical preambles because they were all written by the curate. Historians who attempt preamble-analysis have been aware of these problems, usually arguing that even if preambles are not original personal statements, statistical analysis of sufficiently large samples will reveal important general trends in belief. A more radical assault on the usefulness of the procedure has been attempted by Eamon Duffy, who denies that differences between 'Catholic' and 'Protestant' wills are at all easy to define. There was nothing uniquely Protestant in putting one's trust in the merits of the Passion (examples can be found from before the Reformation), and the bequest to 'Almighty God my maker and redeemer' (which some historians have seen as sympathetic to reform) was in fact uncontroversial, appearing in a sample will in a 1543 *Book of Presidents*. Duffy concedes that there was more to the changes than fluctuations of fashion. Wills were public documents proved in a court of law, and 'early Tudor testators did not lightly include in their wills provisions which they believed might complicate probate or bring trouble on heirs and executors'. Catholics were willing to abandon traditional formulae because they might have no real theological objection to the alternatives.[72] Duffy uses the argument about social pressures on will-making to suggest that wills mask the real strength of Catholic feeling in Edward's reign, though one could argue from the same premise that they underestimate evangelical sentiment under Henry and Mary (as we saw in Section 2.1, William Tracy's will was a salutary warning, though admittedly a unique one, of the dangers of unfettered expression).

Perhaps what is most usefully observed from the testamentary evidence is not the overall incidence of a particular feature within a given town or county, but the relative disparities between different regions. Assuming the progress of one uniform and monolithic 'English Reformation' not only obscures important differences of local experience, but misses a vital dynamic of the Reformation itself, for it was the ability of Protestantism to establish vocal constituencies among particular groups and in particular politically and economically important areas that gave the regime confidence to press ahead with controversial policies. From the testamentary and other evidence, A.G. Dickens posited the existence of a 'great crescent' of Protestant heartlands running from Norwich down to the Sussex coast: the counties of Norfolk, Suffolk, Essex and Kent, with London as the fulcrum. From this, a 'spur' ran up the Thames valley, taking in Buckinghamshire, Oxfordshire and Berkshire, perhaps making contact with the sole western stronghold of Protestantism, Bristol and its Gloucestershire hinterland.

72 Duffy, *Stripping*, ch. 15.

There was a discernible Protestant presence too in Coventry, and in east coast ports like Hull.[73] Protestants were more likely to be found in the south and east, than in the west and north, in towns than in the countryside – though it is as well not to be too determinist about this: there were Protestant outposts in Yorkshire towns like Leeds and Halifax, and despite being major urban centres, Exeter and York were notably hostile to Protestantism. The correspondence of this pattern to the known geography of Lollardy is emphasized by MacCulloch: we are looking at 'something other than a reformation from above: it is a set of independent movements which had begun as dissent from official orthodoxy'.[74] As we have seen, however, it remains deeply contested whether late Lollardy possessed the numerical and organizational strength to provide a springboard in this way. A further apparent dovetailing is with the typology of popular protest in 1549. The demands of the western rebels focussed on the restoration of the mass and images. Those of the East Anglian rising led by Robert Kett were largely concerned with agrarian matters, but where they touched on religion they carried a distinctly evangelical and anticlerical charge: priests were not to interfere in the land market, and were not to be grasping about tithes. They were to be resident on their benefices, to teach the catechism to poor children of the parish, and to 'preach and set forth the Word of God'. Those that could not do so were to be put from their benefices.[75] It is highly unlikely that the camps the rebels established across East Anglia in the summer of 1549 were peopled in the main by committed Protestants. Duffy reminds us that the initial trouble in Norfolk broke out during celebrations of an abolished Catholic feast day, and that some contingents marched to the camps behind their traditional parish banners.[76] Probably nowhere in the 'great crescent' were Protestants numerically preponderant in Edward's reign. Even in London, as Susan Brigden has shown, there was strong conservative feeling throughout the period.[77] But by the end of the 1540s the rhetoric and symbolism of 'the Word of God' were no longer the code words of an underground network; they had entered the mainstream of political discourse and popular consciousness. In 1550 Protestants may still have been a minority, but they were not the kind of minority they had been in 1530.

Perhaps we delude ourselves if we imagine a nation divided into two clearly defined camps: committed defenders of the old faith and zealous advocates of the new. Simple disorientation may have been the most common and natural response to the religious innovations that the Edwardian Reformation brought. A further possibility, suggested by Alec Ryrie, is that the regular evangelical denunciations of 'carnal gospellers'

[73] Dickens, 'Early Expansion', pp. 93–104.
[74] MacCulloch, *Church Militant*, p. 111.
[75] Anthony Fletcher and Diarmaid MacCulloch, *Tudor Rebellions* (4th ed., London, 1997), pp. 144–6.
[76] Duffy, *Morebath*, pp. 130–1.
[77] Susan Brigden, *London and the Reformation* (Oxford, 1989).

who abused the liberty of the gospel should be taken seriously, rather than dismissed as rhetorical clichés. The reformers attacked time-honoured practices such as the requirement to fast, go to confession, pray for the dead or maintain clerical celibacy, social conventions which were potentially burdensome and made sense only when all of society observed them. Many people may have been pragmatically willing to abandon them without undergoing any profound personal conversion. But this 'penumbra' of loose reformist sympathizers could not easily be won back to the old ways.[78] Another target of denunciation for evangelical preachers were the radical sectarians whom historians group together under the loose label of 'anabaptist', and whose beliefs sometimes seem to have been formed in a creative encounter between native Lollardy and heterodox ideas from the continent. (One of the motivations behind the establishment of the London Stranger Church was to police the foreign immigrants who were seen as a potential source of strange heresies). The radicals espoused a variety of ideas anathema to Protestant orthodoxy. Some heresies were 'Christological'. The Kentish woman Joan Bocher was burned in May 1550 for denying that Christ took any flesh from the Virgin Mary. In the following year, a Flemish refugee, George van Parris, was executed for rejecting the divinity of Christ. These were the only executions solely for heresy to be carried out in Edward's reign. Other nonconformists held inadmissible views on salvation: a group of 'freewillers' (who rejected official doctrine on predestination) was discovered meeting at Bocking, Essex, at the end of 1550, and in 1552 Cranmer was ordered by the council to investigate the appearance of a new antinomian sect, which would later be known as the Family of Love.[79] The Freewillers posed a continuing headache for the Protestant leadership in Mary's reign (see Section 4.3); the 'Familists' continued to enjoy a shadowy existence in parts of East Anglia for the rest of the period covered by this book.[80] Such people infuriated and terrified the evangelical establishment in equal measure. They betrayed the cause and played into the hands of the papists, who had always argued that heresy was inevitably fragmentary and corrosive of the social order. Indeed, Protestant propaganda consistently likened popery and anabaptism to each other – they were not opposite ends of a religious spectrum in which the Edwardian Church occupied the middle ground, but manifestations of the same 'false religion' which stood in opposition to the true.[81] Yet the papists may have had a point. As Henry VIII had discovered a decade earlier, it was optimistic simultaneously to

[78] Ryrie, 'Counting Sheep', pp. 99–105.

[79] Jordan, *Threshold*, pp. 326–34. Predestination is the doctrine that humans' actions do not influence whether God sends them to heaven or hell; antinomianism the belief that true Christians are not obliged to observe the moral law.

[80] Christopher Marsh, *The Family of Love in English Society, 1550–1630* (Cambridge, 1994).

[81] Davies, *Religion*, pp. 78–9.

provide the laity with unfettered access to vernacular scripture, and expect them to draw only officially approved conclusions from it.

Summation

All revolutions generate idealism and high hopes; most end in disillusionment and regret. By the time of Edward's death in July 1553, the confidence of Protestant reformers that the cause of the gospel would sweep all before it, transforming not just the Church but all of society, had been badly shaken by the rebellions of 1549, the unresponsiveness of the people, and the cynical opportunism of 'carnal gospellers' among their rulers. The young King's death was interpreted as divine judgement on a people who had not deserved such a monarch.[82] In 1553 the Edwardian Reformation was by any measure an unfinished revolution. Fundamental objectives, such as the reform of canon law, remained unfulfilled. Popery still lurked, not only in the hearts of the people, but also (some reformers thought) in the very structures of the Church itself, its unreliably staffed Church courts, its lavishly endowed cathedrals, the vestments worn by its ministers. Already in the course of the reign alarming divisions had opened up within Protestant ranks about the pace with which such matters needed to be reformed, and about the Church's freedom to choose to retain institutions and observances not explicitly commanded by the Word of God. These divisions did not disappear after 1553, and became part of the dynamic of the Reformation itself. Among future generations of Protestants looking back on the reign, some would see a summons to unfinished business, others a line beyond which it was not proper to advance.

But for an unfinished revolution, the achievements of the Edwardian Reformation were momentous ones. Its essential religious texts, the Forty-Two Articles, Book of Homilies and Book of Common Prayer were (in variously revised forms) to help define the shape of Anglicanism for centuries to come. As MacCulloch has noted, 'the Church of England is the Church of Edward VI more than it likes to admit'.[83] More immediately, its determination to wage war against the forces of darkness had transformed both the outward appearance of places of worship, and the inner obligations placed on worshippers. English people had been expected to understand that religious images were not inspiring aids to devotion, but abominable idolatry; that to pray for the dead was not a pious duty, but a pitiful superstition; that the mass was not a means of making Christ present among them, but a blasphemous counterfeit. The question of how many had learned these lessons, and of how deeply they had imbibed them, was to be put sharply to the test in the years that followed.

[82] Robinson, *Letters*, i. 100.
[83] MacCulloch, *Church Militant*, p. 12.

4

Queen Mary's Reformation 1553–1558

Overview

For a handful of years in the 1550s England was Catholic England once more; the Edwardian Reformation was stopped in its tracks and thrown into reverse. Not so long ago the interpretation of this development seemed clear-cut. The endeavour by Queen Mary and her principal religious advisor, Cardinal Reginald Pole, to reverse the Protestant advances of the preceding decades was simply destined to fail, an attempt to fly in the face of history. The wave of nationalist and anticlerical sentiment which Henry and Edward had ridden could not be held back by the Canute-like pronouncements of a Catholic Queen, and the cruel persecution which her regime initiated merely strengthened the resolve of the Protestant movement and helped swing the uncommitted behind it. In essence, this was the view formulated by the first and greatest historian of the reign, John Foxe, whose accounts of heroic martyrs in the fires of Smithfield in his *Acts and Monuments of the Christian Church* (first published 1563) exercised for centuries a magnetic hold on the English imagination. The intense denominational passions fed by Foxe's stirring narrative have now largely (though not entirely) abated, but historical views of Mary's reign have not become less controversial as a result. Revisionist scholars, notably Jennifer Loach, Christopher Haigh and Eamon Duffy, have rejected a prevailing interpretation which saw Marian religious policy simply as 'reaction', a backward-looking attempt to restore the Church of the early 1520s through an unimaginative blend of legalistic pronouncements and harsh persecution. A.G. Dickens's stern conclusion that Mary 'failed to discover the counter-reformation', that her Church didn't understand the need for positive and enthusiastic Catholic evangelism, has come under sustained attack.[1] The

[1] A.G. Dickens, *The English Reformation* (2nd ed., London, 1989), p. 311.

English Church of the mid-1550s, revisionists argue, was actually an early shoot of the Catholic reform movement, which would flower on the continent after the Council of Trent. Moreover, in keeping with their markedly positive assessments of the strength and vitality of pre-Reformation religious culture, the revisionists detect substantial reserves of popular support for the restoration of Catholicism. But while revisionist reappraisals of the pre-Reformation Church have won a measure of general acceptance, opinion on the Marian Church remains more sharply divided. In second editions of major works appearing in 1989 and 1991, neither Dickens nor David Loades felt the need to revise generally negative assessments.[2] There is a sense in which both sides recognize Mary's reign to have been the hinge moment of the English Reformation. To revisionists, this was the point at which a genuinely English counter-reformation was gathering sufficient momentum to sweep the country permanently back into the Catholic camp – an outcome defeated only by chance political and dynastic circumstance, the early death of the Queen and her failure to produce an heir. The alternative view holds not only that the moment for such a realignment had passed, but that key policies of the regime were clumsily counter-productive and enshrined the virtual inevitability of Protestant victory: 'the reign must still be judged not merely a huge failure, but one likely to have become more monumental with every succeeding year'.[3]

This chapter surveys the main contours of the debate, and attempts a rounded assessment of both Catholic and Protestant reform over the course of the reign. It begins with a narrative account of the main political, financial and diplomatic circumstances that influenced the development of Marian religious policy. It then examines the priorities and potential of Marian Catholicism, both at the higher levels and in the parishes, asking if revisionists are justified in regarding the reign as a period of fruitful Catholic restoration and reform. It concludes with an appraisal of the fortunes of English Protestantism during the reign, and an estimation of the price of persecution, both for those who endured, and for those who imposed it.

4.1 The Politics of Religion

Mary Tudor's accession to the throne in July 1553 has been called 'one of the most surprising events of the sixteenth century'.[4] It was certainly not the

2 Ibid, ch. 12; David Loades, *The Reign of Mary Tudor* (2nd ed., London, 1991), esp. chs. 3, 8, 11.
3 A.G. Dickens, 'The Early Expansion of Protestantism in England, 1520–1558', in Peter Marshall, ed., *The Impact of the English Reformation 1500–1640* (London, 1997), p. 109.
4 Jennifer Loach, *Parliament and the Crown in the Reign of Mary Tudor* (Oxford, 1986), p. 1.

ending that had been scripted in the centres of power as Edward VI lay dying, and in the sixteenth century central authority generally got its way. Under the terms of Henry VIII's will, the line of succession passed from his legitimate son Edward to his (as Henry saw it) illegitimate daughters Mary and Elizabeth. But to the exasperation of her younger half-brother, Mary had flaunted her Catholicism after her father's death, and no one could be in doubt that her accession would lead to the dismantling of the hopes of the Edwardian Reformation. Early in 1553, Edward secretly drew up a 'device for the succession' which provided that in the event of his death without heirs the Crown was to pass to the descendents of his father's sister Mary and her husband the Duke of Suffolk. As the King's health deteriorated in June, the device was altered to exclude Suffolk's daughter and fix the succession on his granddaughter, Jane Grey, conveniently married to Northumberland's son, Guildford. This was a blatant attempt on Northumberland's part to hang on to power, but the King himself may well have been the original inspiration behind the scheme, the last and most significant intervention into politics of the 'godly imp'. When Edward died on 6 July 1553, Jane's proclamation as Queen was supported by the council and the entire political establishment. But the reign of Queen Jane turned out to be the original nine-day wonder. With astonishing ineptitude, Northumberland failed to secure the person of the Princess Mary. She fled to Norfolk, on 10 July proclaimed herself Queen at her house at Kenninghall, and watched a flood tide of support rise in her favour among the commons and provincial gentry of East Anglia and the Thames Valley. When Northumberland moved against her his forces deserted him, and the council in London lost its nerve and declared for Mary. Mary entered the capital in triumph at the beginning of August; Northumberland went to the block a couple of weeks later.

But what sort of triumph was it? Historical opinion is as polarized over the circumstances in which Mary came to power as it is over the ways she subsequently exercised it. The view expressed in the 1950s by T.M. Parker, that 'it was not so much Mary's religion, as her ancestry... which commended her to the nation as a whole', has been followed by the majority of subsequent commentators.[5] Mary's was the only truly successful Tudor rebellion because it was not really a rebellion at all; rather a massive vote in favour of dynastic legitimacy and against political chicanery. But in a critical misinterpretation of the situation, Mary became convinced that there was general and enthusiastic support for the religious counter-revolution she intended to launch: 'from this initial misreading of the facts sprang a whole chain of errors.'[6] The subsequent difficulties encountered by

[5] T.M. Parker, *The English Reformation to 1558* (Oxford, 1950), p. 154.

[6] Ibid. See also Dickens, *Reformation*, p. 285; Loades, *Reign*, p. 17; Rex Pogson, 'The Legacy of the Schism', in Jennifer Loach and Robert Tittler, eds., *The Mid-Tudor Polity, c. 1540–c.1560* (London, 1980), p. 121; Diarmaid MacCulloch, *The Later Reformation in England, 1547–1603* (2nd ed., Basingstoke, 2001), p. 18.

the regime in the implementation of its religious policies can make this interpretation seem persuasive, but the issue is not quite so clear-cut. As Jennifer Loach has pointed out, 'it was not, in fact, primarily in terms of legitimacy and legality that contemporaries saw the struggle'.[7] Government propaganda during the short reign of Queen Jane stressed Mary's attachment to the cause of 'Antichrist', and her earliest and most loyal supporters in East Anglia were drawn almost exclusively from the ranks of the Catholic gentry. There is, moreover, evidence of genuine and spontaneous popular enthusiasm for the expected return to Catholicism. In Yorkshire, Robert Parkyn observed that at the proclamation of Mary 'the whole commonalty in all places in the north parts greatly rejoiced, making fires, drinking wine and ale, praising God'.[8] It was not just north of the Trent, however, but in many parishes of the realm, and even in London, that the Latin mass was rapidly restored, sometimes in advance of an August proclamation allowing both it and the Edwardian service to be legally performed. For Mary's supporters, argues Christopher Haigh, there was no doubt that 'her triumph was the victory of the old religion, and certainly the defeat of the new'.[9] That there was widespread (though by no means universal) support for the halting of the Edwardian Revolution is beyond doubt. The key question in 1553 was not so much whether Catholicism would and should be restored, but what kind of 'Catholicism' it should be. Mary's aim, it is often argued, was to 'turn back the clock'.[10] But should the hands point to 1546 (mass and Six Articles), to 1535 (monasteries and Royal Supremacy), or to 1529 (heresy-hunting and papal supremacy)? The broad spectrum of opinion we can describe as Catholic was far from united on this, though Mary's firm commitment was always for the latter option. The fact that she may have underestimated the difficulties does not mean that the attempt was bound to fail.

It was made more difficult, however, by a factor beyond the Queen's control: her gender. Anxieties about the security of the Tudor dynasty under a queen regnant had been an important element in Henry's disenchantment with his first marriage. A quarter century later, the chicken had come home to roost and rule. We should not let the famously long public virginity of Mary's sister Elizabeth blind us to the universal contemporary expectation that a queen required a consort. Yet this was also a prospect that filled people with apprehension, for it was to be supposed that a husband would exercise power rather than merely influence. In November 1553 a

[7] Loach, *Parliament*, p. 7.

[8] A.G. Dickens, ed., 'Robert Parkyn's Narrative of the Reformation', in Dickens, *Reformation Studies* (London, 1982), pp. 307–8.

[9] Christopher Haigh, *English Reformations: Religion, Politics, and Society under the Tudors* (Oxford, 1993), pp. 204–9.

[10] Gina Alexander, 'Bonner and the Marian Persecutions', in Christopher Haigh, ed., *The English Reformation Revised* (Cambridge, 1987), p. 159; Pogson, 'Legacy', p. 122.

delegation from Mary's first Parliament petitioned the Queen to wed within the realm. They did so in the knowledge that she had already formed the firm intention to marry a foreigner: her first cousin once removed, Philip, shortly to be created ruler of the Netherlands by his father Charles V, and to become, by the latter's abdication in 1556, king of Castile and Aragon. The plan went ahead in spite of opposition from the Lord Chancellor, Stephen Gardiner, who backed the candidacy of Edward Courtenay, Earl of Devon, thus adding to the factional divisions of a council unnaturally enlarged by Mary's inclusion of supporters from the East Anglian Catholic gentry.[11] In matters of foreign affairs, Mary was in any case more inclined to listen to the imperial ambassador, Simon Renard, than to any of her councillors. Not even the most swashbuckling revisionist has sought to suggest that the Spanish marriage enjoyed widespread support in England, though it is hard to see why it should have been quite as unpopular as it seems to have been. Alliance with the Habsburgs was the long-standing default position of early Tudor foreign policy. France was England's traditional enemy; the Armada and the heroics of Drake lay a generation in the future. No doubt the general xenophobia at which the English have for centuries excelled played its part, though a specific anti-Spanish bias was perhaps fed by the fear that Charles V (whose main motive in promoting the marriage was to secure his son's hold on the Spanish Netherlands) would drag the country into war with France. Traditional Anglo-Spanish amity had of course already been rocked by Henry's repudiation of Catherine, and further eroded by the suffering of some English merchants at the hands of the inquisition in the 1540s, as well as by rumours, encouraged by Protestant refugees in Edward's reign, of Spain's cruelty in its New World and Italian possessions. At the same time shifting trade patterns had made the English cloth industry less dependent on the Antwerp market than it once had been.[12] The marriage treaty approved in December 1553 severely limited Philip's powers in England, and excluded him from any claim to the throne if Mary were to die first.

Despite these safeguards, popular and elite disaffection erupted into open rebellion in January 1554. Of a series of planned risings only that in Kent led by Sir Thomas Wyatt got properly under way. For a moment, events looked alarmingly like a mirror image of the previous summer. The Duke of Norfolk was sent against Wyatt, but his troops deserted to the rebels, who made it into the suburbs of London. Mary, however, held her nerve and rallied the capital with a rousing oration in which she protested that she

11 Courtenay's social ineptitude after spending his entire youth in the Tower of London made him in the end an unrealistic candidate: Loades, *Reign*, pp. 59–60.

12 Loach, *Parliament*, pp. 182–4; Dickens, *Reformation*, p. 289; Peter Marshall, 'The Other Black Legend: The Henrician Reformation and the Spanish People', *English Historical Review*, 116 (2001).

would never consent to the marriage if she thought it at all harmful to the commons. Casting herself as the mother of the nation, she delivered a performance to set alongside Elizabeth's better-known speech to the troops at Tilbury during the Armada 34 years later.[13] As with the 'religious' versus 'secular' debates over the risings of 1536 and 1549, the extent to which Wyatt's should be considered a Protestant rebellion has sparked disagreement. David Loades has insisted that 'the main reasons which lay behind the rising were secular and political' and he fails to find evidence of disproportionate Protestant commitment among either the commons or the gentry leadership. The contrary case has been made by M.R. Thorp and A.G. Dickens.[14] Mary herself in her speech at the Guildhall argued that 'the matter of the marriage seemed to be but a Spanish cloak to cover their pretended purpose against our religion', and a number of Protestant clergy, including the erstwhile bishop of Winchester, John Ponet, are known to have been involved. The intent of the rebels was not merely to prevent Mary from marrying, but to replace her with Elizabeth. Jane Grey was executed in a tidying up operation after the rising, though nothing could be proved against Elizabeth, and in a triumph of principle over pragmatism, Mary allowed her to live. Dickens's contention that 'Marian Catholicism was stifled in its infancy through becoming linked in the minds of Englishmen with the idea of Spanish overlordship' is undoubtedly a severe exaggeration.[15] But a seed of the idea that was to burst into full bloom in Elizabeth's reign may have been planted by Wyatt's rebellion.

By the time the marriage took place at Winchester in July 1554, a second major issue was casting a shadow between the aspirations of the political elites and the religious policies of the Crown. The mass had been restored and Edwardian ecclesiastical legislation repealed without great difficulty in the Parliament of 1553, but Mary's over-riding ambition was to undo her father's work by restoring the realm to full communion with the See of Rome. She loathed the title 'Supreme Head', and refused to use it, though ironically she was obliged to exercise the Royal Supremacy to reinstate Catholic worship. The main instrument to bring about reconciliation with Rome was to be Mary's (other) cousin, Reginald Pole, *bête noire* of the Henrician and Edwardian regimes, whom the Pope appointed legate for this purpose in August 1553. But Pole did not arrive in England to end the schism until November 1554; the delay of fourteen months from the start of the reign looks in retrospect like precious time wasted. Twenty years of continuous

[13] The text of the speech is given by John Foxe, *Acts and Monuments*, ed. S.R. Cattley and G. Townsend (8 vols.,1837–41), vi. 414–15.

[14] David Loades, *Two Tudor Conspiracies* (2nd ed., Bangor, 1992), pp. 92–5; M.R. Thorp, 'Religion and the Wyatt Rebellion of 1554', *Church History*, 48 (1979); Dickens, *Reformation*, pp. 289–90.

[15] Ibid., p. 291.

propaganda against the Pope made it unlikely there would be warm enthusiasm for the restoration of Roman obedience, though the iconoclastic excesses of Edward's reign had convinced some conservatives (among them the former anti-papalists Gardiner and Bonner) that the link with Rome was a necessary safeguard against doctrinal deviation (the position Thomas More had taken in 1535). It was not so much the papal primacy itself, however, that caused alarm in English ruling circles, but rather its implications for the status of the monastic and chantry lands that the English gentry, Catholic and Protestant alike, had been avidly purchasing since the late 1530s as fast as the Crown had put them on the market. By investing in monastic estates, the English landowning classes had effectively bought shares in the Royal Supremacy: they wanted guarantees before they were prepared to see ownership of the company change. An initial papal brief to Pole in July 1554 was rejected by the council as too imprecise, and it was only in November that Pole was able to return bearing the necessary concessions, and in a moving ceremony absolve the realm from the sin of schism. Parliament, which had rejected the restoration of the heresy laws earlier in 1554, was now prepared to pass them, and to repeal all the religious legislation enacted since 1529. But the Church lands question was a niggle that never entirely went away. Pole had only with great difficulty been persuaded to agree to any concession at all, and he made his feelings clear in a sermon preached in 1557: though the Church like an indulgent mother had allowed laymen to keep ecclesiastical property, God the father would take a sterner line. Some wondered whether subsequent popes would feel themselves bound by Julius III's concession. Alarm bells rang in 1555 when the newly elected Paul IV issued a bull denouncing the alienation of Church property, and Pole was obliged to petition him for a second statement specific to the situation in England. Small wonder that some lay proprietors of former Church lands took the precaution of acquiring individual bulls of indulgence from Rome.[16]

After the cathartic triumph of the reconciliation with Rome, a number of intractable problems, and some simple bad luck, dogged the progress of Catholic restoration. Historians are no longer convinced that Mary faced an organized opposition in Parliament, but there was a mood of periodic truculence, not entirely dispelled by the concession over monastic lands. Difficulties were made over the bill restoring to the Church 'first fruits and tenths' (an annual 10 per cent income tax imposed on the clergy by Henry VIII), and over a bill confiscating the property of religious exiles.[17] It has been argued that at the root of many of the problems of Marian Catholic revival was the 'question of money'.[18] Progressive impoverishment of the

[16] Loach, *Parliament*, pp. 129, 175.

[17] Ibid., pp. 148, 173, 174.

[18] Rex Pogson, 'Revival and Reform in Mary Tudor's Church: A Question of Money', in Haigh, *Reformation Revised*. See also Loades, *Reign*, pp. 289–92.

Church had taken place under Henry and Edward: the loss of monastic and chantry lands, increasingly heavy taxation, the stripping of episcopal estates and the confiscation of parish property. As a result of the monastic dissolution, much of the income from impropriated benefices (parishes in the hands of religious houses) now went to the Crown, or other 'lay rectors'. Pole's plans for Catholic revival could not be carried out on the cheap. They presupposed a restoration of lavish ecclesiastical ritual and furnishing, and the creation of a well-educated (and therefore well-financed) clerical ministry in the parishes. The Crown was highly supportive in principle, but its hands were tied by its own financial difficulties. The return of spiritual revenues (tenths, tithes, patronage rights in parishes) was in practice delayed until 1556, and even then was not an unmixed blessing for the Church, as it brought with it the responsibility to pay pensions to the former religious. Mary handed back some monastic estates, but, like her father and brother, carried on selling others. At the parish level, commissions were launched to track down the treasures sold, lost or embezzled in Edward's reign, and met with a mixture of success and obstruction.

The financial weakness of the Church was a long-standing structural problem which the authorities were taking steps to overcome, but in May 1555 Mary and Pole received an unforeseen and cruel blow: the election of Cardinal Giampietro Carafa as Pope Paul IV. Carafa was an old enemy of Pole's, who regarded the Englishman's views on justification as tantamount to Lutheran heresy. Moreover, he was fanatically hostile to the Spanish (colonial masters of his Neapolitan homeland). By September 1556, Paul had provoked Philip into war, and early in the following year he recalled his legates from all Habsburg territories. Pole was not only deprived of his legatine powers, but also summoned to Rome to face heresy charges, and only prevented from going by the insistence of Mary, now ironically cast in the role of political enemy of the Pope. The conflict created endless administrative delays, most crucially in the filling of vacant bishoprics – the depleted strength of the episcopal bench was to prove politically important at the start of Elizabeth's reign. Meanwhile, persistent provocation by Henry II of France led to war in 1557, and national humiliation with the loss of England's last remaining French possession, Calais, in January 1558. Though Mary's foreign policy was not in fact in thrall to Philip's, this disaster seemed to vindicate all the doomsayers of the Spanish marriage.[19]

What some have regarded as fatal weaknesses at the heart of the Marian polity, a more tolerant interpretation might see as teething problems, which could have been overcome in time. Without doubt the most serious political handicap of the Marian regime was identical to the one that in the end had crippled its Edwardian predecessor: an inability to send out convincingly reassuring signals about the succession. Mary's failure to conceive a child by

[19] Robert Tittler, *The Reign of Mary I* (London, 1983), pp. 66–8.

her marriage to Philip (despite an optimistic pregnancy announcement in 1555) was a personal tragedy and a political catastrophe. Given the emphatic exclusion of Philip under the terms of the marriage treaty, there was no plausible Catholic candidate as heir to the throne. No one at this stage wanted to press the claims of Mary Stuart, granddaughter of Henry's sister, Margaret, but doubly unwelcome as Queen of Scots and spouse of the French Dauphin. The heir under the terms of Henry VIII's will was Mary's half-sister Elizabeth, and when Mary died on 17 November 1558 (followed a few hours later by Reginald Pole), no voices were raised against Elizabeth's accession. Once again Anne Boleyn had triumphed over Catherine of Aragon.

4.2 The Shape of Restoration

That the Marian attempt to restore Catholicism faced considerable difficulties, and that it ultimately failed, are beyond dispute. The heated debates which have enlivened the recent study of the topic centre primarily on the questions of priorities and potential. What were the leaders of the Marian regime actually aiming to accomplish, and how realistic were their aspirations? What credit should they be given for their achievements in the short time available, and how much popular support were they able to draw on and sustain? For historians who see little evidence of achievement or potential, the charge at the head of the indictment sheet is that 'both Mary and Pole saw the future in terms of the past'.[20] Because they laboured under the misapprehension that the English schism was the work of a handful of malicious heretics leading astray a fundamentally orthodox Catholic nation, the emphases of their policy were profoundly misdirected. What the English Catholic cause needed was an imaginative campaign of reconversion and evangelism; what it got, it is argued, was an 'arid legalism', whose priorities were the reinstatement of the constitutional position of the Church, the restitution of traditional ritual, and a highly counter-productive campaign of persecution.[21] Pole, it is alleged, may have been a reformer, but, in exile since 1532, his perception of reform was a generation out of date. His outlook was that of the Christian humanism of the 1520s, ethical, intellectual and elitist. He regarded the laity as 'little children', to be moulded in good habits by obedient participation in sacraments and ceremonies, and not to be stirred up by unnecessary preaching.[22]

20 Loades, *Reign*, p. 288.

21 Dickens, *Reformation*, pp. 307–9.

22 Pogson, 'Legacy', p. 122; David Loades, 'The Spirituality of the Restored Catholic Church (1553–1558) in the Context of the Counter-Reformation', in Thomas McCoog, ed., *The Reckoned Expense: Edmund Campion and the Early English Jesuits* (Woodbridge, 1996), p. 13.

Thus, when in 1555 Ignatius of Loyola offered to send members of the recently founded Jesuit order to assist the Catholic cause in England, Pole failed to respond, missing the opportunity, in the anti-revisionists' view, to inject some counter-reformation zeal into the moribund English Church. Another unfortunate result of Pole's complacent restorationist outlook was 'the Marian regime's failure to understand the importance of printing'.[23] Despite their difficult circumstances, English Protestant exiles managed to produce a greater quantity of polemical books and pamphlets than did Catholics in England, and some historians have been inclined to regard the Catholic literary output as distinctly outclassed in the battle for hearts and minds, comprising mainly 'devotional works or sermons with little combative force'.[24] The one truly effective Marian propagandist was a London hosier called Miles Huggarde, who wrote witty anti-Protestant verse, but received little official patronage.[25]

Revisionist historians, however, have regarded much of this criticism as misplaced. Far from looking a Jesuit gift-horse in the mouth, Pole may have been wise to offer a cool response to Ignatius's overture. What he needed most was effective leadership on the part of bishops and parish priests (posts which Jesuits were barred by their rules from accepting). Jesuits could preach, but there were hardly any English-speakers among them in the mid-1550s. They were also at this date strongly associated with Spain, and Pole might therefore expect more credit for his arm's length attitude from historians who often accuse the regime of ignoring the depth of anti-Spanish feeling in England.[26] Nor does revisionist scholarship accept that the regime was self-evidently bested in the 'battle of the books'. Rather than failing to grasp the opportunity that printing offered, it simply had different priorities from its Protestant critics, for example sponsoring propagandist works in Latin to persuade an overseas audience. At home, the parishes were in desperate need of replacement service books, which the Marian presses produced in huge numbers, along with new editions of the devotional primers for the use of the laity. The Protestant resort to polemic and satire was, revisionists suggest, the strategy of a minority desperate to stir up division and debate, and the authorities may have been wise not to play them too much at their own

23 J.W. Martin, 'The Marian Regime's Failure to Understand the Importance of Printing', in his *Religious Radicals in Tudor England* (London, 1989).

24 Dickens, *Reformation*, p. 311. See also Tittler, *Mary I*, pp. 40–9; Loades, *Reign*, pp. 280–8.

25 J.W. Martin, 'Miles Hogarde: Artisan and Aspiring Author in Sixteenth-Century England', in his *Religious Radicals*.

26 Thomas M. McCoog, 'Ignatius Loyola and Reginald Pole: a Reconsideration', *Journal of Ecclesiastical History*, 47 (1996). Thomas Mayer, 'Pole, Loyola and the Jesuits in England', in McCoog, *Reckoned Expense*, adds an emphasis on personality clashes, and Pole's pre-existing commitment to other new orders, such as the Theatines.

game.[27] More generally, the alleged failure of the Marian Church to 'discover' the Counter-Reformation raises problems of chronology and definition. Arguably, there was not much counter-reformation around for Mary to discover: the Council of Trent did not complete its work before 1563, and its decrees did not make much of an impact in large parts of Catholic Europe for decades thereafter. Even the Jesuits, it is now claimed, were not in the 1550s the counter-reformation 'shock troops' they were later to become.[28] Pole's most recent biographer, Thomas Mayer, goes so far as to assert that the cardinal rather 'invented than failed to discover the Counter-Reformation', an assessment shared by Eamon Duffy, who argues that the religious priorities of the Marian regime 'closely parallel much that is often thought to be most characteristic of the Counter-Reformation'.[29]

The case for constructive and far-sighted reform places great weight on the decrees of the legatine synod which Pole summoned to meet in London in 1555, having as its primary objective the revitalization of the clergy. Priests were admonished to be resident, and bishops were ordered to undertake regular visitations and to monitor diocesan finances. There was to be a new book of homilies, catechism, and (at last) an approved translation of the New Testament. The synodal decree with perhaps the greatest potential was the order for seminaries to be established in every diocese to train candidates for the priesthood (a process that had been entirely hit-and-miss in the later Middle Ages). The need for systematic clerical education was a nettle the reformers in Edward's reign had signally failed to grasp, and the decree anticipated by several years what was to be one of the most important reforms of the Council of Trent. In the event, Pole's reforms had little chance to bear fruit. The Marian regime inherited a serious shortage of parish clergy, and though ordinations picked up encouragingly after the dearth of the Edwardian years, the Church's local representatives were in the main the same body of fairly undistinguished men who had conformed under Henry and Edward. The clergy were, of course, again required to be celibate, and in a concerted campaign from 1554 around 800 married priests were deprived and separated from their 'pretensed wives'. But the continuing manpower shortage meant that most of them then had to be permitted to take up parishes elsewhere. More could be done to change the character of the bishops. Mary purged the episcopal bench of opponents more quickly than Edward had: the deprived Catholic bishops were restored

[27] Jennifer Loach, 'The Marian Establishment and the Printing Press', *English Historical Review*, 101 (1986); Haigh, *Reformations*, pp. 216–17; Eamon Duffy, *The Stripping of the Altars: Traditional Religion in England 1400–1580* (New Haven and London, 1992), pp. 529–30.

[28] John W. O'Malley, *The First Jesuits* (Cambridge, MA, 1993) argues convincingly that Jesuit ideals were mainly pastoral in the early years of the order.

[29] Thomas F. Mayer, *Reginald Pole: Prince and Prophet* (Cambridge, 2000), pp. 298, 354; Duffy, *Stripping*, p. 525.

and seven Protestant bishops removed (four of them for marriage) in the first months of the reign. Among the familiar Henrician faces (Gardiner, Bonner, Tunstall), 13 new appointments to bishoprics were made by Mary. These were men who conformed to Pole's vision of a resident pastoral episcopate, rather than to the typical pre-Reformation model of career royal bureaucrat. Most were trained in theology rather than canon law, and some were individuals of real talent: Thomas Watson of Lincoln, for example, was author of an effective set of homilies on the sacraments, *Holesome and Catholyke Doctryne*. A couple (like Pole himself) were returning exiles: Richard Pate of Worcester had participated in the opening session of the Council of Trent and Thomas Goldwell of St Asaph had joined the Theatines, a new and austere religious order, in Italy.[30] By the end of the reign, death (there was an influenza epidemic in 1557–8) and delays in consecrations had thinned the ranks: 10 sees were vacant at Elizabeth's accession. But it is a tribute to the *esprit de corps* of the Marian bishops that (with one exception) all declined to accept Elizabeth's religious Settlement, a refusal to bend with the prevailing wind unique in the course of the English Reformation. In time, a reformed Marian episcopate might have delivered real pastoral and administrative change in the dioceses. A further investment in the future health of the Church (and not an altogether wasted one) took place in the universities, where Pole exercised close oversight as chancellor of both Oxford and Cambridge. Three new colleges were established, and new and reliable heads of houses were chosen for old ones. Oxford proved particularly amenable to the reimposition of orthodoxy. After the accession of Elizabeth a striking number of fellows (men like William Allen, Thomas Harding and Thomas Stapleton) fled abroad to produce anti-Protestant propaganda and organize Catholic resistance (see Section 7.1).[31]

Yet it is perhaps in the parishes that assessments of the viability of Marian Catholic restoration must stand or fall. Here revisionists are obliged to confront the argument that the erosion of traditional Catholicism had simply gone too far to be reversed, both in a negative sense (the destruction of artefacts and furnishings, and popular disengagement from traditional practices and thought-patterns), and in a more positive one (the advance of Protestant sentiment). As we have seen, the portents at the start of the reign looked promising, with enthusiasm for the restoration of the mass. But the scale of the task was daunting. Parish churches had been reordered for

30 Philip Hughes, *The Reformation in England* (3 vols., London, 1950–4), ii. 232–3.

31 Pogson, 'Legacy', p. 132; James McConica, 'The Catholic Experience in Tudor Oxford', in McCoog, *Reckoned Expense*; Elizabeth Russell, 'Marian Oxford and the Counter-Reformation', in Caroline Barron and Christopher Harper-Bill, eds., *The Church in Pre-Reformation Society* (Woodbridge, 1985).

Protestant worship in Edward's reign in a fashion which (though often painful) was at least relatively cheap and simple to implement: superfluous Catholic furnishings were sold or destroyed, walls were whitewashed, rood-lofts hacked down, altars replaced by simple communion tables. Reversing the process was a more substantial undertaking, as Bishop Bonner's London visitation Injunctions of 1554 suggest: all parishes were to ensure that, among other things, they had a proper stone altar, rood and rood-loft, holy-water stoup, full set of vestments for the priest and surplices for the clerk, altar coverings, candlesticks, processional cross and banners, eight liturgical books of various kinds, a receptacle for the reserved sacrament.[32] The extent to which parishes were able (or willing) to respond to these considerable financial and logistical demands can be inferred from the evidence of churchwardens' accounts and episcopal visitations, sources from which historians have drawn radically different conclusions. Rex Pogson, for example, considered the visitation records of Bath and Wells, Canterbury and Salisbury to reveal 'lists of devastated churches and in many cases little or no improvement from the opening of the reign'. Moreover, the Edwardian plunder of the churches had created hostility to commissioners of any sort, and the Marian visitors encountered obstruction and lack of co-operation.[33] Revisionist historians have been much more inclined to regard the glass as half full. From his study of the surviving churchwardens' accounts, Ronald Hutton suggests that most parishes managed to redecorate their churches up to and beyond the bare legal requirement. Christopher Haigh uses the visitation evidence to point out that 86 per cent of parishes in the diocese of Bath and Wells had a proper altar and all the requisite books by 1557, and that 85 per cent in Chester had an altar, rood and images as early as 1554 (clearly some items supposed to be destroyed in Edward's reign had been hidden and now retrieved.)[34] The most detailed visitation evidence comes from Cranmer's (now Pole's) diocese of Canterbury, inspected by Archdeacon Nicholas Harpsfield in 1557. In this, perhaps the most heavily Protestantized county, the work of iconoclasm had been particularly thorough, and the visitation revealed major gaps in the provision of liturgical furnishings and images. Yet, even here, it has been argued, we are looking at a Marian success story: virtually every parish had by 1557 acquired a stone altar, vestments and at least the basic mass books.[35] Even the most optimistic reading of the visitation evidence is open to the objection that it reveals, not the popularity of Catholic revival, but

[32] Duffy, *Stripping*, pp. 543–4.

[33] Pogson, 'Revival', p. 146; 'Legacy', p. 133. For a similarly negative assessment, see Hughes, *Reformation*, ii. 236–7.

[34] Ronald Hutton, 'The Local Impact of the Tudor Reformations', in Marshall, *Impact*, p. 154; Haigh, *Reformations*, pp. 211–12.

[35] Duffy, *Stripping*, pp. 555–64.

the characteristic compliance of parish communities to the wishes of outside authority, a feature of the Henrician and Edwardian Reformations. The counter-argument is that it was considerably cheaper to hack down a carved rood than to commission a new one, that the Marian regime was making demands that could only have been met if there was considerable local support for the policy. A generation later, a churchwarden of the London parish of St Andrew Holborn looked back over the Marian accounts, observing that the parishioners 'were at great charges... to erect and set up all manner of superstitious things again in the church'. Yet 'so ready they were to maintain idolatrous service... and in so short a space, that it is wonderful to read or hear, and shall condemn the coldness and slackness of some now in the time of the gospel'.[36]

No historian of Mary's reign has suggested that parish churches and parish devotions refashioned themselves exactly as they had been before the break with Rome. All agree that Marian Catholicism was distinct from the pre-Reformation variety, but historians differ over whether this was a sign of health or of terminal weakness. According to Hutton, there were two 'abiding casualties' of the Henrician and Edwardian reforms: 'the cult of the saints and the provision for souls in purgatory.'[37] The great pre-Reformation shrines and pilgrimage centres – Walsingham, Glastonbury, Canterbury – were not revived. Parishes restored their images of the crucified Christ, of the Virgin, and of the patron of their church, but not the plethora of statues of more minor saints who attracted local cults before 1529. Few lights burned before images, other than those on the rood-loft. Obits and bede-rolls were a much less common feature of Marian than of pre-Reformation accounts, and very few fraternities were founded or refounded in the course of the reign; in London only one of the dozens of suppressed guilds was restored.[38] In wills, too, intercession for the dead did not return to anything like its former level: in the south-west, 18 per cent of Marian wills requested masses and prayers; in the northern counties, around 15 per cent did so, and in Gloucestershire, only 4 per cent. A mere handful of perpetual chantries were founded, by prominent figures such as Viscount Montague.[39] All this might seem to indicate the waning of Catholic belief, and the waxing of Protestantism, though in recognizing the phenomenon revisionists are apt to stress pragmatism rather than conviction: experience had demonstrated the vulnerability of

[36] Thomas Bentley, 'Some Monuments of Antiquities worthy memory', in E. Griffith, *Cases of Supposed Exemption from Poor-rates* (London, 1831), p. xviii.

[37] Hutton, 'Local Impact', p. 131.

[38] J.J. Scarisbrick, *The Reformation and the English People* (Oxford, 1984), pp. 37–8; Robert Whiting, *Local Responses to the English Reformation* (Basingstoke, 1998), p. 50; Susan Brigden, *London and the Reformation* (Oxford, 1989), p. 582.

[39] Peter Marshall, *Beliefs and the Dead in Reformation England* (Oxford, 2002), pp. 115–16.

arrangements for funding intercessory prayer to the attentions of a permanently impecunious Tudor State, and it was widely understood that the heir presumptive, the Princess Elizabeth, was not an orthodox Catholic. Occasionally we get an insight into otherwise hidden calculations of risk and benefit through wills like that of the Kentish yeoman Alan Wood, who established an anniversary service for his soul with the proviso that 'if the same obit by order of law be abrogated hereafter', the money was to go to the poor'.[40] A more intangible, but equally significant consideration here is that the relief of souls in purgatory had always been a very long-term process, dependent upon a whole variety of interlocking social structures. All of these had been swept away under Edward, and the system (like much else in Mary's reign) needed time to reassert itself.[41] The loss of this 'vital dimension of continuity', thinks Duffy, must be the main reason for the 'surprising' failure of the Marian laity convincingly to re-establish the former cult of the dead.[42]

There are clear financial and practical reasons why important aspects of pre-Reformation Catholicism could not be fully re-established after 1553. Most obviously, the determination of the laity to retain the lands of the religious houses meant that Marian monasticism was a shadow of its former self. Of more than 800 abbeys and priories dissolved by Henry, only seven were refounded, and only Westminster (with over 30 monks) on an imposing scale.[43] Only 100 or so of perhaps 1,500 ex-religious in England returned to monastic life, and the initiative came almost entirely from the Crown: Mary's hope that laymen would follow her example and voluntarily return lands to re-establish monasticism was a disappointed one. This was a clear case of thwarted ambition. Pole 'had big plans for the restoration of the monasteries', and to assist the project he tried to bring over advisers from the reformed Italian Benedictine congregation of Monte Cassino (of which he was cardinal protector) – a marked contrast to his response to the offer of Jesuit help.[44] In other areas, however, it has been claimed that discrepancies between the Catholicisms of the 1550s and the 1520s resulted from the deliberate implementation of new priorities, not the

40 Duffy, *Stripping*, pp. 553–4.

41 See Marshall, *Beliefs*, pp. 117–18 for evidence that provision for intercession was beginning to rise after 1555.

42 Duffy, *Stripping*, p. 495.

43 Mayer, *Pole*, p. 288 points out that another five or more restorations of Augustinian houses were planned, and may have been implemented. There were, in addition, at least two spontaneous unofficial refoundations in the north, as well as plans, thwarted by Mary's death, for the re-establishment of the major Benedictine house at St Albans: Claire Cross, 'The Reconstitution of Northern Monastic Communities in the Reign of Mary Tudor', *Northern History*, 29 (1993); James Clark, 'Reformation and Reaction at St Albans Abbey 1530–58', *English Historical Review*, 115 (2000).

44 Mayer, *Pole*, p. 283; David Knowles, *The Religious Orders in England III: The Tudor Age* (Cambridge, 1959), pp. 424–5; Pogson, 'Legacy', p. 134.

frustration of old ones. Marian parish churches typically had only their high altar, and perhaps one other, where a generation earlier they had housed numerous side-altars; their images were often limited to the rood (with accompanying figures of Mary and John), and of patronal saint; worship was confined to the regular parish mass recited by the vicar, in place of the profusion of chantry and guild masses once intoned by a plethora of privately engaged chaplains. But all of this could be regarded as in line with official preference for greater parochial uniformity, and a more Christ-centred style of devotion. Duffy notes that in Kent Archdeacon Harpsfield invariably stipulated that the Passion of Christ should be the image displayed on altar hangings and the pax (a plate kissed as a sign of peace during mass).[45] Such reflections strengthen the case for Marian England anticipating the developments of the later continental Counter-Reformation, in which the suppression of local cults, more centrally directed patterns of piety, and the subjection of lay fraternities to greater clerical control were all to be marked elements.[46]

There is a temptation here to make too great a virtue out of necessity. The leaders of the Marian 'Counter-Reformation' were clearly not, like some later Italian or Spanish bishops, faced with the problem of taming and channelling an over-exuberant popular piety. Rather, their challenge was to heal the wounds of a Church emerging from 20 years of schism, and to provide guidance for 'a silent majority of confused conservatives'.[47] Indeed, the leaders of the Marian Church were themselves emerging from schism; among the bishops, only Pole had been in principled exile from the first moments of the break with Rome. There is an intriguing third possibility between the idea of Marian Catholicism as blind medieval reaction, and as Tridentine counter-reform avant la lettre. This is the suggestion that religious policy in the reign was indebted in important ways to what had preceded it, that the leaders of the Marian Church were prepared to take what they thought was best from the Henrician and Edwardian reforms. There seems to have been an acceptance that vernacular scripture was here to stay: English Bibles were withdrawn from the churches, but possession of one was no longer a heretical offence, and, as we have seen, the authorities planned a new Catholic translation. The primers produced for the laity in Mary's reign largely abandoned the miracle stories that had incited such evangelical derision, and they even retained prayers from the Henrician and Edwardian versions. Duffy has pointed to the importance of the *Profitable and Necessary Doctrine* produced by Edmund Bonner and his chaplains, which Pole ordered all parishes to acquire. This contained a clear and

45 Duffy, *Stripping*, p. 564. See also Haigh, *Reformations*, p. 215.

46 Hutton, 'Local Impact', pp. 156–7; John Bossy, 'The Counter Reformation and the People of Catholic Europe', *Past and Present*, 97 (1970).

47 Pogson, 'Legacy', p. 121.

orthodox summary of Catholic doctrine, though it was based to a large extent on the *King's Book* of 1543. This element of continuity with the regime of Henry VIII was psychologically important for the conservatives who had rallied round the *King's Book* and Six Articles in Edward's reign. Attached to Bonner's book were thirteen approved homilies for less educated clergy to read to their parishioners, an idea evidently copied from Cranmer's Homilies of 1547. Two of the homilies (on charity and on the misery of mankind) were revised versions of those to be found in the 1547 book.[48]

What then might Marian Catholicism have been like had it been able to grow to maturity? Loades has argued that to Mary and Pole 'the notion that the English Church might develop its own distinctive spirituality along traditional lines was unthinkable', and Dickens insisted that there was little chance of a 'broadly acceptable English Catholicism' developing over the course of the reign.[49] Such judgements seem too emphatic in light of the most recent and thoughtful research, particularly since historians of continental Catholicism are increasingly rejecting a one-size-fits-all Counter-Reformation in favour of distinctive national and regional styles of development.[50] A rounded understanding of conservative religion in Mary's reign has in the past undoubtedly suffered at the hands of approaches analysing it solely for symptoms of impending failure. Revisionism has alerted us to the elements of imagination, flexibility and popularity in Marian religious policy, and encouraged us to shake off an inherited whiggish presumption that the future of England was preordained to be Protestant. It has not done so without opening itself to charges of special pleading. With some justice, Dickens took Jack Scarisbrick to task for providing only seven words on the Marian persecution of Protestants in his *The Reformation and the English People*.[51] But, as Duffy points out, Dickens himself in *The English Reformation* devoted over ten times as many pages to Protestantism, persecution and opposition to the Spanish marriage, as he did to the positive achievements of the Marian Church.[52] There appear to be two distinct 'narratives' of Marian Catholicism which modern accounts of the reign struggle to reconcile coherently. But without an equal

48 Duffy, *Stripping*, pp. 527–43. The argument is taken considerably further in a recent study which argues that the Marian Church is best characterized as 'reformist', a blend of Christian humanism and Henrician Catholicism with priorities very different from that of the later Counter-Reformation: Lucy Wooding, *Rethinking Catholicism in Reformation England* (Oxford, 2000), ch. 4.

49 Loades, 'Spirituality', pp. 11–12; Dickens, *Reformation*, p. 315.

50 See David M. Luebke, 'Editor's Introduction', in id., ed., *The Counter-Reformation: Essential Readings* (Oxford, 1999).

51 Dickens, 'Early Expansion', p. 86.

52 Duffy, *Stripping*, p. 524. Duffy absolves himself from the requirement to consider the martyrdoms: 'a study of the restoration of traditional religious practice is not the place for a survey of the pursuit of heresy' (p. 559).

alertness to the significance of primers and prisons, martyrs and mass books, and a dispassionate understanding of how policies promoting one related to those producing the other, the historiography of the reign threatens to remain a dialogue of the deaf.

4.3 The Price of Persecution

No aspect of Mary's short reign has seemed as significant as the fact that during it almost 300 men and women were burned at the stake. To successive generations, Mary I has been 'Bloody Mary', an epithet as burned into the English historical consciousness as the unreadiness of Ethelred, or the greatness of Alfred. Assigning primary responsibility for the persecution, however, has been an uncertain historical exercise. Subsequent Protestant mythology had little doubt that Spanish cruelty and fanaticism fanned the flames, yet in fact Philip's ambassador Reynard was deeply worried about the destabilizing effect of executions. Pole has seemed an obvious architect of the policy, though John Foxe's surprisingly lenient verdict that he was 'none of the bloody and cruel sort of papists' has been endorsed by Mayer's recent biography.[53] Gardiner pressed vigorously for the reintroduction of the heresy laws, but perhaps rather to restore full powers to the episcopate than to launch a reign of terror; he proved in practice a rather ineffective inquisitor. Even Bonner of London, in whose diocese the greatest number of Protestants were burned, and who plays the starring villain's role in Foxe's *Acts and Monuments*, has been partially let off the hook by modern research. He had little control over the way heretics were delivered to him by justices and royal commissioners, and his bullying tactics were designed to get suspects to recant rather than face the flames.[54] Some modern authorities are agreed that it was the Queen herself driving the policy forward. Mary had a highly principled detestation of heresy, and she felt a particular animus against Cranmer as the instrument of her own and her mother's humiliation in Henry's reign.[55] Yet once it was underway, a characteristic of the campaign of persecution appears to be a lack of overall direction, and the build-up of a momentum that no one had quite foreseen. The decision to open proceedings with a series of show-trials of the Edwardian clerical leadership proved to be significant. The regime hoped to repeat its success

[53] Mayer, *Pole*, pp. 272–83. Dickens, *Reformation*, p. 294 comes to the curious conclusion that 'whatever the truth regarding Pole's active participation, he must bear much of the moral responsibility'.

[54] Alexander, 'Bonner'.

[55] Dickens, *Reformation*, p. 293; David Loades, *Mary Tudor: A Life* (Oxford, 1989), pp. 335–6; Diarmaid MacCulloch, *Thomas Cranmer. A Life* (New Haven and London, 1996), p. 618.

with Northumberland in 1553, and to secure a succession of humiliating recantations, propaganda victories that would undermine Protestant morale. The thinking behind the policy of persecution was therefore entirely consistent with that informing other aspects of the Catholic restoration: the realm was in a state of confused schism, rather than irredeemably sunk into heresy. The minority of inveterate troublemakers should be punished; their misguided followers would fall away and in time be reinculcated with virtuous piety.

It didn't turn out that way. With some exceptions, the Edwardian leaders held firm, creating a template of heroic martyrdom for their humbler co-religionists to emulate. The first burning, that of the Bible translator John Rogers, took place at Smithfield on 4 February 1555, followed by that of the celebrated preacher Rowland Taylor at Hadleigh (Suffolk) on 9 February; Hooper was burned at Gloucester the same day. Other high-profile victims followed. Ridley and Latimer were executed together at Oxford in October after a rigged disputation. The third of the 'Oxford martyrs', Thomas Cranmer, went to the stake in March 1556 after recanting his recantation, a botched propaganda opportunity for the regime. Increasingly thereafter the victims were more ordinary folk, many of them skilled craftsmen, and many of them young; 51 of them were women. The geographical dispersal of their deaths corresponds broadly to the 'great crescent' of Protestant heartlands discussed in Section 3.3. Of the 280-odd martyrs (the exact figure is disputed), 113 were burned in the diocese of London (Essex, Middlesex and the City), 52 in Canterbury (Kent), 32 in Norwich (Norfolk and Suffolk), and 27 in Chichester (Sussex). There were a handful of burnings in Lichfield, Leicester and Coventry, but only one in the north (at Chester) and one in the south-west (Exeter).[56] The pattern is less regular than at first appears: there is a Gloucestershire blip in the West Country where Hooper's successor James Brooks condemned ten heretics to the flames, and a distinct unevenness within the Protestant heartlands themselves: in Norwich diocese, twice as many executions took place in Suffolk as in Norfolk, all but three of the Chichester burnings were in East Sussex, and half the London total are accounted for by Essex. The burden of enforcing the persecution, rounding up the suspects, delivering them to the bishops for interrogation, and then arranging for sentences to be carried out, fell principally on the local secular authorities, the sheriffs and justices of the peace. These took to the task with highly varied degrees of enthusiasm. Some (like Anthony Brown and the brothers Edmund and Henry Tyrrel in Essex) were zealous in their pursuit of heretics, others were foot-draggers, needing chivvying from the Privy Council to arrange or assist at executions.[57]

56 Hughes, *Reformation*, ii. 263 has a useful map.
57 David Loades, 'The Enforcement of Reaction, 1553–1558', *Journal of Eclesiastical History*, 16 (1965); MacCulloch, *Later Reformation*, p. 21; Alexander, 'Bonner', p. 165.

The variations help to focus the question of contemporary reactions to the burnings, and whether they served merely to stoke resentment against the Marian authorities, and by association, the Catholic faith. Modern readers may well instinctively share Dickens's exasperation with 'the madness of a system which would burn a virtuous human being for his inability to accept a metaphysical theory of the eucharist', but such moralizing does little to further the cause of historical understanding.[58] The context for assessing the Marian persecution is a society where capital punishment was commonplace for a wide range of offences, where the concept of freedom of conscience in religious matters was anathema to all right-thinking people, and where the principle that dogged persistence in heresy merited death was almost universally accepted by religious theorists on both sides of the divide (John Foxe is an interesting exception to this). In the 1950s the Catholic historian Philip Hughes argued that the association of Catholicism with bloodthirstiness did not originate in the actual experience of Mary's reign, but in the subsequent popularizing of Foxe's propagandist version: 'for the mass of the nation the burnings were simply a few more capital executions than usual'.[59] More recent revisionists have been inclined to agree, pointing out that outside of London and Essex, many burnings seem to have passed off without trouble, and that Foxe's accounts of outpourings of popular sympathy for the martyrs cannot always be taken at face value. 'The persecution was not a disaster: if it did not help the Catholic cause, it did not do much to harm it'.[60]

Such approaches bring a welcome sense of perspective to bear on cherished national myths, but it is wise not to push them too far. It is sometimes alleged that the number of victims was small beer in the broader context of European religious persecution. Across the early modern period as a whole, there is something in this, but in the 1550s, England noticeably stood out among the Catholic states in Europe for the frequency of its executions for heresy.[61] It is significant too that the great majority of Marian martyrs were not anabaptist extremists, whose punishment might have been sanctioned by Catholic and Protestant regimes across Europe, but 'mainstream' Protestants upholding what had only recently been the religion established by law in the land (at their executions, some victims

58 Dickens, *Reformation*, p. 199.

59 Hughes, *Reformation*, ii. 278–82.

60 Jennifer Loach, 'Mary Tudor and the Re-Catholicisation of England', *History Today* (Nov. 1994); Duffy, *Stripping*, p. 559; Haigh, *Reformations*, pp. 230–4 (quote at p. 234).

61 Andrew Pettegree, *Marian Protestantism: Six Studies* (Aldershot, 1996), p. 161. See also William Monter, 'Heresy Executions in Reformation Europe, 1520–1565', in Ole Grell and Bob Scribner, eds., *Tolerance and Intolerance in the European Reformation* (Cambridge, 1996).

pointed out that those presiding had seemed in Edward's reign to hold precisely the same opinions as they). The fact that many were too young ever to have practised Catholicism as an adult may have made their treatment as pertinacious heretics seem to be morally, if not legally dubious. Even allowing for exaggerations in Foxe, a number of burnings clearly did involve popular protests, both those of high-profile clerics like Rogers, or the preacher John Cardmaker (who like Cranmer had recanted his recantation), and those of ordinary lay folk, for example when six local Protestants were burned outside Colchester in July 1557. It is hard to avoid concluding that burnings were often socially divisive, especially where pastors and lay people were executed in their own communities. Early modern people may have had few qualms about the judicial killing of deviant 'outsiders', foreign-born sectaries or witches (and perhaps late medieval Lollards fell into this category). But it was a different matter where, as with the Edwardian bishops, the victims were 'persons of high respect and generally acknowledged decency'.[62] Moreover, during the preceding 20 years many communities had learned, reluctantly, to live with the fact of religious division. Even those with no sympathy for their opinions may have felt little enthusiasm for the slaying of heretics who were also respectable local craftsmen and neighbours.

There is broad historical agreement that in the end the persecution did little for the Marian regime other than to blacken its posthumous reputation. The question of whether it might have worked in the longer term prompts predictably differing responses.[63] Continental parallels are frequently invoked here. The persecution of heretics in both France and the Netherlands in the later sixteenth century contributed to the outbreak of civil war, and the long-term toleration of Protestants. In Spain, by contrast, persecution eliminated the fledgling Protestant movement, and by the mid-seventeenth century, powerful Protestant communities had been crushed in both Bavaria and Austria. None of the parallels are exact enough to settle the argument. Tudor England had a markedly stronger system of centralized control than Valois France, and the element of external colonial rule present in the Spanish Netherlands was effectively absent. On the other hand, the Spanish people, unlike the English, had been conditioned to loathe heresy by long years of nationalist crusading fervour against Muslims and Jewish *conversos* (suspected fifth-columnists). The Habsburg emperors' success in suppressing Protestantism in their central European territories came on the back of victory in war. In the end, it makes more sense to focus on what the campaign did achieve, than on what it might have delivered in a hypothetically extended reign. In laying the foundations for a long tradition of

62 Pettegree, *Protestantism*, p. 157.

63 Compare Loach, 'Mary Tudor' with Dickens, *Reformation*, p. 297 and Pettegree, *Protestantism*, pp. 152–3.

popular anti-Catholicism, the Marian burnings were of immense cultural significance. They also effectively signalled the abandonment of future attempts to coerce the English people into a total uniformity of religious belief. Queen Elizabeth's government after 1558 resembled virtually all early modern regimes in demanding conformity of religious practice. But there was no attempt to launch a Protestant version of the discredited policy of inquisition and persecution; indeed the Elizabethan regime made propaganda capital out of the fact that it punished Catholics for political disloyalty, not inner belief (see Section 7.2). In one sense, therefore, the Marian burnings were deeply counter-productive. In another, they arguably helped create the conditions under which post-Reformation Catholicism was able to survive.

Only a small minority of English Protestants were actually executed for their faith under Mary. The others found ways of enduring the reign, and English Protestantism as a whole emerged deeply marked by the experience. Those who could not stomach the return of the idolatry of the mass and saint-worship fled the realm, a thousand or so seeking refuge in the Protestant towns of Frankfurt, Wesel, Geneva, Zurich, Strassburg and Emden.[64] Like the welcome extended to refugees from the continent in Edward's reign, the phenomenon is a reminder of the international-mindedness of mid-Tudor Protestantism, and an invitation to view the developments in England as part of the ebb-and-flow of the fortunes of European Protestantism more generally. Where the martyrs were predominantly humble folk, the exiles were usually a cut above, gentry, merchants, and educated clergy. They maintained an impressive output of both Latin and English polemic against the regime at home, successfully vindicating their own decision to flee as a legitimate and admirable response to persecution, as well as producing the first open justifications of tyrannicide (the right of subjects to resist, even depose and kill, an ungodly idolatrous ruler) in treatises by John Ponet, Christopher Goodman and John Knox.[65] Exile bred in the expatriates a contentiousness not wholly expended in attacks upon the Antichrist of Rome. In Edward's reign the evangelical movement had inherited the medieval English Church, partially refashioned it, and then lost it again. Suddenly bereft of bishops, courts, cathedrals and parishes, what organizational form should the Protestant congregations in exile take, and what forms of worship should they follow? Disputes about

[64] The standard work is Christina Garrett, *The Marian Exiles* (Cambridge, 1938). Her figure of around 800 exiles is modified by Pettegree, *Protestamntism*, ch. 1.

[65] Jonathan Wright, 'Marian Exiles and the Legitimacy of Flight from Persecution', *Journal of Ecclesiastical History*, 52 (2001); Gerry Bowler, 'Marian Protestants and the Idea of Violent Resistance to Tyranny', in Peter Lake and Maria Dowling, eds., *Protestantism and the National Church in Sixteenth Century England* (London, 1987).

these matters erupted in the English Church in Frankfurt, where in 1554–5 the congregation remodelled itself on the principles of Calvin's Geneva, electing deacons and ministers (including John Knox) and rewriting the 1552 Prayer Book to omit the litany of saints, vestments and other obnoxious elements. A group under Prince Edward's former tutor Richard Cox demanded, however, that they ought to 'do as they had done in England'. A period of unedifying factional infighting resulted in the 'Knoxians', unable to win the support of the Frankfurt magistrates, departing for Geneva.[66]

The exiles at least had more freedom to proceed openly in these matters than those attempting to maintain Protestant worship secretly at home. From Foxe and other sources we know of a number of Protestant cells, the best organized of which were in Colchester and in the capital. The London congregation kept on the move from one safe house to another, but nonetheless numbered 'sometimes forty, sometimes a hundred, sometimes two hundred'. It maintained membership lists, and administered a relief fund for prisoners and its own impoverished members.[67] Here too necessity and opportunity encouraged developments out of line with later 'Anglican' orthodoxy. A.G. Dickens was firm in his insistence that nothing funny was going on in the Marian London congregation: 'despite its congregational form there can be no doubt that the London church was an Anglican body and used the Prayer Book services'.[68] Yet recent research has established that in 1557 the congregation on its own authority granted (non-episcopal) orders to Thomas Simpson as its pastor, a decidedly 'presbyterian' move.[69]

Ironically, the one place where Edwardian Protestants could fairly openly continue to proclaim their faith was in the prisons awaiting execution. Here the clerical leadership preached, performed services, and wrote consolatory and instructive letters to co-religionists on the outside. But the spirit of contention was not absent, for incarcerated with them were the lay leaders of 'freewiller' congregations and other radicals who rejected the orthodox predestinarian theology of the Edwardian Church. As Thomas Freeman has demonstrated, the Protestant clerics devoted huge efforts to confounding and converting the (generally less well-educated) freewillers. Foxe later airbrushed these bitter quarrels from his account of the reign, but the persecution-within-a-persecution appears to have been remarkably successful. In

[66] Dickens, *Reformation*, pp. 344–9; MacCulloch, *Later Reformation*, pp. 70–1.

[67] Alexander, 'Bonner', p. 167; Brigden, *London*, pp. 602–3; J.W. Martin, 'The Protestant Underground Congregations of Mary's Reign', in his *Religious Radicals*.

[68] Dickens, *Reformation*, p. 302.

[69] Brett Usher, '"In a Time of Persecution": New Light on the Secret Protestant Congregation in Marian London', in David Loades, ed., *John Foxe and the English Reformation* (Aldershot, 1997). Bishop Grindal of London, an exile, later accepted the expedient.

the confused situation after 1553 the freewillers looked like they might become a serious rival to 'orthodox' Protestantism, but few traces are found of them in Elizabeth's reign.[70] The soon-to-be-martyrs in the London prisons, and the not-quite-martyrs in continental exile delivered the same uncompromising message to sympathizers at liberty in England: they must not pollute themselves by acceding to the wishes of the bishops, in particular they must steer clear of participation in the mass. The stridency and frequency of the message points to a conclusion which historians have often ignored in their concentration upon martyrs and exiles; that there must have been many of these timorous and reluctant conformists, known disparagingly as 'Nicodemites' after the Pharisee Nicodemus who had kept secret his admiration for Jesus. But Andrew Pettegree has urged us to take more seriously the Nicodemite contribution to the survival and development of the Protestant cause.[71] Those who conformed under Mary included the three most significant figures in the creation of a Protestant settlement in 1559: Elizabeth's first minister, William Cecil (who was in touch with the exiles, and played a part in defeating the bill ordering confiscation of their property in 1555); her first archbishop of Canterbury, the former dean of Lincoln, Mathew Parker; and Elizabeth herself, who had played the part of a good Catholic, while letting those who mattered know what her real feelings were. Given the Queen's experiences in her sister's reign, it is unsurprising that there was little recrimination against the more faint-hearted Protestants after 1558. But as we shall see, Elizabeth never had much fellow feeling for those who returned to England high on the ideologically pure air of Strassburg or Geneva.

The Protestant legacy from Mary's reign was a mixed one. Paradoxically, English Protestantism was in several ways strengthened during this, its darkest hour. There is a sense in which the Marian persecution managed to save the Edwardian Reformation from itself. The blood of the martyrs washed away memories of the cynical opportunism of Northumberland's government, and of the clerical squabbles which wracked the Edwardian establishment: Hooper and Ridley were remembered not as scheming political opponents, but as heroes dying in a common cause.[72]

The years between 1553 and 1558 provided (thanks largely to Foxe) the foundation-myth of English Protestantism. They also made it possible to begin to argue plausibly for an intrinsic association of Englishness with Protestantism, and foreignness (especially Spanishness) with Catholicism –

[70] Thomas Freeman, 'Dissenters from a Dissenting Church: The Challenge of the Freewillers, 1550–1558', in Peter Marshall and Alec Ryrie, eds., *The Beginnings of English Protestantism* (Cambridge, 2002).

[71] Pettegree, *Protestantism*, ch. 4.

[72] Diarmaid MacCulloch, *Tudor Church Militant: Edward VI and the Protestant Reformation* (London, 1999), p. 179.

an equation that would have seemed bizarre a quarter century earlier, yet was being taken increasingly for granted a quarter century later. At the same time, however, the calamity that overtook the Reformation in Mary's reign reinforced the element of perpetual paranoia in the English Protestant psyche. The possibility that Rome might again return had to be vigilantly guarded against, and the suffering of the martyrs provided a yardstick against which all commitment to the gospel had to be fastidiously measured. For the best part of a century, the progress of the Reformation was to be dogged by disputes between reformers willing to countenance some compromise with England's popish past, and those unprepared to consider it, between those who felt that Cranmer and Ridley's legacy had merely to be preserved in aspic, and those who felt that to stand still in religious matters was to move backwards. These were tensions crystallized in the experiences of compromise, exile and martyrdom.

Summation

The contested historiography of Marian religion is evident from the very chapter headings: 'reaction', 'restoration', 'renewal' or 'counter-reform'?[73] In recent times the smoke from the martyrs' pyres has cleared sufficiently for us to view the reign with a more objective eye, though the fire of strong historical empathy with the rival protagonists of the Marian drama has not been entirely extinguished (which may be no bad thing). There is, moreover, an instinctive sense on the part of many historians that the reign of Mary Tudor fits the description for that rather old-fashioned concept, a turning-point in history, when one line of national development is closed and another opened up. Few can resist the lure of counter-factual speculation when it comes to the Marian period. If, against the odds, Philip's sojourn in England had produced a three quarters Spanish princeling, or if Mary had been spared to occupy the throne for anything like the 45 years allotted to her younger sister, might not England have become a North Atlantic bastion of the Counter-Reformation, and in time the possessor of a vibrantly baroque Catholic culture? Categorical assertions that such an outcome was simply impossible now seem unconvincing, close to the position satirized many years ago by the ever-incisive humorists Sellar and Yeatman: 'England is bound to be C. of E., so all the executions were wasted'.[74] Revisionism has

[73] Loades, *Reign*, ch. 8; Tittler, *Mary I*, ch. 5; Wooding, *Rethinking Catholicism*, ch. 4; Christopher Haigh, *Reformation and Resistance in Tudor Lancashire* (Cambridge, 1975), ch. 12.

[74] W.C. Sellar and R.J. Yeatman, *1066 And All That* (new ed., London, 1984), p. 65. This effectively is the position of Dickens, *Reformation*, pp. 314–15. More cautious scepticism is expressed in Pogson, 'Legacy', p. 136, and Loades, 'Spirituality', p. 17.

made a strong case that the prospects for a permanent return to Catholicism were good, a steady process of restoration at parish level combining with sensible long-term planning for the education and edification of clergy and laity. The burnings had achieved little by 1558, but given time and resources, persecution is not, sad to relate, self-evidently self-defeating. Such alternative histories go to the heart of radically divergent assessments of the vitality of English Protestantism in the first three decades of the Reformation, but they must not become substitutes for evaluating the outcome which actually was delivered in 1558.

Some decisive things had happened by then, but it is now clear that one of them was not the arrival of match point for the English Reformation. The idea that Mary's reign represented the last desperate gasp of Catholicism, allowing Protestantism to step triumphantly forward and erect the Elizabethan Settlement over the corpse is no longer convincing. Indeed the intractableness of conservative forces looks if anything greater after the bracing experience of restored Catholicism. Not only did the higher clergy prove distinctly less biddable than on previous changes of regime, but after 1558 local communities seem to have been slower to respond to the wishes of government than they had been under Henry or Edward (see Section 5.2). In part, this was likely due to wariness (and weariness) about the trouble and expense of yet more reversals of policy, but another factor may have been the way that Mary's reign had helped to clarify issues at stake, and to sharpen confessional identities. It was in the mid-1550s that evangelicals decisively adopted 'Protestant' as their identifying label, while their opponents made great efforts to assert sole copyright to the term 'Catholic'.[75] If there had ever been such a thing as 'Catholicism without the pope', Mary's reign made it difficult to imagine what it might be in the future. In more practical terms, polarization at the local level had been increased by the wholehearted commitment of some of the gentry to the campaign of burnings, and by the non-participation or hostility of others. Mary had purged unreliable JPs from the county commissions. Later governments would follow suit, but 'no subsequent Protestant government could rely on the undivided co-operation of county elites to the extent that the Edwardian regimes had done.'[76] But if Queen Mary's reformation deepened the crevasse running through the centre of English Christianity, it also highlighted differences among those grouped on either bank of the divide. On the Catholic side, the legacy of the reign included disagreement over whether England was mission territory in need of evangelism, or a schismatic nation requiring orderly ecclesiastical government, as well as

[75] Patrick Collinson, 'Night Schools, Conventicles and Churches: Continuities and Discontinuities in Early Protestant Ecclesiology', in Marshall and Ryrie, *Beginnings*, pp. 230–4.

[76] MacCulloch, *Later Reformation*, p. 22.

over the political (as opposed to spiritual) authority of the pope, and the wisdom of close links with Spain (see Section 7.2). Among the Protestants, intense debates over liturgy, vestments, rituals and Church government had all been aired, and would not thereafter go away. By the end of the reign of the most devout of the Tudors, the ideal of a unified body of English Christian believers had been shown to be irretrievably shattered.

5

Protestantism and Puritanism 1559–1625

Overview

Though no one could have known it for certain at the time, the accession of Anne Boleyn's daughter to the English throne in November 1558 ensured that Catholic England would become a nostalgic dream. The first, most bitterly contested stage of the English Reformation was over, the way opened for gradual consolidation of Protestant gains. Yet the recent historiography of English religion in the reigns of Elizabeth and her successor James I has if anything been yet richer and more complex than that on the preceding period. In part, this is because many historians already have one eye upon those seminal events of English history, the breakdown of royal authority and eruption of civil war in the 1640s. Whether or not the English Civil War can legitimately be described as 'the last of the Wars of Religion'[1], there is an almost universal recognition that tensions over religion were of considerable importance in the political and social polarizations that preceded its outbreak. Some have suggested that destabilizing divisions over religion were a longstanding problem from the later sixteenth century onwards; others argue that the reigns of Elizabeth and James were characterized by broad agreement about fundamentals in religion (among Protestants at least), and that the instability was down to the sudden change in direction sponsored by the Crown in the 1630s away from the priorities of the 'Jacobethan' Church (see Chapter 8). In this context, the question of whether there was a 'Calvinist consensus' in the Church of England after 1559 over the issue of predestination is more than a matter of historical theology. But we should try to read the story forwards, as well as look back from the perspective of the mid-seventeenth century. The strongest argument against considering the religious settlement of 1559 to be the natural conclusion to a study of the English

[1] John Morrill, 'The Religious Context of the English Civil War', in Richard Cust and Ann Hughes, eds., *The English Civil War* (London, 1997), p. 176.

Reformation is that it is deeply untrue to contemporary perceptions. Most English Protestants believed that there was a great deal of 'reformation' still to bring about, both in the structures and rituals of the Church, and in the hearts and minds of the people. They also took extremely seriously the prospect that Rome might yet reassert itself. Yet, as under Edward, there was no unanimity about how best to proceed, about what could legitimately be retained, and what had to be swept away. The dilemma was sharpened by the anomalous position in which the reformers again found themselves, in charge of a Catholic ecclesiastical structure of bishoprics, Church courts and medieval parishes. English Protestantism, it has been aptly remarked, was 'a cuckoo in the nest'.[2] And presiding once again over all, was the Royal Supremacy: simultaneously the instrument for many of the Protestants' ambitions, and the source of many of their frustrations.

At the heart of many of these issues lies the vexed question of 'Puritanism' in the Elizabethan Church. Gallons of ink and mountains of printer cartridges have been expended in debates about what (if anything) the term actually means, about whether Puritanism should be considered a 'movement', and about the significance and depth of the divisions Puritanism promoted both locally and nationally in English society. Once, the matter seemed straightforward enough. Puritans were the opponents of Anglicans. The latter were the religious mainstream, upholders of the moderate Anglican ecclesiastical settlement established by law in 1559 and assailed by papists from the one extreme, and Puritans from the other.[3] This interpretation has fallen dramatically from favour in recent years. Not only was the word 'Anglican' virtually unknown before the mid-seventeenth century, but Anglicanism in the commonly understood modern sense – a distinctive version of Christianity synthesizing Catholic and Protestant strands – simply did not exist in the Tudor period. The leading Elizabethan clergy thought of themselves as Protestants, and of their Church as part of the 'Reformed' family of European Protestant Churches. Even the juxtaposition of 'Protestantism' and 'Puritanism' in the title of this chapter might be misleading. The foremost historian of Elizabethan and Jacobean Puritanism, Patrick Collinson, has argued over many decades that the phenomenon is best understood not as a species of 'opposition', but as a tendency or impulse largely contained within the Protestant mainstream, and sharing many of its concerns.[4] But if

[2] Diarmaid MacCulloch, *The Later Reformation in England, 1547–1603* (2nd ed., Basingstoke, 2001), ch. 3.

[3] For example, M.M. Knappen, *Tudor Puritanism* (Chicago, 1939); J.F.H. New, *Anglican and Puritan: The Basis of their Opposition, 1558–1640* (London, 1964); Richard Greaves, *Society and Religion in Elizabethan England* (Minneapolis, 1981).

[4] The case is most fully set out in his *The Religion of Protestants: The Church in English Society 1559–1625* (Oxford, 1982).

simplistic Anglican/Puritan dichotomies have largely been abandoned as a means of understanding the progress of the later Reformation, there remains huge scope for exploring the divisions and tensions within English society, which the 'Puritan' vision of personal and communal Reformation caused or exacerbated. Social and cultural historians have entered the fray here, debating the extent to which Puritanism is to be associated with the outlook and interests of local social elites, and with an attempted 'reformation of manners', imposing discipline and moral restraint on the disorderly and the poor.

The following four sections combine a narrative of the main developments within the Church of England in the later sixteenth and early seventeenth centuries with analyses of the themes and problems which recent scholarship has found most interesting and most intractable. The chapter begins with an evaluation of Elizabeth's religious settlement of 1559, and goes on to trace the fortunes of attempts to press that settlement further, and to preserve it, through to the accession of James I and beyond. There follows a discussion of whether, beneath the disagreements, churchmen of the period were fundamentally united in a 'Jacobethan consensus' about the most important matters in religion, and the chapter concludes with an attempt to understand the motivation of 'godly' Puritans, and assess their contribution to conflict and division within local communities.

5.1 Elizabethan Settlement

Two Acts of Parliament passed in April 1559, an Act of Supremacy and an Act of Uniformity, defined the character of the Elizabethan Church of England. The former abolished the jurisdiction of the pope and restored Royal Supremacy; the latter reimposed the second (1552) Edwardian prayer book with minor alterations as the official worship of the Church. The Reformation was back on track, ready to pick up where it had been unceremoniously (or perhaps ceremoniously) dragged off course by the accession of Mary. But on track to where? Both the intentions behind these parliamentary declarations, and their practical effects, have been the focus of intense controversy. In the past, historians from within the Anglican tradition were inclined to regard the course set in 1559 as a distinct middle way, a *via media* between the extremes of Geneva and Rome. For many years the most widely accepted scholarly interpretation of the shaping of the Elizabethan Settlement was that of J.E. Neale. In Neale's view, Elizabeth was aiming at the creation of a moderate, consensual Protestantism based around the restoration of the first (1549) Edwardian prayer book, and her real preference may have been for something not unlike the 'Henricianism' of her father's reign. But organized opposition in the Commons, particularly that of a 'Puritan choir' of returned Marian exiles, forced the government's hand, and led to the creation of a more emphatically Protestant settlement than the Queen had desired.[5] Neale wrote at a time when historians were more convinced of the importance of the House of Commons, and of opposition to royal policies within it, than they have since become, and subsequent research, particularly that of Norman Jones, has cast doubt on his assertions.[6] It is clear that there were relatively few Marian exiles (19 in all) elected to the 1559 Parliament, and that they would have had little time to organize 'opposition'. Moreover, a document drawn up within Elizabeth's circle of close advisers in December 1558, a 'Device for the Alteration of Religion' was already recommending a return to the 1552 prayer book: the outcome in 1559 may have been very close to what the Queen and her ministers had wanted all along. The dramatic tension of spring 1559 sprang not from the government's clash with 'Puritans' in the Commons, but with Catholic opposition in the House of Lords, opposition that almost succeeded in derailing the planned settlement. The strength of resistance prompted the decision to split an original single Reformation bill into two separate ones. Restored supremacy was more palatable than the loss of the mass to lay Catholic peers still anxious about the freehold to their monastic lands, and the inclusion of a clause allowing communion in two kinds in the supremacy bill suggests the intention to save at least some religious reform from the wreckage if the uniformity bill was lost. In the event both were passed, but with all the bishops and nine lay nobles voting against the uniformity bill. This squeaked through after Bishops Watson and White had been sent to the Tower, and other bishops intimidated into staying away. For the first time, major ecclesiastical legislation had been implemented without the support of a single churchman.[7]

The Neale thesis has been discredited, but some have argued that it deserves to be turned completely on its head. Elizabeth and her ministers were obliged to accept a settlement considerably less Protestant than they wanted, if not exactly a *via media*, then, in Christopher Haigh's words, a 'Church rather more Catholic than had been planned... a half-hearted Reformation'.[8] Some differences between 1559 and the high point of Edwardian reform seem to support the case. The Supremacy Act declared Elizabeth to be 'Supreme Governor' rather than 'Supreme Head' of the Church of England, and the 1559 prayer book modified 1552 at the most

5 J.E. Neale, 'The Elizabethan Acts of Supremacy and Uniformity, *English Historical Review*, 65 (1950); *Elizabeth I and her Parliaments, 1559–1581* (London, 1953).

6 Norman Jones, *Faith by Statute: Parliament and the Settlement of Religion, 1559* (London, 1982). See also W.S. Hudson, *The Cambridge Connection and the Elizabethan Settlement of 1559* (Durham, NC, 1980).

7 A point made by John Guy, *Tudor England* (Oxford, 1988), p. 262.

8 Christopher Haigh, *English Reformations: Religion, Politics, and Society under the Tudors* (Oxford, 1993), p. 241.

sensitive point of the communion service, the 'words of administration' spoken by the minister to those receiving communion. The formula from 1549 ('The body of our Lord Jesus Christ, which was given for thee, preserve thy body and soul unto everlasting life') was added on to the more uncompromisingly 'memorialist' words of 1552 ('Take and eat this in remembrance that Christ died for thee, and feed on him in thy heart by faith with thanksgiving'). It is by no means evident, however, that these were changes to conciliate religious conservatives. Some Protestants had always felt uneasy about 'headship' of the Church being ascribed to anyone other than Christ, and those anxieties were sharpened when the head in question was on the shoulders of a woman. In any case, Elizabeth's powers were in no way infringed by the rebranding of the royal title. The changed words of administration clearly did lean towards the possibility of belief in some kind of 'real presence' (as did the omission of the black rubric), but it is doubtful if this provided much comfort for Catholics. A more plausible explanation is that account was being taken of developments in continental reformed theology. Not only did Lutherans regard the communion as more than a bare memorial, but Calvin, unlike Zwingli, espoused belief in a real, if spiritual presence of Christ in the hearts of faithful communicants, and since the late 1540s, Zwingli's successors at Zurich had moved closer to this position.[9]

Few historians of the English Reformation would now seriously wish to portray the Elizabethan Settlement as a halfway house between Protestantism and Catholicism. Yet attempts to portray the events of 1559 as an unalloyed triumph for Protestantism are immensely complicated by the vexed question of the religious views of the Queen herself. Was Elizabeth a Protestant? Recent attempts to grapple with this immensely important question have tended towards conclusions of the 'yes, but' variety. Elizabeth was 'a Protestant (of sorts)', 'an odd sort of Protestant', '[not] unequivocally Protestant'.[10] Diarmaid MacCulloch portrays the Queen as an old-fashioned 'evangelical' in the mould of her step-mother, Catherine Parr, which may be as close to a plausible categorization as we are likely to get.[11] Certainly, in the early months of the reign the Queen showed an ability to send out contradictory signals, a talent perhaps honed by her 'Nicodemite' experience in her sister's reign. There were ostentatious displays of commitment to the cause of reform, appointing known

[9] Andrew Pettegree, *Marian Protestantism: Six Studies* (Aldershot, 1996), p. 135; MacCulloch, *Later Reformation*, p. 26.

[10] Haigh, *Reformations*, p. 242; Patrick Collinson, 'Windows into a Woman's Soul: Questions about the Religion of Queen Elizabeth I', in his *Elizabethan Essays* (London, 1994), p. 114; Guy, *Tudor England*, p. 251.

[11] Diarmaid MacCulloch, *Tudor Church Militant: Edward VI and the Protestant Reformation* (London, 1999), pp. 186–7. See also Susan Doran, 'Elizabeth I's Religion: Clues from her Letters', *Journal of Ecclesiastical History*, 52 (2001).

Protestants to preach at Paul's Cross, allowing iconoclasts in the capital to escape unpunished, and sweeping out of mass on Christmas Day 1558 when the host was elevated. Elizabeth's chosen advisers were men like William Cecil, known to have been out of favour with the Marian regime. Protestant reformers joyously hailed Elizabeth as a new Deborah, the biblical ruler who crushed the Canaanites, but the Queen rapidly demonstrated a capacity for disappointing their hopes.

The Uniformity Act placed a small time bomb under Protestant unity: ornaments of the Church and the dress of the clergy were to revert to the forms of 1548, 'until other order shall be therein taken by the authority of the queen's majesty'.[12] The vestments issue, bane of the Edwardian bishops, would return to haunt their successors. In the meantime, the Queen scandalized Protestant opinion by insisting on retaining a cross and candlesticks on the (altar-like) communion table in her chapel royal. These objects of 'idolatry' would daringly be removed or vandalized four times during the reign, but always the Queen replaced them. There are clear difficulties in reconciling this face of Elizabeth with the image of the godly young queen pressing for the restoration of her brother's Church. Andrew Pettegree has attempted to square the circle, arguing that Elizabeth's apparent attachment to ornaments and vestments was 'more symbolic than theological'. Elizabeth was determined to demonstrate her own authority to arrange such matters in the face of expectations that England would be guided by the practice of the 'best reformed churches' (i.e. those of Geneva and Zurich), a determination sharpened by her annoyance at Calvin for permitting the publication at Geneva of John Knox's *First Blast of the Trumpet against the Monstrous Regiment of Women*. Knox's intemperate outburst against the unnaturalness of female rule was directed at the Catholics Mary Tudor and Mary Queen of Scots, but in a masterpiece of bad timing it appeared in 1558, shortly before the accession of Elizabeth.[13] The evidence for Elizabeth's selective religious conservatism, however, runs deeper than mere 'politique' calculation. She took few pains to hide her lifelong distaste for the institution of clerical marriage, something which to Protestants embodied an important statement of theological principle, and which rapidly became widespread in the Church. Yet after Mathew Parker, Elizabeth never appointed another married Archbishop of Canterbury.[14] Another lifelong trait was a distinctly un-Protestant penchant for elaborate church music, the Queen employing Catholic composers like William Byrd in her chapel royal. There was, conversely, little enthusiasm for the necessity of

12 Henry Gee and William Hardy, eds., *Documents Illustrative of English Church History* (London, 1896), p. 466.

13 Pettegree, *Protestantism*, pp. 141–9.

14 Eric Carlson, 'Clerical Marriage and the English Reformation', *Journal of British Studies*, 31 (1992); Helen Parish, *Clerical Marriage and the English Reformation* (Aldershot, 2000), pp. 227–34.

preaching: in 1576 Elizabeth horrified Archbishop Grindal by suggesting that three or four preachers per county were quite enough.[15] Elizabeth's Protestantism, rather like her father's 'Catholicism', was deeply idiosyncratic and always conditioned by a high sense of her own prerogative. But whereas Henry had generally found churchmen eager to second-guess the workings of the royal mind, much of Elizabeth's reign (particularly the earlier part) was characterized by a lack of fit between the outlook of the Queen and that of her leading ecclesiastics. The mass resignation of the Marian bishops compelled Elizabeth to look to the Protestant clergy, amongst whom the most able and obvious candidates for high office were the exiles. Archbishop Parker had remained in England in Mary's reign, but the majority of his new episcopal colleagues had firsthand experience of how things were done in continental centres of Protestantism.[16] As far as Elizabeth was concerned, the partial resuscitation of the Edwardian Reformation in 1559 was precisely a settlement, a line drawn under contentious issues that would (providing people did what they were told) provide the basis for future stability. But the majority of those in authority in the Church in 1559 hoped for a continuation of the policy of ongoing Reformation that had prevailed between 1547 and 1553. In the end, the key to understanding the relationship between Elizabeth and the religious settlement that bears her name is not to imagine that it went further than she wished it to go, but to understand that she did not wish it to go further. Frustration with the Queen's attitude was most marked among those spiritual heirs of Hooper whom historians call Puritans, but it was widely shared among more establishment figures, the heirs of Cranmer and Ridley. In the 1563 meeting of convocation, the bishops were prepared to back sweeping measures for further reform, but the Queen would have none of it.[17]

5.2 Puritan Discontents

To many in the early 1560s, the Church of England was a Church but 'half-reformed'. This was despite the fact that a royal visitation of 1559 aimed at

[15] Patrick Collinson, 'The Elizabethan Church and the New Religion' in Christopher Haigh, ed., *The Reign of Elizabeth I* (Basingstoke, 1984), p. 181.

[16] Two exceptions among the early Elizabethan bishops, who seem to have shared the Queen's conservative sympathies were Edmund Guest of Rochester and Richard Cheyney of Gloucester. See William Haugaard, *Elizabeth and the English Reformation* (Cambridge, 1968), pp. 250–3; Caroline Litzenberger, 'Richard Cheyney, Bishop of Gloucester, an Infidel in Religion?', *Sixteenth Century Journal*, 25 (1994).

[17] David Crankshaw, 'Preparations for the Canterbury Provincial Convocation of 1562–3: A Question of Attribution', in Susan Wabuda and Caroline Litzenberger, eds., *Belief and Practice in Reformation England* (Aldershot, 1998).

thoroughly expunging from the parishes the limited steps towards Catholic restoration that had been taken since 1553. As in 1547, the apparent moderation of the visitation injunctions belied the intentions of the staunchly Protestant visitors. Although largely a reissue of the Edwardian set, the injunctions did not actually demand the removal of all images, and they ordered that altars were to be taken down only with the consent of the curate and churchwardens. There were further minor steps back from Edwardian positions in the requirements to bow reverently at the name of Jesus, to use traditional-style wafers (though without embossed pictures) instead of ordinary bread for the communion, and to allow processions at rogationtide (a time of prayer for the harvest in late spring). But the Marian exiles who acted as visitors insisted on universal destruction of roods and images, and removal of altars. Whatever might be kept in the Queen's chapel royal, Elizabethan parish churches would resemble Edwardian ones in the starkness of their furnishing. Nonetheless, the evidence of churchwardens' accounts and episcopal visitations through the 1560s suggests a slower rate of compliance than under Edward. Particularly in the northern dioceses of York, Lincoln and Chester, as well as in Wales, altars and images were still being discovered up to the end of the decade. Whether Catholic loyalty had been strengthened by Mary's reign, or whether uncertainty about the succession made parishes reluctant yet again to destroy expensive furnishings and fittings, it appeared that 'the ability of the Tudor state to make its subjects alter their religious habits on demand had slightly declined'.[18]

Elizabeth was finding this to be the case with her Protestant as well as Catholic subjects. The 1559 Injunctions clarified the open-ended ornaments clause in the Uniformity Act by insisting that the clergy should use 'such seemly habits' as were observed in the last year of Edward's reign. This meant, above all else, the wearing of a surplice to celebrate church services. To many ministers (especially those with experience of the more austere clerical attire in continental churches) the wearing of surplices was not a trivial or indifferent matter. It seemed to imply a continuing attachment to the Catholic notion of a separate priestly caste, running counter to the Reformation's insistence on 'the priesthood of all believers'. But for Elizabeth, this was a matter of order and obedience, and in 1565 Archbishop Parker was instructed to crack down. His 'Advertisements' of March 1566 ordered that at public prayer every minister should wear 'a comely surplice with sleeves', thus reopening the wounds of the Hooper investment controversy, and the 'troubles at Frankfurt'. For refusing to comply, 37 London clergy were suspended. The dissidents included many of

[18] Ronald Hutton, 'The Local Impact of the Tudor Reformations', in Peter Marshall, ed., *The Impact of the English Reformation 1500–1640* (London, 1997), pp. 157–61 (quote at p. 159).

the most able and diligent ministers, among them the martyrologist, John Foxe and the distinguished theologian, Thomas Becon. The authorities won a tactical victory in the 'Vestiarian Controversy', but it left a divisive legacy. Disgust with the action of the bishops led to the formation of the first breakaway Protestant congregation from the Elizabethan Church: a group led by deprived ministers and former Marian exiles were discovered meeting secretly at Plumbers Hall in London in June 1567. It was at this time, too, that the first instance of the derisive label 'Puritan' appears in the records.[19]

Vestments were an itch on the conscience of godly ministers that never went away, but as the 1570s dawned, tensions between the bishops and their critics came to encompass a wider range of issues. Amongst these, the question of Church government loomed increasingly large. Under the Queen, the governance of the English Church retained its long-standing medieval form: hierarchical rule by bishops presiding over large dioceses centred on cathedral cities. But in the Protestant towns where Marian exiles had sought refuge (and in the refugee 'Stranger' Church, now restored in London) there were alternative models: free-standing congregations, electing their own elders (for discipline), deacons (for relief of the poor) and ministers (for preaching and the sacraments), with oversight in the hands of regional presbyteries and synods. The epitome of this 'presbyterian' system was Calvinist Geneva, and the Genevan model was becoming the norm in the later sixteenth century throughout much of the Protestant world: in south-west Germany, Scotland and Eastern Europe, among the Protestant congregations of France and the Netherlands. Many of its English advocates were convinced that presbyterianism was commanded in the New Testament, while episcopacy was contaminated by its associations with popery (only somewhat ameliorated by the witness of the Protestant martyr-bishops under Mary).

A second phase of internecine conflict in the Church was inaugurated in the spring of 1570 by a series of Cambridge lectures delivered by the Lady Margaret Professor of Divinity, Thomas Cartwright, arguing for the equality of all ministers and the establishment of a presbyterian Church order. Cartwright was forced into Genevan exile, but the campaign was continued by a group of radical ministers led by Thomas Field and John Wilcox, whose increasing support among sections of the influential laity led them to shift the focus of their agitation to Parliament. In 1571 a bill was introduced (unsuccessfully) for the removal of objectionable ceremonies from the Book of Common Prayer, and in 1572 Field and Wilcox published an intemperate *Admonition to the Parliament*, which denounced bishops as 'antichristian and devilish', and accused the prayer book of being full of abuses 'picked out of that popish dunghill, the mass book'. (These included

[19] Patrick Collinson, *The Elizabethan Puritan Movement* (London, 1967), pp. 86–8.

saints' days, kneeling to receive communion, the burial service, the ceremony of 'churching' women after childbirth, the 'idolatrous' use of rings in the marriage ceremony, and of course, the surplice.)[20] The 'Admonition Controversy' which ensued has been described as 'a struggle for the "soul" of mainstream Protestantism', with Cartwright weighing in on the side of Field and Wilcox, and the bishops being defended by the rising 'conformist' star, the Master of Trinity College Cambridge, John Whitgift.[21] The ceremonies which Cartwright regarded as backdoors to popery, Whitgift saw as helpful gateways to order and uniformity; there could be little meeting of minds.

Yet the common ground had by no means been evacuated. Many 'moderate Puritans' were appalled by the confrontational tone of the *Admonition*, and many of the bishops shared the view that numerous abuses in the Church awaited reformation, particularly the failings of non-resident, non-preaching parish clergy. There was also widespread concern about the Church turning in on itself at a time when internationally popery looked to be on the ascendant (the massacre of French Protestants on St Bartholomew's Day 1572 was a shocking wake-up call). There seemed the possibility of a fresh start in 1575, when Elizabeth appointed Edmund Grindal as Parker's successor. Grindal was a Marian exile, formerly Bishop of London (where he had gone easy on vestiarian nonconformists) and Archbishop of York (where he had been tough on papists). Whether or not Grindal can legitimately be termed a 'Puritan' archbishop, he was certainly one who hoped to harness the energies of Puritans in the task of evangelizing the nation, and he enjoyed the backing of most of Elizabeth's leading councillors, including both Cecil and the most high-profile lay champion of 'godly' reformation, the Earl of Leicester. But his primacy came spectacularly to grief over the issue of 'prophesyings'. Less exciting than the name suggests, these were meetings bringing the clergy of a locality together on a fortnightly or monthly basis to preach in turn and have their preaching assessed by their fellows, with lay people occasionally in attendance. They were flourishing across much of the province of Canterbury in the mid-1570s with considerable episcopal support. From one perspective, prophesyings were 'subtly subverting the whole hierarchic structure envisaged by the Queen's programme'; from another they were merely 'locally arranged clerical seminars designed to improve teaching standards in her Church'.[22] The Queen, distrustful of exotic-sounding religious ventures not provided

20 David Cressy and Lori Anne Ferrell, eds., *Religion and Society in Early Modern England: A Sourcebook* (London, 1996), pp. 82–90.

21 Peter Lake, *Anglicans and Puritans? Presbyterianism and English Conformist Thought from Whitgift to Hooker* (London, 1988), ch. 1 (quote at p. 24).

22 Wallace MacCaffrey, *Elizabeth I* (London, 1993), p. 318; MacCulloch, *Church Militant*, p. 194.

for in her 1559 Settlement, ordered Grindal to suppress them. He refused: 'Bear with me, I beseech you, Madam, if I choose rather to offend your earthly Majesty than to offend the heavenly majesty of God'.[23] The price for this courageous stand was suspension from office in 1577, and effectively the end for hopes that the bishops themselves would spearhead the drive for further reformation.

When Grindal died in 1583, his successor was a man of very different outlook, Cartwright's old adversary John Whitgift. In broad terms, the second half of Elizabeth's reign witnessed a more conservative, disciplinarian character to the episcopal bench, as the generation of Marian exiles died out, and concerns resurfaced about the subversive potential of clerical nonconformity. There was renewed confrontation when Whitgift demanded that all ministers subscribe to three articles, the second of which, declaring that the prayer book 'containeth nothing. . . contrary to the word of God', was particularly designed to smoke out nonconformists. But leading councillors, including Cecil, were alarmed by the scale of opposition: some 3–400 ministers were suspended for non-subscription, and were receiving the vocal backing of many gentry in the localities. Whitgift was forced into a partial climb down, accepting promises from individual ministers simply to use the prayer book. This isolated a hard core of non-subscribers, but Whitgift's policy of getting these to incriminate themselves through use of the *ex officio* oath (a legal procedure which removed the right to silence) further antagonized members of the Privy Council. By 1584 Sir Walter Mildmay and Sir Francis Knollys were prepared to act as parliamentary patrons of what can now be termed a 'presbyterian movement', backing a bill, which proposed the introduction of a modified presbyterian system. The Queen swiftly forbade further discussion of this, but outside Parliament, something like a shadow presbyterian structure for the Church was nonetheless being created under the leadership of Field, with groups of ministers meeting in local conferences or *classes*, and reporting to county synods. The best documented of these gatherings took place at Dedham on the Essex–Suffolk border between 1582 and 1589, though it is likely that here and elsewhere many ministers taking part may have been 'responding to an intensely felt and practical desire to share their theological and pastoral problems', rather than expressing dogmatic presbyterianism.[24] 'Godly' ministers were birds of a feather: Puritan 'surveys of the ministry' produced for many parts of the country in the mid-1580s claimed that large numbers of the parish clergy were 'dumb dogs', unable to preach, while others were drunkards or 'subject to the vice of good fellowship'.[25] A

[23] Patrick Collinson, *Archbishop Grindal 1519–1583: The Struggle for a Reformed Church* (London, 1979), p. 242.
[24] Collinson, *Religion*, p. 120.
[25] Collinson, *Puritan Movement*, pp. 280–2.

presbyterian high-water mark was reached in 1586–7, with another attempt to introduce a Genevan system through Parliament, and the publication of a *Book of Discipline* laying down the form a presbyterian Church of England should take. But all these waves broke ineffectually against the rock of the Queen's determination to maintain the status quo. Whitgift was able to go more forcefully on to the counter-attack after the clandestine publication in 1588–9 of the 'Marprelate tracts', scurrilously satirical attacks on the bishops, which deeply embarrassed the Puritan leadership. In the hunt for the author and presses, evidence of earlier synods was uncovered, and Cartwright and other leaders were arrested, brought before the courts of High Commission and Star Chamber, and forced to swear not to hold future 'conferences'. By the early 1590s, presbyterianism as an organized movement had run its course. Field had died in 1588, and several of the powerful laymen who had provided some degree of protection – Leicester, Mildmay and Sir Francis Walsingham – also died in 1588–90. Whitgift meanwhile was making propaganda capital out of associating presbyterianism with separatism. Since the discovery of the Plumbers Hall conventicle in 1567, a trickle of other Protestants had broken all ties with the Church of England. These tended to be called 'Brownists' after the Cambridge don, Robert Browne, whose followers formed a succession of fractious congregations in the Netherlands in the 1580s, and who was author of *A Treatise of Reformation without Tarrying for Any* (1582). The 'any' in question was the secular authority, and it was for seditious denial of the Royal Supremacy rather than any doctrinal heresy that separatists were punished by the Elizabethan State. In 1587, Whitgift arrested the separatist leader Henry Barrow, and in 1593, at the height of anti-presbyterian oppression, Barrow was executed for treason along with two other separatists, John Greenwood and John Penry.

It is usual to detect a sea change in the outlook of English Puritanism after the debacle of the early 1590s. The 'movement' (if it can any longer be called that) turned inwards, away from political activism, and towards local evangelism and the cultivation of an intense, interiorised Puritan piety.[26] Yet many ministers and godly lay people had lost none of their distaste for the ceremonial aspects of the prayer book, and there is scattered evidence for the continuation of unauthorized fasts and conferences through the 1590s.[27] Nor was the hope for reform of the structure and worship of the Church from the top entirely dead. The crux, as always, was the succession. The prospect of a convincing Catholic claim to the throne had sharply receded

26 Patrick Collinson, 'Ecclesiastical Vitriol: Religious Satire in the 1590s and the Invention of Puritanism', in John Guy, ed., *The Reign of Elizabeth I: Court and Culture in the Last Decade* (Cambridge, 1995), p. 152; Guy, *Tudor England*, p. 307; MacCulloch, *Later Reformation*, pp. 50–1.

27 John Spurr, *English Puritanism 1603–1689* (Basingstoke, 1998), pp. 57–8.

after 1587, when Elizabeth agreed (to immense Protestant relief) to execute her cousin Mary Queen of Scots. Mary had been in confinement in England since fleeing Scotland in 1568, and was up to her elbows in plots with Catholic conspirators (see Section 7.2). As Elizabeth's own life drew to a close, it became increasingly clear that the only feasible successor was Mary's son, James VI of Scotland, who had been brought up in the faith of the Calvinist and presbyterian Kirk of Scotland. 'In the history of English religion', it has been claimed, 'the passing of Elizabeth made very little difference'; 1603 was an 'almost irrelevant date'.[28] Puritans at the time would have been dismayed to hear it; they pinned immense hopes on James, and reactivated the tactics of the 1580s, gathering together in clerical conferences and setting in motion a concerted petitioning campaign. On his way south in March 1603, James was presented with a 'Millenary Petition', which purported to represent the views of a thousand ministers. Radical demands for the abolition of episcopacy were scrupulously excluded from this document, which focussed on the language of the prayer book and the vestments issue. It was a hopeful sign when the King agreed to call a meeting of bishops and Puritan leaders at Hampton Court in 1604 to discuss the demands, but in the event this produced only disappointment. The Puritans had misjudged their man. Though a Calvinist in theology, James had suffered indignity at the hands of Scots presbyterians prepared to remind him that he was a simple member of Christ's Kirk like other lay Christians, and may have taken alarm at the scale and sophistication of the Puritan petitioning campaign that greeted him in England (the tendency to become easily alarmed was characteristic of James throughout his reign). At Hampton Court he seized the opportunity to make clear his commitment to episcopacy in the celebrated outburst, 'no bishop, no king'. There were minor concessions to Puritan concerns about the financing of the ministry as well as the commissioning of a new translation of the Bible (the 'Authorized Version' of 1611), but otherwise the conference produced 'little more than an endorsement of the Elizabethan *status quo*'.[29] Moreover, it heralded a return to the 1583 subscription policy, the King working closely with Whitgift's successor, the fiercely anti-Puritan Archbishop Richard Bancroft, to harry nonconformists. Around 80 ministers were deprived (four-fifths of them in 1605–6), though James was keen not completely to alienate 'moderate' Puritans, and bishops were allowed discretion about whom to pursue.[30]

[28] Collinson, 'Elizabethan Church', p. 194.

[29] Patrick Collinson, 'The Jacobean Religious Settlement: The Hampton Court Conference', in Howard Tomlinson, ed., *Before the English Civil War* (Basingstoke, 1983), p. 32.

[30] Spurr, *Puritanism*, pp. 60–2; Kenneth Fincham, *Prelate as Pastor: The Episcopate of James I* (Oxford, 1990), pp. 214–7, modifying the view of greater severity in Collinson, 'Jacobean Religious Settlement', p. 45.

After the King had made his point; there was little active persecution of dissenting ministers in Jacobean England, particularly after George Abbot was appointed to succeed Bancroft at Canterbury in 1611. Abbot was a prelate in the Grindal mould, sympathetic to the aspirations of moderate Puritanism, and prepared to turn a blind eye to infringements such as omission of the surplice. The King, however, continued to disappoint Puritan hopes. His issuing of the 'Declaration of Sports' in 1618, which gave official sanction to the pursuit of 'harmless recreations' after Sunday worship, offended the strong 'sabbatarian' instincts of the godly, who believed that only religious activities were permissible on the Sabbath. In addition, his determination to pursue a pacific foreign policy in the early stages of the Thirty Years War seemed shameful to those who felt that England should assume the mantle of Protestant leadership against the forces of the Catholic Habsburgs. But there was no return to full-blooded Cartwrightian agitation. In Collinson's careful formulation, James's reign witnessed, not the end of Puritanism, but 'the end of the Puritan movement in the form of a concerted effort mounted from within the Church to alter the fundamental terms of the Elizabethan settlement by political means'. Thereafter Puritanism operated 'like leaven in the lump', seeking gradual moral and spiritual transformation of the nation.[31] It did so, moreover, in an often supportive ecclesiastical climate. Collinson notes the widespread diffusion of an ideal of 'Grindalian episcopacy' in the Jacobean Church, and Kenneth Fincham identifies several 'evangelical' bishops, men, including both Abbot of Canterbury and Archbishop Toby Mathew of York, who did not regard Puritanism as subversive, and who shared at least something of the Puritan outlook.[32] Yet we have also been warned that 'it would be unwise to overlook the disruptive potential of even moderate Puritanism' in Jacobean England.[33] At this point we should attempt to weigh in the balance the elements of conflict and consensus within English Protestantism, as they manifested themselves over the reigns of Elizabeth and James.

5.3 Calvinist Consensus?

After discussion of protests, petitions and deprivations, it may seem curious to consider the possibility that the most important characteristic of the

[31] Ibid., pp. 45, 30.

[32] Collinson, *Grindal*, pp. 290–3; id., *Religion*, pp. 79–91; Fincham, *Prelate*, pp. 253–61. Peter Lake goes further, arguing that Matthew Hutton, Archbishop of York 1595–1606, should be described as a 'Puritan bishop': 'Matthew Hutton – a Puritan Bishop?', *History*, 64 (1979).

[33] Spurr, *Puritanism*, p. 71. See also Arnold Hunt, 'Laurence Chaderton and the Hampton Court Conference', in Wabuda and Litzenberger, *Belief and Practice* for the argument that 'moderate' Puritans conformed to ceremonies with extreme reluctance after 1604.

English Church in its 'Jacobethan' phase was a powerful underlying internal stability. Yet this notion has been extremely influential in framing recent approaches to the history of the later Reformation. In addition to Collinson's emphasis on the overlapping outlook of bishops and 'Puritans', their common concern for the advancement of the gospel, historians can point to other unifying factors. According to Nicholas Tyacke, the most important of these was doctrinal. Belief in the Calvinist doctrine of predestination was a 'common and ameliorating bond' uniting the outlook of bishops, clergy, and the more educated among the laity, one which, while it did not stop Whitgift harassing Puritans, imposed limits on the extent of his persecution.[34] Another source of ideological cement was the universal fear and hatred of Catholicism found among English Protestants: the depth and significance of 'anti-popery' has been explored by a number of recent scholars.[35] If Rome was a focus of hostility, then almost by definition, the Royal Supremacy became a shared symbol of loyalty. Despite the frustration reformers sometimes felt with royal policy, the Crown throughout the period exhibited a clear commitment to Protestant unity and inclusiveness. James in particular, it is argued, was astute at defusing conflict by promoting churchmen of differing outlooks, and by demanding minimal conformity from Puritans.[36] All of this points towards two conclusions: that the old 'Anglican versus Puritan' approach distorts understanding of the late sixteenth- and early seventeenth-century Church, and that the explosion of religious conflict in the mid-seventeenth century was far from inevitable – its causes need to be sought in the 1630s and in the policies of Charles I. The latter claim will be examined more closely in Chapter 8, but here it is important to consider the possibility that these forces for 'unity' held within them the seeds of conflict – that the 'consensus' binding the forces of the Reformation was more fragile than some approaches have suggested.

The idea (it is now indeed an orthodoxy) that the English Church of 1559–1625 was a 'Calvinist' Church has seemed odd to those who find it hard to associate Calvinism with bishops, cathedrals and the early history of

[34] Nicholas Tyacke, 'Puritanism, Arminianism and Counter-Revolution', in Conrad Russell, ed., *The Origins of the English Civil War* (London, 1973), p. 121; id., *Anti-Calvinists: The Rise of English Arminianism c. 1590–1640* (Oxford, 1987).

[35] Peter Lake, 'Anti-Popery: the Structure of a Prejudice', in Cust and Hughes, *Civil War*; Alexandra Walsham, '"The Fatall Vesper": Providentialism and Anti-Popery in Late Jacobean London', *Past and Present*, 144 (1994); Arthur Marotti, ed., *Catholicism and Anti-Catholicism in Early Modern English Texts* (London, 1999).

[36] Peter McCullough, *Sermons at Court: Politics and Religion in Elizabethan and Jacobean Preaching* (Cambridge, 1998), pp. 2–5; Kenneth Fincham and Peter Lake, 'The Ecclesiastical Policy of King James I', *Journal of British Studies*, 24 (1985); id., 'The Ecclesiastical Policies of James I and Charles I', in Kenneth Fincham, ed., *The Early Stuart Church, 1603–1642* (Basingstoke, 1993).

'Anglicanism'. But in late sixteenth-century Europe, Calvin's name was linked above all with the doctrine of predestination, the belief that irrespective of human merits, God had preordained some of mankind to salvation, and that these members of the 'elect' could never finally fall from grace. Calvin's successor at Geneva, Theodore Beza, made the doctrine still more central to Calvinist thought. Beza laid more emphasis on double predestination (the 'reprobate' were predestined for hell, as the elect were for heaven), and on God's decision for each individual soul having been made even before the fall of Adam (technically, *supralapsarian* predestination). Whereas Calvin believed that Christ died for all men (though only interceding for the elect), Beza insisted on the idea of 'limited atonement', Christ dying for the elect only. This meant that people could not look simply to the sacrifice of Christ to feel a sense of 'assurance' of their salvation (the earlier evangelical or Lutheran view), but had to look deep inside themselves to see if God was at work within them.[37]

The extent to which Calvinist concepts of predestination actually dominated the thinking of the Elizabethan Church is open to debate. Diarmaid MacCulloch reminds us that the liturgy and formularies adopted after 1558 were largely inherited from the Edwardian Church, and that for Edwardian Protestants, Calvin was less of a name to conjure with than Bucer or Bullinger.[38] It is noteworthy that although the seventeenth of the Thirty-Nine Articles adopted by the Church in 1563 taught that God had chosen to elect some to salvation 'before the foundations of the world were laid', it maintained silence about a decree of reprobation. Some scholars, most notably Peter White, have denied that there was a 'Calvinist' monopoly of views about grace and salvation, arguing instead for a broad spectrum of views and diverse continental Protestant influences.[39] But the evidence for the growing dominance of Calvin over the thought of English theologians and churchmen remains powerfully convincing. By the end of the sixteenth century, more editions of Calvin's works had been translated into English than into all other languages combined. Tyacke establishes that the doctoral theses in divinity maintained in Elizabethan and Jacobean Oxford regularly upheld Calvinist views of predestination, and that the sermons dealing with election preached at the 'official' pulpit of Paul's Cross before 1632 virtually all took an orthodox Calvinist line.[40] Not just 'evangelical' bishops like Abbot, but the two successive 'anti-Puritan' archbishops of Canterbury, Whitgift and Bancroft, were Calvinist predestinarians. In controversies with

[37] R.T. Kendall, *Calvin and English Calvinism to 1649* (Oxford, 1979), chs. 1–2.
[38] MacCulloch, *Later Reformation*, p. 60.
[39] Peter White, *Predestination, Policy and Polemic: Conflict and Consensus in the English Church from the Reformation to the Civil War* (Cambridge, 1992). See also the debate between White and Tyacke in *Past and Present*, 115 (1987).
[40] Tyacke, 'Puritanism', p. 120; *Anti-Calvinists*, p. 249.

Cartwright, Whitgift was just as likely as his opponent to cite Calvin and Beza, and in 1595 (in an intervention in a theological dispute in Cambridge) Whitgift drafted an uncompromising statement of double predestination, the Lambeth Articles.[41] Tyacke and others do not seek to deny the existence of conflict in the Elizabethan and Jacobean Church, but they minimize its potential for inflicting serious damage: before Charles I changed the rules, 'nonconformists and even presbyterians were never regarded as being totally beyond the pale: they were seen instead as aberrant brethren deserving of some indulgence.'[42]

However, the insight that 'Puritans' and 'conformists' had a common theological base invites the question of whether they set off from it in broadly the same direction. There is a growing recognition that there were different types of 'Calvinist' in the Elizabethan and Jacobean Church. In an important distinction first formulated by R.T. Kendall in 1979, Calvinist predestinarians might be of the 'credal' or of the 'experimental' variety.[43] 'Credal' Calvinists (Whitgift is a pre-eminent example of the type) held firmly to the formal doctrine of predestination, but tended to regard the identity of the elect and the reprobate as unknowable in this life, and worried about the disruptive social consequences if there were too much concentration on the doctrine in popular preaching. As the Thirty-Nine Articles warned, for the ungodly 'to have continually before their eyes the sentence of God's predestination, is a most dangerous downfall, whereby the devil doth thrust them either into desperation, or into wretchlessness of most unclean living'.[44] Since the godly and ungodly could not be told apart, it made more sense to concentrate on the importance of the Church as a visible institution encompassing both types, than on an invisible 'true Church' of the elect. 'Experimental' Calvinists, by contrast, made predestination the very centre of their piety, and turned reflection on it into a highly developed form of 'practical divinity'. Since Christ died for the elect only, it was incumbent upon faithful Christians to seek signs of 'assurance' that they were part of that privileged company. There was an emphasis on what the theologians termed 'sanctification', the cultivation of a godly lifestyle, which would make manifest the 'marks of election' in an individual believer. The leading exponent of experimental Calvinist divinity was the Cambridge theologian William Perkins (1558–1602), whose works were published in 76 editions in his lifetime, and who was one of very few English authors to

41 The first of these read: 'God from eternity has predestined some men to life, and reprobated some to death': White, *Predestination*, p. 107.

42 Tyacke, 'Puritanism', p. 121.

43 Kendall, *Calvinism*, pp. 1–13. See also Peter Lake, 'Calvinism and the English Church 1570–1635', *Past and Present*, 114 (1987).

44 E.J. Bicknell, *A Theological Introduction to the Thirty-Nine Articles of the Church of England* (2nd ed., London, 1925), p. 278.

be widely translated and read abroad. Perkins advocated an intense religious self-scrutiny, sharpened by his development of the Calvinist concept of 'temporary faith' – the alarming idea that even those who seemed to be irreproachably godly might in reality be reprobates and fall away before the end. Perkins's works showed no interest in elders, deacons or the forms of Church government that had been the concerns of the classical movement of the 1580s. Experimental Calvinism did not necessarily imply presbyterianism, rejection of episcopacy or separatism. But its interest in the identity of the elect in this world provided the logic for a kind of semi-separatism, for the godly to seek out each other's company and to shun the wicked. It implied too a temptation to exclude the ungodly from fully active membership of the visible Church. Some of the consequences of this for neighbourly relations and for local power structures will be considered in Section 5.4. But it should be apparent that even within a predestinarian 'consensus', impulses towards exclusion and the authority of the demonstrably godly might be at odds with an emphasis on inclusion and hierarchical order.

A similar set of paradoxes is to be found in another unifying characteristic of English Protestantism, its intense anti-popery. Few Protestants in the period lost sight of the fact that their real enemy was the pope and his minions, backed by the massed forces of the Catholic powers abroad and a fifth column of papists at home. If they were ever tempted to forget, events would periodically remind them: the rebellion of the Catholic Northern Earls in 1569, plots to depose and assassinate Elizabeth in 1571, 1584 and 1585, the Spanish Armada in 1588 and the Gunpowder Plot in 1605. There is no doubt that on one level the task of combating the popish threat 'promoted general Protestant solidarity'.[45] Endless tomes of anti-Catholic polemic were produced in this period, by Puritans and conformists alike. Attacking Rome in print was a way that 'moderate Puritans' in particular could simultaneously discharge their godly conscience and demonstrate their loyalty to the regime.[46] Even at the height of his conflict with Whitgift, the exiled Cartwright was recruited by a consortium of Puritan divines to produce a confutation of the recent Catholic translation of the New Testament. Up until the 1620s at least, the overwhelming majority of Protestant divines, in England as elsewhere, were convinced that the pope of Rome was the Antichrist foretold by scripture, an identification that was at once deeply threatening and somewhat reassuring. It provided a justification for the course the Reformation had taken to date, a rallying call for national resistance against Spain and other limbs of the Antichrist, and, in the schemes of apocalyptic history being worked out by writers such as John

[45] Fincham, 'Introduction', in id., *Early Stuart Church*, p. 12.

[46] Peter Lake, *Moderate Puritans and the Elizabethan Church* (Cambridge, 1982), chs. 4–6.

Foxe, a guarantee that the Antichrist would eventually be overthrown.[47] MacCulloch has remarked that 'such a monstrous foe made imperfections in the English Church seem comparatively trivial'.[48] Yet there is a sense in which the opposite may sometimes have been the case, for while Protestants agreed that popery was the enemy, they did not always agree about what popery actually was. Among Puritan divines like the Cambridge theologian William Whitaker, there was a tendency to regard any lapse from strict Calvinist orthodoxy as tantamount to popery. Out in the parishes, Puritan ministers were often prone to label opponents of their preaching and strict programmes of moral reformation as 'papists', irrespective of whether they displayed any kind of sympathy for Rome.[49] Some of this was mere name-calling ('papist' the throw-back insult for 'Puritan'), but an expanding definition of the extent of popery was also promoted by the common tendency in this period to view the structure of the world in terms of binary oppositions and inversions. This phenomenon has been most thoroughly explored in the study of early modern witchcraft persecution: contemporaries convinced themselves that there *must* be a counter-society of devil-worshipping witches to mirror the Christian Church giving honour to God.[50] But the same logic was sometimes applied to tensions within Christianity itself: whatever was not explicitly commanded of Christ, was of Antichrist, ergo popery. There was thus a potentially dangerous gulf between conformist bishops and writers who employed a narrow, legalistic definition of popery as the act of being in communion with the Church of Rome, and those Puritans for whom popery was a dangerous, pervasive force which might infect the structure and ceremonies of the Church of England itself.[51] This mentality was a religious landmine, one liable to explode if the time ever came when the actions of leaders of Church and State could plausibly be portrayed as a manifestation of the secret power of the Antichrist.

Such a time did come. In the 1630s, religious policies associated with Archbishop Laud, and the views of theologians patronized by the King

47 Peter Lake, 'The Significance of the Elizabethan Identification of the Pope as Antichrist', *Journal of Ecclesiastical History*, 31 (1980); Christopher Hill, *Antichrist in Seventeenth-Century England* (Oxford, 1971), ch. 1; Anthony Milton, *Catholic and Reformed: The Roman and Protestant Churches in English Protestant Thought 1600–1640* (Cambridge, 1995), ch. 2.

48 MacCulloch, *Later Reformation*, p. 67.

49 Lake, *Moderate Puritans*, p. 286; Alexandra Walsham, *Church Papists: Catholicism, Conformity and Confessional Polemic in Early Modern England* (London, 1993), pp. 111–18.

50 See particularly Stuart Clark, 'Inversion, Misrule and the Meaning of Witchcraft', *Past and Present*, 87 (1980); id., *Thinking with Demons: the Idea of Witchcraft in Early Modern Europe* (Oxford, 1997).

51 Conrad Russell, *The Causes of the English Civil War* (Oxford, 1990), pp. 75–82; Lake, 'Anti-Popery'.

himself, seemed to some designed to cast England back into the net of papistry (see Section 8.3). But 'Laudians' did not emerge in the 1630s out of a spaceship from a far-away galaxy. Looking back even to the early years of Elizabeth's reign, we can identify diverse trends and individuals which, taken together, constituted the materials for constructing a version of English Protestantism very different from that of William Perkins or Archbishop Abbot. It is not, in other words, an entirely pointless exercise to begin looking in this period of 'Calvinist consensus' for the roots of what would later be called 'Anglicanism'. The soil allowing this plant to grow was, once again, the essentially Catholic Church structure inherited in 1558. The anti-Puritan or conformist positions taken in the first half of Elizabeth's reign (by Whitgift and others) tended towards a rather negative or at least neutral defence of the wearing of surplices, kneeling to receive communion, or the institution of episcopacy itself. These things were merely 'not unlawful', matters of decency and order, which properly constituted authority might legitimately insist on. But (as the godly had perhaps feared) the retention of elements of pre-Reformation tradition began over time to encourage a more positive assessment of their place in the life of the Church. This had clearly happened by the last decade of Elizabeth's reign with respect to the office of bishop, partly in indignant response to the presbyterians' accusation that episcopacy was positively unchristian. In 1587 the Dean of Salisbury, John Bridges, published a weighty treatise propounding the (for Protestants) novel opinion that bishops were required in the Church *iure divino*, by divine law. The idea appealed strongly to Whitgift's successor, Richard Bancroft, and was defended in the 1590s by a clutch of anti-Puritan writers including Thomas Bilson, Matthew Sutcliffe and Hadrian Saravia (a refugee from Dutch presbyterianism).[52] To its proponents, belief in *iure divino* episcopacy did not imply any backsliding from the cause of the Reformation: Bridges and Sutcliffe were noted anti-Catholic controversialists, and Bancroft was a firm Calvinist on the issue of predestination. In James's reign *iure divino* became an increasingly orthodox opinion, accepted by Abbot and other 'evangelical' bishops.[53] Nonetheless, the assertion of *iure divino* episcopacy was a potential danger to Protestant unity, narrowing the range of 'things indifferent' over which concessions might be made and accommodations reached. It also implied a degree of distance from continental Protestant Churches which lacked this God-given instrument of government, as well as a stronger sense of institutional continuity with the medieval Church.

That continuity was accentuated by institutions situated (almost literally) in the bishops' backyards: the cathedrals. Ruled by a dean and chapter often virtually independent of the authority of the bishop, and with large numbers

[52] Lake, *Anglicans and Puritans?*, pp. 90–6.
[53] Fincham, *Prelate*, p. 261; Milton, *Catholic and Reformed*, p. 456.

of attached clergy, the English cathedral typically kept much more of its traditional furnishings and devotional style than did the parish church. This was particularly true of music. In their elaborate sung services performed by professional musicians, cathedrals underlined something which made many Protestants uncomfortable: that the liturgies in Cranmer's Book of Common Prayer could be made to look and sound very conservative indeed. Reformers sometimes demanded to know what cathedrals were for in a Protestant Church, and to this, other than the defence that they could serve as centres of preaching, there was no very compelling answer. The anomaly was most striking in the high-profile case of Westminster Abbey, a church under the special jurisdiction of the Crown, and a cathedral in all but name. Under the long rule of the very moderately Protestant Gabriel Goodman (Dean, 1561–1601) Westminster retained its medieval vestments, as well as the use of wafers for the communion (the norm in parish churches was to follow the rubrics of the prayer book rather than the Injunctions on this, and to use 'common bread'). Goodman's Jacobean successors Lancelot Andrewes and Richard Neile were equally 'ceremonialist' in their instincts, and the abbey enjoyed the patronage and protection of the leading ministers William Cecil and his son Robert. Julia Merritt has identified Westminster as a 'cradle of Laudianism', and Diarmaid MacCulloch speaks of a 'Westminster movement', an Elizabethan precursor in the Church of England to the Catholicizing tendencies of the nineteenth-century Oxford Movement.[54]

By the 1590s, this running thread of an un-Calvinist devotional style was being intertwined with a more direct doctrinal challenge to the dominant orthodoxy on predestination. At the universities, a handful of theologians – Antonio del Corro in Oxford, William Barrett, Peter Baro and John Overall in Cambridge – stirred controversy by openly attacking Calvin's views on election. These dissidents were termed 'Arminians', after the Dutch theologian Jacobus Arminius (1560–1609), who had broken ranks with strict Calvinism by teaching that Christ had died for all, and that humans possessed the free will to resist God's grace. Arminius's views were condemned at the Synod of Dort (Dordrecht) in 1618–19, to which an English delegation was sent. In the meantime, Whitgift had attempted to close the issue down by issuing the ultra-Calvinist Lambeth Articles (1595), but the failure of these to be ratified by the Queen was a significant signal that the anti-Arminians could not rely on complete and unquestioning support from the Crown. Proponents of the 'Calvinist Consensus' model rightly insist that anti-predestinarian views were publicly espoused only by a small minority of Protestants in Elizabeth's reign.[55] But more than predestination was at issue

[54] Julia Merritt, 'The Cradle of Laudianism? Westminster Abbey, 1558–1630', *Journal of Ecclesiastical History*, 52 (2001); MacCulloch, *Church Militant*, pp. 210–13.

[55] Russell, *Causes*, p. 91.

in the growing challenge to the dominant pattern of Protestant 'churchmanship': there were questions of the importance of sacraments and ceremonies, and of the relationship of the Church of England to its own past. These themes were powerfully developed in the writings of Richard Hooker (c. 1554–1600). Hooker has traditionally been regarded as the Anglican theologian *par excellence*, but, as Peter Lake suggests, a convincing case can be made that 'Anglicanism' came into existence 'largely because Hooker invented it'.[56] Unlike earlier 'conformists', Hooker presented a highly positive view of ceremonies and rituals as instruments of spiritual growth for the participants, an essential complement to preaching. This led to a much stronger reverence for the visible Church as the channel through which such 'edification' was made available. Whitgift had defended the visible Church on the grounds that the invisible 'true' Church of the elect was unknowable. But Hooker broke more radically with the view, expressed most powerfully by John Foxe, that the true Church's historical continuity was with a succession of individuals and groups who had held out against the Antichrist of Rome. Rather, Hooker insisted on an unbroken succession of the Church of England from its medieval predecessor: its ceremonies were not an embarrassing left-over, but a treasured inheritance. He was even prepared to concede that the Roman Church of his own day, though corrupt, was a part of Christ's visible Church. Here he was opening a can of worms. As we have seen, differing assessments of the threat posed by Rome always potentially threatened to divide English Protestants. Under Elizabeth, Hooker was something of a voice in the wilderness, and only part of his seminal *Laws of Ecclesiastical Polity* was published in his lifetime. But his concerns were nurtured by a group of divines increasingly influential at the Jacobean Court. Peter Lake labels their style of piety 'avant-garde conformity', and identifies as the pivotal figure the renowned preacher Bishop Lancelot Andrewes, friend of Hooker and patron of Arminian clerics, 'the necessary link in the chain... which runs between Hooker and Laud'.[57] While steering clear of direct attacks on predestination, Andrewes and a handful of other court preachers stressed the importance of sacraments and outward reverence in worship. A clear subtext of their message was an attack on a very broadly defined 'Puritanism' – obsessed with predestinarian theorizing, spiritually lifeless and politically subversive.[58] Preachers like Andrewes had no monopoly of the King's ear, and they had to proceed carefully when they were bending it. James has been praised for

[56] Lake, *Anglicans and Puritans?*, p. 227.

[57] Peter Lake, 'Lancelot Andrewes, John Buckeridge, and Avant-garde Conformity at the Court of James I', in Linda Levy Peck, ed., *The Mental World of the Jacobean Court* (Cambridge, 1991), quote at p. 131.

[58] Ibid., pp. 116–20. For detailed treatment of the frequently 'political' character of court preaching, see Lori Anne Ferrel, *Government by Polemic: James I, the King's Preachers, and the Rhetorics of Conformity, 1603–1625* (Stanford, 1998); McCullough, *Sermons*.

maintaining unity by balancing his patronage of 'proto-Arminian' churchmen with continued support for more orthodox Calvinists, and by tolerating a degree of ceremonial nonconformity on the part of Puritans.[59] But there are indications that towards the end of the reign the line was increasingly difficult to hold, and that the King was becoming more open to persuasion about the need to constrain the energies of godly Protestantism. James was alarmed by the extent of opposition to his 1622 proposal for a marriage between Prince Charles and a Spanish Princess, and by the popular rejoicing that greeted Charles's return from Madrid (without a Catholic bride) the following year. Royal chaplains, bishops, and even Archbishop Abbot had agitated against the planned union. In 1622 James issued a set of directions for preachers, which forbade parading the 'deep points' of predestination in front of the people. In 1624 he commended the Bishop of Norwich, Samuel Harsnett, for introducing religious imagery in the churches of his diocese, and he permitted the publication of a provocative work by one of the most audacious anti-Calvinists, Richard Montague. *A New Gagg for an Old Goose* attacked the doctrine of double predestination, and the identification of the pope as Antichrist.[60] All of this hardly amounts to full-scale religious warfare. But there is no doubt that attention to the elements of 'consensus' in Jacobean Protestantism needs to be balanced by a recognition of the ever-present potential for conflict – conflict which in no small measure arose out of the ambiguities built into the Elizabethan Settlement itself.

As a brief postscript to this section we should take note of another of those dynastic accidents that regularly punctuate the narrative of the Reformation in England from the time of Prince Arthur's untimely death in 1502. In 1612, James's eldest son Prince Henry died suddenly of typhoid fever. Henry had been a zealous Protestant, an advocate of militant action against the Catholic powers in Europe. The 'avant-garde conformist' preachers that the King tolerated in the chapel royal had no place in Henry's household at St James's. Had Henry lived to succeed his father in 1625, religious conflicts would have taken an entirely different and probably less disastrous course. Like Henry VIII, Charles I should never have been king.[61]

5.4 Godly Identity

A marked feature of the tensions in the Elizabethan and Jacobean Church was the expression of anti-Puritanism. Hostile stereotypes of Puritans abounded in Elizabethan and Jacobean England. The most famous ones are

59 See works cited in n. 36 above.

60 William Hunt, *The Puritan Moment. The Coming of Revolution in an English County* (Cambridge, MA, 1983), pp. 175, 179–80; Spurr, *Puritanism*, pp. 80–1.

61 See Roy Strong, *Henry, Prince of Wales: England's Lost Renaissance* (London, 1986).

literary: the hypocritical Malvolio in Shakespeare's *Twelfth Night*, the fanatical killjoy Zeal-of-the-Land Busy in Ben Jonson's *Bartholomew Fair*.[62] Puritans were portrayed as self-regarding frauds, 'busy' interferers in their neighbours' affairs, as well as disobedient and subversive. The purpose of this section is to explore what correspondence there was between such images and reality, and to investigate the social and cultural implications of the theological differences between Puritans and non-Puritan Protestants.

Yet to some extent it is misleading simply to ask whether the stereotype fitted the reality, for the two are not in practice easily separable. The most sophisticated recent work in this area has insisted that 'Puritanism' was not a thing in itself but a fluid 'identity' created through the experience of religious and social conflict, and processes of religious labelling. As Patrick Collinson has put it, Puritanism was 'only one half of a stressful relationship'.[63] Contemporaries used the word 'Puritan' as an insult, with connotations of hypocrisy and sanctimoniousness. The people to whom it was applied tended to refer to themselves as 'the godly', though it is wise to remember that 'self-descriptions are as polemically loaded as labels applied by others'.[64] The imprecision of the term 'Puritan', and the heavily value-laden way in which it has been employed has persuaded some historians it would be better simply to abandon it as a concept of analysis.[65] But this may be to miss the point: the fact that there were people whom others began to call Puritans helped in turn to fashion powerful social bonds among the people so maligned. This gets us past the difficulty of trying to employ an external checklist of beliefs and attributes to decide whether an individual was or was not a 'Puritan'. Those conventionally identified as such could hold differing doctrinal and liturgical positions (most significantly, over

62 Patrick Collinson, 'Ben Johnson's *Bartholomew Fair*: The Theatre Constructs Puritanism', in D. Smith, R. Strier and D. Bevington, eds., *The Theatrical City: Culture, Theatre and Politics in London, 1576–1649* (Cambridge, 1995). Collinson argues that the word 'Puritan' came into everyday usage as a result of a wave of satire responding to the Marprelate tracts, though note Peter Lake's argument that anti-Puritan satire was effective precisely because the stereotypes were so instantly recognizable: Peter Lake with Michael Questier, *The Antichrist's Lewd Hat: Protestants, Papists and Players in Post-Reformation England* (New Haven and London, 2002), pp. 568–9, 604.

63 Patrick Collinson, *The Birthpangs of Protestant England: Religious and Cultural Change in the Sixteenth and Seventeenth Centuries* (Basingstoke, 1988), p. 143.

64 Tom Webster, *Godly Clergy in Early Stuart England* (Cambridge, 1997), p. 4. In the course of time, 'Puritans' became increasingly willing to adopt the label as a badge of pride: Peter Lake, '"A Charitable Christian Hatred": The Godly and their Enemies in the 1630s', in Christopher Durston and Jacqueline Eales, eds., *The Culture of English Puritanism 1560–1700* (Basingstoke, 1996), pp. 154–5.

65 See Durston and Eales, 'Introduction', in id., *Puritanism*, pp. 1–2; Kenneth Parker and Eric Carlson, *'Practical Divinty': The Works and Life of Revd Richard Greenham* (Aldershot, 1998), pp. 121–6.

whether to remain in or separate from the Church of England), and their concerns changed over time. Thus issues of Church government exercised the godly in the 1580s in a way they did not in the early 1600s. Probably the most useful approach is to think of 'Puritanism' in terms of a common outlook, ethos or culture, and to note the helpful thumbnail definition provided by John Spurr: 'that which Puritans saw in each other'.[66]

But what did they (and others) see? Puritans based their lives on a distinctive spirituality rooted in the experimental Calvinist tradition. It was their duty to convince themselves that they belonged to the elect, but given humans' general depravity, utter certainty about this was impossible. Introspection and self-discipline were thus the hallmarks of Puritan piety, finding expression in frequent recourse to prayer and fasting, an interest in individual conversion experiences, and in recording fluctuations of pious intensity in spiritual journals or diaries. The idea that Puritans were deeply psychologically damaged individuals may be an unwarranted extrapolation from a handful of well-known cases, such as that of the London artisan Nehemiah Wallington, who attempted suicide ten times because he took lustful feelings as a sign of reprobation.[67] But Protestants who felt quite at ease with themselves can hardly qualify as Puritans. In certain key ways, the religion of Puritans was 'hotter' than that of other Protestants. All Protestants regarded scripture as the basis of their faith: 'the Bible, the Bible only I say, is the religion of Protestants' declared the early Stuart writer, William Chillingworth.[68] But the biblicism of Puritans was peculiarly intense, and explains their dislike of ceremonies in the prayer book, which had no explicit sanction in scripture. Puritans were notable too for preferring the 1560 Geneva Bible (with its extensive Calvinist marginal notes and directions) to the officially encouraged Bishops' Bible of 1568 and Authorized Version of 1611.[69] A more fundamentalist biblicism shone through in attitudes to the keeping of the Ten Commandments, particularly the second (no graven images) and the fourth (respect the Sabbath). Modern scholarship has made clear just how central iconoclasm was to the mainstream Reformation. But after the iconoclastic purges of the mid-Tudor decades Puritans went beyond other Protestants in their acute sensitivity to

[66] Spurr, *Puritanism*, p. 7. For similar attempts to define Puritanism in broad cultural rather than narrowly political or ecclesiastical terms, see Peter Lake, 'Defining Puritanism – again?', in Francis Bremer, ed., *Puritanism: Transatlantic Perspectives on a Seventeenth-Century Anglo-American Faith* (London, 1993); Durston and Eales, *Puritanism*; Webster, *Godly Clergy*.

[67] Paul Seaver, *Wallington's World: A Puritan Artisan in Seventeenth-Century London* (1985), pp. 22–3.

[68] Collinson, *Religion*, p. viii. Chillingworth was an Arminian sympathizer, and Laud's godson.

[69] Ian Green, *Print and Protestantism in Early Modern England* (Oxford, 2000), ch. 2.

the continuing dangers of 'idolatry'. They detested, for example, the husband's vow in the marriage ceremony ('with my body I thee worship') on the grounds that it made an idol out of his wife. Some believed that the Elizabethan authorities had been unforgivably lax in permitting stained-glass windows to be retained in churches, and in exempting funeral monuments from the general ban on three-dimensional images.[70] Protestants in general regarded the injunction to observe the Sabbath as a binding divine law rather than a dispensable ecclesiastical edict, and a study by Kenneth Parker has argued that there was nothing specifically Puritan about the phenomenon of 'sabbatarianism'.[71] But by insisting there was an obligation on all Christians to spend the entire day in religious exercises and to give up all leisure pursuits, sports or pastimes, Puritans increasingly identified themselves with strict sabbatarianism. A divergence in outlook among Protestants was widened after James I permitted Sunday recreations in the 1618 Declaration of Sports. Actions as well as attitudes bound the godly to each other. A Puritan religious subculture found expression in communal fasting (ad hoc occasions, detached from the fast days of the medieval Church), in the singing of versified or 'metrical' psalms (the only form of church music the godly would tolerate), and above all in 'gadding' to sermons – the preaching of competent godly ministers (not the reading of printed homilies and services) was *the* essential instrument of spiritual awakening.[72]

Puritans were religious individualists who clung together for safety and support. They perceived themselves as a beleaguered minority, surrounded by hordes of the ungodly. Though the number of the elect was unknowable, it was usually assumed to be small. The Jacobean preacher John Denison thought perhaps one in ten might be saved; his contemporary Nicholas Byfield was sure that 'almost all that we meet with are malefactors under sentence. . . unquenchable fire kindled against them'.[73] But, paradoxically, people who thought of themselves as a persecuted minority were often in positions of power and influence in Elizabethan and Jacobean England. Where Puritan ministers acquired the support of powerful local lay people, parishes, and even whole towns, could acquire a distinctly Puritan character

70 Margaret Aston, 'Puritanism and Iconoclasm, 1560–1660', in Durston and Eales, *Puritanism*; Peter Marshall, *Beliefs and the Dead in Reformation England* (Oxford, 2002), pp. 168–80.

71 Kenneth Parker, *The English Sabbath: A Study of Doctrine and Discipline from the Reformation to the Civil War* (Cambridge, 1988).

72 Patrick Collinson, 'Elizabethan and Jacobean Puritanism as Forms of Popular Religious Culture', in Durston and Eales, *Puritanism*. Note that alongside preaching godly ministers might hold sacraments, particularly the eucharist, in high regard: Arnold Hunt, 'The Lord's Supper in Early Modern England', *Past and Present*, 161 (1998); Webster, *Godly Clergy*, pp. 113–21.

73 Marshall, *Beliefs*, p. 196.

and reputation. Detailed local case studies, like David Underdown's examination of Dorchester (Dorset) in the early seventeenth century, have shown how godly ministers and magistrates aspired to turn their communities into 'new Jerusalems', beacons of godly piety and order.[74] Here the historiography has become especially controversial, as historians debate the precise relationship between Puritanism and patterns of social control, in a society experiencing population growth and increasing poverty. In particular, there is disagreement about whether Puritanism was the driving force behind a 'reformation of manners', the attempt to regulate and discipline the poor through attacking their raucous traditional culture of festivals, sports and 'ales', and policing their moral behaviour. Puritanism, it has been argued, was a religious ideology which suited the social and economic interests of the industrious 'middling sort'. In an influential study of the Essex village of Terling, Keith Wrightson and David Levine showed how a clique of Puritan yeomen monopolized the local offices of churchwarden, village constable and overseer of the poor, making strenuous efforts to stamp out drunkenness and fornication among the poor at a time when economic divisions in the parish were widening. William Hunt has argued that Puritan motivation lay behind the drive to reform 'manners' across the county of Essex as a whole.[75] These models owe something to the earlier suggestions of R.H. Tawney and Christopher Hill that since Puritan self-discipline and obsession with 'assurance' could produce worldly success, Puritanism appealed particularly to the upper and middling ranks in society, and was a factor in the early development of capitalism.[76]

There has been sharp criticism of these approaches, partly because they seem to imply a rather 'functionalist' or 'reductionist' model of religious belief. It has been pointed out that Puritanism was not exclusively the religion of the 'middling sort', but won adherents from across the social spectrum (something Wrightson or Hunt would not seek to deny, though they insist on a 'disproportionate' appeal to parish elites). In a direct attack on the 'Terling thesis', Margaret Spufford has argued that the impulse to tighten social regulation (particularly of sexual behaviour) was not specific to Puritans, but took place whenever economic circumstances were difficult (for example, in the early fourteenth century). In a parallel study of the Wiltshire village of Keevil, Martin Ingram found evidence of a 'reformation

[74] David Underdown, *Fire from Heaven: Life in an English Town in the Seventeenth Century* (London, 1992). Other centres of active municipal Puritanism included Salisbury, Gloucester and Colchester: Paul Slack, *Poverty and Policy in Tudor and Stuart England* (London, 1988), pp. 150–2.

[75] Keith Wrightson and David Levine, *Poverty and Piety in an English Village: Terling 1525–1700* (London, 1979); Hunt, *Puritan Moment*.

[76] R.H. Tawney, *Religion and the Rise of Capitalism* (London, 1926); Christopher Hill, *Society and Puritanism in Pre-Revolutionary England* (London, 1964).

of manners' similar to that taking place in Terling, though Keevil was a community over which Puritanism exercised little or no influence.[77] In other words, if social divisions in English communities were increasing in this period, Puritanism should not be made to shoulder so much of the blame. In some of his most recent work, Collinson has demonstrated that Puritan preachers were capable of castigating the wealthy and showing a real compassion for the poor.[78] Even the existence of a wide cultural gulf between the mentality of Puritans and that of the common people is now being questioned. The involvement of Puritan ministers in performing exorcisms (of which conformists like Bancroft and Harsnett strongly disapproved) has been presented as an example of the way in which the gap might be bridged.[79] (see also Section 6.3).

But we should not underestimate the potential of Puritanism as an agent of social division. It is notable, for example, that though both Terling and Keevil witnessed a drive against pre-marital sex (a potential drain on the resources of the parish), concerns about alehouses were much more prominent in the former. Drunkenness symbolized the ease with which people's carnal appetites might overwhelm their slender capacity for godliness: for Puritans it was, writes Hunt, 'the emblem of original sin'.[80] Where Puritans were influential there was much less tolerance for the traditional festive culture of ales, wakes and maypoles, though (a problem for any simplistic 'social control' thesis) these were often defended by other members of the local elite.[81] Where there was a strong Puritan presence there was almost bound to be division. Strict sabbatarianism proved virtually impossible to impose on non-Puritans (though Puritans invariably tried), and Collinson writes of 'wars of religion' in towns like Banbury, where Puritan and anti-Puritan factions clashed over maypoles and Morris dancing, and over

77 Margaret Spufford, 'Puritanism and Social Control?', in Anthony Fletcher and John Stevenson, eds., *Order and Disorder in Early Modern England* (Cambridge, 1985); Martin Ingram, 'Religion, Communities and Moral Discipline in Late Sixteenth- and Early Seventeenth-Century England', in Kaspar von Greyerz, ed., *Religion and Society in Early Modern Europe, 1500–1800* (London, 1984).

78 Patrick Collinson, 'Christian Socialism in Elizabethan Suffolk: Thomas Carew and his *Caveat for Clothiers*', in Carole Rawcliffe, Roger Virgoe and Richard Wilson, eds., *Counties and Communities: Essays on East Anglian History* (Norwich, 1996); 'Puritanism and the Poor', in Rosemary Horrox and Sarah Rees Jones, eds., *Pragmatic Utopias: Ideals and Communities, 1200–1630* (Cambridge, 2001).

79 Thomas Freeman, 'Demons, Deviance and Defiance: John Darrell and the Politics of Exorcism in Late Elizabethan England', in Peter Lake and Michael Questier, eds., *Conformity and Orthodoxy in the English Church, c. 1560–1660* (Woodbridge, 2000).

80 Hunt, *Puritan Moment*, p. 128.

81 Jeremy Goring, *Godly Exercises or the Devil's Dance? Puritanism and Popular Culture in Pre-Civil War England* (London, 1983), pp. 8–9.

whether or not the famous market crosses should be allowed to stand.[82] We are back here to our earlier definition of Puritanism as a religious identity forged in conflict and name-calling. Puritans became identifiable because they attempted to impose their vision of godly discipline and moral reformation on the rest of society. As Hunt wittily puts it, 'a Puritan who minds his own business is a contradiction in terms'. [83] And even in conducting their own business, Puritans seemed to offer rebuke to others, where possible shunning the company of the 'ungodly'. Indeed, it has been argued that precisely because the great majority of Puritans remained inside the Church of England they felt impelled to keep themselves pure by practising a kind of 'separation within the Church'. In some parishes in Kent, Sussex and Northamptonshire at the end of the sixteenth century, the godly's children were marked off with such exotic names as 'Praise-God', 'Sure-Trust' and 'Bethankful'. A few Puritan ministers carried internal separatism to an extreme by trying to restrict access to the communion in their parishes to a network of the godly.[84] Jesus warned his disciples that he came 'not to send peace, but a sword'. It was a teaching many Puritans had internalized all too well.

Summation

One insight which draws together many of the divergent approaches to Elizabethan and Jacobean religion in recent scholarship is a recognition that this period belongs at the heart of 'the Reformation' as a unit of meaningful historical analysis, that its religious quarrels and tensions were not, as was once thought, 'residual problems' to be cleared up backstage after the Elizabethan Settlement had brought down the curtain on the main show. 'The Reformation', Collinson is prepared to assert, 'was something which happened in the reigns of Elizabeth and James I'.[85] This was certainly so if we think of the Reformation as the attempt to turn the mass of the people

[82] Spurr, *Puritanism*, p. 183; Collinson, *Birthpangs*, pp. 137–41, here conceding that the picture of consensual Calvinistic Protestantism presented in his *Religion of Protestants* 'runs the risk of undervaluing both the scale and the intensity of localised conflicts'.

[83] Hunt, *Puritan Moment*, p. 146.

[84] Patrick Collinson, 'The Cohabitation of the Faithful with the Unfaithful', in Ole Grell, Jonathan Israel and Nicholas Tyacke, eds., *From Persecution to Toleration: The Glorious Revolution and Religion in England* (Oxford, 1991); Nicholas Tyacke, 'Popular Puritan Mentality in Late Elizabethan England', in his *Aspects of English Protestantism c. 1530–1700* (Manchester, 2001); Collinson, *Religion*, p. 269.

[85] Collinson, *Birthpangs*, p. ix. 'Residual Problems' is the penultimate chapter in A.G. Dickens, *The English Reformation*, (2nd ed., London, 1989).

into convinced Protestants, a process begun, but in some places barely begun, before 1559. The success (or otherwise) of reformers in Protestantizing the beliefs and culture of the nation as a whole is the subject of the next chapter. But to contemporaries the question of whether the institutions and liturgies of the Church itself had been sufficiently Protestantized remained a distinctly moot point. The Settlement of 1559 (enacted before even the Protestant leadership of the Church had been put into place) sought to close down all discussion of this, at least as Elizabeth (and in general James too) understood it. It was as if the referee had come on to the pitch to blow the final whistle just after the start of the second half. Many could not accept that the game was over, but it was not a matter of 'Puritans' crying foul from the sidelines, as 'Anglicans' carried off the ball in triumph. Modern research has allowed us to feel confident that 'Anglicanism' was a later *interpretation* of the Elizabethan Settlement rather than its self-evident essence; confident too (thanks largely to Patrick Collinson) that Puritans were important shareholders in the Church, and sometimes members of the Board, not disenfranchised outsiders. But any talk of 'consensus' requires considerable qualification and subtlety of definition. The Jacobean Church was no ecclesiastical Garden of Eden, but rather 'riven with friction and disagreement'.[86] In paying greater attention to the processes of name-calling by which 'Puritans', 'papists' or 'Arminians' were identified, historians are coming to understand how factionalism and polarization in the Church were to a considerable degree self-fulfilling prophecies. But the spaces in which such rancour could find oxygen were provided by the ambiguities of the 1559 Settlement itself, a set of distinctly *unsettled* questions about what the Church of England was, had been, and should become. According to Peter Lake there was really no such thing as a unitary Elizabethan settlement, 'but merely a number of competing readings of a series of inherently ambiguous, even unstable, legal, social, institutional and theological "texts"'. In more homely fashion, Conrad Russell has described the years between 1559 and 1625 as the setting for an ongoing 'custody battle' for ownership of the Church.[87] That battle would intensify sharply after 1625, with the added and immensely complicating factor that the Crown itself seemed to have become a party to the dispute, rather than the judge presiding over the case.

86 Fincham, 'Introduction', p. 11.
87 Lake, 'Defining Puritanism', p. 29; Russell, *Causes*, p. 84.

6

Religions of the People 1560–1630

Overview

The English Reformation did happen. As Patrick Collinson wittily puts it, there comes a point when 'the insomniac historian needs to start counting a minority of Catholics rather than a gaggle of Protestants in order to get to sleep'.[1] There is a growing consensus among historians that this transition should be dated no earlier than the second or third decade of Elizabeth's reign. But as the historiography of the Reformation enters its 'post-revisionist' phase, it is increasingly the quality rather than the quantity, or simple fact of English Protestantism, that is becoming the key point. In a formulation positively begging to be placed on examination papers with 'Discuss' tagged on to it, Christopher Haigh sees the achievement of Elizabethan reformers as 'creating a Protestant nation, but not a nation of Protestants'.[2] Any student attempting the question would be well advised to start by noting that it depends what you mean by 'Protestant'. The definitions and perspectives involved are both our own, and those of contemporary commentators, many of whom were quick to insist that 'the people' were hardly touched by the essential message of the gospel, and were at best 'cold-statute Protestants' who attended church in accordance with the law, and with a hazy notion that being a Christian involved trying to avoid sinfulness and trying to get on with your neighbours.

This chapter surveys the evidence about the beliefs and practices – the religious culture – of those English people who were neither the godly (discussed in the last chapter) nor self-consciously Catholics (the subject of the

1 Patrick Collinson, 'Anti-Papist, Anti-Puritan', in Henry Chadwick, ed., *Not Angels, but Anglicans* (Norwich, 2000), p. 144.

2 Christopher Haigh, *English Reformations: Religion, Politics, and Society under the Tudors* (Oxford, 1993), p. 280.

next). Such people were surely in numerical terms a majority through most, if not all, of this period, but we should resist the temptation to suppose that they necessarily comprised a coherent third category, in some sense the normative default position of English Christianity. Terms and definitions are the necessary tools of historical understanding, but here they are particularly difficult to use without the risk of hammering one's thumb. Is the religion(s) of the people the same as 'popular religion'? The latter is a very useful shorthand expression, but one that risks implying an intrinsically oppositional relationship to 'elite' or 'official' religion, as well as a fundamental uniformity of outlook among subordinate groups.[3] The subject can be recast as 'conformity' or 'conformist religion', an apparently more neutral formulation, but one fraught with its own interpretative problems. Conformism might signify a mere pattern of behaviour, doing what one is told irrespective of inner conviction, or it might betoken an ideological commitment to a particular ideal of Church order. Under both definitions, its forms and meanings would shift over time. Definitional difficulties are compounded by evidential ones. Since, by their very nature, conformists tend not to antagonize the authorities, they do not generate anything like the volume of records produced in the course of disciplining nonconformists and deviants. Nonetheless, an increasing body of scholarship, which we can loosely term post-revisionist, is attempting to enter the mindset of those who absorbed and adapted to the later English Reformation – a necessary complement to the attention traditionally lavished on the people ('papists and Puritans') who actively resisted or aggressively promoted it. Post-revisionists, while usually conceding the case for the strengths of traditional Catholicism, are disinclined to accept that Protestantism and popular culture were simply naturally antithetical, unable to find 'points of contact' with each other. Decisive changes in English cultural life – such as the growth of popular anti-Catholicism – were discernible within a generation or two of the Elizabethan settlement, and make it possible to identify the English Reformation as a success, even (in Diarmaid MacCulloch's phrase) 'a howling success'.[4] But, as with debates in the 1970s and 80s about success and failure in the German Reformation, meaningful assessments require an acknowledgement of whose criteria for success and failure is being adopted. In an influential article, Gerald Strauss argued that the educational and spiritual attainments of Lutheran parishioners in the 1570s fell dramatically short of what Luther would have considered acceptable, a template Christopher Haigh applies to the Reformation in England at the end of the sixteenth century: 'by the standards evangelical ministers set themselves, it

[3] See Christopher Marsh, *Popular Religion in Sixteenth-Century England: Holding their Peace* (Basingstoke, 1998), introduction.

[4] Diarmaid MacCulloch, 'The Impact of the English Reformation', *Historical Journal*, 38 (1995), 152.

had failed'.[5] There is an irony in the fact that historians who are more optimistic about the long-term potential of Protestant teachings to strike a chord with the populace (such as Robert Scribner for Germany, or Peter Lake, Alexandra Walsham and Tessa Watt for England) have attributed this success in large measure to an accommodation to traditional preoccupations, a willingness to employ 'images and elements from pre-Reformation religious culture'.[6] This begs the question not only of whether reformers of the first generation would have approved, but also of whether the resultant synthesis really deserves to be termed 'Protestant' at all.

It is around these poles of continuity/discontinuity and success/failure that assessments of the English Reformation as a process of cultural transformation are currently revolving. The first section of this chapter discusses the chronology and methods of attempts to 'Protestantize' the people. The second looks at recent approaches to the issue of 'conformity', and the various forms it may or may not have taken. The third examines how historians have increasingly been turning to a close reading of literary and printed sources in an attempt to penetrate the 'inner' aspects of popular religious belief. Distilling all these complex issues and approaches might leave the following agenda for discussion: how (and when) did the mass of the English people become Protestant, and how Protestant did they actually become?

6.1 Protestantizing the People

The country Elizabeth inherited in 1558 was certainly not 'a nation of Protestants'. If it were to become one, the primary impetus would need to come from a reformed ministry, able to preach the Word, and instruct parishioners in the essentials of the Protestant faith. Yet the parish clergy might seem to be part of the problem rather than the solution. The fact that the vast majority of them were prepared to conform outwardly to the Elizabethan Settlement (only about 300 nationwide were deprived for refusing the oath of supremacy) was a distinctly double-edged triumph for the authorities. In countless parishes, the official representative of the Church was a man who had taken orders under Henry or Mary, with the expectation that his ministry would involve saying mass and hearing confessions, rather than regular preaching. Some of these we have met already. Robert Parkyn, the deeply conservative chronicler of religious

[5] Gerald Strauss, 'Success and Failure in the German Reformation', *Past and Present*, 67 (1975); Christopher Haigh, 'Success and Failure in the English Reformation', *Past and Present*, 173 (2001), 49.

[6] Robert Scribner, *Popular Culture and Popular Movements in Reformation Germany* (London, 1987), p. 353. See Section 6.3.

reform remained in his Yorkshire parish till his death in 1569; Christopher Trychay, vicar of Eamon Duffy's Morebath, was in post from 1520 to 1574.[7] Such men were not necessarily actively working against the Reformation, but the authorities viewed them with suspicion. A 1571 Act of Parliament required explicit subscription to the Thirty-Nine Articles from any clergyman ordained under Henry or Mary, and an examination of parish clergy undertaken in 1575 for Archbishop Grindal of York distinguished between those who were 'minister' (ordained since 1559), and those who were 'sacerdos pontificius' (papal priest).[8] The problem was compounded by a serious clergy shortage inherited from the troubled mid-Tudor decades: many non-preaching curates acquired parish livings as rectors and vicars in the 1560s when the Church could not afford to be choosy, and were often still there decades later. In the little East Yorkshire parish of Carnaby, John Otes (a priest ordained under Mary) was appointed vicar in 1568 and died in office in 1600, having spent the intervening years locked in tithe disputes with his parishioners, and failing to provide them with sermons or catechism classes. In the meantime, the Reformation passed Carnaby by.[9]

As Haigh has noted, for a long time the Church of England was 'a Protestant Church with many Catholic, or at least conservative, clergy'.[10] But this striking continuity may not always simply have inoculated communities against the impact of change. Puritans, like the returning Genevan exile Anthony Gilby, fulminated against 'old monks and friars, and old popish priests. . . allowed in the place of true and faithful pastors', but the presence of such familiar faces could make the introduction of new services more palatable, and smooth the transition to the new order. Mark Byford has produced a fascinating case study of the ministry of one former monk, William Sheppard, vicar of Heydon in Essex between 1541 and 1586, and (unlike Otes of Carnaby) a devoted pastor, who spent considerable sums on charitable works in his parish, and made the effort to preach. Byford concludes that though Sheppard never underwent a formal Protestant conversion, his later life was shaped by 'a series of conforming experiences', and that by the end of his life 'he had long left many aspects of the old world

7 A.G. Dickens, *The English Reformation* (2nd ed., London, 1989), p. 30; Eamon Duffy, *The Voices of Morebath: Reformation and Rebellion in an English Village* (New Haven and London, 2001), p. 190.

8 Patrick McGrath and Joy Rowe, 'The Marian Priests under Elizabeth I', *Recusant History*, 17 (1984–5), 65; Peter Marshall, *The Face of the Pastoral Ministry in the East Riding, 1525–1595* (York, 1995), p. 2.

9 Peter Marshall, 'Discord and Stability in an Elizabethan Parish: John Otes and Carnaby, 1563–1600', *Yorkshire Archaeological Journal*, 71 (1999).

10 Christopher Haigh, 'The Church of England, the Catholics, and the People', in Peter Marshall, ed., *The Impact of the English Reformation 1500–1640* (London, 1997), p. 237.

behind'.[11] The same could surely be said for many of his parishioners, and of lay people right across Elizabethan England.

In any case, the old priests did not live forever. A generational turnover can be discerned in the 1570s/80s with the arrival of large numbers of new clergy who had been brought up as Protestants. With the easing of the mid-century recruitment crisis, these were increasingly likely to be university graduates. At Cambridge, the new colleges of Sidney Sussex and Emmanuel were founded in the 1580s with the explicit purpose of 'rendering as many persons as possible fit for the sacred ministry' – a Protestant (in Emmanuel's case, markedly Puritan) counterpart to the Catholic seminaries set up by the Council of Trent. The 'graduatization' of the clergy was a slow and uneven process, a kind of ripple effect outwards from the two universities, which meant that most Yorkshire incumbents were non-graduate even at the close of the sixteenth century. But by the 1620s, graduates were in a majority everywhere, and in some dioceses held an effective monopoly.[12] Graduates could (in theory) do what a minister was supposed to do: preach. As we have seen, Queen Elizabeth was no fan of unfettered preaching, preferred the reading of the official *Homilies*, and had suppressed the 'prophesyings' which Archbishop Grindal considered such a valuable pastoral exercise. But if Protestantizing the people meant preaching to them, there was a lot of Protestantizing going on by the early seventeenth century, particularly in market towns, where clergy from the vicinity often took turns to supply sermons on a formal basis ('lectures by combination'), and where local authorities often appointed town 'lecturers', who could concentrate on preaching free from the constraints of parish responsibilities.[13]

But did preaching necessarily create Protestants? Christopher Haigh thinks not. Sermons were long and tedious. Where they dealt with predestination, they were likely to alarm and mystify their hearers; where they attacked traditional festive culture, they antagonized them. 'The preaching campaign had produced only a small minority of godly Protestants, leaving the rest in ignorance, indifference or downright apathy'.[14] Furthermore,

11 Mark Byford, 'The Price of Protestantism: Assessing the Impact of Religious Change on Elizabethan Essex: The Cases of Heydon and Colchester' (Oxford D.Phil. thesis, 1988), quotes at pp. 35, 82.

12 Rosemary O'Day, *The English Clergy: The Emergence and Consolidation of a Profession 1558–1642* (Leicester, 1979), pp. 133–4; Marshall, *Pastoral Ministry*, p. 13; Patrick Collinson, *The Religion of Protestants: The Church in English Society 1559–1625* (Oxford, 1982), pp. 94–5.

13 Patrick Collinson, *Godly People: Essays on English Protestantism and Puritanism* (London, 1983), pp. 467–98. See also the essays in id. and John Craig, eds., *The Reformation in English Towns* (Basingstoke, 1998).

14 Haigh, 'Church of England', pp. 243–6. Yet for evidence that sermons could be entertaining and emotionally exciting, see Francis Bremer and Ellen Rydell, 'Performance Art? Puritans in the Pulpit', *History Today* (Sep. 1995); Alexandra Walsham, *Providence in Early Modern England* (Oxford, 1999), pp. 315–19.

Haigh has argued that the 'professionalization' of the parish ministry involved the distancing of pastors from parishioners. University education, rising social status, and an extremely high incidence of intermarriage among clerical families, led to the emergence of a new clerical 'caste', and a clericalist insistence on the rights and dignity of the clergy, which in turn provoked growing anticlericalism. By the early seventeenth century there was no shortage of clerical writers ready to affirm that 'there was never more. . . contempt of the ministry'.[15] Haigh's pithy insistence that anticlericalism was a result not a cause of the English Reformation (see Section 1.2) has not convinced all critics. He can be accused of applying different standards of interpretation to pre- and post-Reformation examples of 'anticlericalism' (the former untypical, the latter representative), and of paying disproportionate attention to disruptive Puritan ministers, when more pastorally sensitive colleagues kept out of the limelight (and the courts). Complaints that the ministry was held in contempt had been common for centuries.[16] But though it is important to note continuities, it is undeniable that the interaction of pastors and people in the Elizabethan and Jacobean Church took place in a changed context. The Protestant clergy had surrendered the claim to status based on a unique ability to perform the miracle of the mass, and unsurprisingly sought to reclaim it by stressing their dignity as 'ministers of the Word'.[17] The loss of another pre-Reformation sacramental function, the hearing of confessions, was equally significant, removing an occasion for individual regulation and pastoral oversight of all members of the community. An Essex parishioner, commenting in 1570 on the clergy's difficulties in collecting personal tithes, thought it was 'by reason of auricular confession then moving their good conscience in those days more than good preaching can do now'.[18] The long-term effects of confession's demise are difficult to gauge. Collinson goes so far as to suggest that its disappearance, without the institution of an effective disciplinary replacement, is the closest thing to a sole explanation of why eventually the Church of England 'found itself ministering to a largish sect rather than a nation'.[19] Confession had provided an opportunity for testing the religious knowledge of parishioners, as well as for dishing out

15 Christopher Haigh, 'Anticlericalism and the English Reformation', in id., ed., *The English Reformation Revised* (Cambridge, 1987), pp. 58, 73–4; 'Anticlericalism and Clericalism, 1580–1640', in Nigel Aston and Mathew Cragoe, eds., *Anticlericalism in Britain, c. 1500–1914* (Stroud, 2000), p. 18.

16 Marsh, *Popular Religion*, pp. 91–2; Peter Marshall, *The Catholic Priesthood and the English Reformation* (Oxford, 1994), p. 227.

17 Eric Carlson, 'The Boring of the Ear: Shaping the Pastoral Vision of Preaching in England, 1540–1640', in Larissa Taylor, ed., *Preachers and People in the Reformations and Early Modern Period* (Brill, 2001).

18 Byford, 'Price of Protestantism', p. 86.

19 Patrick Collinson, 'Shepherds, Sheepdogs, and Hirelings: The Pastoral Ministry in Post-Reformation England', *Studies in Church History*, 26 (1989), p. 219.

spiritual advice, and for both reasons many ministers felt something significant had been lost. Some, like the godly Cambridgeshire pastor Richard Greenham, encouraged people in their congregations with troubled consciences to come for private 'conferring', but as with all forms of voluntary self-improvement, this must have had little impact on those thought to be most in need of it.[20]

If preaching was often to the converted, and conferring was limited to those already in the team, one aspect of the post-Reformation pastoral effort had an effect in theory on all members of the parish community: the teaching of the catechism. Catechisms were summaries of essential Christian knowledge, in question-and-answer format. An official version was included in the 1559 prayer book, and bishops' Injunctions demanded that weekly catechism classes be held for the parish youth, and that no one be admitted to communion who did not know the catechism's contents.[21] By the early seventeenth century England was awash with catechisms. The leading historian of the subject, Ian Green, estimates that about half a million copies of the official catechism were in circulation, as well as over three-quarters of a million copies of the numerous alternative versions that ministers had produced in response to the perceived inadequacies of the former.[22] It is hard to believe that such a torrent of educational print had no cultural impact, even if we cannot assume that people believed exactly what the catechism told them to. Indeed, Haigh, whose earlier work emphasized the unpopularity and ineffectiveness of catechizing, has more recently conceded that the teaching of the catechism was the 'one great educational success' of the Church of England. Comparing visitation reports of the 1570s with those of the 1600s, he finds evidence that the age of those being reported for ignorance was falling, as well as a suggestion in the language being used by churchwardens that such ignorance was more socially unacceptable. But this was an ambivalent success. The official catechism demanded knowledge of a small number of key texts – the Creed, Ten Commandments and Lord's Prayer – and had nothing on the doctrines of justification and predestination which godly ministers considered essential for the development of a true Protestant faith.[23] There was a broader range of treatment in the unofficial catechisms, but here too Green has found that

20 Eric Carlson, '"Practical Divinity": Richard Greenham's Ministry in Elizabethan England', in id., ed., *Religion and the English People 1500–1640* (Kirksville, MO, 1998), pp. 173–4.

21 W.H. Frere and W.M. Kennedy, eds., *Visitation Articles and Injunctions of the Period of the Reformation*, (3 vols, London, 1910), iii. 22, 88, 101, 166, 258–9.

22 Ian Green, '"For Children in Yeeres and Children in Understanding": The Emergence of the English Catechism under Elizabeth and the Early Stuarts', *Journal of Ecclesiastical History*, 37 (1986), 425; *The Christian's ABC: Catechisms and Catechizing in England, c. 1530–1740* (Oxford, 1996).

23 Haigh, 'Success and Failure', pp. 46–7.

'hard' doctrines like predestination were downplayed in the best-selling titles.[24] Again, a judgement as to whether catechizing helped produce a nation of Protestants depends upon the definition of Protestant we are prepared to accept.

In the lowest common denominator sense of Protestant as 'not Catholic', there are good reasons for looking to the 1580s as the time when Collinson's 'birthpangs of Protestant England' actually produced the baby.[25] As we have seen, it was around now that the remnants of the Catholic parish clergy were dying off, giving way to younger Protestant replacements, something of course also true of the population as a whole. The generation which came to adulthood in the 1580s had no personal memory of Catholic England, even in its brief Marian encore.[26] The visitation reports and court records of this decade also supply the last examples of some traditional Catholic practices taking place within the parish, most notably the ringing of church bells at Halloween for the souls of the dead.[27] At the same time, war with Spain, culminating in the national deliverance from Philip II's Armada in 1588, was strengthening the identification of popery with perfidy, and Protestantism with patriotism.

Yet is it appropriate to think about the beliefs of the people simply as a swapping of allegiance, the tenets of Catholicism for those of Protestantism? An influential interpretation points towards a vital third dimension here: an array of popular beliefs about the supernatural, distinct from (and sometimes incompatible with) the orthodoxies of both Protestantism and Catholicism, a world of 'magic' rather than 'religion'. In his monumental study *Religion and the Decline of Magic*, Keith Thomas produced a mass of (admittedly anecdotal and impressionistic) evidence for widespread belief in magical healing, astrology, prophecy, the abilities of 'cunning men' and 'wise women', signs and omens, ghosts, fairies and (above all) witchcraft. Moreover, it was Thomas's contention that an effect of the Reformation was to drive a greater wedge between official and 'popular' belief. In the Middle Ages, the rituals and sacraments of the Church (holy water and candles, images, relics, the mass itself) had constituted a 'vast reservoir of magical power', which, with some semi-official connivance, ordinary people could draw upon to guard themselves against the forces of evil and mishap

24 Green, 'English Catechism', 406; *Christian's ABC*, pp. 356–86.

25 Though Collinson points slightly earlier, to the 1570s, as the time when Protestants ceased being a minority: *The Birthpangs of Protestant England: Religious and Cultural Change in the Sixteenth and Seventeenth Centuries* (Basingstoke, 1988), p. ix.

26 The importance of generational turnover as the key element in the implementation of the Reformation is emphasized by Norman Jones, *The English Reformation: Religion and Cultural Adaptation* (Oxford, 2002).

27 Peter Marshall, *Beliefs and the Dead in Reformation England* (Oxford, 2002), pp. 128–32.

in the world (see Section 1.1). But the Protestant reclassifying of all of these as unacceptable 'superstitions' left people bereft of plausible protection through the agency of the Church, and more likely to seek the advice of village conjurors, as well as to instigate legal action against those they suspected of trying to harm them through supernatural means – an at least partial explanation for the intensified witchcraft persecution of the later sixteenth and early seventeenth centuries.[28]

There is no doubt that interest in various types of 'magical' explanation was commonplace in Elizabethan and early Stuart England, and by no means confined to the lower orders – Elizabeth herself consulted the astrologer John Dee, and like other early modern monarchs, she encouraged the belief that the royal touch was an effective remedy for the glandular disease scrofula ('the king's evil').[29] The question is rather how important such beliefs were to the people who entertained them, and whether they constituted a significant rival to the explanations provided by official Protestant Christianity. Certainty is likely to elude us here. On the basis of sources revealing the preoccupations of the elite – court proceedings, private letters – Diarmaid MacCulloch declares himself 'impressed by how little talk there is of witches and magic'.[30] Ronald Hutton has argued that beliefs about ghosts and the 'magical' properties of hallowed candles, Easter crosses and cakes ('hot-cross buns') survived to become 'folklore' because the Protestant authorities by and large did not view them as important enough to persecute with any vigour.[31] Historians of Mediterranean societies have been able to paint a more vivid picture of a range of unorthodox beliefs because the Catholic Inquisitions had the job of policing popular 'superstition'.[32] But the English Church courts did not pursue people for holding irregular views about the supernatural, so long as they came to church regularly and paid their tithes.

What we can say is that large elements of the 'magical' outlook of common people were not incompatible with the orthodox faith taught by theologians. Thus, Protestant authorities had no difficulty accepting that

28 Keith Thomas, *Religion and the Decline of Magic: Studies in Popular Beliefs in Sixteenth- and Seventeenth-Century England* (London, 1971).

29 David Starkey, *Elizabeth* (London, 2000), pp. 263–4; Thomas, *Religion*, pp. 227–8.

30 Diarmaid MacCulloch, *The Later Reformation in England, 1547–1603* (2nd ed., Basingstoke, 2001), p. 140.

31 Ronald Hutton, 'The English Reformation and the Evidence of Folklore', *Past and Present*, 148 (1995).

32 For example, David Gentilcore, *From Bishop to Witch: The System of the Sacred in Early Modern Terra d'Otronto* (Manchester, 1992); Carlo Ginzburg, *The Cheese and the Worms: The Cosmos of a Sixteenth-Century Miller*, tr. John and Anne Tedeschi (London, 1980); Henry Kamen, *The Spanish Inquisition: A Historical Revision* (London, 1997), ch. 12.

spirits, angels, demons and ghosts were at work in the world – though they usually insisted that the latter were delusions of the devil not souls of the dead.[33] Most significantly, belief in the dangers posed by witchcraft was shared cultural ground between elites and commons. The persecution of witches was a broader European phenomenon, but in England (where up to 500, mainly women, were put to death under the terms of successive statutes in 1542, 1563 and 1604) it looks like a genuinely collaborative effort between the law, Protestant divinity and the fears of the people. Priorities and emphases differed: English villagers were most exercised by the witches' ability to cause harm to their children and livestock through the performance of wicked spells ('maleficium'), while theologians were more concerned about their abandoning the worship of God for that of the devil – the ultimate heresy. But the most sophisticated recent research reveals the potential for two-way traffic and the interpenetration of elite and popular ideas: the theologians' interest in pacts made with the devil were increasingly entering popular testimony by the end of the sixteenth century, while the 'folkloric' notion of witches' 'familiars' (pet spirits in animal shape) was coming to be taken seriously in the conduct of trials.[34] We should resist the temptation to collapse altogether into one another the categories of popular magic and lay Christianity – people who visited the local cunning man to find out the whereabouts of stolen goods were doing something of which the minister disapproved, and likely knew it. But to suppose that the average rural dweller was Christian in name only, inhabiting a universe governed absolutely by the rules of sympathetic magic – a thesis that has been advanced in the context of the European Counter-Reformation – is unconvincing.[35] Christopher Marsh may have it about right when he characterizes alternative 'magical' culture as 'one part of a syncretic blend that was dominated by more orthodox Christianity'.[36] Nor should we overlook the possibility that Protestantism was capable of generating its own methods for understanding and controlling the supernatural world – new (or adapted) forms of 'magic' (see Section 6.3 below).

Perhaps, however, the alternative to orthodox Protestantism was more prosaic than a rich mesh of magical beliefs. It was a preacher's commonplace that at sermon time the church would be empty and the alehouse full.[37] In the view of some historians, ignorance, indifference and irreverence were serious problems confronting the Church, and absenteeism from

[33] See the essays in John Newton, ed., *Early Modern Ghosts* (Durham, 2002).
[34] Among the vast recent scholarship, James Sharpe, *Instruments of Darkness: Witchcraft in England 1550–1750* (London, 1996) is the surest guide.
[35] Jean Delumeau, *Catholicism between Luther and Voltaire: A New View of the Counter-Reformation*, tr. Jeremy Moiser (London, 1977).
[36] Marsh, *Popular Religion*, p. 154.
[37] Collinson, *Religion*, pp. 203–4.

services was endemic. Keith Thomas observed that some churches were too small to house even half their potential congregations, and took the view that many of the poorer sorts simply never became regular churchgoers.[38] The view was buttressed by Ronald Marchant's study of Church courts in the large diocese of York, which suggested that considerable numbers of people were formally cut off from the Church through excommunication (often for failing to attend court): such inveterate non-attendees and their families may have amounted to 15 per cent of the population – a subculture of 'ethical dissenters' who scorned ecclesiastical discipline and conventional morality.[39] Those who did attend may often have behaved badly; Thomas collated enough complaints of sleeping, jostling, chatting and sarcastic interruption to conclude that 'the tone of many Elizabethan congregations seems to have been that of a tiresome class of schoolboys'.[40]

But more recent assessments have tended to be more optimistic, and to be sceptical of a widespread irreverence at odds with the norms of official Christianity. If there is substance to the notion of an 'alehouse culture' flaunting drunkenness and fornication in opposition to the values of respectable churchgoing society, the divide was most likely along generational rather than social or ideological lines. Historians have become increasingly aware of the existence of a subculture of disorderly youth in early modern England, but one that hardly threatened to overthrow the status quo, as its members continually graduated into householding respectability.[41] The opposition of church and alehouse was a homilist's cliché, before the Reformation as after it, but we need not assume that the same people could not frequent both: the seventeenth-century antiquary John Aubrey noted the custom in one North Yorkshire parish for the parishioners to troop to the alehouse after receiving the sacrament to 'drink together as a testimony of charity and friendship'.[42] There are certainly examples of boorish or inattentive behaviour in church, before the Reformation as well as after, though we should note that these were offences for which people were reported by fellow parishioners, and can hardly have been the norm. Low levels of church attendance may also have

[38] Thomas, *Religion*, pp. 189–90. See also Christopher Hill, 'Irreligion in the "Puritan" Revolution', in J.F. McGregor and B. Reay, eds., *Radical Religion in the English Revolution* (Oxford, 1984), pp. 192–4; Peter Clark, 'The Alehouse and the Alternative Society', in Donald Pennington and Keith Thomas, eds., *Puritans and Revolutionaries* (Oxford, 1978).

[39] Ronald Marchant, *The Church under the Law: Justice, Administration and Discipline in the Diocese of York, 1560–1640* (Cambridge, 1969), pp. 227, 243.

[40] Thomas, *Religion*, pp. 191–2.

[41] Paul Griffiths, *Youth and Authority: Formative Experiences in England 1560–1640* (Oxford, 1996), pp. 390–402; Martin Ingram, *Church Courts, Sex and Marriage in England, 1570–1640* (Cambridge, 1987), pp. 354–5, 365.

[42] Marshall, *Priesthood*, p. 91; Marsh, *Popular Religion*, p. 50.

been less common than Thomas assumed. Martin Ingram's study of the Church courts in the post-1570 period modified Marchant's pessimistic view to reveal an impressive level of compliance with summonses to appear (in some archdeaconries exceeding 90 per cent). Overall, Ingram considered the prestige and efficiency of the Church courts to be rising in the later sixteenth century (after a mid-Tudor dip), and observed them increasing their efforts, in conjunction with local authorities, to enforce regular church attendance, something 'far more widely accepted by the 1620s and 1630s than. . . in the middle years of Elizabeth's reign'.[43] Sets of diocesan communicants' returns for Ely and London in 1603 suggest only 1–2 per cent of eligible communicants staying resolutely away from church.[44]

Weekly church attendance was never uniform, but it was a social norm (particularly for householders) and not all absentees were in the alehouse: one Cambridgeshire man, presented by the churchwardens for irregular churchgoing, explained that he and his wife staggered their attendance so one of them could look after their two young children. The case against him was dismissed.[45] We can be reasonably sure that by the last years of the sixteenth century the great majority of the adult population came fairly regularly to church, had some exposure to formal Protestant teaching, and considered themselves to be orthodox Protestant Christians. One Somerset curate, questioned about the beliefs of a deceased parishioner in the 1630s, replied that she 'was for ought he knew a Protestant, for she came ordinarily and duly to church'.[46] But was this enough to make her so?

6.2 Ways of Conforming

How can we begin to understand the religious experience of those conformists who did come ordinarily and duly to church, but otherwise left little or no mark upon the records? Some of them (the more substantial among them) left wills, and these usually included a statement of faith, but the formulaic nature of the language employed makes it difficult to distinguish between the heartfelt and the merely conventional.[47] But if conformist churchgoers do not tell us much about themselves, there was no shortage of

43 Ingram, *Church Courts*, pp. 350–1, 107–8.

44 Margaret Spufford, 'Can We Count the "Godly" and the "Conformable" in the Seventeenth Century?', *Journal of Ecclesiastical History*, 36 (1985), pp. 435–6.

45 Eric Carlson, 'The Origins, Function and Status of the Office of Churchwarden, with Particular Reference to the Diocese of Ely', in Margaret Spufford, ed., *The World of Rural Dissenters* (Cambridge, 1995), p. 173.

46 Peter Marshall, 'Old Mother Leakey and the Golden Chain: Context and Meaning in an Early Stuart Haunting', in Newton, *Ghosts*, p. 97.

47 Christopher Marsh, '"Departing Well and Christianly": Will-Making and Popular Religion in Early Modern England', in Carlson, *English People*.

others ready to put words into their mouths. The late sixteenth and early seventeenth centuries witnessed a flurry of what can be termed 'Puritan complaint literature', in which godly ministers vented their frustration at the religious complacency of conformist neighbours and parishioners. Two of the best-known examples (by the Essex ministers George Gifford and Arthur Dent) take the form of dialogues, in which rural types with symbolic, if unlikely names ('Atheos', 'Asunetus') are allowed their say before being put right by learned and earnest ministers.[48] Interestingly, these characters are not closet papists, or alehouse scoffers, but well-meaning churchgoers who say their prayers at night, and know at least the basics of the catechism. Their principal values are social ones – the importance of good fellowship, charity and peace among neighbours – yet they had managed to miss the point of the Reformation, believing that men would be saved by their good works, and even that all in the end might go to heaven. An instinctive sympathy for this evident good-heartedness should not obscure that these were meant to be unflattering portraits. As John Craig has put it, 'to men like Dent and Gifford, the Protestant defined by ecclesiastical authority was little better than an atheist, for no demands were placed upon his heart or his conscience'.[49] Nonetheless, a number of historians have been inclined to think that these sketches of the 'country divinity' of the people got it about right, one going so far as to award Gifford the honorary title of 'Tudor anthropologist'.[50] Others warn of the dangers of accepting a polemical and satirical genre as an approximation of social reality, a vision of the world with the 'godly' on one side, the 'multitude' on the other, and not much of a spectrum in between. It has been pointed out that these works served an important function in Puritan identity-formation, the simple and apparently appealing Christian profession of the 'unregenerate' a temptation more dangerous to the godly than open persecution.[51]

[48] George Gifford, *A Briefe Discourse of Certaine Points of the Religion which is among the Common Sort of Christians which may be termed the Countrie Divinitie* (London, 1583); Arthur Dent, *The Plaine Mans Path-way to Heaven* (London, 1601, and many subsequent editions).

[49] John Craig, *Reformation, Politics and Polemics: The Growth of Protestantsism in East Anglian Market Towns, 1500–1610* (Aldershot, 2001), p. 20.

[50] Alan Macfarlane, 'A Tudor Anthropologist: George Gifford's Discourse and Dialogue', in Sidney Anglo, ed., *The Damned Art: Essays in the Literature of Witchcraft* (London, 1977). See also Marsh, *Popular Religion*, pp. 145–6; Martin Ingram, 'From Reformation to Toleration: Popular Religious Cultures in England, 1540–1690', in Tim Harris, ed., *Popular Culture in England, c.1580–1850* (Basingstoke, 1995), p. 109.

[51] Craig, *Politics and Polemics*, pp. 12–24; Peter Lake with Michael Questier, *The Antichrist's Lewd Hat: Protestants, Papists and Players in Post-Reformation England* (New Haven and London, 2002), p. xvi; Frank Luttmer, 'Persecutors, Tempters and Vassals of the Devil: The Unregenerate in Puritan Practical Divinity', *Journal of Ecclesiastical History*, 51 (2000).

Haigh has made extensive use of the complaint literature to advance a challenging thesis about the nature of lay religion in the post-Reformation Church. Quite rightly, he observes that those of whom the godly disapproved can hardly be dismissed as the ungodly, but the views attributed to Atheos, Asunetus and their ilk were nonetheless 'not Protestantism'. Their real-life counterparts were the parishioners who can be found in the records presenting Puritan ministers to the authorities for omission of ceremonies and the surplice, and who insisted on kneeling to receive the communion. By the end of Elizabeth's reign, though their opponents might accuse them of 'popery', such people were not Catholics. As we shall see (Section 7.2), Haigh considers the Catholic mission beginning in the 1570s as a missed opportunity, which neglected a potential reservoir of support in the parishes. Those whom the godly had failed to enthuse with their brand of evangelical Protestantism were 'the spiritual leftovers' of the English Reformation. They clung to the rites and ceremonies which the Church of England still sanctioned. But they were not all 'mere conformists'. Haigh identifies an active and assertive strand of conformity within the Elizabethan and Jacobean Church, and has a name for its proponents – 'parish anglicans'.[52] There is a longer-term agenda here: if such people existed in considerable numbers in the early seventeenth century, then the ceremonialist programme imposed by Archbishop Laud in the 1630s may have enjoyed more grass-roots support than historians have usually assumed (see Section 8.2).

One valuable aspect of Haigh's interpretation is to remind us that the most recurrent exposure lay people had to authorized religion was in the form of the liturgy, the set services and litanies of Cranmer's Book of Common Prayer (something historians' traditional preoccupation with preaching has been inclined to obscure). Most Elizabethan English people may have acquired their familiarity with the language of religion not through a dramatic experience of personal conversion, but through a kind of osmosis. Collinson has alerted us to the importance of the 'almost imperceptible penetration of the language of Bible and Prayer Book as heard and absorbed in parish worship'. And Eamon Duffy, in the elegiac conclusion to his *Stripping of the Altars*, imagines how for Elizabethan men and women 'Cranmer's somberly magnificent prose, read week by week, entered and possessed their minds, and became the fabric of their prayer, the utterance of their most solemn and their most vulnerable moments'.[53] But Duffy, like Haigh, believes that this

[52] Haigh, 'Church of England', quotes at pp. 249, 253. The argument is developed in his 'The Taming of Reformation: Preachers, Pastors and Parishioners in Elizabethan and Early Stuart England', *History*, 85 (2000), which suggests that pressure from parishioners pushed clergy to be less rigidly predestinarian, and to provide more varieties of ceremony.

[53] Patrick Collinson, *Elizabethan Essays* (London, 1994), pp. 27–8; Eamon Duffy, *The Stripping of the Altars: Traditional Religion in England 1400–1580* (New Haven and London, 1992), p. 593.

was Protestantism's pyrrhic victory. Prayer book observance became a hallmark of traditionalism, the bugbear of the properly reformed outlook. An interpretation both building on and challenging these approaches is that of Judith Maltby.[54] Maltby looks at those same 'conformists from conviction' with whom Haigh is concerned, but the 'parish anglicans' are rechristened 'prayer book Protestants', an adjustment of more than merely semantic significance. A vocal Puritan minority, Maltby argues, should not be allowed to define Protestantism for us on its own terms. Two sets of sources are employed: cases in the Church courts where parishioners took action against Puritan or negligent ministers for omitting or truncating prayer book services; and the series of around 30 petitions in support of episcopacy and the prayer book produced across the country between the summoning of the Long Parliament in 1640 and the outbreak of the Civil War (these were often critical of Archbishop Laud's 'innovations' of the 1630s, which Haigh's parish anglicans ought to have been supporting). Maltby's suggestion of a substantial constituency, self-consciously Protestant, but firmly attached to the liturgy, is a compelling one, but raises some questions. We cannot always be sure that parishioners reporting nonconforming ministers were motivated by idealism. Some charges may have been a convenient cover for disputes of a more personal nature (and a number of those against whom cases were brought do seem to have been negligent and disagreeable characters). Nor can we be completely certain that strident local opponents of Elizabethan Puritan ministers were not nostalgic ceremonialists in the Haighian mould, or even 'Church papists' whose hearts really did belong to Rome. ('They do make the book of common prayer a cloak for their papistry', claimed one Suffolk minister in 1590.[55]) It is noteworthy that support for the prayer book seems most often to have focussed on where it fulfilled the very traditional role of sanctifying anxious points in the life-cycle: communion of the sick, baptism, burial. The evidence from the early 1640s appears less ambiguous, but was this proto-Anglican consciousness the culmination of a continuous tradition, or the creation of the unprecedented crisis? (see Section 8.3)

Perhaps the shape of conformist religious experience should be sought in mundane day-to-day transactions, rather than ideologically charged confrontations between prayer book-toting parishioners and surplice-spurning ministers. The duty of keeping the parish church well equipped and repaired devolved on Elizabethan and Jacobean lay people, just as it had on their Catholic grandparents. As an index of lay enthusiasm and commitment, this is difficult to read: post-Reformation churches did not require the same level of expenditure on furnishings and ornaments (many of which had been sold, broken up or thrown away in the mid-Tudor decades), and did not get it. In

[54] Judith Maltby, *Prayer Book and People in Elizabethan and Early Stuart England* (Cambridge, 1998).

[55] Craig, *Politics and Polemics*, p. 32 n.

Herefordshire, for example, nearly 60 per cent of testators left bequests to their parish church in the 1530s, and fewer than 20 per cent did so in the 1590s.[56] Some contemporaries believed things had slipped badly. In 1593 the godly writer Philip Stubbes considered 'lamentable' the condition of parish churches that were once 'stately edifices', a view of the neglect of church fabrics that has been endorsed by modern authorities.[57]

But others have questioned whether lay commitment to the physical surroundings of worship really waned so calamitously, and identify a renewed effort in the decades around 1600. Andrew Foster's survey of a sample of 100 early seventeenth-century churchwardens' accounts reveals 'an impressive degree of restoration work of a major structural kind. . . galleries, new seating, towers, and bells'. Julia Merrit demonstrates that at least 63 parish churches in London were either rebuilt or substantially repaired and refurbished in James I's reign: historians' failure to recognize the achievement comes from accepting at face value polemical Laudian claims about the calamitous state of churches, used to justify the remodelling campaign of the 1630s (see Section 8.1).[58] Much of this work involved the levying of compulsory local rates – but we need not assume that people gave unwillingly. The parish church, though stripped of its Catholic imagery, continued to perform many of the same communal functions. Indeed in some ways its significance as a hub of local identity was enhanced through the Reformation decades, as rival sites of religious adherence (monasteries, friaries and guild chapels) were removed or converted to secular use. In the Elizabethan and Jacobean decades a growing number of tombs and monuments were placed in parish churches – a development facilitated by the whitewashing of murals that created space for a new style of hanging wall monument, and encouraged the commemoration of a wider range of local worthies. Changes in the technology of bell-casting and hanging from the latter part of Elizabeth's reign allowed the performance of more elaborate change-ringing – a development that accounts for much of the rebuilding work, as church towers required improving and strengthening.[59]

56 Marsh, *Popular Religion*, p. 67.

57 Patrick Collinson, 'The Elizabethan Church and the New Religion', in Christopher Haigh, ed., *The Reign of Elizabeth I* (London, 1984), pp. 170–1; David Palliser, 'Introduction: the Parish in Perspective', in Susan Wright, ed., *Parish, Church and People: Local Studies in Lay Religion 1350–1750* (London, 1988), p. 14.

58 Andrew Foster, 'Churchwardens' Accounts of Early Modern England and Wales', in Katherine French, Gary Gibbs and Beat Kümin, eds., *The Parish in English Life 1400–1600* (Manchester, 1997), pp. 87–8; Julia Merritt, 'Puritans, Laudians, and the Phenomenon of Church-Building in Jacobean London', *Historical Journal*, 41 (1998). See also Diarmaid MacCulloch, 'The Myth of the English Reformation', *Journal of British Studies*, 30 (1991), 13.

59 Marshall, *Beliefs*, pp. 289–90; A. Woodger, 'Post-Reformation Mixed Gothic in Huntingdonshire Bell Towers and its Campanological Associations', *Archaeological Journal*, 141 (1984).

The question of how regularly people attended their parish churches has been considered already. A related, but perhaps more pertinent issue is that of how often, and in what numbers they took communion there, for this was a devotional and religious act in a way that mere attendance was not. 'Church papists' were often prepared to attend services to avoid statutory fines, but not to receive communion, a merely ecclesiastical offence. There is an intriguing paradox here: levels of participation in the communion seem to have been high, but the event itself was infrequent. The prayer book and the ecclesiastical canons of 1604 required people to receive communion three times per year, but almost everywhere the medieval custom of a single annual communion at Easter persisted (perhaps in part because the cost of providing wine for the entire parish was too daunting to contemplate more frequently).[60] Though people were supposed to be reported to the Church courts for failing to communicate without good reason, we usually cannot be certain about the precise level of participation. An exception is the surviving evidence for a handful of urban parishes, which operated a token system (tokens issued upon payment of Easter tithes were returned when people came to receive communion). In a celebrated article, Jeremy Boulton has shown a participation rate at the turn of the seventeenth century of 80–90 per cent in the London parishes of St Botolph without Aldgate and St Saviour's Southwark (the sort of large suburban parishes which one would not expect to be tightly controlled).[61] This is impressive evidence of compliance with the (minimal) demands of official religion. But it is difficult to know what further it tells us about faith. It is not the case, as was once widely assumed, that a concern with receiving the sacrament was a quintessentially 'Anglican' instinct – the minority who communicated more regularly than the annual norm were as likely to be the godly as anyone else.[62] In any case, the reception of communion was an act of more than narrowly devotional significance. To receive communion as an adult was to assert one's place in the community. Before and after the Reformation it was described as 'receiving one's rights'. It also defined one's place. Just as where parishioners sat in church reflected the hierarchical order of the parish, people came to receive in order of social precedence. In some parishes two sorts of wine were served: fine muscadine for the better sort, malmsey for the hoi polloi. However, the communion was not just an occasion for reinforcing distinction, but for resolving tension. In another continuity across the Reformation divide, no one was supposed to be admitted to communion

60 Arnold Hunt, 'The Lord's Supper in Early Modern England', *Past and Present*, 161 (1998), 41; MacCulloch, *Later Reformation*, p. 116.

61 J.P. Boulton, 'The Limits of Formal Religion: The Administration of Holy Communion in Late Elizabethan and Early Stuart London', *London Journal*, 10 (1984).

62 Hunt, 'Lord's Supper', pp. 51–4.

who was 'out of charity' with their neighbour (see Section 1.1). For some (especially Catholics) this was an ideal excuse for not taking part, and for others an opportunity to publicly disgrace rivals as they knelt preparing to receive. But given the social importance attached to the ceremony, it could provide a real incentive to patch up quarrels, and restore what John Bossy has called 'the social miracle'.[63]

Arguably, (then as now) a concern with the finer points of theology was not essential to playing a full part in the life of the Church of England. Patrick Collinson remarks that 'the trick in making a Protestant settlement of religion stick was to sell it to that social majority for whom 'religion' was part and parcel of good-neighbourhood'.[64] Martin Ingram has underlined the extent to which participation in church services, like holding office as churchwarden or overseer of the poor, was closely intertwined with local status and respectability. It was therefore probably the middling sort and the middling aged who were most closely 'locked... into the system of corporate worship'. But Ingram sees age rather than class as the main determinant of religious commitment: poorer householders too had a real stake in the community. Rather than exuberant piety or scoffing indifference, an 'unspectacular orthodoxy' was the characteristic tone of Elizabethan and early Stuart parish religion.[65] Christopher Marsh's survey of *Popular Religion in Sixteenth-Century England* concludes that charity, neighbourliness, and the preservation of peace were the dominant values of the 'commonplace piety' of English communities, either side of the Reformation.[66] No doubt it was ever thus, but too emphatic a steer in this direction runs the risk of implying that in the end the Reformation did not matter so very much, and avoiding the question of what religion may actually have meant to individual believers – concentrating on the social functions of faith at the expense of its actual contents. So what did the people really believe?

6.3 Reading the Reformation

Perhaps the question is simply unanswerable: 'We shall never know *in detail* what ordinary people believed because there was no systematic official attempt to find out. The stress in the English Church was on outward conformity'.[67] In recent years, however, complete pessimism on this issue has

63 Ibid., 49; Christopher Haigh, 'Communion and Community: Exclusion from Communion in Post-Reformation England', *Journal of Ecclesiastical History*, 51 (2000), 738–9; Ingram, 'Reformation to Toleration', pp. 117–18; John Bossy, *Christianity in the West 1400–1700* (Oxford, 1985), ch. 4.

64 Patrick Collinson, 'Anti-Papist', p. 144.

65 Ingram, *Church Courts*, p. 123; 'Reformation to Toleration', p. 113.

66 Marsh, *Popular Religion*, p. 26 and *passim*.

67 Ingram, 'Reformation to Toleration', p. 109.

abated, as historians have turned to a close study of printed texts, and particularly 'cheap print', to recover the mix of religious ideas and motifs that may have appealed to a broad reading public. It may seem paradoxical to use literary sources to illuminate 'popular religion' in what was a largely illiterate society. In 1500 only about 10 per cent of men and 1 per cent of women were able to write their names. Over the course of the century, however, this rose sharply, to perhaps a total of 30 per cent of the population, a development that can reasonably be considered, in part at least, both cause and consequence of the spread of Protestantism, the quintessential religion of the book. Moreover, it is probable that a significantly larger percentage of the population had acquired the skill of reading without needing to learn how to write. In any case, the world of text was not a sealed one. Reading aloud and in company was normal behaviour, and oral and literate culture overlapped and interpenetrated in numerous ways: ballads were printed, but were designed to be memorized and sung.[68]

One of the most important contributions here has been Tessa Watt's study of piety in the cheap print of the later sixteenth and early seventeenth centuries: the single-sheet 'broadside' ballads (which retailed at a penny or less), and the slightly more substantial chapbooks, which increased in popularity through the seventeenth century. Of course, not all cheap print was concerned with religious themes, but a considerable proportion was, and by studying the genre, particularly the items that became publishers' 'stock' (i.e. frequently reprinted), Watt suggests we can gain 'insight into the inarticulate beliefs of "the multitude".'[69] With the provisos that we have little direct evidence for how this material was received or understood, and that the audience may not have been entirely 'popular' (i.e. lower or middling sort), this methodology yields interesting results. Watt finds themes of traditional or pre-Reformation piety still present, but substantially modified, not a straightforward replacement of Catholic by Protestant doctrine, but a gradual modification, a 'dialogue'. Some lessons had been learned: there is an awareness of the importance of repentance and salvation through faith, an absence of saints, an obvious interest in Protestant martyrs, and a greater emphasis on the Old Testament. But at the same time, the ballads about Marian martyrs are more concerned with their sufferings and adventures than with their doctrine (making them read rather like pre-Reformation saints' lives).There is an immoderate interest in the

[68] Margaret Spufford, 'First Steps in Literacy: The Reading and Writing Experiences of the Humblest Seventeenth-Century Autobiographers', *Social History*, 4 (1979); David Cressy, *Literacy and the Social Order: Reading and Writing in Tudor and Stuart England* (Cambridge, 1980); Adam Fox, *Oral and Literate Culture in England 1500–1700* (Oxford, 2000).

[69] Tessa Watt, *Cheap Print and Popular Piety, 1550–1640* (Cambridge, 1991) p. 83.

miracle of the virgin birth, and a recurrent stress on practical morality, with lists of good and bad behaviour. Most prominently of all, there is death and judgement: highly traditional depictions of hell, and an evident concern with issues of last-minute repentance and a 'good death' that sits uneasily with orthodox predestinarianism. Where other historians stress the increasingly iconoclastic, even 'iconophobic' outlook of English Protestantism in the last decades of the sixteenth century, Watt finds a greater openness to the impact of the visual: woodcut illustrations were a standard feature of religious ballads, and almost certainly broadened their appeal.[70] Ultimately, and in a memorable formulation, Watt concludes that 'the resulting patchwork of beliefs may be described as distinctively "post-Reformation", but not thoroughly "Protestant".'[71]

If this was the world-view of the typical lay Protestant, then godly preachers must have viewed it with distinctly ambivalent feelings (it seems not a million miles away from Gifford's 'country divinity'). But there may have been a closer fit between popular religious culture and the preoccupations of the godly than the latter were prepared to admit. Alexandra Walsham identifies just such a 'point of contact' in the theory of providentialism, the view that everything that happened on earth did so in accordance with the will of God, that God's judgements on individuals and communities could be read in dramatic events, often calamities, occurring in the natural world. Where earlier commentators (such as Keith Thomas) saw an intense interest in providence as the preoccupation of a pious minority, Walsham (surveying a vast array of pamphlets, sermons and tracts) argues for its roots in a variety of medieval notions, and its ability to function as a 'cultural cement' between the learned culture of Protestant elites and the culture of the people. A dramatic case study is provided by the 'fatal vesper' of October 1623, when 90 Catholics secretly attending a sermon in Blackfriars fell to their deaths through a collapsing floor. Protestant authors rushed into print with elaborate explanations of the symbolic meanings of the event (under the Gregorian calendar used in Catholic Europe, the day was November 5 – the anniversary of the Gunpowder Plot), but the London mob were equally convinced that divine judgement had been delivered, and survivors were stoned as they crawled from the wreckage. A flexible and adaptable system of explanation, providentialism allowed a long-standing popular fascination with the bizarre and the supernatural (deformed births, freak weather, apparitions) to be channelled into relatively safe Protestant forms.[72]

70 Ibid., chs. 4–5. Cf Patrick Collinson, 'From Iconoclasm to Iconophobia: The Cultural Impact of the Second English Reformation', in Marshall, *Impact*.

71 Watt, *Cheap Print*, p. 327.

72 Walsham, *Providence*; '"The Fatall Vesper": Providentialism and Anti-Popery in Late Jacobean London', *Past and Present*, 144 (1994).

Similar conclusions have been reached by Peter Lake in a series of studies examining the related genre of murder pamphlets, topical and sensationalist accounts of 'true crime', often with titillating elements of sex and violence – surely 'popular' literature in all senses of the term. But these texts (which were sometimes composed by clergymen) were also deeply moralistic, often included a providential exposure of the murderer, and usually finished with a penitent declaration from the gallows. Lake considers the genre as one which allowed Protestant authors an entry point into the mental world of the people, in so far as conventional elements in the pamphlets lent themselves to a Protestant reading, and indeed Protestant of the 'hot' rather than watered-down variety. Predestination, the doctrine that Christopher Haigh feels the people simply couldn't swallow, often underpins the drama. For instance, when captured felons obstinately refused to make a declaration of guilt this was taken as a sign of preordained damnation.[73]

Though sharing the perception that Protestantism had considerable potential to overlap with the world-view of 'the people', the post-revisionists are not entirely of one mind. Ian Green, who has undertaken the most comprehensive survey of 'print and Protestantism' in the early modern period, criticizes Tessa Watt for exaggerating the extent to which cheap print achieved a successful fusion of traditional and Protestant piety. In his view, 'godly' ballads which encouraged an old-fashioned interest in miracles, and a religion of good-neighbourliness unwilling to get to grips with more difficult teachings, constituted 'a serious rival rather than a support to many of the central thrusts of the new religion'. Similarly, he feels that Walsham overestimates the extent to which educated Calvinists and unlettered parishioners held the same view of providential occurrences – not so much a cultural cement as 'a shared frontier which looked and functioned very differently according to where one was standing'.[74] But Green in his turn has been attacked by Lake for propagating too bland and consensual a view of the varieties of Protestant belief. Green set himself the task of identifying the most essential and enduring features of English Protestantism in the sixteenth and seventeenth centuries by examining all religious works going through more than five editions in 30 years. But, as Lake points out, this leads to 'an almost complete omission of all the discordant notes in contemporary church

[73] Peter Lake, 'Deeds Against Nature: Cheap Print, Protestantism and Murder in Early Seventeenth-Century England', in Kevin Sharpe and Peter Lake, eds., *Culture and Politics in Early Stuart England* (Basingstoke, 1994); id., 'Popular Form, Puritan Content? Two Puritan Appropriations of the Murder Pamphlet from Mid-Seventeenth-Century London', in Anthony Fletcher and Peter Roberts, eds., *Religion, Culture and Society in Early Modern Britain* (Cambridge, 1994); id., *Lewd Hat*, chs. 1–5. Cf Haigh, 'Success and Failure', 49: the predestinarian theology of evangelical ministers 'defined their own defeat'.

[74] Ian Green, *Print and Protestantism in Early Modern England* (Oxford, 2000), pp. 471, 437–8.

and society' by passing over short-term crises, scandals, and polemical disputes. It also misses out texts such as murder pamphlets, whose specific subject matter was 'time-sensitive', but which conformed to a familiar and recurring formulaic pattern. Like Green, however, Lake takes Walsham to task for conflating too much the outlook of godly Protestants and the style of popular providentialism discernible in cheap print, thus implying 'a consensual, univocal, providentialist, anti-catholic "religion of protestants"'. His own preference is for a less than exact fit, 'a bundle of attitudes, assumptions and expectations... left strewn about the cultural landscape by the Tudor century', only some of which could be appropriated by godly evangelists. The categories of 'popular' and 'Puritan' were not utterly unbridgeable, but neither were they on the same side of the river.[75]

Despite these differences of emphasis, an overall result of the work undertaken over the last decade on the huge volume of religious and quasi-religious print has been to challenge the view that Protestantism and popular culture were like oil and water which could not mix. It is beyond dispute that the Reformation was deeply hostile to some forms of popular culture, but Protestant England was not without its own 'festive' occasions. In one of the earlier 'post-revisionist' studies, David Cressy examined the ways in which the Reformation remodelled people's experience of the calendar, the 'ritual year'. Of course, the large number of religious feast days and saints' days, holy days which were also holidays, was mostly swept away. But using the evidence of churchwardens' accounts which record expenditure on the ringing of church bells and the lighting of festive bonfires, Cressy has traced the process by which a new more secular and Protestant calendar was laid over the previous one, with its own opportunities for popular celebration – November 17, the anniversary of Queen Elizabeth's accession, and most importantly, November 5, the anniversary of the foiling of the Gunpowder Plot. There were other occasions too when popular Protestant celebrations spilled out into the streets: the defeat of the Spanish Armada in 1588, or the return of Prince Charles from Madrid in 1623 without the Catholic Spanish bride he had gone there to seek (see Section 5.3).[76] To take part in the kind of celebrations Cressy describes did not require sophisticated religious understanding, but the people who participated may well have thought that they were good Protestants.

In other ways too, historians are beginning to ask questions about the potential of early modern Protestantism as a vehicle for popular cultural expression. Until recently, music has represented a shamefully missed opportunity to explore the intersection between 'religion' and 'culture'. Though

[75] Lake, *Lewd Hat*, pp. 14, 325 n, 317, 154. See also Collinson's review of Green in *Times Literary Supplement* (Jun. 29, 2001), 29, noting the oddity of excluding Foxe's *Acts and Monuments* on the grounds it managed only 4 editions in 1563–83.

[76] David Cressy, *Bonfires and Bells: National Memory and the Protestant Calendar in Elizabethan and Stuart England* (London, 1989).

the liturgical reforms of the sixteenth century ended the rich polyphonic tradition of English parish churches (cathedrals were another matter), churchgoers were soon provided with an unprecedented musical opportunity to participate rather than listen. The congregational singing of psalms, in the metrical or versified version produced by Thomas Sternold and John Hopkins in Edward's reign, seems to have been taken up with alacrity. It has been suggested that 'Sternhold and Hopkins' was the most frequently published work in the early modern period, and MacCulloch has described the metrical psalm as a 'secret weapon of the English Reformation'.[77] The psalms were of course just one way in which the language of the Bible became increasingly familiar to ordinary English people over the course of the later Reformation. Late Tudor and early Stuart England was a society saturated with scripture – a cultural sea change from the early Tudor world. The scrupulous calculations of Ian Green suggest that by 1640 around 280 editions of the complete Bible and 175 editions of the New Testament had been produced, with print runs often in the thousands. Green speculates that 'by the mid-seventeenth century the owning of a Bible and perhaps to a lesser extent the regular reading of that Bible had become a firmly established habit, at least among those who were relatively well-to-do or devout or both.'[78] William Shakespeare perhaps hardly qualifies as an ordinary English person, and there has been sustained debate about whether he qualifies as a Protestant. But critics have long been aware of the extent to which his plays 'resound with echoes of the Bible': language and imagery drawn from no fewer than 42 scriptural books. It is significant that biographers remain undecided about the extent to which Shakespeare actively read the Bible for himself, or merely allowed it to penetrate his consciousness through the drip-feed of weekly church attendance.[79] The text which best equips us for 'reading the Reformation' as an agent of cultural transformation may therefore be the Bible itself. But this by no means removes the ambiguities and paradoxes surrounding the reception of the Reformation at a popular level. A seventeenth-century Bible owner piously inscribed into his or her copy the couplet: 'who reads a chapter when he rises, shall not be troubled with ill eyes'. Two centuries earlier, this kind of 'magical' efficacy had been widely attributed to the act of gazing on the elevated host at mass: 'thine eyes from their sight shall not blind'.[80] Was this a transformation or not?

77 MacCulloch, *Later Reformation*, p. 138; Green, *Print*, p. 503; id., '"All People that on Earth do Dwell, Sing to the Lord with Cheerful Voice": Protestantism and Music in Early Modern England', in Simon Ditchfield, ed., *Christianity and Community in the West* (Aldershot, 2001).

78 Green, *Print*, pp. 50–3, 99. And we should not forget here the appearance of the New Testament (1567) and complete Bible (1588) in Welsh: Glanmor Williams, *Wales and the Reformation* (Cardiff, 1997), ch. 13.

79 Collinson, *Elizabethan Essays*, pp. 251–2.

80 Green, *Print*, p. 100 n; Duffy, *Stripping*, p. 100.

Summation

We have seen repeatedly in the course of this chapter that to ask whether the Reformation succeeded in turning the mass of the population into good Protestants does not lend itself to a straightforward answer, for reasons that are partly to do with problems of evidence, and partly with problems of definition. Revisionists argue that genuine Protestant teaching was an intellectually and culturally daunting obstacle that caused the bulk of the populace to refuse at the first fence, while post-revisionists insist that we should lower the hurdle, and allow those who classed themselves as Protestants to finish the race with the others. Yet arguably it is not the most appropriate course for historians to decide whether Puritan authors were being objective social commentators, or unreasonable bigots, when they railed against the godlessness, ignorance and 'country divinity' of the multitude. Rather we should recognize that deep divisions about what it was necessary to do or think in order to be a good-enough member of a national Protestant Church were at the heart of the contemporary religious experience.[81] Debates about what it meant to be a Protestant continued up to the Civil War, itself a kind of violent referendum on the sort of Protestant nation England ought to be and become. We should not cast these issues in over-simplistic polar terms. If too rigid a distinction is proposed between a minority of evangelical activists and a majority of 'parish Protestant' conformists ('the godly and the multitude'), there is a risk of allowing the old discredited 'Anglicans and Puritans' dichotomy in by the back door. Much of the work surveyed in this chapter has lessened the temptation, by identifying the common ground, the points of entry between godly Protestantism and the evolving religious culture of the people. But the alternative temptation, of discovering an all-embracing post-Reformation synthesis, which defined the essential character of lay Protestantism, is to be resisted too. Haigh's characteristically bold assertion that in Elizabeth's reign 'the English people *could not* be made Protestants' certainly begs some questions, but he is surely correct to discern that they could not all be made into the sort of Protestants that a substantial proportion of the parish ministry wished.[82] The previous chapter questioned the view that there was a clear 'consensus' in the theology of the Elizabethan and Jacobean Church, and we should not expect to find one at the level of the parish and of 'popular' religious culture. It is legitimate and valuable to posit the existence of 'parish Anglicans', 'prayer book Protestants', 'Church papists', 'unspectacularly orthodox' parishioners, so long as we do not imagine this as a multiple-choice test in which one such label must be the 'correct' characterization of the broad conformist mass of the people. Martin Ingram

[81] A point made by Haigh, 'Success and Failure', pp. 48–9.
[82] Haigh, 'Church of England', p. 249.

is right to talk of 'popular religious cultures' (plural) in the sixteenth and seventeenth centuries.[83] Religion is always a complex social dynamic, and it became more so as a result of the Tudor Reformations, as the opportunity to make individual confessional and ideological choices cut across traditional Christian imperatives towards unity and uniformity, and as the language of religious division (and hostile labelling) lent itself to a variety of social and cultural conflicts. Underlying much of this was an awareness that even after decades of Protestant evangelization, Catholic England had not finally gone away, that the adherents of the Antichrist were taking their chances and biding their time.

83 Ingram, 'Reformation to Toleration'. See also Lake, *Lewd Hat*, pp. 713–14, Peter Lake and Michael Questier, 'Introduction', in id., eds., *Conformity and Orthodoxy in the English Church, c. 1560–1660* (Woodbridge, 2000), pp. xiv–xix.

7

Catholics in Protestant England 1560–1625

Overview

While a Protestant nation, and perhaps even a nation of Protestants, was being forged through the reigns of Elizabeth and James, another decisive development in English religious history was simultaneously taking place: the emergence of a sizeable body of Christians who rejected the Church of England's claim to their allegiance and reaffirmed the medieval and Marian Churches' acknowledgement of the spiritual authority of the pope in Rome. Papists (as their enemies called them) or Catholics (as they called themselves) were to be an important, if often unsettling presence in the English religious landscape through to modern times. Yet while Puritan critics of the Church of England have been firmly assimilated into mainstream narratives of the Reformation, these other, more radical nonconformists have been relatively neglected. The study of Catholicism remains the poor stepsister of mainstream Reformation historiography, not quite part of the family. Historically, the reasons for this are not hard to discern. Until comparatively recently, the subject was firmly claimed by the heirs of the Catholic tradition themselves, resulting in an introspective 'confessional history' which concerned itself principally with the themes of heroic suffering and survival – martyrdom and priests' holes – as well as with a localist interest in the continuity of Catholic communities and traditions within particular counties and regions.[1] Avoidance of the subject by non-Catholic historians was in part the consequence of a continuing distaste for Catholicism itself among many English intellectuals through the nineteenth and earlier twentieth centuries, and in part the reflection of a 'whiggish' understanding of historical progress and causation. Protestantism and Puritanism were

[1] Despite its often inward focus, much of this work is scholarly and reliable. See in particular the valuable research which continues to be published in the journal *Recusant History*.

associated with change and modernity, the rise of individualism, the middle class, and the nation state – a narrative in which the survival of a fundamentally 'backward' religion had little obvious relevance. In a work as recent as the second edition of Dickens's *English Reformation*, Elizabethan Catholics are allocated no more than two pages in a chapter devoted to 'residual problems'. Even today, when denominational passions among practising historians have generally cooled or dissolved, the study of post-Reformation English Catholicism still has something of the feel of the 'specialist subject' about it.[2]

Yet in any persuasive portrayal of the English Reformation, Elizabethan and early Stuart Catholics deserve to emerge from the wings to the main stage, and not just because a more developed historical sensibility is teaching us to pay attention to 'losers' as well as 'winners'. If (as argued in this book) the English Reformation was a process which continued through the early decades of the seventeenth century, then the fact that it not only failed to convert, but also positively alienated, a significant minority of English people is something demanding careful explanation. Moreover, English Catholicism did not develop in isolation or along lines determined solely from within. It was an oppositional and a persecuted movement (though the opposition was often qualified, and the persecution frequently tempered), the product of a relationship that deeply affected both parties. Indeed, the very process of attempting to define what English Catholicism *was* is one of defining its relationship to the State and wider society. There is a tendency to treat as synonyms the terms 'Catholic' and 'recusant' – the latter (from Latin *recusare*, to refuse) signifying those who refused to attend the services of the Church of England. But the matter is not quite so straightforward: self-definitions and those supplied by others did not always coincide, and scholars have become increasingly aware of the continued existence of those whom contemporaries disparagingly termed 'Church papists', people who conformed to varying degrees with the legal demands of the Church of England, but stubbornly refused to internalize its doctrines. It was partly because Catholicism was not in this period clearly and totally separated from the established Church that it remained a focus of intense anxiety. An important reason for taking Catholics seriously is that they featured so prominently in the perceptions of others. Anti-Catholicism in Elizabethan and Jacobean England was, as we have seen (Section 5.3) a powerful ideological and cultural 'construct'. But we should not lose sight of the fact that anti-Catholicism depended on the actual existence of Catholics, some of whom were actively working to bring about the downfall of the Protestant regime.

[2] A.G. Dickens, *The English Reformation* (2nd ed., 1989), pp. 365–7. For an illuminating discussion of the marginalization of Catholic themes in mainstream academic study, see the introduction to Alison Shell, *Catholicism, Controversy and the English Literary Imagination, 1558–1660* (Cambridge, 1999).

The following discussion breaks the history of English Catholicism between the lost opportunity of Mary's reign and the (perhaps) new opportunities opened up in Charles I's, into three broad periods, each of which usefully frames a number of issues and debates. The first section examines the experience of Catholics from the accession of Elizabeth to about 1580, the period in which something that began as late medieval English Christianity reinvented itself as a separate and distinct religious identity – 'Roman Catholicism'. The controversy over whether this was a process characterized by 'continuity' or 'discontinuity' will be assessed, and related to broader questions about the progress and potential of the later Reformation. We then move on to the period between 1580 and the death of Elizabeth – the years of most intense persecution for English Catholicism, but ones which, paradoxically, ensured its long-term survival. The question of whether the form of that survival (as a gentry-based or 'seigneurial sect') had been irrevocably fixed, and the significance of controversies among the Catholics themselves about the way their society should be organized, will be brought into focus. Finally, we explore the political dilemmas of English Catholics, and the nature of English Catholic culture, in the apparently easier conditions brought about by the accession of James I. Here it will be argued that despite a growing Catholic acceptance of their minority status, and a broad retreat from the political activism of earlier decades, an appreciation of the position of Catholics in a Protestant nation, and of the fears and misunderstandings that it generated, is vital for understanding the English Reformation as a whole.

7.1 The Creation of a Community

What happened to English Catholics after their massive political defeat in 1558–9? If we allow a broad definition of Catholicism, one embracing those who hankered after the Latin mass and the calendar rituals of the medieval Church, and who disliked iconoclasm and the new breed of Protestant preachers, then there was clearly a lot of it about in 1560, but it was not very clear where it ought to be going. After the twin disasters of the deaths of Mary and Cardinal Pole in November 1558, a crisis of leadership descended on English Catholics for the better part of a decade. Mary's bishops, as we have seen, almost to a man courageously refused to subscribe to the 1559 Settlement, though the regime shrewdly decided to confine them under semi-comfortable house arrest, rather than to make inspiring martyrs of them on the Cranmer-Ridley model. There is evidence that some of them (David Poole of Peterborough, Bonner of London, Watson of Lincoln) kept in contact and offered guidance to recusant priests on the outside, but the practical leadership they could offer was minimal.[3] The policy of the Counter-Reformation papacy to the new situation in England

[3] J.J. Scarisbrick, *The Reformation and the English People* (Oxford, 1984), pp. 138–40.

was initially characterized by dither and delusion. Pius IV had unrealistically high hopes that Elizabeth might not turn out such a hopeless heretic after all. Papal nuncios were despatched to the English Court (though not received) in 1560 and 1561, and it was even rumoured that Pius had offered to confirm the 1559 liturgy, if Elizabeth acknowledged papal jurisdiction.[4] Meanwhile Philip II was using his considerable diplomatic muscle to head off any papal moves to condemn or excommunicate Elizabeth. He had initial hopes of resuming the dynastic marriage alliance that had brought England into the Habsburg orbit, and even when these fell through he had no desire to see England driven into the arms of his arch-rival, France. Remarkably, not until 1563 did Rome authoritatively decree that English Catholics should stay away from Church of England services, and there was little serious attempt to publicize the prohibition before 1566, when the priest Laurence Vaux arrived in Lancashire with a 'definitive sentence' from the Pope.[5]

In the meantime, conservative priests and lay people were having to work out for themselves the extent of permissible compromise with the demands of the times. Whether or not 'Catholic priests and traditionalist laity were in large majorities' in the parishes at the start of the reign, they were certainly very numerous.[6] Throughout the 1560s, episcopal visitors found many cases of 'idolatrous' Catholic furnishings surviving in churches (altars, crosses, holy water stoups), as well as decidedly un-Protestant patterns of behaviour. In 1567, for example, over a dozen clergy in Yorkshire and Nottinghamshire were discovered who 'useth the communion for the dead'.[7] Such delinquency was particularly prevalent in the north: in Yorkshire, Lancashire and Durham (the latter received an influx of militantly Catholic Scottish clergy after the Protestant takeover of 1562).[8] But conservative sentiment was not confined to fringe and highland regions. Early Elizabethan bishops encountered entrenched conservatism in Hampshire and Sussex (particularly West Sussex), even in Suffolk.[9] When

4 Edward Norman, *Roman Catholicism in England from the Elizabethan Settlement to the Second Vatican Council* (Oxford, 1986), p. 10; Alexandra Walsham, *Church Papists: Catholicism, Conformity and Confessional Polemic in Early Modern England* (Woodbridge, 1993), p. 17.

5 Christopher Haigh, *Reformation and Resistance in Tudor Lancashire* (Cambridge, 1975), p. 249.

6 The suggestion of Christopher Haigh, *English Reformations: Religion, Politics, and Society under the Tudors* (Oxford, 1993), p. 252.

7 Peter Marshall, *Beliefs and the Dead in Reformation England* (Oxford, 2002), p. 126.

8 David Marcombe, 'A Rude and Heady People: The Local Community and the Rebellion of the Northern Earls', in id., ed., *The Last Principality: Religion and Society in the Bishopric of Durham 1494–1660* (Nottingham, 1987), p. 137.

9 Ralph Houlbrooke, *Church Courts and the People during the English Reformation 1520–1570* (Oxford, 1979), pp. 245–52; Roger Manning, *Religion and Society in Elizabethan Sussex* (Leicester, 1969), pp. 34–59; Diarmaid MacCulloch, *Suffolk and the Tudors: Politics and Religion in an English County 1500–1600* (Oxford, 1986), pp. 181–91.

the government undertook a nationwide survey of Justices of the Peace in 1564, classifying magistrates as 'favourable', 'neutral' or 'unfavourable' towards the Elizabethan Settlement, nearly a third were found to be unfavourable, although a purge of the more overtly Catholic justices had already taken place.[10] It is fairly clear, however, that throughout the first decade of Elizabeth's reign, the tendency for which historians generally use the somewhat disparaging label 'survivalism' was largely contained within the Church of England. As A.G. Dickens once remarked, 'no recusant problem existed during the early years of the reign'.[11] This may be putting it too strongly, but there were compelling reasons for Catholics not to vote with their feet and absent themselves from the services of the established Church. Unlike some modern historians, Catholics in the 1560s could hardly have seen the triumph of Protestantism as the inevitable verdict of history. The times had changed before, and might do so again. Elizabeth was unmarried (and almost died of smallpox in October 1562). In the meantime they could hold their noses and bide their time, attending church in accordance with the law, but showing scant respect for what went on there. In the diocese of Chichester in 1569, Archbishop Parker's commissary noted with disgust that 'many bring to church the old Latin popish primers, and use to pray upon them all the time when the lessons are being read'.[12] 'Church papists' might come to services but either refuse to receive, or find excuses for not receiving, the communion. Where parish clergy were sympathetic to the old ways (and there was an overwhelming continuity of personnel from Mary's Church), they could make the experience of the Protestant services less alien and uncongenial by chanting them in the manner of a mass or by employing the (technically legal) expedient of using wafers rather than ordinary bread for the communion. There were even priests whom historians have termed 'biconfessional incumbents' or 'liturgical hermaphrodites' – men who outwardly conformed but also said Latin masses for the disaffected in secret.[13] It is important here not to underestimate the strength of the social pulls and pressures that helped to keep people within the orbit of their ancient parish church. To cease worshipping with one's neighbours and move into recusancy was an act of extreme nonconformity in a more than religious sense. For the gentry in particular, to withdraw themselves from the churches where their honourable ancestors lay buried, and of which they themselves were often patrons, must have been psychologically painful, as well as seeming (in John Bossy's words) 'a grave dereliction of social duty... a shocking example to sectaries and

10 Alan Dures, *English Catholicism 1558–1642* (Harlow, 1983), p. 6.

11 A.G. Dickens, 'The First Stages of Romanist Recusancy in Yorkshire, 1560–1590', in his *Reformation Studies* (London, 1982), p. 179 (and coining the term 'survivalism' at p. 183).

12 Manning, *Sussex*, p. 46.

13 Walsham, *Church Papists*, p. 15; Haigh, *Reformations*, p. 253.

separatists'.[14] For the more humble too, there were strong practical arguments for continued conformity: the blessing of marriage, the baptism of children, and burial in consecrated ground.

Nonetheless, a process of withdrawal did begin. Had it not done so it is probable that English Catholicism as a distinct religious identity would over time have diluted and dissolved, becoming a kind of 'high-church' residue within the Church of England – a pattern which can be observed, for example, in the Scandinavian kingdoms. Recusancy gathered pace from the 1570s and 80s.The deaths of old Marian clergy and the repeated investigations of the bishops combined to make the parishes less hospitable habitats for 'survivalist practices', while missionary priests from the continent were arriving to bolster the papal condemnation of 'schismatics' and to provide an alternative ministry. But there are indications that the process started earlier, particularly in Lancashire, where it has been estimated that as many as fifty clergy were recusant mass-providers by the start of the 1570s.[15] At first, the risks were not so very great. Under the 1559 Act of Uniformity, lay people faced a fine of 12d for not attending church, and though the penalties for priests were greater, they were sparingly applied. Before 1577, no priest was executed for saying mass. The punishment for a second refusal of the Oath of Supremacy was death, but since Elizabeth ensured that the Oath was never actually offered twice, there were no new Bishop Fishers or Thomas Mores.

Towards the end of the 1560s, however, events combined to sharpen the issues of spiritual and political allegiance facing English Catholics, and to increase the suspicion with which they were viewed by the authorities. The first of these was the flight into England in May 1568 of Mary Stuart, deposed Queen of Scots and (Catholic) heir presumptive to the throne of her cousin, Elizabeth. Almost at once, Mary began what was to be a twenty-year career as the focus of doomed Catholic plots. But the first of these was by some way the most serious, indeed the most significant internal challenge to Elizabeth's authority over the course of her 45-year reign. In November 1569, alienated by exclusion from office, and fearing arrest after a summons to court, the Catholic earls of Northumberland and Westmorland raised rebellion in Yorkshire and County Durham. This 'Rising of the Northern Earls' failed in its immediate objective of freeing Mary from captivity at Tutbury (she was rapidly moved south) and collapsed in the face of an advancing royalist army at the end of the year. But the rising had graphically revealed the strength of militant Catholic sentiment in parts of the north. The banner of the Five Wounds was again unfurled (as in 1536 and 1549), Protestant prayer books were destroyed in scores of Yorkshire churches, and mass was solemnly said

[14] John Bossy, *The English Catholic Community 1570–1850* (London, 1975), p. 124.

[15] Haigh, *Reformations*, p. 256.

in Durham Cathedral, where the participants were absolved from the sin of schism 'in the name of Christ and Bishop Pius of Rome'. The rebellion was on a much smaller scale than that of 1536 (perhaps 5–6000 were in arms), and large parts of the north remained quiet – recent scholarship is divided over whether it should be considered a genuinely populist religious rising, or a last flexing of social muscle by the fading feudal aristocracy.[16] Either way, the consequences for England's Catholics were momentous, most particularly because of a delayed echo of the revolt reverberating the following year. In February 1570, Pius V, anxious to lend moral support to the English rebels and unaware the rising had already been crushed, promulgated the bull *Regnans in Excelsis*, an exercise of the long cherished, but by now rather anachronistic papal power of deposing sovereigns. Elizabeth was declared to be a heretic and excommunicated, and English Catholics were ordered to withdraw their allegiance from her at the risk of being excommunicated themselves. It was, to say the least, a rather impractical document. There were no realistic mechanisms for enforcement (the Catholic powers were not consulted in advance) and English Catholics could hardly be expected to carry it out on their own. A few years later, Pius's successor Gregory XIII was prevailed upon to issue a clarification: the bull was not binding on Catholics in current circumstances, but only when 'the public execution of the said bull can be carried out.'[17] Nonetheless, the document understandably alarmed Elizabeth's government, and added considerable plausibility to the claim that Catholics, by virtue of being Catholics, were traitors to the Crown.

Another event of the late 1560s was decisive for the future of English Catholicism, and for the identification of loyalty to Rome with disloyalty to the Crown. This was a crucial shift of policy on the part of the English clerical exiles. The years after 1559 witnessed a repeat of the phenomenon that followed Mary's accession: the voluntary removal of scores of clergy loyal to the supplanted regime to hospitable centres abroad. Like the Marian exiles before them, the early Elizabethan exiles (who included fifteen heads of Oxford and Cambridge colleges and both Regius professors of divinity) aimed to swamp the government at home under a wave of print. Their Geneva was the university town of Louvain in the Spanish-controlled Netherlands, where between 1564 and 1568 scholars like Thomas Harding (former Oxford Professor of Hebrew), Nicholas Sanders and Thomas Stapleton produced over 40 works of theology and polemic. The prompt for many of these was Bishop John Jewel's 'Challenge sermon' of 1559–60, in which he defied the Catholics to prove the antiquity of their practices from scripture or the early fathers – something they were more than happy to try

16 For the former view, see Scarisbrick, *Reformation*, pp. 145–7; Haigh, *Reformations*, pp. 257–8; for the latter, Susan Brigden, *New Worlds, Lost Worlds: The Rule of the Tudors 1485–1603* (London, 2000), pp. 236–7.

17 Patrick McGrath, *Papists and Puritans under Elizabeth I* (London, 1967), p. 162.

and do.[18] One of the most active of the 'Louvainists' was a Lancashire and Oxford man, William Allen, who finally settled on the continent in 1565. In 1568 Allen established a college for the training of English priests at Douai (just inside present-day France, but then in Spanish Flanders). Douai was planned initially as a purely educational establishment (of the kind which Cardinal Pole had hoped to establish in Marian England), but under the influence of a new wave of exiles in the late 1560s, the college was reconceived as a missionary institution for training young men to return secretly to work in their homeland. Allen himself, through to his death in 1594, remained deeply committed to the missionary enterprise and to the 'reconversion of England', even if this involved the assistance of foreign soldiery. His position as de facto leader of English Catholicism was recognized by Gregory XIII in 1581 when he was created 'Prefect of the Mission', and in 1587 he was made a cardinal. By the middle of the 1570s there were 240 students in residence at Douai, and in 1574 the first of them were sent back into England – a trickle soon to become an alarming flood, as far as the Elizabethan authorities were concerned. By 1580, when the Jesuits joined the English mission (a full generation after Ignatius had offered their talents to an unenthusiastic Cardinal Pole) some 100 'seminary priests' had already come back. Over Elizabeth's reign as a whole, around 500 foreign-trained Catholic clergy are known to have worked in England. Douai (temporarily relocated to Rheims between 1578 and 1593 because of the war in the Low Countries) remained of central importance, but was supplemented by a number of other institutions. In 1576 the old hospice for English pilgrims in Rome was converted into 'the English College', and, after a brief power struggle between Allen's supporters and those who wished it to remain a house of academic studies, it became a second missionary training centre. In 1586 control was formally passed to the Society of Jesus, and the supervision of the superior of the Jesuit mission to England, Robert Persons, a man who shared Allen's conviction that only an 'activist' policy of missionary endeavour, combined with diplomatic and military support from the Catholic powers, could return England to the faith. At Persons' instigation, an English seminary was established at Valladolid in 1589 and another at Seville in 1592. It did not escape the notice of Elizabeth's ministers that, bar Rome, all the English colleges were established on Spanish territory, and Fr Persons, a confidante of Philip II, rapidly acquired the status of Public Enemy Number One in the eyes of the Elizabethan authorities.[19]

[18] Ibid., pp. 59–63; Peter Milward, *Religious Controversies of the Elizabethan Age* (Lincoln, NB, 1977), pp. 1–25.

[19] This may not have been unmerited: a recent study concludes that Persons was ready to contemplate or advocate the assassination of Elizabeth: John Bossy, 'The Heart of Robert Persons', in Thomas McCoog, ed., *The Reckoned Expense: Edmund Campion and the Early English Jesuits* (Woodbridge, 1996). For a more uncritical appraisal, see Francis Edwards, *Robert Persons: The Biography of an Elizabethan Jesuit* (St Louis, MO, 1995).

There is little doubt that the missionary effort which began in the mid-1570s in some sense saved English Catholicism, and set it along the lines that would characterize its history until the transforming effects of Irish immigration in the nineteenth century. But there has been considerable disagreement about how exactly this took place, and how great a moment of rupture it represented. Did the seminarists and Jesuits pick up the baton from a flagging survivalist Catholicism that had nonetheless run a good race through the first two decades of Elizabeth's reign, or were they required to build from scratch a new 'Counter-Reformation' Catholic community over the grave of an earlier Catholic culture and identity that had simply ceased to exist? The issue has traces of an old theological conundrum about it: is Anglicanism or Roman Catholicism the 'real' heir of the medieval English Church? But more pertinently from our point of view, it relates to recent revisionist concerns about the vitality of Marian Catholicism and the potential of Protestantism to erode traditional religious values in the localities. It is thus unsurprising to find A.G. Dickens concluding in his early work on Yorkshire that 'only the slenderest of threads connect the old reaction with the new... Between survivalism and seminarism little or no connection existed.'[20] But the interpretation of this issue has never simply followed denominational lines. The eminent Catholic historian of Yorkshire recusancy, Hugh Aveling, conceded that post-Reformation English Catholicism had its pioneers before 1570, but believed that 'Catholicism was practically dying' by that date.[21] The most persuasive and developed presentation of the theme came in John Bossy's 1975 book, *The English Catholic Community*, a work which broke new ground in distancing itself from the hagiographical stance of much Catholic history, and in adopting a sociological analysis of early modern English Catholicism as 'a branch of the English nonconforming tradition'. Entitling the first section of his book, 'The Death of a Church', Bossy argued that the medieval English Church, and realistic hopes of its revival, had ceased to exist before the Douai-trained missionaries arrived, that this was indeed a necessary precondition for a viable post-Reformation Catholic community to emerge. The moving spirits of the missionary endeavour, men like Persons, Edmund Campion or Gregory Martin, were fundamentally 'Elizabethans' – they had first gone to Oxford after 1559, and had no ties with the old Marian establishment. They had no hankering after monasticism, or a settled hierarchy, and they increasingly came to accept that pending a political Catholic restoration, their mission was to a minority sect in a Protestant land. In the longer term, Bossy argues, there was to be only a very fragmentary geographical continuity between the distribution of the post-Reformation Catholic community and the areas of greatest traditional devotion in pre-Reformation England. The modern history of

20 Dickens, 'Romanist Recusancy', pp. 182–3.

21 J.C.H. Aveling, *The Handle and the Axe: The Catholic Recusants in England from Reformation to Emancipation* (London, 1976), p. 52.

English Catholicism began not with the survival of a continuous tradition across the troubled Reformation decades, but with 'the withdrawal of a separating body from the Church of England'.[22]

Bossy's bold thesis has not passed unchallenged. It raises at least two important questions: that of whether strict recusancy was the characteristic mark of the post-Reformation Catholic community (something to which we will return) and whether a decisive movement into recusancy happened only after the arrival of seminarist priests. Christopher Haigh in particular has argued against the latter proposition, suggesting that the old 'Marian clergy' had initiated the withdrawal from Protestant services before the English mission was underway, or *Regnans in Excelsis* had been promulgated. In Hampshire, for example, charges of recusancy were brought against only three individuals in 1561–5, but against 15 in 1566 and 13 in 1568. Numbers of recorded recusants nationally were growing rapidly in the late 1570s before the missionary priests were present in force. Haigh accuses Bossy of taking at face value Robert Persons's 'propagandist Jesuit version of Tudor Catholic History', which denigrated the achievements of the Old Church in order to accentuate the contribution of the mission. And in Haigh's own case-study county of Lancashire the continuities between late medieval piety and later recusancy seem fairly apparent.[23] Other historians, such as Patrick McGrath, Joy Rowe, and Jack Scarisbrick, have joined Haigh in emphasizing the real contribution the Marians made to the survival of Elizabethan Catholicism. According to Bishop Edwin Sandys of Worcester in 1564, such 'popish and perverse priests which misliking religion have forsaken the ministry' were being welcomed in gentlemen's houses 'and have great estimation with the people'. When the seminarists arrived, the Marians worked alongside them and shared their sufferings: at least 130 of them were imprisoned under Elizabeth. Those ordained legally in England before 1559 were, however, usefully shielded from the most draconian parts of the penal legislation, which designated as traitors only those who had been made priests abroad. There is no doubt that priests who had been part of the abortive Marian Counter-Reformation helped lay the foundations for future Catholic survival, yet, as Scarisbrick observed, 'their fatal shortcoming was that they had no way of replacing themselves.'[24] Over the longer term, without the infusion of leadership and fervour provided by the missionaries, the prospects for a mass movement of popular Catholicism seem little better than those of late medieval

[22] Bossy, *Catholic Community*, quotes at pp. 7, 15, 107, 144.

[23] Haigh, 'The Continuity of Catholicism in the English Reformation', in id., ed., *The English Reformation Revised* (Cambridge, 1987); *Reformations*, pp. 259–60.

[24] Patrick McGrath and Joy Rowe, 'The Marian Priests under Elizabeth I', *Recusant History*, 17 (1984–5); id., 'The Imprisonment of Catholics for Religion under Elizabeth I', *Recusant History*, 20 (1991); Scarisbrick, *Reformation*, pp. 141–5; Michael Mullett, *Catholics in Britain and Ireland 1558–1829* (Basingstoke, 1998), pp. 9–10.

Lollardy without the arrival of the evangelicals. A further analogy is of relevance here. Just as the apparent 'rise' of Lollardy in the early sixteenth century may be a function of greater episcopal efforts to find Lollards, so the rise of recorded recusancy from the later 1570s may reflect, in the light of the scare provided by the arrival of the missionaries, a greater pressure on officials and communities to identify individuals who had earlier been quietly getting away with it.

The continuity/discontinuity debate about the early history of the post-Reformation Catholic community may now have run its course, and come to rest in a middle position. It is clear that by about 1580 a new and distinctive English (Roman) Catholic community was coming into existence, and that both 'survival' and 'rebirth' played a part in the process. Attention must now turn to the issue of how such an entity negotiated the terms of its existence with the English (Protestant) state, and the related question of how it understood (and argued about) its own identity as the heir of pre-Reformation, Catholic England.

7.2 The Paradoxes of Persecution

The Elizabethan State had no intention of allowing a separated Roman Catholicism to go about its business undisturbed – it could hardly do so when much of that business seemed to involve the subversion, even the overthrow of the State itself. An optimistic hope in government circles that popery would wither away of its own accord was shattered by the 1569 Rising and the 1570 papal excommunication. Succeeding events seemed merely to confirm that Catholicism, at home and abroad, was an insidious and pervasive threat. In 1571 a plot centred on the Florentine banker Roberto Ridolfi involved a projected marriage between Mary Queen of Scots and the Duke of Norfolk, backed by Spanish troops and papal money. The arrival of the first Douai missionaries followed hard on the heels of the 1572 St Bartholemew's Day Massacre, in which thousands of French Protestants were slaughtered by the Parisian mob. The temperature dropped still further after 1580. In that year the first Jesuits, Edmund Campion and Robert Persons, joined the missionary enterprise in England. Campion was caught and died a martyr, protesting that his mission was purely pastoral and devoid of any political purpose. But it has been argued that Persons was looking to build up support for the overthrow of Elizabeth, having high (but as it turned out fruitless) hopes that James VI was on the verge of declaring for Catholicism.[25] Certainly, it became

[25] Michael Carafiello, 'English Catholicism and the Jesuit Mission of 1580–81', *Historical Journal*, 37 (1994). For the opposing view that Persons only turned 'political' after the failure of the mission and execution of Campion, see Thomas McCoog, *The Society of Jesus in Ireland, Scotland, and England 1541–1588* (Leiden, 1996), pp. 129–77, 266–7.

an article of faith among Protestants that Jesuits favoured the use of force to restore Catholic power. In the mid-1580s, violent Catholic schemes (most of which were hare-brained and half-baked) seemed to come with almost monotonous regularity: the plan of a Warwickshire squire, John Somerville, to assassinate Elizabeth in 1583, the Throckmorton Plot of the same year, the Parry Plot of 1585, the Babington Plot of 1586 (Mary Queen of Scots' proven knowledge of which brought her to the scaffold in the following year). War with Spain, which began in 1585 and continued for the rest of the reign, inevitably heightened the sense of threat posed by English Catholics, particularly in the invasion year of 1588.

The consequence of all of this was increasingly harsh legislation aimed at eliminating the Catholic clerical leadership and forcing the laity back into conformity with the Church of England. In 1571, in the wake of the papal excommunication, it became treason to call the Queen a heretic or to introduce any papal bull, and an offence to import any kind of Catholic devotional object. Still harsher legislation was introduced in 1581, increasing the fines for non-attendance at church to a swingeing £20 per month, and making it a treasonable offence to convert anyone or be converted to Rome if the intention was to withdraw allegiance to the Crown. The logic of this was extended in 1585 when it was decreed that any priest ordained overseas was by definition guilty of treason when he arrived in England, and that lay people could be put to death for harbouring priests. An Act of 1587 tightened up the collection of recusancy fines, and in 1593 recusants' movements were restricted to within five miles of their dwelling. This was a draconian set of legislative measures, and out of it emerged a real persecution. The first seminary priest to be executed was Cuthbert Mayne in 1577, and a further 123 of his fellows had suffered the same fate before the end of Elizabeth's reign. This was a high rate of attrition: about half the total that arrived in England were arrested, and about half of these were put to death, along with 59 lay helpers. For centuries to come, the veneration of the martyrs, the prizing of their relics and of their memory, deeply entered into the psyche of English Catholics, became their 'most sacred centre of communal self-consciousness'.[26]

Assessing the impact of the Elizabethan penal legislation, Fr Philip Hughes remarked in the mid-1950s that 'the great achievement of this policy of persecution was that it made the life of the ordinary Catholic a very nightmare of insecurity'.[27] Yet what is interesting about the Elizabethan penal legislation is how intermittently and selectively it was applied. There was no general holocaust of Catholics, and no inclination on the part of Elizabeth and her ministers to initiate one. Some high-profile Catholic landowners (like Lord Vaux or Sir Thomas Tresham) were

26 Norman, *Roman Catholicism*, p. 16. See also Anne Dillon, *The Construction of Martyrdom in the English Catholic Community 1535–1603* (Aldershot, 2002).

27 Philip Hughes, *The Reformation in England*, (3 vols., London, 1950–4), iii. 369.

crippled by cumulative recusancy fines, but others were not pursued with the same vigour. The treason legislation was seldom applied against the laity. On a crude layperson-killed-per-annum scale, Elizabeth's persecution of Catholics over her reign was something like 38 times less intense than Mary's persecution of Protestants. Even the clergy, who were more harshly treated, were in considerably greater danger at some times than others. Over half of the total of the priestly martyrs were put to death in the crisis years of 1586–92, no fewer than 21 of them in the second half of 1588 alone, as the Armada teetered round the English coastline. Thereafter, the persecution eased somewhat: 33 priests were executed in Elizabeth's last decade, but others were simply expelled from the country.[28]

Simple administrative incompetence has often been cited as an important reason why many English Catholics were able to get on with their lives in relative peace and security. The Church courts had little coercive power over those who regarded their most serious sanction, excommunication, as a spiritual irrelevance. The exchequer, which administered the fines for recusancy, was notoriously inefficient: its lists were often inaccurate and out-of-date, and its procedures for seizing the wealth of those unwilling or unable to pay the £20 fines were cumbersome and open to abuse. But Michael Questier has argued that when they worked in a co-ordinated way, the enforcement mechanisms available to the Elizabethan authorities were powerful ones; the institution of the ecclesiastical commission, for example, gave bishops power to imprison or fine which they did not ordinarily possess. The reasons why Catholics were not *en masse* forced to become Protestants were more complex, involving the mismatch of 'religious' and 'political' motives for enforcing conformity. Elizabethan and Jacobean bishops were genuinely interested in the souls and consciences of Catholics; when they could, they required recusants returning to the Church of England to participate in special liturgical rituals repudiating Rome as a heretical Church. But, other than during the alarm-ridden 1580s, when genuine religious conversion seemed a prerequisite of political loyalty, the secular authorities were more interested in conformity as a token of outward obedience, in accordance with Queen Elizabeth's famous disinclination to make 'windows into men's souls'. (Hence the repeated failure of the bishops to get legislation through Parliament stipulating punishment for non-communicants.)[29] Indeed, it was a recurrent insistence of the regime that Catholics were punished not for reasons of spiritual conscience, but for political disloyalty: the priests were hanged for treason, not burned for heresy. This may have seemed a rather technical distinction to the victims, but to the authorities it offered both a shrewd propaganda ploy, and

28 Haigh, *Reformations*, p. 263; McGrath, *Papists*, pp. 202–3.
29 Michael Questier, *Conversion, Politics and Religion in England, 1580–1625* (Cambridge, 1996), chs. 5–6.

possession of the moral high ground. The case was set out in a tract of 1583, *The Execution of Justice in England*, by no less a personage than William Cecil.[30] The strategy, however, placed limits on the actions the government might take, and it opened opportunities for Catholics publicly to contest the regime's approved version. In a fascinating discussion of the events and rituals surrounding the execution of priests, Peter Lake and Michael Questier have shown that these occasions were far from straightforward celebrations of the power of the monarchy. From the scaffold, priests often proclaimed that they died for religion, and insisted on wearing their vestments to make the point. Some achieved a propaganda coup in converting to Catholicism the ordinary criminals with whom (appropriately, in the State's view) they were being hanged. A consequence of the State's propensity for dismembering the bodies of traitors and putting the parts on display was to make it easier for supporters to acquire relics of the martyrs. The prisons were another apparent instrument of official repression and control which opened up opportunities for Catholic 'agency'. Most of the seminarists who worked in Elizabethan England are known to have been incarcerated at some point, in the London gaols of Newgate, Marshalsea and the Clink, and in almost 50 others nationwide. The concentration of priests in some places, combined with the often lax 'privatized' administration of the prison system, meant prisons became *de facto* mass-centres to which lay Catholics flocked, and to which newly arrived priests often headed in order 'to touch base with one of the most symbolic and practical centres of Catholic activity'.[31]

Another consequence of the government's (at least partial) willingness to discriminate between religious and political allegiance, however, was to open up space for division among the Catholics themselves. These divisions had been present from the very beginnings of the mission (for example, over the purpose of the English College in Rome), but were less apparent during the persecution of the 1580s, a period which has been called a 'puritan moment' in English Catholicism, when wide sections of the Catholic clergy and laity threw their support behind the aims and methods of the Jesuits.[32] But as the intensity of oppression eased, disagreements increasingly came to the surface about what measure of compromise was possible with the regime, and about what kind of Catholic community the mission was trying to create. Appropriately enough, dissension first flared up in the prisons,

30 William Cecil, *The Execution of Justice in England*, ed. R.M. Kingdom (Ithaca, NY, 1965), pp. 1, 7–10, 20–1, 36–7.

31 Peter Lake and Michael Questier, 'Agency, Appropriation and Rhetoric under the Gallows: Puritans, Romanists and the State in Early Modern England', *Past and Present*, 153 (1996); id., 'Prisons, Priests and People', in Nicholas Tyacke, ed., *England's Long Reformation 1500–1800* (London, 1998), quote at p. 202.

32 Peter Lake with Michael Questier, *The Antichrist's Lewd Hat: Protestants, Papists and Players in Post-Reformation England* (New Haven and London, 2002), p. 285.

places where large numbers of argumentative clerics were thrown together with time heavy on their hands. At Wisbech Castle in Cambridgeshire (the main government holding-centre outside London) a party led by the Jesuit William Weston clashed in the mid-1590s with a group headed by the secular priest, Christopher Bagshaw. Weston objected to what he saw as the lax moral conduct of the seculars, and to traditional Christmas entertainments involving Morris dancers and a hobbyhorse. For their part, the seculars were affronted by the Jesuit practice of making decisions by majority vote and, worse, by their sitting where they liked at dinner, rather than arranging places by order of seniority – 'a disgrace to all degree of learning and fit for Anabaptists'.[33] These petty clerical disputes were in fact microcosms of larger issues. The secular priests emphasized tradition and hierarchy because they regarded themselves as being in unbroken line of continuity with the medieval Catholic Church in England. Their principal objectives were to re-establish the structures of that Church, and minister sacraments to the faithful in an orderly and traditional fashion. This would inevitably involve a degree of official or unofficial government sanction, something that madcap Jesuit schemes involving Spanish arms could only irreparably damage. The Jesuits, by contrast, saw England as mission territory, more akin to other frontiers of the Counter-Reformation such as Mexico or Japan, than to the settled Catholic territories of Italy or Spain. Their ethos was a fundamentally 'evangelical' one, which emphasized conversion and the operation of divine grace above formal hierarchical structures. There is an analogy here that did not fail to impress itself upon contemporaries. Bagshaw called his opponents 'puritans, precisians, Genevans', and a range of conformist Protestant commentators (notably James I) habitually drew comparisons between the arrogant zealotry of Puritan and Jesuit.[34]

Matters came to a head over the issue of leadership after the death of Allen in 1594. The seculars petitioned Rome for the appointment of a bishop for England, but were disappointed when in 1598 the papacy followed Persons' suggestion and employed the novel expedient of an 'Archpriest', George Blackwell, with limited jurisdiction and instructions to consult closely with the Jesuits. The seculars instantly appealed against the decision to the Pope, and through the last years of Elizabeth's reign an 'Appellant' party was locked in bitter dispute with the Jesuits, the two sides pouring out vitriol against each other in letters and in print. Some degree of compromise was reached in 1602 when Clement VIII ordered Blackwell to

[33] Arnold Pritchard, *Catholic Loyalism in Elizabethan England* (London, 1979), ch. 5.

[34] Lake and Questier, *Lewd Hat*, p. 288; Caroline Hibbard, 'Early Stuart Catholicism: Revisions and Re-Revisions', *Journal of Modern History*, 52 (1980), 26–7. Questier, *Conversion*, pp. 79–84 notes how converts to and from the Society of Jesus in fact often were Puritans.

cease consulting with the Jesuits and to take three leading Appellants as his assistants. But in the meantime the Appellants, convinced that Catholic misfortunes were caused by understandable government suspicion of the violent and subversive outlook of the Jesuits, had been negotiating for toleration at home: free practice of religion in exchange for assurances of political trustworthiness. An oath of loyalty proposed by the priest William Watson was rejected by fellow Appellants, though thirteen of them did sign a Protestation of Allegiance to Elizabeth in January 1603. These hopes were in the end unrealistic. The only legally sanctioned recognition of more than one confession in a major West European state, the toleration of Huguenots in France under the 1598 Edict of Nantes, had been extorted by three decades of bloody civil war. The Appellant priests had no such leverage, and the government was prepared to go no further than a promise of personal immunity from the treason laws for priests prepared to repudiate the papal deposing power. The authorities were, however, more than happy to mischief-make, Bishop Bancroft of London allowing the printing of Appellant anti-Jesuit works in order to deepen and publicize the divisions in Catholic ranks.[35]

English Catholicism thus entered the seventeenth century with a split personality, two contrasting visions of what the Church should be, and of its relationship to its own past (visions which have a clear historiographical afterlife in the Haigh–Bossy 'continuity' debate). But what sort of society had English Catholicism in practice become? Here Bossy and Haigh find themselves in broad agreement. Increasingly, the Catholic community had come to depend on the gentry and on gentry households, and had evolved into a predominantly 'seigneurial Catholicism'. The reasons are not hard to fathom. Known 'safe' gentry houses constituted a ready-made communications network for priests entering the country, and from them priests could minister with a modicum of safety both to the Catholic elite and to their neighbours and tenants (even if it required occasional confinement in a well-constructed priest-hole). Presented for not coming to his parish church in Bedfordshire in 1581, Lord Vaux 'did claim his house to be a parish by itself'. In such 'parishes', however, there was a tendency for the priest to take on the characteristics of a domestic chaplain, one of the upper servants.[36] Traditionally, Catholic historians have celebrated the resilience and survival-against-the-odds of the recusant families, but more modern scholarship has recognized there was a price to be paid. Bossy saw the instinctive loyalism and hierarchical outlook of the

[35] Dures, *Catholicism*, pp. 36–8; Pritchard, *Catholic Loyalism*, pp. 171, 191; Alexandra Walsham, '"Domme Preachers"? Post-Reformation English Catholicism and the Culture of Print', *Past and Present*, 168 (2000), 92.

[36] John Bossy, 'The Character of Elizabethan Catholicism', in Trevor Aston, ed., *Crisis in Europe 1560–1660* (London, 1965), p. 225.

gentry as always in tension with the clerical activism of the Allen–Persons school, and concluded that in the end the former won out. The history of Elizabethan Catholicism was 'a progress from inertia to inertia in three generations'.[37]

Haigh is even more inclined to see a glass half empty, or rather a glass whose contents had been carelessly and needlessly spilled. The corollary of his emphasis on the vitality of survivalist and 'Marian recusant' Catholicism in the early years of Elizabeth is the proposition that the seminary priests squandered the opportunity to build a mass popular movement, particularly in the areas of greatest traditionalist sentiment in north and west England, and in Wales. They were left merely with a rump community, 'a seigneurial sect'. Haigh points out that in the middle of Elizabeth's reign over half the priests were based in London, Essex and the south Midlands, areas which had fewer than 20 per cent of recorded recusants, an imbalance that had been redressed but by no means corrected by the end of the reign. The mismatch was in part a necessary function of the arrival of priests in the east coast ports, and of the mechanics of the distribution agency being operated from London by the Jesuit Henry Garnet. But it was also a matter of deliberate choice on the part of the missionary priests, sons of gentry families who preferred to live and work in some comfort and security among their social equals. The typical priest in the second half of Elizabeth's reign was ensconced in an Oxfordshire manor house; the typical lay Catholic, in a rural parish in Cornwall, Yorkshire or North Wales, had been left to his or her own devices, and to eventual absorption as a 'parish anglican' into the Church of England.[38] Critics, in particular Patrick McGrath, have regarded Haigh as unduly censorious, and unrealistic about the choices open to the missionary priests. Charges of timidity and seeking an easy life are difficult to reconcile with the high clerical casualty rate, and there were other reasons for congregating among the gentry of the south and east. For as long as there were hopes of a political restoration, concentrating resources near the geographical and social centres of power made sense (a point Haigh concedes). While Haigh highlights the limited aims of the seminary priests, insisting that they were 'not missionaries' but rather directed solely to sustain the faith of existing Catholics, McGrath points out that there are numerous examples of priests converting 'heretics' when they

37 Ibid., p. 246.

38 Christopher Haigh, 'From Monopoly to Minority: Catholicism in Early Modern England', *Transactions of the Royal Historical Society*, 5th ser. 31 (1981); 'Continuity of Catholicism'; 'The Church of England, the Catholics, and the People', in Peter Marshall, ed., *The Impact of the English Reformation 1500–1640* (London, 1997); 'Revisionism, the Reformation, and the History of English Catholicism', *Journal of Ecclesiastical History*, 36 (1985); *Reformations*, ch. 15.

got the chance.[39] Nonetheless, he does not substantially contest the picture of a Catholicism which was becoming contracted and domesticated, restricted largely to the gentry and a small penumbra of their tenants and dependents. Haigh speaks about the 'collapse of Catholicism among the lower orders' by the end of Elizabeth's reign, while Diarmaid MacCulloch argues that 'a Catholic group of yeomen or of the "middle sort" hardly existed'.[40]

Yet from a number of sources it is possible to build up a picture of a late Elizabethan Catholicism more diverse and more fluid than the above portrayal would suggest, and as a result more relevant to the mainstream of English social and ecclesiastical life. The existence of a continuing strand of 'plebian Catholicism' has been asserted by Jack Scarisbrick, Alexandra Walsham, Michael Mullett and Marie Rowlands. Of 820 individuals cited for recusancy for the first time in 1615, only 50 were gentlemen, while 239 were 'yeomen, labourers and mechanicals'.[41] Catholics in London could hardly enjoy seigneurial protection: they were numerous enough to alarm the Privy Council, but have been neglected by modern historians. Over 20 years ago, Caroline Hibbard noted the distortion caused by 'the almost total omission of London' from Bossy's picture of the Catholic community, and the subject is still awaiting thorough investigation.[42] The notion of an introspective, enclosed Catholic world of stubbornly recusant gentry families is further problematized by Michael Questier's work on conversion, showing how considerable numbers of individuals passed in and out of allegiance to Rome, and how many families were divided by religion. A revealing source here is the record of family backgrounds collected from entrants to the English College at Rome. Of 124 Jesuits who passed through the College between 1598 and 1640, 49 said that they had formerly been heretics (as opposed to schismatics) and gave the names of those who had converted them.[43]

But it is in renewed exploration of the permeable boundaries between recusancy and conformity that some of the most important recent contri-

[39] Patrick McGrath, 'Elizabethan Catholicism: a Reconsideration', *Journal of Ecclesiastical History*, 35 (1984).

[40] Haigh, *Reformations*, p. 265; Diarmaid MacCulloch, *The Later Reformation in England, 1547–1603* (2nd ed., Basingstoke, 2001), p. 125.

[41] Scarisbrick, *Reformation*, pp. 156–9; Walsham, *Church Papists*, pp. 92–3; Mullett, *Catholics*, p. 21; Marie Rowlands, 'Hidden People: Catholic Commoners, 1558–1625', in id., ed., *English Catholics of Parish and Town 1558–1778* (Catholic Record Society, 1999).

[42] Hibbard, 'Early Stuart Catholicism', 6n. Though see now Michael Gandy, 'Ordinary Catholics in Mid-Seventeenth Century London', in Rowlands, *Parish and Town*.

[43] Questier, *Conversion*; '"Like Locusts over all the World": Conversion, Indoctrination and the Society of Jesus in Late Elizabethan and Jacobean England', in McCoog, *Reckoned Expense*.

butions have been made. The suggestion of Bossy and others that 'church papistry' had effectively run its course as a significant phenomenon before the end of Elizabeth's reign has been questioned by Alexandra Walsham, who argues that 'articulate Catholicism within the Church of England was a lasting feature of a complex contemporary religious scene', rather than a brief episode in the posthumous history of pre-Reformation Christendom.[44] Catholic clerical writers condemned 'schismatics', just as Protestant writers had castigated the 'Nicodemites' of Mary's reign. But informally, many priests were prepared to condone churchgoing in certain circumstances. It can be shown that individuals moved in and out of recusancy under local pressures and harassment, many returning to it after long periods of conformity when conditions eased under the early Stuarts. Well into the seventeenth century, Protestants worried about church popery, 'feigned conformity'. In 1607 the Yorkshire Puritan Francis Bunny argued church papists to be 'as dangerous as they that come not', and Sir Edward Giles urged a parliamentary committee to introduce a law against them in 1621. As Questier puts it, 'papistry was regarded as a threat precisely because of its malleability, its capacity to adapt and its readiness to integrate.'[45] These insights have been supplemented by Bill Sheils' close-focus study of recorded recusancy in Jacobean Yorkshire. Women and the elderly predominate among the lists, but the fact that many of these seem only to have been recusants for a short time is striking, suggesting a 'life-cycle' pattern in outward conformity: people became (or were reported as) recusants when they had less to lose.[46] The old assumption that 'Catholic' and 'recusant' are virtually synonymous terms is becoming impossible to sustain.

By the end of Elizabeth's reign, most English Catholics were coming to terms with their minority status. Even in clerical and Jesuit circles the hope of reversing the Reformation with one swift blow involving foreign invasion and domestic rebellion was starting to fade. But it would be a mistake to suppose that Catholicism had simply withdrawn from the national stage, noteworthy only because of the role it played in the paranoid and overheated imaginations of Protestant zealots. The accession of a new dynasty in 1603 seemed to offer real hopes of a revival for English Catholics, and when those hopes were disappointed, the response of some of them was to prepare to greet the new century not with a whimper, but with a bang.

44 Bossy, *Catholic Community*, p. 124; Dures, *Catholicism*, p. 39; Walsham, *Church Papists*, p. 95.

45 Michael Questier, 'The Politics of Religious Conformity and the Accession of James I', *Historical Research*, 71 (1998), 26, 30; Walsham, *Church Papists*, p. 96.

46 W.J. Sheils, 'Household, Age, and Gender among Jacobean Yorkshire Recusants', in Rowlands, *Parish and Town*. See also his 'Catholics and their Neighbours in a Rural Community: Egton Chapelry 1590–1780', *Northern History*, 25 (1998).

7.3 The Trials of Toleration

The rule of James I was a period of relative toleration for English Catholics (only 19 missionary priests died, compared to 124 under Elizabeth), but during the reign relations between the Catholics and the English State remained complex and difficult. On his accession, the new King (who was, after all, the son of Mary Queen of Scots) showed signs of favours to individual Catholics, and brought a halt to the execution of priests. The fractious Jesuit William Weston was released from imprisonment, and the Jesuit superior in England, Henry Garnet, wrote of 'a golden time', 'great hope is of toleration'.[47] Church popery now reached the highest places in the land, for James's wife, Anne of Denmark, had been secretly received into the Catholic Church shortly before her husband's accession, and ostentatiously did not receive communion at the coronation in Westminster Abbey.[48] But Catholic, like Puritan, expectations of James were to be disappointed. Just as the Puritan activism of 1603–4 had alarmed the King, so the open displays of Catholic confidence and revival prompted a crackdown; priests were expelled and recusancy fines reimposed. The immediate result was an attempt by a small group of minor gentry to assassinate James and the assembled Lords and councillors at the opening of Parliament on November 5 1605, by detonating a massive explosion in a cellar under the House of Lords – a desperate plan encouraged by the realization (after the Anglo-Spanish Peace Treaty of 1604) that military assistance from Spain could no longer be counted on. Though the Gunpowder Plot is indelibly associated with the name of Guy Fawkes, the leader was Robert Catesby, a gentleman from Warwickshire (Shakespeare's county was a long-standing centre of 'hot' Catholicism). After the plot was discovered, Catesby and three others were killed resisting arrest, and a further nine were executed, including Henry Garnet who seems to have had prior knowledge of the plans under the seal of confession – confirmation of both Protestant and Appellant convictions about the perfidy of Jesuits.[49] There was, however, no general purge of Catholics, and the most significant long-term consequence of the affair was its contribution to a tradition of popular anti-popery, careful ever after to 'remember, remember, the fifth of November'. James instead took the occasion to attempt to force from

[47] Antonia Fraser, *The Gunpowder Plot: Terror and Faith in 1605* (London, 1996), pp. xxxiv–v.

[48] Peter McCullough, *Sermons at Court: Politics and Religion in Elizabethan and Jacobean Preaching* (Cambridge, 1998), pp. 169–74.

[49] The best general survey of these events is Fraser, *Gunpowder Plot*. Suggestions, e.g. by Francis Edwards, *Guy Fawkes: The Real Story of the Gunpowder Plot* (London, 1969), that the plot was planned by James's chief minister, Salisbury, to discredit the English Catholics are improbable, though it seems likely that Salisbury knew about it sometime before the arrest of Fawkes on the night of 4/5 November.

Catholics an explicit declaration of allegiance, hoping in the process to exploit the long-standing divisions within the Catholic community. An Act of 1606 'for the better discovering and repressing of Popish Recusants' not only imposed penalties on non-communicants for the first time, but set out the form of an Oath of Allegiance which all indicted recusants (barring the nobility) were required to take, describing the deposing power of the pope as 'blasphemous and heretical'.[50] A handful of clergy (including the Archpriest Blackwell) took the oath; lay Catholics were in practice seldom called upon to do so. But its overt antipapalism was too much for even the leading Appellants, and a damaging schism among the Catholic clerical body was in the end avoided.[51]

After the King's fears of imminent assassination had subsided, Catholic fortunes tended to fluctuate with the directions of James's foreign policy, which were, to the chagrin of many of his Protestant subjects, usually pacific ones. At the time of Prince Charles's projected marriage to a Spanish princess in 1622–3 the penal laws were temporarily suspended, and Archbishop Abbot (no doubt through gritted teeth) was made to order preachers to avoid 'bitter invectives and railing speaches' against the Church of Rome.[52] In 1625 James secured the marriage of his son to another foreign Catholic Princess, Henrietta Maria of France. In a generally safer environment, Catholics were more likely to emerge into full recusancy, thus fuelling an alarming perception of growing numbers on the part of Protestant observers. Catholics, claimed Abbot in 1624, 'go by the thousand to mass'.[53] The recusancy laws themselves, meanwhile, were increasingly coming to be regarded by the exchequer as a source of additional revenue, rather than a means of compelling papists into conformity. Within the Catholic community, the Appellants' ideal of orderly hierarchical government was making progress, particularly after the death of Persons in 1610. By 1621 the Archpriest system had effectively broken down, and in 1623 episcopal oversight was finally achieved with the appointment of one of the original Appellants, called (appropriately) William Bishop. A system of vicars-general, archdeacons and deans was set up, giving institutional embodiment to the claim that the Catholic secular clergy were a group 'legally and historically speaking identical with the *Ecclesia Anglicana* as it

[50] G.W. Prothero, ed., *Select Statutes and Other Constitutional Documents Illustrative of the Reigns of Elizabeth and James I* (4th ed., Oxford, 1913), pp. 258–9.

[51] John Bossy, 'The English Catholic Community 1603–1625', in Alan G.R. Smith, ed., *The Reign of James VI and I* (Basingstoke, 1973), pp. 92–3.

[52] Thomas Cogswell, 'England and the Spanish Match', in Richard Cust and Ann Hughes, eds., *Conflict in Early Stuart England* (London, 1989), p. 118.

[53] Norman, *Roman Catholicism*, p. 34. Bossy estimates the number of the 'more or less regular clientele of the missionary priests' as c. 35,000 in 1603, and c. 60,000 in 1640: 'English Catholic Community', p. 101.

had stood before the Reformation.'[54] But this did not signify an eclipse of the religious orders. Jesuit numbers in England increased from 16 in 1598 to 40 in 1606, rising to 123 in 1623 and 193 in 1639, and they were increasingly joined by other regulars such as the Benedictines. A significant English contribution to religious life in the Roman Catholic Church was the foundation in 1610 by the Yorkshirewoman Mary Ward of the Institute of the Blessed Virgin Mary – an active order of nuns modelled on the Jesuits. Overcoming papal and indeed Jesuit suspicion, the order came to play an important role in educational and missionary work in England and on the continent.[55]

Thus confidence and expansion, rather than ossification or decline from a heroic mid-Elizabethan peak seems to characterize the Catholic experience in the decades before the Civil War. By the 1630s the ratio of priests to people was higher than it was to be for over another two centuries; there were numerous opportunities for Catholic education abroad, and, less certainly, at home; the quality and quantity of Catholic literature was high.[56] Perhaps it is impossible, however, to identify a single English Catholic culture. The world of Catholic or crypto-Catholic peers like James's favourite Henry Howard, Earl of Northampton (there were eight or nine Catholic nobles in 1603, and 18 in 1625) was very different from that of the stubbornly 'country' recusant gentry, and more so from that of Catholic artisans or yeomen. Some Catholic gentry, perhaps those with Jesuit chaplains, were more in tune with a Counter-Reformation devotional ethos stressing frequent communion and confession; elsewhere a more traditional emphasis on the round of feasts and fasts of the medieval year may have prevailed. But we should be wary of exaggerated contrasts between, for example, gentry 'formed by the modernized Catholicism of the Counter-Reformation, and the poorer Catholics who remained in unreformed ignorance and superstition'.[57] The 'Counter-Reformation' Jesuits, most notably William Weston, were deeply involved in the 'popular' practice of exorcism (another parallel with the Puritans), and in 1605, on the eve of the Gunpowder Plot, the Jesuit Henry Garnet led a thoroughly 'medieval' pilgrimage to the shrine of St Winifred at Holywell in North Wales.[58] Walsham has recently convincingly demonstrated (against some traditional preconceptions) the extent of the reliance of post-Reformation Catholicism on the printed word. Books brought with them the thought-world of wider Catholicism, and could to a

[54] Ibid., p. 97.

[55] Mullett, *Catholics*, p. 26; Marie Rowlands, 'Recusant Women 1560–1640', in Mary Prior, ed., *Women in English Society 1500–1800* (London, 1985), pp. 168–73.

[56] Hibbard, 'Early Stuart Catholicism', pp. 10–13.

[57] Bossy, 'English Catholic Community', p. 104.

[58] F.W. Brownlow, *Shakespeare, Harsnett, and the Devils of Denham* (London and Toronto, 1993); Fraser, *Gunpowder Plot*, pp. 134–5.

degree compensate for the absence of the close episcopal oversight and clerical discipline experienced by Catholics on the continent, but they were not in themselves an automatic agent of Tridentine modernization. There is evidence of texts and printed pictures being treated as intrinsically sacred objects, talismans to ward off evil spirits and bad weather.[59]

There is one feature of English Catholic culture about which historians seem agreed – its notably feminized character. The prominence, and often preponderance of women in recusant lists is striking, and many Catholic gentry households displayed a clearly 'matriarchal' character (i.e. the religious observances were arranged by a recusant wife, while the husband attended Church of England services). Bossy has suggested that Catholic nonconformity may have been particularly attractive to women alienated by the 'domestic authoritarianism' implicit in the Protestant teaching on the priesthood of all believers, the emphasis on literacy as almost a condition of salvation, and the loss of ritual functions connected with fasting and abstinence.[60] There were some genuinely 'mixed marriages', but in many other cases more strategic calculations were involved: church papist husbands conformed, to preserve the estate against recusant fines, and perhaps to maintain public duty, while wives carried out conscientious resistance in the 'private' sphere of the household.[61] Contemporaries did not fail to notice the phenomenon. A preacher in Cambridge in the early 1620s warned darkly that because 'that sex is more fit and apt to delude', women were particularly targeted by the papists, and that because 'women rule more in the hearts of children... within these few years their number is increased here among us exceedingly'.[62] Before dismissing this as paranoid misogyny, we should remember that both sons of one important mixed marriage, Charles II and James II, converted to the religion of their mother in adult life.

This abrupt swing back into the world of the Court and high politics invites reflection on the complex relationship between 'popery' and 'antipopery' in the early Stuart period. By some objective standards, the sense of threat expressed by many Protestants seems out of proportion. Interest in direct action to topple the regime (the Allen–Persons project) had almost totally waned, despite a final flare-up in 1605 (of which many Catholics vehemently disapproved). Whether one takes a maximalist or minimalist view of the size of the Catholic community based on recusancy statistics, Catholics were a small percentage of the population as a whole,

59 Walsham, 'Domme Preachers'.

60 Bossy, *Catholic Community*, p. 158.

61 Rowland, 'Recusant Women', p. 161; Walsham, *Church Papists*, p. 81. Though men with recusant wives were not exempt from outside pressure, see Questier, *Conversion*, p. 146.

62 Robert Jenison, *The Height of Israel's Heathenish Idolatrie* (London, 1621), p. 112.

save in a few exceptional areas such as Lancashire. We have seen, moreover, that lay Catholics seldom experienced sustained and heavy persecution under Elizabeth, and even less so under James. A number of scholars have emphasized how ordinary Catholics were integrated into their local communities, and often tacitly exempted, or even protected from the full severity of the law: 'anti-Catholicism was an ideological construct, passionate in the abstract or at isolated flashpoints, rather than something that was applied on a daily basis to the people next door'.[63] The minister of Faversham in Kent, reproved for making laudatory remarks in a funeral sermon of 1625 about a parishioner 'inclined to the Romish religion', retorted that it was quite proper to suppose God might have mercy upon 'a simple-hearted papist'.[64]

Yet we should be cautious before accepting the experience of Catholics as evidence that English society was generally 'tolerant' of deviants who did not rock the boat. For English Catholicism, notwithstanding Bossy's refreshing perspective, was never just another branch of nonconformity, a sect like the Family of Love. Though Catholics were often politically quiescent, or even actively loyal to the English Crown, it is probably the case that, as Edward Norman puts it, most of them 'consciously regarded their condition as abnormal, and awaited the change of political and dynastic fortunes which would lead to a national restoration of the faith'.[65] Most importantly, they were distinct from all other seventeenth-century dissenting groups in the strength of their international ties. English Catholics had strategies for coping with an intermittent and unpredictable supply of priests, but without them, and the sacraments they provided, they simply could not in the end remain Catholics. The priests were all trained overseas. Caroline Hibbard has aptly observed that 'no other English group has been tied by an umbilical cord to the continent of Europe for over 200 years', and that, ultimately, 'the friendly, familiar face of English Catholicism' could not be completely disassociated from 'the dark, unknown, frightening side – the spectre of international Catholicism'.[66] Protestants did not need to be delusionally paranoid to feel concerned by the continuing clandestine cross-channel traffic with the Spanish Netherlands, by the apparent greater numbers and confidence of recusants in the localities, by the presence at Court of at first a covertly, and then an openly Catholic queen – and also by

[63] Marsh, *Popular Religion*, p. 189. See also Robin Clifton, 'Fear of Popery', in Conrad Russell, ed., *The Origins of the English Civil War* (London, 1973), pp. 163–5; Anthony Milton, 'A Qualified Intolerance: the Limits and Ambiguities of Early Stuart Anti-Catholicism', in Arthur Marotti, *Catholicism and Anti-Catholicism in Early Modern English Texts* (Basingstoke, 1999).

[64] Marshall, *Beliefs*, p. 209.

[65] Norman, *Roman Catholicism*, p. 31.

[66] Hibbard, 'Early Stuart Catholicism', pp. 29–30.

the suspicion (which modern research is confirming to be accurate) that significant numbers of closet papists sat (or snored) along with them in church each Sunday. The 'toleration' of Catholics in early Stuart England was a deeply ambivalent and unstable phenomenon, and an important element in the unravelling of the Reformation Settlement that took place in the 1640s (see Section 8.3).

Summation

Recent scholarship has tended to show more interest in anti-Catholicism than in Catholicism itself, though in truth (and as common sense would suggest) the two themes are really inseparable. Catholicism has an internal social history, which Bossy and Aveling (assisted by an army of local Catholic historians) have done a vast amount to illuminate. But the development of the English Catholic community was shaped, more than anything else, by the legal, social and cultural pressures operating upon it from outside (in other words, by persecution). At the same time, hostility to Catholicism, and on occasion, to Catholics, was a formative influence on English Protestant identity, perhaps the single most important influence. The persecutors themselves *felt* persecuted: by the memories of the Marian fires of Smithfield, by the impression of an infiltrating army of Jesuits, by apprehensions about the presence of papists in high places. Though it seems clear with hindsight that the 'activist' phase of English Catholicism had passed after the 1590s, this may not have been so evident to contemporaries, who were only too aware that the first half of the seventeenth century was the flood-tide of the Counter-Reformation. Elsewhere in Europe, heavily Protestantized lands (such as Bohemia) were being forcibly re-Catholicized.[67] Another reason for the sense of insecurity was a deep anxiety about how many Catholics there were in England, where they were to be found, how they were to be identified – perceptions less paranoid than traditional histories of 'recusancy' would have us believe. It may be going too far to suggest, as Michael Questier does, that there was no such thing as a unitary 'English Catholicism', only 'a series of dissident oppositional expressions of religious motive'.[68] But it is certainly true that the size and shape of 'the English Catholic Community' is exceptionally hard to define. Marie Rowlands has usefully observed that 'Roman Catholicism was a belief and value system; popery was a social and political construct; recusancy was a legal offence which had to be proved'.[69] Greater method-

67 Jonathan Scott, *England's Troubles: Seventeenth-Century English Political Instability in European Context* (Cambridge, 2000), pp. 29–30, 56–8.
68 Questier, *Conversion*, p. 204.
69 Marie B. Rowlands, 'Introduction', in id., *Parish and Town*, p. 4.

ological sophistication in the interpretation of recusancy statistics, and a greater appreciation of the significance of church popery, have problematized the view that Elizabethan Catholicism fairly rapidly transformed itself into an inward-looking, and rather insignificant 'sect'. It has become easier to understand why, when identified recusants constituted less than 2 per cent of the population, some early seventeenth-century Protestants were apt to see popery all over the place, and also why the terms 'papist' and 'church papist' could become so dangerously imprecise, applicable even to the policies of a Protestant king. In short, the study of post-1559 Catholicism is more than an interesting, if obscure, by-way on the map of Reformation England. Arguably, it is a signpost towards a much broader thoroughfare (though one whose very existence historians dispute): the 'high road to civil war'.[70]

70 G.R. Elton, 'A High Road to Civil War?', in C.H. Carter, ed., *From the Renaissance to the Counter-Reformation* (London, 1965).

8

Charles I's Reformation 1625–1642

Overview

In the years after 1625, the course of the English Reformation took a strange and fateful turn. Once again, the Royal Supremacy was invoked to bring about a thorough reform of the worship and theology of the Church, and of the fabric and furnishings of churches. Yet while the reformations of the Tudor period were either on their own terms broadly successful (Henry and Elizabeth) or terminated by the accident of the monarch's death (Edward and Mary), the ecclesiastical reformation (or counter-reformation) sanctioned by Charles I was, uniquely, halted and reversed by opposition from his subjects. The manner and scope of that failure set the terms for England's future religious (and political) development. It is, however, still somewhat unusual to pose the issues in this way. The later 1620s and 1630s are the point at which historians whose interests lie in the reception of the Reformation conventionally pass the torch to those whose principal concern is to explain the outbreak of civil war in 1642. The student travelling across this traditional boundary is likely to notice an abrupt shift of gear, for the historiography of the immediate background to the English Civil War (or, more properly, British Civil Wars) is of an exceptional richness and complexity. While few would contend that the conflicts were solely about religious issues, the role of religion has always loomed large in this scholarship, and has if anything become more prominent in recent years. A tradition, originating in the nineteenth century, which regarded the events of the 1640s as a 'Puritan Revolution' against an Anglican establishment, came under sustained attack from the 1970s by an interpretation which presented Charles I and his bishops as the real revolutionaries, heaven-bent on overturning long-established Protestant agreement over matters of doctrine and practice with a novel 'Arminian' theology and insistence on (popish-seeming) ceremonial innovations. This interpretation has in its turn generated a wave of critical responses: we have seen already (Section 5.3) that much of this controversy hangs on whether there was a fundamental 'consensus' within the Jacobean Church to be attacked or undermined in the 1630s.

Unlike the people they study, historians have the advantage of knowing what comes next, though this can be a dangerously double-edged knowledge. Just as medievalists distrust an approach to the early sixteenth-century Church that has one eye fixed on the coming Henrician Reformation, some Stuart historians warn of the risk of distortion caused 'by viewing the period before 1640 in the light of the dramatic events of the 1640s'. Not only is there the temptation to regard all instances of religious conflict as feeding inevitably into the coming conflagration, but also to underplay the continuing unspectacular advance of mainstream Protestant reform: the ongoing production of catechisms and bibles, the growing efficiency of the Church courts, the increasingly graduate character of the parish clergy.[1] A concern with the causation of major events, however, is surely the historian's business. The adoption of a broader perspective here benefits both 'Reformation' and 'Civil War' specialists. For the crisis of the 1640s was in large measure the crisis of the English Reformation itself, a time when long submerged tensions came to the surface, forcing answers and demanding decisions. Developments in the 1630s bring sharply into focus many themes already surveyed in this book: the potential and limits of the Royal Supremacy, the ambiguities of the Elizabethan Settlement and the subversive or conservative character of Puritanism, the potency of anti-popery, the implementation of religious reform in the parishes, the religious instincts of the conformist majority.

The first section of this chapter combines a narrative of the first dozen or so years of Charles I's reign with an analysis of the development of official religious policies. The question of the relative novelty or familiarity of these will be considered, as will that of who was primarily responsible for their formulation. The next section examines the implementation of Caroline religious directives in the localities, assessing the effectiveness with which they were imposed and the amount of resistance and support that they encountered. The last section attempts to explain why Charles I's religious policies came so dramatically off the rails at the end of the 1630s, and why, more than a century after Henry VIII's break with Rome, religion was an issue over which the English (or some of them at least) were prepared to go to war.

8.1 Laudian Policy: Origins and Objectives

There were no signs of approaching war at Charles's accession in March 1625, though informed contemporaries had reason to believe a significant

[1] Ian Green, '"England's Wars of Religion?" Religious Conflict and the English Civil Wars', in J. van den Berg and P.G. Hoftijzer, eds., *Church, Change and Revolution* (Leiden, 1991), quote at p. 107.

change of direction in ecclesiastical affairs might be in the offing. After Prince Charles returned from Madrid in 1623, one of the chaplains who accompanied him – the anti-Calvinist Mathew Wren – was summoned to a meeting at the palace of his patron, Bishop Lancelot Andrewes of Winchester. Here he was quizzed by Andrewes and two other prominent sacramentalist churchmen, Bishop Richard Neile of Durham, and William Laud, Bishop of St David's, about 'how the Prince's heart stands to the Church of England, that when God brings him to the Crown, we may know what to hope for'. Wren replied that 'for upholding the Doctrine and Discipline, and the right Estate of the Church, I have more Confidence of him, than of his Father'.[2] Historians dispute the significance of this episode. Kevin Sharpe thinks it suggests only that Charles had a conventionally conservative attachment to discipline and order, while Nicholas Tyacke uses it to date Charles's commitment to a distinctly Arminian theology. To Andrew Foster it reveals 'both the existence of an Arminian party and the fact that they sought to manipulate the crown', precisely the situation many would come to suspect in succeeding years.[3]

There is little doubt that the type of churchman to whom James had been showing signs of favour in his latter years flourished after the accession of Charles, and rapidly came to acquire a virtual monopoly of ecclesiastical promotions at the highest level. Andrewes (who died in 1626) was an inspiration, but the 'godfather' of the group was Richard Neile, whose London home at Durham House provided a base of operations for anti-Calvinist clergy during Neile's tenancy of the bishopric of Durham between 1617 and 1628. Their leading lay patron was the Duke of Buckingham, a favourite of James's who retained the confidence of his son (and the perpetual distrust of the House of Commons). In February 1626, Buckingham convened a conference at York House in London after pressure from anti-Arminians to condemn the writings of Richard Montague (who, as we saw in Section 5.3, had attacked predestination and suggested Rome was a true, if flawed Church). The conference ended without any condemnation of Montague, and boosted the confidence of the 'Durham House' Arminians taking part. It was a signal that the Jacobean policy of balance between factions, while allowing the overall dominance of conformist Calvinism, was starting to change. With royal backing, Buckingham secured election as Chancellor of Cambridge in 1626, and Calvinist teaching there was effectively prohibited.

2 Peter McCullough, *Sermons at Court: Politics and Religion in Elizabethan and Jacobean Preaching* (Cambridge, 1998), p. 208.

3 Kevin Sharpe, *The Personal Rule of Charles I* (New Haven and London, 1992), pp. 279–80; NicholasTyacke, *Anti-Calvinists: The Rise of English Arminianism c. 1590–1640* (Oxford, 1987), pp. 113–14; Andrew Foster, 'Church Policies of the 1630s', in Richard Cust and Ann Hughes, eds., *Conflict in Early Stuart England* (London, 1989), p. 211.

A royal proclamation of the same year banned the promotion of 'new opinions... differing from the sound and orthodoxal grounds of the true religion': despite its conservative and even-handed tenor, it was widely used to silence Calvinists, as was a Declaration against 'unnecessary disputations' prefixed to a reissue of the Thirty-Nine Articles in November 1628. Tyacke notes that Calvinist themes in the sermons preached at the 'official' pulpit of St Paul's Cross (at least in those that were printed) while common in the Elizabethan and Jacobean periods, disappear completely after 1628.[4] Meanwhile, the anti-Calvinists were going places. Neile was made Archbishop of York in 1632, while Laud secured promotion to London in 1628 and Canterbury in 1633 (the veteran Calvinist Archbishop Abbot had in practice been sidelined for many years). The most provocative of the anti-Calvinists, Montague, was made a royal chaplain and then bishop of Chichester in 1628. Indeed, Arminians dominated the promotion lists to the extent that only three recognizably Calvinist bishops were appointed between 1625 and 1641.[5]

In the meantime alarm bells were ringing among the country's Protestant elites. Complaints against Arminianism surfaced in Parliament in 1625 and 1626. In 1629, a subcommittee of the Commons complained, naming Montague and others, that persons maintaining 'papistical, Arminian, and superstitious opinions and practices... are countenanced, favoured and preferred', and a Protestation was passed (while the Speaker was held physically in his chair) announcing that anyone promoting popery or Arminianism should be 'reputed a capital enemy to this Kingdom and Commonwealth'.[6] This was something of a last hurrah, for after 1629 the opportunity to air such grievances in the forum of Parliament was taken away. Charles had become deeply frustrated with parliamentary opposition to his methods of raising taxation, particularly since the money was needed to finance wars against France (to force Louis XIII to fulfil the terms of the treaty accompanying Charles's marriage to Henrietta Maria) and against Spain (to retake lands seized from Charles's brother-in-law the Elector of the Palatinate) – precisely the kind of 'Protestant' foreign policy the godly had longed for under James. With the return of peace, Charles determined to govern without Parliament, and inaugurated the period once known to historians as 'the eleven years tyranny', but now (less judgementally) as 'the Personal Rule'. It was in the 1630s that anti-Calvinism came into its own, and began attempting to reshape the English Church in its image.

4 Tyacke, *Anti-Calvinists*, pp. 248–65.

5 Kenneth Fincham and Peter Lake, 'The Ecclesiastical Policies of James I and Charles I', in Fincham, ed., *The Early Stuart Church, 1603–1642* (Basingstoke, 1993), pp. 37–8.

6 S.R. Gardiner, ed., *Constitutional Documents of the Puritan Revolution* (Oxford, 1906), pp. 81, 83.

The ecclesiastical policies of the Personal Rule proceeded along a twin track: to restore the wealth and status of the Church (and churchmen), and to insist upon a greater reverence and order in worship, to rediscover 'the beauty of holiness'. In an effort to bolster the economic position of the Church, bishops were ordered to maintain residence in their dioceses, to preserve their estates, and not to renew leases of land after they were appointed to a new bishopric. At the same time, there was an effort to exalt the status of the clergy: a Jacobean tendency to appoint bishops and ministers as justices of the peace was accelerated, and when Bishop William Juxon of London was appointed Lord Treasurer in 1636, he became the first ecclesiastic to hold the office in more than a century. The bishops were encouraged to send in regular reports from their dioceses, acting, Andrew Foster notes, rather like the *Intendants* who were the prime instruments of royal centralization in seventeenth-century France.[7] Another face of this increased clericalism was the attempt to control and discipline nonconformist, and even conforming godly clergy. Royal Instructions to the bishops in 1629 ordered that parish catechizing should replace Sunday afternoon sermons in parishes, and to make sure that town lectureships were not being used as a bolt-hole for nonconformists, lecturers were ordered to read the prayer book service before beginning to preach. Godly preaching came under further attack in 1633, when Charles and Laud banned the activities of the 'Feoffees for Impropriations', a group of Puritan clerics and laity who had been buying up parish livings to fund urban lectureships from the tithes.[8] A deep suspicion of the subversive potential of Puritan preaching, inherited from his father, and strengthened by his own experience of the Spanish Match agitation, underlay Charles's actions. An anti-Puritan agenda is evident also in the King's 1633 reissuing of James's Book of Sports, the *bête noire* of godly sabbatarian ministers, who were now required to read it from the pulpit. The Laudian antidote to the Puritan poison in the bloodstream of the Church was not so very different from that prescribed by Cardinal Pole in the 1550s: the promotion of reverent, communal and sacramental worship, centred on the parish church. Considerable effort went into surveying and rectifying the fabric of parish churches (though Laudians were apt to underestimate or undervalue the degree of restoration that had taken place in the Jacobean period). It has been calculated that roughly 65 per cent of the churches and chapels under Archbishop Neile's jurisdiction were ordered to make repairs of some kind in the 1630s.[9] Within the churches themselves, there was encouragement to reintroduce religious images of the kind that had been swept out of the

7 Andrew Foster, 'The Clerical Estate Revitalised', in Fincham, *Early Stuart Church*, pp. 141, 156–9; id., 'Church Policies', pp. 198–9, 209.
8 Nicholas Tyacke, 'Archbishop Laud', in Fincham, *Early Stuart Church*, pp. 66–7.
9 Foster, 'Church Policies', pp. 201–3.

parishes by Edwardian and Elizabethan iconoclasm, surviving in James's reign only in the chapel royal and a handful of private chapels.[10]

Most controversial, however, was the policy with regard to the placing and arrangement of 'altars', Laud and his associates provocatively insisting on the medieval term in contradistinction to the accustomed Protestant nomenclature of 'Lord's Table'. The Injunctions of 1559 had required communion tables to be kept at the east end of churches 'in the place where the altar stood', though they were to be brought into the chancel for the celebration of communion. The Prayer Book, however, implied that tables should permanently 'stand in the body of the church' and made it clear that they should be pointed east–west, rather than the north–south alignment traditionally used for altars.[11] In practice most parishes had adopted this latter course, keeping the table in the middle of the chancel rather than ferrying it back and forth for communion services. The 1630s, however, saw a concerted campaign to have tables situated permanently at the east end of churches, placed 'altarwise' (i.e. north–south) and surrounded by a rail (marking them off as pieces of particularly sacred space). The catalyst was the case of St Gregory's, a London church standing next to St Paul's Cathedral but refusing to obey the cathedral authorities and move its altar to the east end of the chancel. In November 1633, Charles himself ruled on the case, declaring such matters were not to be 'left to the discretion of the parish', but should follow 'the cathedral mother church'.[12] The subsequent repositioning and railing of altars nationwide was, suggests Nicholas Tyacke, 'the most obvious and symbolic religious act of the Caroline regime', an exalting of the importance of sacraments and ceremony over preaching. That this was Laud's own view can hardly be doubted. He once remarked that 'the altar is the greatest place of God's residence on earth, greater than the pulpit; for there 'tis *Hoc est corpus meum*; but in the other it is at most *Hoc est verbum meum*, This is my word.' In Tyacke's view, these policies taken together constituted nothing less than an 'Arminian revolution', a radical overthrowing of long-established Protestant verities, and one bound to provoke a widespread hostile reaction.[13]

Tyacke's interpretation of the religious history of the 1630s turned the established 'Puritan Revolution' thesis on its head, and has been hugely influential (it is completely accepted, for example, by the doyen of early

10 Margaret Aston, *England's Iconoclasts* (Oxford, 1988), pp. 461–2; Fincham, 'Introduction' in id., *Early Stuart Church*, p. 14.

11 W.H. Frere and W.M. Kennedy, eds., *Visitation Articles and Injunctions of the Period of the Reformation*, 3 vols (London, 1910), iii. 27–8; John E. Booty, ed., *The Book of Common Prayer 1559* (Washington, 1976), p. 248.

12 Gardiner, *Constitutional Documents*, pp. 104–5.

13 Tyacke, 'Archbishop Laud', p. 68; 'Puritanism, Arminianism and Counter-Revolution', in Conrad Russell, ed., *The Origins of the English Civil War* (London, 1973), pp. 130, 143.

Stuart political historians, Conrad Russell.[14]) But from the early 1990s it has faced considerable criticism from, among others, George Bernard, Julian Davies, Ian Green, Kevin Sharpe and Peter White – a group of historians confusingly identified as 'revisionists', though their views diverge sharply from the earlier revisionism of the Tyacke–Russell school.[15] An important assertion of this revisionary second wave is that there was no 'Calvinist consensus' in the Elizabethan and Jacobean Church for Charles I to disrupt, an issue we have examined already (Section 5.3). Regarding the 1630s themselves, the critique of Tyacke can be summarized in a couple of key propositions: the ceremonial changes of the 1630s had no connection with Arminian theology, reflecting rather a more traditional concern with decency and order, and Charles I, not Archbishop Laud, was the primary mover behind them. There was no 'rise of Arminianism', other than in the exaggerated perceptions of some Puritans and extreme anti-Catholics. Thus, Bernard notes that churchmen with the views of Laud and Neile had been promoted before 1625, and regards the policy pursued by Charles and Laud as a direct continuation of the 'monarchical view of the Church' held by Elizabeth and her archbishops Whitgift and Bancroft. The religious disputes of the early 1630s were no more bitter than the vestments controversy of the 1560s, or the subscription campaign of the early 1600s.[16] Similarly, Kevin Sharpe sees the basis of the campaign to restore ceremonies as an enforcement of the ecclesiastical canons of 1604, having 'little connection with theology, and certainly little evidence of a connection with the Arminian doctrine of free will.' It seemed innovatory simply because it followed the lax archiepiscopal regime of Abbot, during which conformity had not been insisted on. The altar campaign was a case in point – the insistence on rails (which had gone up in some places before the 1630s) was about decency and dignity, keeping dogs and badly behaved boys away from the holy table. In all of this, Sharpe sees the hand not of Laud (whose commitment to Arminianism he in any case disputes), but of the King, stressing, for example, his initiative in the St Gregory's case. Charles had little interest in the finer points of theology, but was deeply committed to a vision of peace and unity in a revitalized Church. This vision was threatened by the divisive attitudes of a Puritan minority; hence his advocacy of the Book of Sports, bringing the community together in lawful festive recreation.[17] This insistence on the leading role of Charles (an interesting parallel to the debates about 'King or Minister' in the Henrician Reformation) is made yet

[14] Conrad Russell, *The Causes of the English Civil War* (Oxford, 1990), p. 109.

[15] To add to the confusion, 'post-revisionist' in the context of Civil War historiography usually refers to historians who see longer-term, structural factors as significant causes of the conflict.

[16] George Bernard, 'The Church of England, c. 1529–c.1642', *History*, 75 (1990), 195, 201–4.

[17] Sharpe, *Personal Rule*, ch. 6.

more forcefully by Julian Davies, who denies that Charles was ever converted to Arminianism; 'the role of doctrine was negligible' as an explanation for his actions. Charles was determined to undermine Puritanism, to exalt the primacy of liturgy and discipline over preaching, and to assert his divine right to rule through a 'sacramental notion of kingship'– an ideological package which Davies terms 'Carolinism', and of which Laud was merely a pragmatic and uncertain follower (though he became the scapegoat for it in 1640).[18] Davies is more ready than Sharpe or Bernard to accept that these policies stirred up widespread opposition, but the thrust of all their arguments is to suggest that since there was nothing shockingly new about the policies of the 1630s, there was no reason why they should not have been effectively implemented and accepted. The reasons for the dramatic change of direction in 1640–2 must be located in the short-term crisis leading to the recall of Parliament in 1640, rather than in a decade of pent-up frustrations and tensions. Reactions to the policies in the localities will be considered more closely below (Section 8.2), but first we should note some critical responses to this barrage of 'monarchical' revisionism.

Tyacke and his supporters have hit back, accusing the (re-)revisionists of resurrecting the anachronistic notion of an Anglican *via media* under threat from Puritanism.[19] The notion that Charles was the real author of policy, and Laud merely the bureaucrat carrying out his wishes, has been subject to particular scrutiny. Kenneth Fincham has examined Laud's exercise of ecclesiastical patronage, and concluded that he played a crucial role in selecting the royal chaplains from among whom future bishops were recruited, and ensuring that committed Laudians were placed in hundreds of Crown livings. At his trial Laud failed to deny the accusation that he had secured episcopal promotions for the leading anti-Calvinists Neile, Wren and William Piers. But Fincham argues that to reassert Laud's importance does not devalue that of Charles. As chief patronage broker, Laud was the King's trusted lieutenant; together they formed 'a partnership of prince and prelate unparalleled since the Reformation'.[20] A similar template has been applied to the altar policy. That Charles became committed to it is not in doubt, but it seems unlikely the policy originated with the King. As dean of Gloucester, Laud had moved the cathedral's communion table to the position of the pre-Reformation altar in 1617, a move mirrored by his close ally Richard Neile at Durham. Indeed, Neile had begun to enforce the policy of railed east-end altars across the northern province in 1632–3, in advance of

18 Julian Davies, *The Caroline Captivity of the Church: Charles I and the Remoulding of Anglicanism 1625–1641* (Oxford, 1992), esp. pp. 288–305.

19 Fincham, 'Introduction', pp. 5–6; Nicholas Tyacke, 'Anglican Attitudes', in his *Aspects of English Protestantism, c. 1530–1700* (Manchester, 2001).

20 Kenneth Fincham, 'William Laud and the Exercise of Caroline Ecclesiastical Patronage', *Journal of Ecclesiastical History*, 51 (2000), quote at 93.

the St Gregory's case. Though sometimes prepared to proceed more tactfully over the issue than zealous Arminians like Bishop Wren, the evidence suggests Laud had long favoured a permanent altarwise position for the table, communion at the rails and bowing to the altar, practices he sought to enforce when in office.[21] To portray Laud as merely the executor of royal policy in the 1630s is in the end little more convincing than attempts to do the same with Thomas Cromwell in the 1530s. Tyacke has described Laud as 'among the greatest archbishops of Canterbury since the Reformation'; Patrick Collinson as 'the greatest calamity ever visited upon the Church of England'.[22] The two judgements are not necessarily incompatible.

Despite the best efforts of the revisionists, therefore, it looks as if 'Laudianism' is here to stay as a description of what was happening in the 1630s. But the term (unknown to contemporaries) begs some questions of interpretation. Alexandra Walsham has remarked that historians can become too fixated on doctrines of grace, that theories of salvation were not the main source of discord in the 1630s. There were 'other items on the Laudian agenda': clericalism, anti-sabbatarianism, the campaign for conformity and order, and a concern with liturgy and ceremony that was not always linked to theological preferences.[23] Andrew Foster, by contrast, feels that limiting oneself to the term 'Laudian' runs the risk of stressing only the effects of policies at the expense of their rationale. He argues that 'what made this a coherent programme rather than just a collection of policies was an Arminian outlook which stressed different attitudes towards God, to the nature of worship and to the sacraments'.[24] Unsurprisingly, the perception that 'Laudian' policies were firmly rooted in 'Arminian' theology is shared by Tyacke: the heightened emphasis on the sacrament of holy communion, for example, reflected an outlook in which God's saving grace was available to all penitent sinners, and not restricted to a predestined elect.[25] A possible objection to this approach is that, individually, many policies of the 1630s were not unprecedented: the Book of Sports had been issued by James I, the altar policy could (and did) claim authorization from the Elizabethan Injunctions and the canons of 1604, and even the 'altarwise' positioning reflected long-standing practice in the chapel royal. Here Peter Lake has made an important contribution, arguing that more important than the parentage of individual policies or opinions was 'the overall package', the

21 Id., 'The Restoration of Altars in the 1630s', *Historical Journal*, 44 (2001); Foster, 'Church Policies', pp. 210–11; Tyacke, 'Archbishop Laud', pp. 68–9.

22 Ibid., p. 51; Patrick Collinson, *The Religion of Protestants: The Church in English Society 1559–1625* (Oxford, 1982), p. 90.

23 Alexandra Walsham, 'The Parochial Roots of Laudianism Revisited: Catholics, Anti-Calvinists and 'Parish Anglicans' in Early Stuart England', *Journal of Ecclesiastical History*, 49 (1998), 622–3.

24 Foster, 'Church Policies', pp. 215–16.

25 Tyacke, 'Archbishop Laud', p. 62.

synthesis of a variety of political, cultural and religious attitudes that he terms 'the Laudian style'. Thus, a Laudian insistence on the house of God as a place of special divine presence drew together the concern with church fabrics and with the ceremonial and liturgical aspects of worship, particularly the altar policy. The emphasis on the status of the clergy similarly sprang from a 'worship-centred view of the world', in which the clergy's monopoly of the administration of sacraments meant more than their role as preachers. The anti-sabbatarianism implicit in the Book of Sports reflected the confidence of a Church which felt itself able to demarcate holy times. Furthermore, Laudians defined their identity against a counter-image of Puritan deviance. Merely formal conformity (combined with some tolerance of nonconformist practices) of the kind that had been secured from moderate Puritans under James was not sufficient. There had to be full inward conformity to the ceremonies prescribed by the Church because there was little sense that these might be things indifferent, adiaphora. What all this added up to was 'a coherent, distinctive and polemically aggressive vision of the Church', something very different from 'a conventional conformist pursuit of uniformity and obedience' in the Whitgift or Bancroft mould.[26] Another way in which the Laudian outlook diverged from that of the 'conformist' wing of the Elizabethan and Jacobean Church has been illuminated by Anthony Milton: their manner of speaking and writing about both the Roman Church and the other Reformed Churches of Europe. As we have seen (Section 5.3), it was a theological commonplace at the start of the seventeenth century to assert that the pope was the Antichrist, but Laud, Montague and others openly rejected this identification. Rome was a true, though corrupted Church. A corollary of this was that Laudians increasingly claimed a direct institutional continuity with the pre-Reformation Catholic Church (some of whose practices they were seeking to revive) rather than searching for ancestry among the pockets of medieval 'true believers' (Lollards and others) in the tradition of John Foxe. (In this, the Elizabethan writings of Hooker were an important intellectual resource.) At the same time, the strong sense, formed under Edward VI and maintained through Elizabeth's reign, of belonging to a family of 'Reformed' European Churches was being jettisoned. The Jacobean Church had organized collections for the relief of beleaguered co-religionists in Geneva, but under Charles they were coming to seem members of a different faith, and Laud adopted a much frostier and more suspicious attitude than his predecessors to the 'Stranger Churches' in England. Like other recent scholars, Milton is sensitive to the existence of stresses and tensions within the Jacobean Church, but he argues that an important unifying factor before 1625 was

[26] Peter Lake, 'The Laudian Style: Order, Uniformity and the Pursuit of the Beauty of Holiness in the 1630s', in Fincham, *Early Stuart Church*, quotes at pp. 162, 173.

the existence of a 'common style of discourse', a 'symbolic orthodoxy' of anti-Romanist and pro-Calvinist language.[27] This was a form of political correctness the Laudians flagrantly refused to observe.

In the ongoing debate over whether the Laudians were the conservatives or the 'revolutionaries' in the early Stuart Church, a modified version of the Tyacke thesis looks likely to hold the day. The royally sanctioned episcopal policies of the 1630s represented an abrupt discontinuity with those of the early 1600s and, more importantly, were perceived to do so by large numbers of contemporaries. Yet it is important to recognize that the tensions of the 1630s were a family quarrel *within* English Protestantism, the boiling over of simmering ambiguities inside the cauldron of the English Reformation itself. The heat had been removed suddenly at the death of Edward in 1553 and the warming over of the Elizabethan 'settlement' had produced a predominantly Calvinist Church of a distinctly odd character, with bishops, ornate cathedrals and a prayer book whose ceremonial and sacramental characteristics could seem to jar with the orthodoxies of unconditional predestination.[28] The fact that the Elizabethan prayer book and Injunctions seemed to contradict each other over the use of ordinary bread or wafers for the communion, and over the positioning of the communion table, enabled both the ceremonially inclined and the ceremonially averse to appeal to precedent and established authority. In this sense the label 'Arminian' is misleading if it implies something simply imported from the continent without English roots. Though their enemies frequently charged them with maintaining 'popery', Arminians were not crypto-Catholics. Laud was the author of a piece of effective antipapal polemic, and in due course both he and Charles would claim to die in the 'Protestant Religion'.[29] Nor is it necessarily the case that they consciously thought of themselves as innovators or (metaphorical) iconoclasts. At the end of the parliamentary session of 1629, Charles announced that he would authorize nothing 'whereby any innovation may steal or creep into the Church', but was determined 'to preserve the unity of doctrine and discipline established in the time of Queen Elizabeth, whereby the Church of England hath stood and flourished ever since'.[30] No doubt he was sincere in this, but, as Conrad Russell has observed, 'in all the ambiguities of which the Elizabethan

[27] Anthony Milton, *Catholic and Reformed: The Roman and Protestant Churches in English Protestant Thought 1600–1640* (Cambridge, 1995), esp. chs. 2, 3, 9, conclusion; Conrad Russell, 'The Reformation and the Creation of the Church of England 1500–1640', in John Morrill, ed., *The Oxford Illustrated History of Tudor and Stuart Britain* (Oxford, 1996), p. 288.

[28] For example, the persistent complaint that the language of the burial service seemed to promise salvation indiscriminately: see Peter Marshall, *Beliefs and the Dead in Reformation England* (Oxford, 2002), pp. 151–6.

[29] Sharpe, *Personal Rule*, pp. 285–6; Milton, *Catholic and Reformed*, p. 382.

[30] Russell, *Causes*, p. 196.

Settlement was full, Charles saw only one side of the argument, and never fully understood that there was another'.[31] Those who did not share the Laudian world-view were increasingly stereotyped as 'Puritans', religiously delinquent and politically disloyal. It was to be in large measure a self-fulfilling prophecy.

8.2 Laudian Policy: Impact and Implementation

Like the Tudor reformations which preceded it, the real measure of the Caroline religious programme is perhaps not so much the coherence with which policy was formulated at the centre, as the effectiveness with which it was implemented in the localities, though there have been fewer detailed studies of the local impact of Laudianism in the 1630s than of Henrician reform in the 1530s or the Edwardian and Marian brands in mid-century.[32] One parallel with the earlier reformations immediately suggests itself: the extent to which the full implementation of initiatives emanating from the centre varied according to the enthusiasm of local bishops. While some diocesans – Laud, Neile, Wren of Norwich, Piers of Bath and Wells – were zealous enforcers of Laudian reforms, some others were foot-draggers, or adopted a pragmatic non-confrontational approach. Thus Bishops Robert Wright of Coventry and Lichfield, and John Thornborough of Worcester, needed sharp prodding to take action against nonconforming ministers, while the moderate Calvinist Joseph Hall of Exeter never rigorously imposed the altar rail policy; a significant number of Devon churches still lacked them in 1640.[33] Nevertheless, the consensus of recent scholarship is that Laudianism was remarkably effective in transforming the appearance of parish churches, particularly after Laud's metropolitan visitation of 1634–5 (another point of similarity with the Tudor campaigns). In Warwickshire, for example, a county that lacked notably zealous episcopal oversight, new altar rails had been erected by 1639 in nine of the 13 parishes for which churchwardens' accounts survive. In Norfolk, 18 out of 24

[31] Russell, 'Reformation', p. 288.

[32] See, however, Anthony Fletcher, *A County Community at Peace and War: Sussex 1600–1660* (London, 1975), ch. 4; Margaret Stieg, *Laud's Laboratory: the Diocese of Bath and Wells in the Early Seventeenth Century* (East Brunswick, NJ, 1982); John Fielding, 'Arminianism in the Localities: Peterborough Diocese 1603–1642', in Fincham, *Early Stuart Church*; Darren Oldridge, *Religion and Society in Early Stuart England* (Aldershot, 1998).

[33] Oldridge, *Religion*, pp. 37–47; Kenneth Fincham, 'Episcopal Government 1603–1640', in id., *Early Stuart Church*, pp. 84–6. Julian Davies's claim that the Calvinist Bishop Davenant of Salisbury was a enthusiastic implementer of the altar policy has been sharply questioned by Tyacke, 'Anglican Attitudes', pp. 191–2.

parishes acquired rails after Wren's arrival in 1635, and in the dioceses of London and Chichester, too, rails appear to have become the norm.[34] Parishes were also being urged to acquire new vestments, altar covers and communion plate, and to spend heavily on the repair and decoration of chancels. Laudian religious policies resembled those of Mary in imposing a heavy financial burden on English parishes, and this at a time when communities were having to deal with rising demands for the relief of the poor, and a variety of forms of extra-parliamentary taxation. In the York parish of St Martin's Micklegate the annual rate for church maintenance increased threefold in the 1630s from an average of £11 per year in the 1620s; at St John's Ousebridge it rose from an average of £17 to one of £37.[35]

Unsurprisingly, therefore, many scholars have concluded that Laudian policies were intrusive and disruptive, and not merely for religious reasons. The campaign to instil reverence for the beauty of holiness involved interference with a variety of customary arrangements in English parish life. In particular, the 1630s witnessed the first concerted official effort to insist upon uniformity in the construction and arrangement of church seating, patterns of which had evolved gradually in many places to reflect intricate understandings of local hierarchy and precedence. In 1637, Bishop Francis Dee of Peterborough flatly ordered a standard height of three feet for every pew in the diocese, and in consequence at least 120 high pews belonging to the aristocracy and gentry were hacked down.[36] Such actions undoubtedly provoked resentment. One consequence of the altar policy was the attempt to get rid of seats from the chancel. As a consequence of Jacobean patterns of reception around a centrally positioned 'tablewise' communion table, seating in a number of parishes had extended round the chancel walls, including the far east end, anathema to Laudian sacramentalists. 'Do you think you are worthy to sit above the Lord's board in his house?' Neile asked rhetorically in 1632. A concern with the proper ordering of prayerful space also sometimes involved interference with the lavish funeral monuments which were sources of local pride and family reputation in many churches.[37] It has been eloquently argued by David Cressy that Laudian ceremonialist reforms were deeply unpopular and divisive, not on theological or even primarily religious grounds ('Arminianism was not the issue'), but because the

34 Oldridge, *Religion*, pp. 53, 56; Sharpe, *Personal Rule*, p. 342.

35 William Hunt, *The Puritan Moment. The Coming of Revolution in an English County* (Cambridge MA, 1983), p. 261; Foster, 'Church Policies', pp. 215–16.

36 Fielding, 'Peterborough Diocese', p. 106.

37 Christopher Marsh, 'Sacred Space in England, 1560–1640: The View from the Pew', *Journal of Ecclesiastical History*, 53 (2002), 290–99; Foster, 'Church Policies', pp. 204–5; Marshall, *Beliefs*, p. 296.

intransigent insistence on uniformity infringed parochial custom and wrecked long-established local mechanisms for resolving conflict. The Jacobean period had been marked, not by an ideological consensus, but by a practical agreement to tolerate diversity of practice, a 'willingness to wink' on the part of the authorities, and a local determination to let charity and neighbourliness take priority over uniformity and order. But this 'culture of consensus and accommodation' was destroyed by an inflexible insistence on such matters as the use of the sign of the cross in baptism (often silently omitted before 1625), the placing of fonts at the south-west door of churches, the wearing of veils by women for the ceremony of 'churching' after childbirth (optional in the Jacobean period) and, most of all, by the Laudian altar policy: 'Who would have thought there would be such fuss about where you put the furniture!'[38]

But it is questionable whether opposition to the Laudian programme was usually so resolutely non-ideological in nature. In the words of a Colchester churchwarden, 'turning communion tables into altars and placing them altarwise is a popish practice and backsliding to popery'.[39] There is considerable evidence that the requirement to move communion tables to the east end, and to turn them through 90 degrees, to receive communion kneeling at the altar rails, and to bow in the direction of the altar, were the most widely resisted aspects of the Laudian programme. In the archdiocese of York, many parishes (particularly in the Puritan cloth towns of the West Riding) evaded detection at Neile's visitation of 1632–3, and it required special commissioners (often returning several times) to compel them to move their tables. Some parishes mounted legal challenges through the ecclesiastical courts. In a famous test case, the churchwardens of Beckington (Somerset) appealed to the superior court of the province of Canterbury known as the Court of Arches against Bishop Piers's order to move their table. The arguments they employed were not just legal, but religious ones, appealing to 'the reformation of King Edward's time, of blessed memory'.[40] In 1630s Essex, a number of churches became 'arenas for gestural conflict': while some parishioners were prepared to bow to the altar or receive kneeling at the rails, others inverted the symbolism by keeping their hats on, or remaining seated when others stood.[41]

38 David Cressy, 'Conflict, Consensus, and the Willingness to Wink: The Erosion of Community in Charles I's England', *Huntington Library Quarterly*, 61 (1998). See also his *Travesties and Transgressions in Tudor and Stuart England* (Oxford, 2000), ch. 12.

39 John Walter, 'Anti-Popery and the Stour Valley Riots of 1642', in David Chadd, ed., *Religious Dissent in East Anglia* (Norwich, 1996), p. 129.

40 Fincham, 'Altars', 919; Foster 'Church Policies', pp. 203–5; Tyacke, *Anti-Calvinists*, p. 204.

41 John Walter, 'Confessional Politics in Pre-Civil War Essex: Prayer Books, Profanations, and Petitions', *Historical Journal*, 44 (2001), 683–4.

Was the local opposition to ceremonial conformity recognizably 'Puritan' in motivation? There has been a trend in recent research to reassert an older perception that Puritanism did not simply dissolve into a Jacobean Protestant mainstream after the 1590s; that despite the absence of organized pressure for a presbyterian system, a 'Puritan continuum' was channelled through books, family traditions and patronage networks.[42] Nonetheless, it is hard not to conclude that Laudianism radicalized and politicized godly opinion, placing intense pressure on the moderate Puritans and 'Calvinist conformists' who had earlier been relatively comfortable with their place in the Church. As John Spurr has remarked of the 1620s, 'many who had been merely Protestant at the beginning of the decade would see themselves, and be seen by others, as Puritans before its close'.[43]

Parliamentary agitation was a route closed to Puritanism in the 1630s, but this did not mean the godly voice was silenced completely. It was easier for the Laudian authorities, using visitations and the ecclesiastical courts, to impose reforms on church interiors, than it was for them to control preaching, which might involve confrontation with powerful urban corporations. Darren Oldridge's study of Warwickshire shows that lectureships continued at Coventry, Birmingham, Nuneaton, Warwick and Stratford through the 1630s, providing a platform for preachers unsympathetic to Laudian policies.[44] Even where the authorities were able to curtail the practice of weekly lectures, some ministers cheekily took advantage of the new stress on holy days. By observing all the liturgical feast days, the Essex Puritan minister Stephen Marshall was able to preach on another 27 days in addition to sabbaths and Protestant anniversaries such as November 5. Tom Webster's survey of Puritan 'trajectories of response to Laudianism' concludes that many ministers were prepared to make compromises (wearing the surplice, using the sign of the cross) in order to retain the liberty to preach.[45] The 'persecution' of Puritanism under Charles and Laud was, in fact, on a rather limited scale. Only about 30 ministers were actually deprived of their livings in the 1630s, markedly fewer than during Bancroft's subscription campaign of 1605–6. But a changed context is reflected in the fact that many of the most irreconcilable opponents of Caroline policy took themselves off to voluntary exile in the Netherlands or New England. The

[42] Jacqueline Eales, 'A Road to Revolution: The Continuity of Puritanism, 1559–1642', in Christopher Durston and Jacqueline Eales, eds., *The Culture of English Puritanism 1560–1700* (Basingstoke, 1996); Nicholas Tyacke, 'The Fortunes of English Puritanism, 1603–40', in his *English Protestantism* (where Tyacke concedes he underestimated this phenomenon in his earlier work on Arminianism).

[43] John Spurr, *English Puritanism 1603–1689* (Basingstoke, 1998), p. 79.

[44] Oldridge, *Religion*, pp. 55–8.

[45] Tom Webster, *Godly Clergy in Early Stuart England* (Cambridge, 1997), pp. 167–80, 247.

pressures on those who stayed were real enough: hundreds of godly ministers were hauled in front of the ecclesiastical courts for omitting aspects of ceremonial dress or practice, and open criticism of the bishops carried genuine risks. In 1637 three authors of anti-episcopal pamphlets, the lawyer William Prynne, the doctor John Bastwick, and the preacher Henry Burton, were sentenced in Star Chamber to have their ears cropped, and remain in perpetual imprisonment. Their fate provided the opposition with the martyrs every cause needs: large crowds cheered them at their punishment, and hagiographical copies of Prynne's portrait circulated widely.[46]

Yet there were some who welcomed Prynne's punishment, and even thought it too light. The question of positive support for Laudianism among lay society and in the localities has, until fairly recently, been a neglected dimension of the historiography, stranded between the traditional interest in 'Puritan revolution' and the Tyackean model of Laudianism as the property of a radical clerical clique. Yet could Laudianism have accomplished the decisive changes to parish worship and church fabrics that it did if those who were called upon to implement the policies had uniformly detested it? There certainly seems to have been a sizeable Laudian constituency among the parish clergy. After his visitation of Norwich in 1636, Bishop Wren had little problem in finding 58 clergymen prepared to act as 'standing commissioners' to enforce ceremonial discipline. Interestingly, the majority of these had been ordained under Elizabeth or James, suggesting that Laudianism exercised an appeal not just to recent products of the universities, but to an older generation of ministers, perhaps attracted by the anti-Puritanism and the increased emphasis on the dignity of a sacramental priesthood.[47] The suggestion that Laudian ascendancy was enabling long-standing critics of Calvinism among the clergy to air their views is underlined by Peter Lake's case study of Peter Studley, vicar of St Chad's in Shrewsbury. After a local Puritan yeoman went mad in 1633 and killed his brother and mother with an axe, Studley published a pamphlet arguing that such complete lack of moral restraint was the inevitable consequence of predestinarian theology and Puritan piety. Studley was not a product of the Personal Rule – he had been vicar of St Chad's since 1620 – 'but what the Personal Rule did do was let radical anti-Puritans like Studley off the leash'.[48]

The identification of a body of Laudian support among the laity, however, is fraught with evidential problems – it is those who attempt to frustrate, rather than those who approve of official initiatives who end up in the records of the courts, a phenomenon we have encountered at various stages in this book. Christopher Haigh has argued (see Section 6.2) that the

46 Cressy, *Travesties*, ch. 13.

47 Fincham, 'Episcopal Government', pp. 89–90.

48 Peter Lake, 'Puritanism, Arminianism and a Shropshire Axe-Murder', *Midland History*, 15 (1990), quote at p. 59.

'parish anglicans' who were left high and dry after the twin failures of godly evangelists to convert them to meaningful Protestantism, and missionary priests to retain them for recusant Catholicism, formed an obvious bedrock of support for attempts to create a more ritualized and sacramental style of worship in the parishes, though he has yet to substantiate this with detailed published research. In the meantime, Kevin Sharpe finds it significant that churchwardens' accounts recording the erection of altar rails often describe them as 'comely', 'handsome' or 'fine', indicating they might be objects of genuine local pride.[49] One aspect of Laudian (or Caroline) policy in the 1630s surely had a widespread, though not universal, popular appeal: the resanctioning of traditional festive culture through the reissuing of the Book of Sports. David Underdown describes how months before the 1633 promulgation of the Book, news of it spread through Somerset villages that had seen their ales and revels banned by local Puritan authorities, with disorder ensuing in several places. Puritan ministers hated the Book, and read it through gritted teeth, but Laudian clerics might glory in the licence now permitted to their parishioners, like the minister of Rockland St Peter's (Norfolk), who turned up to shout 'well played!' at Sunday afternoon football matches.[50] An enthusiasm for village-green football hardly equates to an affirmation of Arminian doctrines of grace, but here and elsewhere Laudian policy was serving to reignite the local tensions and cultural conflicts caused by strict sabbatarianism and 'reformation of manners' (see Section 5.4).

A further, and intriguing, possibility of lay support for Laudianism has been suggested by Alexandra Walsham: the appeal it may have exercised for a number of the 'church papists', who, as we saw in Section 7.2, remained a distinct feature of the religious scene well into the Stuart period. Laudians frequently justified their employment of ritual and ceremony as a means of preventing waverers from defecting to Rome, and of drawing Catholics into full conformity with the Church of England. At his trial in 1644, Laud supplied the names of over 20 upper-class Catholics he had personally managed to convert. It is known that in the Elizabethan period, Catholic gentry in East Anglia were promoting 'avant-garde conformists' to parish livings within their gift, and the possibility exists (though it remains to be researched) that something similar was happening in the 1630s. Church papist Members of Parliament, and crypto-Catholic aristocrats at the Court, were among those defending Richard Montague when his views came under attack in the 1620s. But Laudian attempts to entice Catholics into the fold had the effect of encouraging many Protestants in their suspicion that Arminianism was tantamount to popery by another name, fears confirmed

49 Sharpe, *Personal Rule*, p. 342.

50 David Underdown, *Revel, Riot and Rebellion: Popular Politics and Culture in England 1603–1660* (Oxford, 1985), pp. 67–8.

by the fact that some clerics associated with the Durham House group later defected to Rome.[51] More than anything else, it was the perception that the religious policies of Charles and Laud were a front for the reintroduction of Catholicism that helps to explain why in the end those policies were frustrated and overthrown.

8.3 Laudian Policy: Containment and Collapse

In the late 1630s Laudianism was riding high. Opposition had been muted or exiled, and the reordering of churches and worship in accordance with ceremonialist principles was continuing apace. A new set of canons issued by convocation in May 1640 gave unambiguous sanction to the railing of east-end altars, and to bowing in their direction. Yet by the end of the year Archbishop Laud was in prison and his policy in tatters. Within two years of that, the kingdom was at war with itself. The sequence of events here can be rehearsed fairly briefly, though their interpretation is more uncertain and contentious. By universal agreement, however, it was the affairs of Scotland that precipitated the dramatic reversal of fortunes. Charles's obsession with order and uniformity was affronted by the fact that the Church in his northern kingdom operated on different principles (James had established a compromise system which combined the Kirk's presbyterianism with limited episcopacy). Charles had been promoting Arminians to Scottish bishoprics through the 1630s, and in 1637 the attempt was made to bring the Kirk more firmly into line by the promulgation of a Scottish prayer book, employing the more 'Catholic' 1549 communion formula (see Section 5.1) and imposed without consultation with the Scottish Parliament or Kirk assembly. The outcome was rebellion, widespread subscription to a 'National Covenant' swearing resistance to innovations attempting 'the subversion and ruin of the true reformed religion', and the abolition of episcopacy north of the border.[52] The ensuing 'Bishops' Wars' were militarily and financially disastrous for Charles, and spelled the end of the Personal Rule. The 'Short Parliament' which met in April–May 1640 refused to fund the expenses of the Scots War without the redress of grievances, grievances which were increased when convocation decided to impose on clergy an oath of loyalty to the government of the Church by 'archbishops, bishops, deans and archdeacons etcetera'. Many were alarmed at what precisely 'etc.' might mean. In the meantime, the Scots had invaded, routed an English army at the Battle of Newburn in August 1640, and occupied Newcastle. There was no alternative to the resummoning of Parliament, and the 'Long Parliament' (it sat until 1653) which convened in November 1640 set about a comprehensive rolling-

[51] Walsham, 'Parochial Roots', 639–49.
[52] Gardiner, *Constitutional Documents*, p. 132.

back of the Laudian programme, under the leadership of figures like the Earl of Essex in the Lords and John Pym in the Commons. The latter's keynote speech in November 1640 warned of conspiracies to erect tyranny in England and subject the nation to Rome.

In December 1640 the Commons ruled that the ecclesiastical canons were illegal, impeached Laud of treason and sent him to the Tower, along with the Earl of Strafford, Charles's formidable Lord Deputy of Ireland, who had been recalled by the King in 1639 and was urging him to take a tough stand. Strafford, suspected of planning to bring over an Irish army to use against Parliament, was executed in May 1641; Laud, 'the sty of all pestilential filth' according to one MP, languished in prison until trial and execution in 1645.[53] The hand of the radicals in Parliament was strengthened by the presentation of a petition in December 1640, signed by 15,000 Londoners, calling for the abolition of episcopacy 'root and branch', and backed up by similar petitions from the provinces. An attempt to enact this in legislation was narrowly defeated in the Commons, and Charles took care to ensure that new bishops appointed after 1640 were conformist Calvinists in the Grindal–Abbot mould. Yet Charles's inconsistent behaviour during 1641, on the one hand making concessions, on the other attempting to plot with the Scots and with officers in the army, kept tensions high. In May 1641 Pym and his allies drew up a Protestation against schemes to introduce 'arbitrary and tyrannical government', and appended to it an oath or declaration (which was taken widely across the nation) binding signatories to defend with their lives 'the true reformed Protestant religion expressed in the doctrine of the Church of England against all Popery and popish innovation'.[54] In September, the Commons resolved that communion tables be removed from the east end of churches and rails be taken down, that crucifixes and images be abolished, and that bowing to altars and at the name of Jesus cease forthwith. The Book of Sports too was overturned: 'the Lord's Day shall be duly observed and sanctified'.[55] Many of these policies were in any case being enacted unofficially: there was a wave of iconoclasm and destruction of altar rails at the start of the 1640s, particularly in the south and south Midlands. Political temperatures were raised to fever pitch in November 1641 by the news that rebellion had broken out in Ireland, and the reports (exaggerated in detail but real enough in substance) that Catholic rebels were slaughtering the Protestant population. This was the context for the production of a parliamentary Grand Remonstrance itemizing the many misdeeds of

[53] John Morrill, 'The Religious Context of the English Civil War', in Richard Cust and Ann Hughes, eds., *The English Civil War* (London, 1997), p. 166.

[54] David Cressy, 'The Protestation Protested 1641 and 1642', *Historical Journal*, 45 (2002) notes that the ambiguity of the Protestation encouraged radical local action against ceremonies which could be deemed 'popish'.

[55] Gardiner, *Constitutional Documents*, pp. 155–6, 197–8.

Charles's government over the course of the reign, and making much of the now familiar association between Arminianism and popery. But the fact that the Remonstrance passed in the Commons by only 159 to 148 votes was an indication of how polarized opinion was becoming within Parliament itself. It alarmed many in the Lords by seeming to appeal directly to the people. Having ditched Laud, Charles could now more plausibly pose as the defender of the constitution and the Church against dangerous radicals seeking to sweep away episcopacy along with all good order. The numerous county petitions against bishops and popish lords in 1641–2 were mirrored by others defending (non-Laudian) episcopacy and the prayer book. The question of who controlled the country's military force was the immediate catalyst for war in the summer of 1642. The parliamentary Militia Ordinance passed in March was countered by Charles's sending of Commissions of Array to supporters in the localities, authorizing them to muster troops. When the Lords and Commons voted in July 1642 to raise an army, they claimed to be acting for 'the safety of the King's person, defence of both Houses of Parliament. . . and preserving of the true religion.' A few weeks later, after fighting had broken out, the King published a manifesto in which he told his supporters that their enemies were for the most part 'Brownists, Anabaptists and Atheists'.[56] Two rival conspiracy theories – that of an Armininan–Papist plot to subvert the liberties of the kingdom, and that of a Puritan confederacy to undermine all hierarchy and order in Church and State – had come to full and bloody fruition.

John Morrill has famously proposed that 'the English Civil War was not the first European revolution: it was the last of the Wars of Religion'.[57] Critics observe that it is misleading to imply the conflict was about religion and nothing else, and have warned of the dangers of artificially separating religion from other issues: Arminianism (like popery) was associated in the minds of many contemporaries with arbitrary forms of government; active participation in local government was a characteristic of Puritanism, which many of Charles's supporters regarded as politically subversive.[58] In the case of someone like the eventual royalist supporter, the Earl of Dorset – a religious moderate of essentially 'Jacobethan' outlook, and almost obsessive concern with social and political unity – it has been argued that it is impossible to separate out 'religious' and 'political' motivation; they formed part of 'a coherent package'.[59] Yet it is hard to deny that overtly religious language

56 Ibid., p. 261; J.P. Kenyon, *Stuart England* (Harmondsworth, 1978), p. 145.

57 Morrill, 'Religious Context', p. 176.

58 Tyacke, 'Introduction', in his *English Protestantism*, p. 8; Ann Hughes, *The Causes of the English Civil War* (Basingstoke, 1991), pp. 114–15; Green, 'Wars of Religion?', pp. 114–17.

59 David L. Smith, 'Catholic, Anglican or Puritan? Edward Sackville, Fourth Earl of Dorset and the Ambiguities of Religion in Early Stuart England', *Transactions of the Royal Historical Society*, 6th ser., 2 (1992), 120–3.

and issues played a crucial role in the way the sides divided after the summoning of the Long Parliament. Spurred on by their fears of Catholic plotting, many MPs were driven towards an increasingly radical religious stance, feeling that the only safe course was to do away once and for all with the order of bishops (against which God's Providence appeared in any case to have passed judgement). This militancy created a counter-reaction among other parliamentarians in support of something that, in time, would come to be known as 'Anglicanism'.[60] The most compelling evidence of this reaction nationally is the wave of conformist petitions, from more than half the English counties, presented to Parliament in 1640–2, though there is some debate about the extent to which these were authentic expressions of local opinion, or attempts to manipulate and construct public opinion by local elites with links to the Court.[61] These texts extolled the dignity of the prayer book (the first drafters of one Kentish petition wanted to describe it as 'penned by the inspiration of the Holy Ghost'[62]) and defended episcopacy as an institution of apostolic origin, while often being critical of individual bishops and of (Laudian) corruptions in the Church. It is hard to be certain what the petitions tell us about the shape of religious attitudes in the decades before 1640. Judith Maltby argues that they provide evidence of a long-standing tradition of 'prayer book Protestantism', equidistant from Laudianism and Puritanism (see Section 6.2) though she also concedes that the attack on the Church in 1640–2 may have 'created a sense of "group identity" among conformists that had been lacking before.' Morrill writes of a situation 'which created, or at any rate crystallized' a theoretical and practical defence of non-Laudian episcopacy and the prayer book.[63] Yet it has also been argued that we should be wary of taking the anti-Laudianism of the petitions at face value at a time when, for obvious political reasons, almost everybody was eager to disentangle themselves from association with Laud and present the 1630s as the work of a small clique.[64]

Though Morrill's argument is focussed closely on the events of 1640–2, he has no doubt that the origins of religious conflict stretched back into Charles's reign, stressing that 'it is almost impossible to overestimate the damage caused by the Laudians' whose programme was 'offensive to most lay and much clerical opinion'.[65] Other revisionist historians have been less

[60] Morrill, 'Religious Context', pp. 168–9.

[61] Walter, 'Confessional Politics' takes the latter view, in contrast to Judith Maltby, *Prayer Book and People in Elizabethan and Early Stuart England* (Cambridge, 1998).

[62] Russell, *Causes*, p. 122. This was 'upon debate, omitted.'

[63] Maltby, *Prayer Book*, p. 224; Morrill, 'Religious Context', p. 169.

[64] Anthony Milton, 'The Laudian Moment: Conformist Trajectories in the Early Stuart Church', a paper given at the Reformation Studies Colloquium in Exeter in April 2002.

[65] Morrill, 'Religious Context', p. 165.

convinced of this, Kevin Sharpe in particular arguing that after the summoning of the Long Parliament the religious issues changed dramatically, and may have little direct connection with Laudianism in the 1630s. He notes that action to reform matters of ceremony and liturgy emerged rather slowly after November 1640 (because there was no consensus about how to do this), and in any case, debates about Laudian innovations were fairly rapidly overtaken by other more fundamental issues about the nature and government of the Church. The threat to episcopacy itself effected a fundamental realignment of ecclesiastical politics, with the line-up of sides in 1641 very different to that of the 1630s. Sharpe concedes the persistent thread of the fear of popery, something that 'perhaps alone served to connect the religious issues of 1640–2 with Laud and the Caroline regime', though he denies that fixation with a popish plot was really widespread before about 1639. In short, he feels that religious issues did not seriously threaten the stability of the Caroline regime before the outbreak of the Scottish rebellion in 1637, a military crisis that led to a fiscal crisis.[66] An emphasis on the Scottish crisis also characterizes the approach of Conrad Russell, though he is more inclined to locate it in a long-term structural weakness of Stuart royal power, 'the British Problem'. For as long as different ecclesiastical regimes operated in England and Scotland, dissidents in both countries would look across the border for inspiration and support, Scottish Arminians encouraged by the tide of events in England in the 1630s, and beleaguered English Puritans increasingly attracted to the way things were done north of the Tweed. Charles's policies towards the Kirk, and his resort to force, convinced Scottish presbyterians that in order to preserve their own security they would have to bring about a shift of power in England. And it was more than anything 'the attempt to impose a Scottish Reformation on England' that created a royalist-episcopalian party in England by 1642.[67]

But bishop-hating was not simply learned from the Scots. It is possible to see the radical opposition agenda that developed in 1640–2 as a culmination of strands in English religious thought that stretched well back into the Elizabethan period. Tyacke accuses revisionists like Sharpe and Bernard of placing enormous weight on the Scottish rebellion, portraying it as 'a sufficient explanation of all that followed thereafter', and of making Puritans like Pym appear out of virtually nowhere in 1640.[68] We should remember here that a significant part of the English Protestant tradition had never been convinced by the *iure divino* arguments emerging in the 1590s, only ever accepting government by bishops as a means to an end. If the reign of Edward VI (and to a lesser extent, that of James I) had displayed the potential of bishops as

[66] Sharpe, *Personal Rule*, pp. 934–54.
[67] Russell, *Causes*, pp. 109–11, 122–4.
[68] Tyacke, 'Anglican Attitudes', pp. 180, 196.

instruments of godly reformation, the experience of the 1630s revealed the potentially disastrous consequences of sticking with a model of Church government that was popish in its origins. For some, it reignited the aspirations of the Elizabethan presbyterian movement for a system closer to the perceived pattern of the New Testament. To many of the godly, the collapse of Laudianism in the autumn of 1640 was a moment of liberation, of revolutionary possibility. The 'Fast Sermons' delivered before the Long Parliament in 1640–1 repeatedly raised the prospect of going beyond the inadequate compromise of the Elizabethan Settlement. Stephen Marshall called upon parliamentarians to 'throw to the moals and the bats every rag that hath not God's stamp upon it'; Edward Calamy urged them to 'reform the reformation'.[69] In the provinces, godly ministers who had tolerated, though never fully reconciled themselves to services and ceremonies prescribed by the prayer book were now reluctant merely to return to how things had been in the Jacobean Church. In Herefordshire, for example, godly ministers urged their MP, Sir Robert Harley, to push for further reform once the Laudian innovations had been overturned. In many places nationally, clerics and their lay patrons who had been proponents of vigorous moral reform in the 1620s, and opponents of Laud in the 1630s, moved from petitioning against Laudianism in 1640, to campaigning for the abolition of episcopacy in 1641, to forthright support for the parliamentary armies in 1642. In his study of Essex, William Hunt refers to a 'Puritan moment' in order to emphasize the decisive role of religious conviction in bringing about war against the King: 'above all else it was militant Protestantism – called Puritanism by its enemies – that gave rebellion its cultural validation, and that resolved a host of conflicts into the encounter of Roundhead and Cavalier.'[70]

Not all opponents of Laudianism followed this trajectory. The growing clamour for 'root and branch' reform split the parliamentary opposition of 1640 and created the conditions for civil war. Why were some people prepared to push matters so far? There seems little doubt that lending the sense of urgency to the reforming campaign of the early 1640s was the belief in a popish plot, a conspiracy to mislead, if not brainwash the King, with the ultimate aim of returning the kingdom to the thraldom of Rome. In one sense this was a short-term catalyst: rumours of military plots involving Catholic officers, and of planned Catholic uprisings in the localities, multiplied in the fevered political atmosphere of the Long Parliament. It was the Irish Rebellion, and the dreadful fear that Charles himself had sanctioned it, that impelled even moderate Puritans like Richard Baxter to adopt the parliamentary cause in the war.[71] But the widespread belief in an imminent Catholic coup d'etat in 1641 only makes sense in a broader con-

69 Morrill, 'Religious Context', p. 167.
70 Oldridge, *Religion*, pp. 137–43; Hunt, *Puritan Moment*, pp. 311–12.
71 William Lamont, 'Richard Baxter, "Popery" and the Origins of the English Civil War', *History*, 87 (2002).

text of developments over Charles's reign, and a much older preoccupation with the reality of a popish threat, from without and from within.

A perception in the latter years of James I that the number and confidence of English papists was growing (see Section 7.3) intensified after the accession of his son. In fact, Charles's reign was no golden age for English Catholics: though missionary priests were able to go about their business in (relative) safety, the financial pressures on the recusant community as a whole actually increased, as recusancy fines came to provide a regular source of government taxation (particularly during the Personal Rule).[72] But the public profile of Catholics in Caroline England was higher than it had been in two generations. Of fundamental importance here was Charles's marriage in 1625 to a French Catholic princess. Henrietta Maria was no discreet church papist like her predecessor Anne of Denmark, but ostentatiously devout in the practice of her religion, even venturing to Tyburn in 1626 to offer prayers for the Catholic martyrs who had been executed there. Her chapels at St James's palace and Somerset House were staffed by a full complement of French Capuchin friars, who paraded openly in the London streets. Protestant observers were alarmed by a spate of aristocratic conversions at Court, and still more by the way the Queen's household was being used to open informal diplomatic relations with the papacy. From 1634 a succession of papal agents attended upon Henrietta Maria. George Con, a Scotsman who arrived in 1636, was a particular favourite of both Catholic and conformist courtiers. The King freely discussed foreign affairs with him, and William Juxon, Lord Treasurer and Laudian bishop of London, gave a dinner in his honour.[73]

Events on the continent, where in the mid-1630s the tide of the Thirty Years War was flowing strongly against the Protestant cause, intensified and justified anxiety. Catholic rulers like the Habsburg Emperor Ferdinand II aimed at strengthening their rule through greater identification with the authority of the Church, and at the extirpation of Protestantism in their lands. In this context, it has been suggested, it was by no means irrational for contemporaries to see events in England as part of a pattern, the ecclesiastical policies promoted by the leaders of Charles I's Church as belonging to a wider phenomenon of resurgent popery.[74] A Suffolk gentleman asked

72 Michael Mullett, *Catholics in Britain and Ireland 1558–1829* (Basingstoke, 1998), p. 26.

73 Edward Norman, *Roman Catholicism in England from the Elizabethan Settlement to the Second Vatican Council* (Oxford, 1986), pp. 34–5; Robin Clifton, 'Fear of Popery', in Russell, *Origins*; Caroline Hibbard, *Charles I and the Popish Plot* (Chapel Hill, NC, 1983), ch. 3.

74 Jonathan Scott, *England's Troubles: Seventeenth-Century English Political Instability in European Context* (Cambridge, 2000), chs. 2–6, arguing that 'popery' signified to contemporaries not so much specific Roman doctrines as a campaign of anti-Protestantism, and that the 1630s can legitimately be labelled 'Counter-Reformation England'.

by the churchwardens if they should obey the order to erect an altar rail answered, 'the king hath a wife, and he loves her well, and she is a papist and we must all be of her religion, and that's the thing the bishops aim at.' Wren's commissioners at Ipswich in 1637 were met with shouts of 'they would have all his Majesty's subjects to be the Queen's subjects'.[75] As we have seen, Laudian clerics were notably reluctant to employ traditional anti-Catholic rhetoric and were nostalgic for aspects of the ceremony and discipline of the pre-Reformation Church. Already in the Parliament of 1626, Pym and other Calvinist members were charging that Arminianism was a means of introducing popery into the realm, while MPs in the 1629 Parliament, appealing to memories of the Armada and Gunpowder Plot, termed it 'this Trojan horse' and observed that 'an Arminian is the spawn of a Papist'. The writings of Puritans like Henry Burton elaborated the notion of Arminianism as part of a 'popish plot', and by the time of the Grand Remonstrance 'popery' and 'Arminianism' were virtually interchangeable terms – the machinations of 'the Popish party' included the 'oppressions in religion, Church, government and discipline' brought in the 1630s.[76] The wave of rioting against Catholics that broke out in many parts, particularly of the south and east, between 1640 and 1642 was the compounded result of a layering of attitudes and fears. A long-standing culture of popular anti-popery, fuelled by Gunpowder celebrations and traditional xenophobia, could be galvanized into violent action by fears of foreign (Irish) Catholic invasion, backed by the treachery of an internal papist fifth column (of unknowable size). The situation was redolent of 1588, with the spine-chilling twist that this time the sovereign and the bishops were believed to be on the side of the Antichrist.

Summation

If the English Civil War was indeed the last of the European wars of religion, it has the added distinction of being a civil war among Protestants rather than (as in France or the Netherlands) between members of the Reformed Churches and Romanists (though not all protagonists saw it in this light). There was nothing inevitable about such a conflict, which probably owed as much to the mismanagement and poor political skills of Charles I as to any other factor. But surveying the religious tensions of the late 1620s and 1630s, and their rapid deterioration and mutation in 1640–2, one is struck by the extent to which the approach of all sides to the most contentious issues was rooted in memories and perceptions of the nation's sixteenth-century experience. The Laudian canons of May 1640,

75 Walter, 'Anti-Popery', p. 129.

76 Tyacke, 'Puritanism', pp. 134–5; *Anti-Calvinists*, pp. 135, 157–9, 227–8, 243–4; Gardiner, *Constitutional Documents*, pp. 204–5.

which insisted on the placing of the altar at the east end, and the Long Parliament's November arrangements for communion with the table brought into the middle of the church 'according to the rubric', both cited the same authority for their actions – the Injunctions of 1559.[77] From the perspective of 1642 it is easier to see that the 'Elizabethan Settlement' is something of a misnomer, that fundamental questions about the reformation of religion, about the shape of 'Protestant England' were still to be finally addressed. In that sense, the politics of the immediately pre-civil war period belong as much to the history of the English Reformation as to any narrative of the first stirrings of England's modern constitution. The historiography of Caroline religion seems to offer a stark choice. On the one hand, there is the model of a consensual Protestant Church, with 'Puritanism' integrated into the mainstream, torn apart by the imposition of an alien discipline and theology in the 1630s. On the other, a fundamental continuity of conformist episcopal policies, with the ever-present possibility of a radical Puritan challenge. Both versions surely contain elements of truth. Puritanism, or more broadly, the impulse towards further Protestant reformation, was quiescent before 1625, but only to the extent that it was allowed to pursue its mission of preaching and moral reform, and that its conscience was not pressed too hard over matters of dress, ceremony and ritual. Even aside from the theological issue of Arminianism versus Calvinism, Laudian approaches drew inspiration from developments within the Elizabethan and Jacobean period – an emphasis on the authority of a visible institutional Church, and on the role of sacraments and ceremonies in helping people to be good. Conrad Russell's notion of there being from the outset within the Church of England 'two churches struggling to get out' is an attractively perceptive one.[78]

Could this struggle have been resolved differently before 1640? More specifically, if Charles had desisted from taking on his Scottish subjects in 1637, could he and his advisers have succeeded in marginalizing Puritan opposition and thoroughly 'Laudianizing' the buildings and people of the Church of England? The question is as intriguing (and as unanswerable) as that of whether a longer-lived Queen Mary could have restored England permanently to Catholicism in the 1550s and 60s. Mary, though, can be granted the extenuating circumstance of her death, and the failure of Charles to see through his preferred ecclesiastical policies is a conspicuous one. No doubt some of the reasons for this are simply fortuitous. Had the leaders of the Pilgrimage of Grace held their nerve and succeeded in 1536–7, for example, one can imagine Henry VIII undertaking as dramatic a reversal of religious policy as Charles was obliged to in 1640–1. Charles, however, lacked the talent and inclination for persuasion through propaganda and

[77] Russell, *Causes*, p. 86.
[78] Ibid., p. 82.

public display that Henry (and Elizabeth) possessed in abundance, as well as the gut political instincts of his father, James. Yet we should be wary of any solely 'top-down' perspective on this. At every stage of its implementation, redirection and reinvention, the English Reformation involved the co-operation, active or passive, of thousands of local officers, town governors, clergymen and ordinary parishioners. Such people not only enacted, but also learned the Reformation, and were increasingly provided with the means to make devotional and confessional choices. These had to be reconciled with the demands of political obedience, and there were limits to how far English subjects were persuadable in conscience.

After the civil strife of the mid-seventeenth century had been resolved, something rather similar to the sacramentalist, non-Calvinist outlook of the 1630s – 'Anglicanism' – did become the dominant ethos of the Church of England. But the price of this was the departure of Baptists, Congregationalists, Presbyterians and Quakers, to stand alongside the older nonconformity of Roman Catholicism in principled dissent from the established Church. Unity and uniformity within a national Church was the aspiration of every English monarch in the period covered by this book. In neglecting to ensure this outcome, not just Charles, but all of them can be judged to have failed. Yet failure is not the note on which to conclude. For countless numbers of English people, the Reformation imposed unprecedented choices and provided unprecedented opportunities. For some, it activated the power of conviction, bringing forth, even in martyrdom, a triumph of the spirit. For greater numbers of others, it was merely a triumph of endurance. While the imaginative energies of scholars continue to engage passionately with the predicament of the people who lived there, Reformation England will remain a compelling place.

Select Bibliography

This bibliography follows the chapter arrangement of the book. Works are cited only once, though many are relevant to various topics.

General Works

Margaret Aston, *England's Iconoclasts: Laws Against Images* (Oxford, 1988).

Susan Brigden, *London and the Reformation* (Oxford, 1989).

Richard Cust and Ann Hughes, eds., *The English Civil War* (London, 1997).

A.G. Dickens, *The English Reformation* (2nd ed., London, 1989); *Reformation Studies* (London, 1982).

Eamon Duffy, *The Stripping of the Altars: Traditional Religion in England 1400–1580* (New Haven and London, 1992).

Christopher Haigh, *English Reformations: Religion, Politics, and Society under the Tudors* (Oxford, 1993); ed., *The English Reformation Revised* (Cambridge, 1987).

Philip Hughes, *The Reformation in England*, (3 vols., London, 1950–4).

Ronald Hutton, *The Rise and Fall of Merry England: The Ritual Year 1400–1700* (Oxford, 1994).

Norman Jones, *The English Reformation: Religion and Cultural Adaption* (Oxford, 2002).

Peter Lake and Maria Dowling, eds., *Protestantism and the National Church in Sixteenth-Century England* (London, 1987).

Diarmaid MacCulloch, *The Later Reformation in England, 1547–1603* (2nd ed., Basingstoke, 2001).

Christopher Marsh, *Popular Religion in Sixteenth-Century England*, (Basingstoke, 1998).

Peter Marshall, ed., *The Impact of the English Reformation 1500–1640* (London, 1997); *Beliefs and the Dead in Reformation England* (Oxford, 2002); and Alec Ryrie, eds., *The Beginnings of English Protestantism* (Cambridge, 2002).

J.J. Scarisbrick, *The Reformation and the English People* (Oxford, 1984).

Keith Thomas, *Religion and the Decline of Magic: Studies in Popular Beliefs in Sixteenth- and Seventeenth-Century England* (London, 1971).

Robert Whiting, *The Blind Devotion of the People: Popular Religion and the English Reformation* (Cambridge, 1989).

1. Catholic England

Caroline Barron, 'The Parish Fraternities of Medieval London', in id. and Christopher Harper-Bill, eds., *The Church in Pre-Reformation Society* (Woodbridge, 1985).

George Bernard, 'Vitality and Vulnerability in the Late Medieval Church: Pilgrimage on the Eve of the Break with Rome', in John Watts, ed., *The End of the Middle Ages? England in the Fifteenth and Sixteenth Centuries* (Stroud, 1998).

Clive Burgess, '"A Fond Thing Vainly Invented": an Essay on Purgatory and Pious Motive in Later Medieval England', in Susan Wright, ed., *Parish, Church and People* (London, 1988).

Claire Cross, 'Monasticism and Society in the Diocese of York 1520–1540', *Transactions of the Royal Historical Society*, 5th ser., 38 (1988).

R.G. Davies, 'Lollardy and Locality', *Transactions of the Royal Historical Society*, 6th ser., 1 (1991).

J.D.M. Derrett, 'The Affairs of Richard Hunne and Friar Standish', in Thomas More, *The Apology*, ed. J.B. Trapp (New Haven and London, 1979).

A.G. Dickens, 'The Shape of Anticlericalism and the English Reformation', in his *Late Monasticism and the Reformation* (London, 1994).

Ken Farnhill, *Guilds and the Parish Community in Late Medieval East Anglia c. 1470–1550* (York, 2001).

Sean Field, 'Devotion, Discontent, and the Henrician Reformation: The Evidence of the Robin Hood Stories', *Journal of British Studies*, 41 (2002).

Ronald Finucane, *Miracles and Pilgrims: Popular Beliefs in Medieval England* (London, 1977).

Katherine French, *The People of the Parish: Community Life in a Late Medieval English Diocese* (Philadelphia, 2001).

Anthony Goodman, 'Henry VII and Christian Renewal', *Studies in Church History*, 17 (1981).

Steven Gunn, 'Edmund Dudley and the Church', *Journal of Ecclesiastical History*, 51 (2000).

Peter Gwyn, *The King's Cardinal: The Rise and Fall of Thomas Wolsey* (London, 1990).

Christopher Harper-Bill, *The Pre-Reformation Church in England 1400–1530* (London, 1989).

Peter Heath, 'Between Reform and Reformation: The English Church in the Fourteenth and Fifteenth Centuries', *Journal of Ecclesiastical History*, 41 (1990).

Anne Hudson, *The Premature Reformation: Wycliffite Texts and Lollard History* (Oxford, 1988).

Jonathan Hughes, *Pastors and Visionaries: Religion and Secular Life in Late Medieval Yorkshire* (Woodbridge, 1988).

Mervyn James, 'Ritual, Drama and the Social Body in the Late Medieval English Town', *Past and Present*, 98 (1983).

David Knowles, *The Religious Orders in England III: The Tudor Age* (Cambridge, 1959).

Beat Kümin, *The Shaping of a Community: The Rise and Reformation of the English Parish c. 1400–1560* (Aldershot, 1996).

David Loades, 'Anticlericalism in the Church of England before 1558: an "Eating Canker"?', in Nigel Aston and Matthew Cragoe, eds., *Anticlericalism in Britain, c. 1500–1914* (Stroud, 2000).

Peter Marshall, *The Catholic Priesthood and the English Reformation* (Oxford, 1994).

Derek Plumb, 'The Social and Economic Status of the Later Lollards', and 'A Gathered Church? Lollards and their Society', in Margaret Spufford, ed., *The World of Rural Dissenters 1520–1725* (Cambridge, 1995).

Richard Rex, *The Lollards* (Basingstoke, 2002).

Colin Richmond, 'Religion and the Fifteenth-Century English Gentleman', in R.B. Dobson, ed., *The Church, Politics and Patronage in the Fifteenth Century* (Gloucester, 1984); 'The English Gentry and Religion, c. 1500', in Christopher Harper-Bill, ed., *Religious Belief and Ecclesiastical Careers in Late Medieval England* (Woodbridge, 1991).

Gervase Rosser, 'Communities of Parish and Guild in the Late Middle Ages', in Susan Wright, ed., *Parish, Church and People* (London, 1988); 'Parochial Conformity and Voluntary Religion in Late-Medieval England', *Transactions of the Royal Historical Society*, 6th ser., 1 (1991).

Miri Rubin, *Corpus Christi: The Eucharist in Late Medieval Culture* (Cambridge, 1991).

Robert Swanson, *Church and Society in Late Medieval England* (Oxford, 1989).

John A.F. Thomson, *The Early Tudor Church and Society* (London, 1993); *The Later Lollards 1414–1520* (Oxford, 1965).

Walter Ullman, 'This Realm of England is an Empire', *Journal of Ecclesiastical History*, 30 (1979).

2. Henry VIII's Reformation

George Bernard, 'Anne Boleyn's Religion', *Historical Journal*, 36 (1993); 'Elton's Cromwell', *History*, 83 (1998); and 'The Making of Religious Policy, 1533–1546: Henry VIII and the Search for the Middle Way', *Historical Journal*, 41(1998).

Susan Brigden, 'Thomas Cromwell and the "Brethren"', in Claire Cross, David Loades and J.J. Scarisbrick, eds., *Law and Government under the Tudors* (Cambridge, 1998).

John Craig and Caroline Litzenberger, 'Wills as Religious Propaganda: the Testament of William Tracy', *Journal of Ecclesiastical History*, 44 (1993).

David Daniell, *William Tyndale: a Biography* (New Haven and London, 1994).

C.S.L. Davies, 'Religion and the Pilgrimage of Grace', in Anthony Fletcher and John Stevenson, eds., *Order and Disorder in Early Modern England* (Cambridge, 1985).

John F. Davis, *Heresy and Reformation in the South East of England 1520–1559* (London, 1983).

Maria Dowling, 'Anne Boleyn and Reform', *Journal of Ecclesiastical History*, 35 (1984).

G.R. Elton, *Policy and Police: The Enforcement of the Reformation in the Age of Thomas Cromwell* (Cambridge, 1972); 'Politics and the Pilgrimage of Grace', in B. Malament, ed., *After the Reformation* (New Haven, 1980).

John Guy, 'Thomas Cromwell and the Intellectual Origins of the Henrician Revolution', in id., ed., *The Tudor Monarchy* (London, 1997).

Richard Hoyle, 'The Origins of the Dissolution of the Monasteries', *Historical Journal*, 38 (1995); *The Pilgrimage of Grace and the Politics of the 1530s* (Oxford, 2001).

Eric Ives, *Anne Boleyn* (Oxford, 1985); 'Anne Boleyn and the Early Reformation in England', *Historical Journal*, 37 (1994).

Stanford Lehmberg, *The Reformation Parliament 1529–1536* (Cambridge, 1970).

Diarmaid MacCulloch, ed., *The Reign of Henry VIII* (London, 1995).

Peter Marshall, 'The Rood of Boxley, the Blood of Hailes and the Defence of the Henrician Church', *Journal of Ecclesiastical History*, 46 (1995); 'Mumpsimus and Sumpsimus: The Intellectual Origins of a Henrician *Bon Mot*', *Journal of Ecclesiastical History*, 52 (2001).

Glyn Redworth, 'Whatever Happened to the English Reformation?', *History Today* (October, 1987); 'A Study in the Formulation of Policy: The Genesis and Evolution of the Act of Six Articles', *Journal of Ecclesiastical History*, 37 (1986).

Richard Rex, 'The English Campaign against Luther in the 1520s', *Transactions of the Royal Historical Society*, 5th ser., 39 (1989); 'The New Learning', *Journal of Ecclesiastical History*, 44 (1993); and *Henry VIII and the English Reformation* (Basingstoke, 1993).

Alec Ryrie, 'The Strange Death of Lutheran England', *Journal of Ecclesiastical History*, 53 (2002).

J.J. Scarisbrick, *Henry VIII* (London, 1968).

Ethan Shagan, 'Print, Orality and Communications in the Maid of Kent Affair', *Journal of Ecclesiastical History*, 52 (2001).

Carl Trueman, *Luther's Legacy: Salvation and the English Reformers 1525–1556* (Oxford, 1994).

Robert Whiting, 'Abominable Idols: Images and Image-breaking under Henry VIII', *Journal of Ecclesiastical History*, 33 (1982).

3. Edwardian Revolution

J.D. Alsop, 'Religious Preambles in Early Modern English Wills as Formulae', *Journal of Ecclesiastical History*, 40 (1989).

Michael Bush, *The Government Policy of Protector Somerset* (London, 1975).

Catharine Davies, *A Religion of the Word: The Defence of the Reformation in the Reign of Edward VI* (Manchester, 2002).

Eamon Duffy, *The Voices of Morebath: Reformation and Rebellion in an English Village* (New Haven and London, 2001).

W.K. Jordan, *Edward VI: the Young King* (London, 1968); *Edward VI: the Threshold of Power* (London, 1970).

Alan Kreider, *English Chantries: The Road to Dissolution* (Cambridge, MA, 1979).

Caroline Litzenberger, 'Local Responses to Changes in Religious Policy Based on the Evidence from Gloucestershire Wills', *Continuity and Change*, 8 (1993).

Jennifer Loach, *Edward VI* (New Haven and London, 1999).

Diarmaid MacCulloch, *Thomas Cranmer: A Life* (New Haven and London, 1996); *Tudor Church Militant: Edward VI and the Protestant Reformation* (London, 1999).

Helen Parish, *Clerical Marriage and the English Reformation* (Aldershot, 2000).

Andrew Pettegree, *Foreign Protestant Communities in Sixteenth-Century London* (Oxford, 1986).

Glyn Redworth, *In Defence of the Church Catholic: The Life of Stephen Gardiner* (Oxford, 1990).

Ethan Shagan, *Popular Politics and the English Reformation* (Cambridge, 2003).

Joyce Youings, 'The South-Western Rebellion of 1549', *Southern History*, 1 (1979).

4. Mary I's Reformation

James Clark, 'Reformation and Reaction at St Albans Abbey 1530–58', *English Historical Review*, 115 (2000).

Claire Cross, 'The Reconstitution of Northern Monastic Communities in the Reign of Mary Tudor', *Northern History*, 29 (1993).

Jennifer Loach, *Parliament and the Crown in the Reign of Mary Tudor* (Oxford, 1986); 'The Marian Establishment and the Printing Press', *English Historical Review*, 101 (1986); and 'Mary Tudor and the Re-Catholicisation of England', *History Today* (Nov. 1994).

David Loades, 'The Enforcement of Reaction, 1553–1558', *Journal of Eclesiastical History*, 16 (1965); *Mary Tudor: A Life* (Oxford, 1989);

The Reign of Mary Tudor (2nd ed., London, 1991); and *Two Tudor Conspiracies* (2nd ed., Bangor, 1992).

Rex Pogson, 'The Legacy of the Schism', in Jennifer Loach and Robert Tittler, eds., *The Mid-Tudor Polity, c. 1540–c.1560* (London, 1980).

J.W. Martin, *Religious Radicals in Tudor England* (London, 1989).

Thomas McCoog, ed., *The Reckoned Expense: Edmund Campion and the Early English Jesuits* (Woodbridge, 1996); 'Ignatius Loyola and Reginald Pole: a Reconsideration', *Journal of Ecclesiastical History*, 47 (1996).

Thomas F. Mayer, *Reginald Pole: Prince and Prophet* (Cambridge, 2000).

Andrew Pettegree, *Marian Protestantism: Six Studies* (Aldershot, 1996).

Elizabeth Russell, 'Marian Oxford and the Counter-Reformation', in Caroline Barron and Christopher Harper-Bill, eds., *The Church in Pre-Reformation Society* (Woodbridge, 1985).

M.R. Thorp, 'Religion and the Wyatt Rebellion of 1554', *Church History*, 48 (1979).

Robert Tittler, *The Reign of Mary I* (London, 1983).

Brett Usher, '"In a Time of Persecution": New Light on the Secret Protestant Congregation in Marian London', in David Loades, ed., *John Foxe and the English Reformation* (Aldershot, 1997).

Lucy Wooding, *Rethinking Catholicism in Reformation England* (Oxford, 2000).

Jonathan Wright, 'Marian Exiles and the Legitmacy of Flight from Persecution', *Journal of Ecclesiastical History*, 52 (2001).

5. Protestantism and Puritanism

Eric Carlson, 'Clerical Marriage and the English Reformation', *Journal of British Studies*, 31 (1992).

Patrick Collinson, *The Elizabethan Puritan Movement* (London, 1967); *Archbishop Grindal 1519–1583: The Struggle for a Reformed Church* (London, 1979); and 'The Jacobean Religious Settlement: The Hampton Court Conference', in Howard Tomlinson, ed., *Before the English Civil War* (Basingstoke, 1983); 'The Elizabethan Church and the New Religion' in Christopher Haigh, ed., *The Reign of Elizabeth I* (Basingstoke, 1984); *The Religion of Protestants: The Church in English Society 1559–1625* (Oxford, 1982); *The Birthpangs of Protestant England: Religious and Cultural Change in the Sixteenth and Seventeenth Centuries* (Basingstoke, 1988); 'The Cohabitation of the Faithful with the Unfaithful', in Ole Grell, Jonathan Israel and Nicholas Tyacke, eds., *From Persecution to Toleration: The Glorious Revolution and Religion in England* (Oxford, 1991); *Elizabethan Essays* (London, 1994); 'Ecclesiastical Vitriol: Religious Satire in the 1590s and the Invention of Puritanism', in John Guy, ed., *The Reign of Elizabeth I: Court and Culture in the Last Decade* (Cambridge, 1995); 'Ben

Johnson's *Bartholomew Fair*: The Theatre Constructs Puritanism', in D. Smith, R. Strier and D. Bevington, eds., *The Theatrical City: Culture, Theatre and Politics in London, 1576–1649* (Cambridge, 1995); and 'Puritanism and the Poor', in Rosemary Horrox and Sarah Rees Jones, eds., *Pragmatic Utopias: Ideals and Communities, 1200–1630* (Cambridge, 2001).

David Crankshaw, 'Preparations for the Canterbury Provincial Convocation of 1562–3: A Question of Attribution', in Susan Wabuda and Caroline Litzenberger, eds., *Belief and Practice in Reformation England* (Aldershot, 1998).

Susan Doran, 'Elizabeth I's Religion: Clues from her Letters', *Journal of Ecclesiastical History*, 52 (2001).

Christopher Durston and Jacqueline Eales, eds., *The Culture of English Puritanism 1560–1700* (Basingstoke, 1996).

Lori Anne Ferrel, *Government by Polemic: James I, the King's Preachers, and the Rhetorics of Conformity, 1603–1625* (Stanford, 1998).

Kenneth Fincham, *Prelate as Pastor: The Episcopate of James I* (Oxford, 1990); and Peter Lake, 'The Ecclesiastical Policy of King James I', *Journal of British Studies*, 24 (1985).

Thomas Freeman, 'Demons, Deviance and Defiance: John Darrell and the Politics of Exorcism in Late Elizabethan England', in Peter Lake and Michael Questier, eds., *Conformity and Orthodoxy in the English Church, c. 1560–1660* (Woodbridge, 2000).

Jeremy Goring, *Godly Exercises or the Devil's Dance? Puritanism and Popular Culture in Pre-Civil War England* (London, 1983).

William P. Haugaard, *Elizabeth and the English Reformation* (Cambridge, 1968).

Christopher Hill, *Society and Puritanism in Pre-Revolutionary England* (London, 1964).

W.S. Hudson, *The Cambridge Connection and the Elizabethan Settlement of 1559* (Durham, NC, 1980).

Arnold Hunt, 'The Lord's Supper in Early Modern England', *Past and Present*, 161 (1998).

William Hunt, *The Puritan Moment. The Coming of Revolution in an English County* (Cambridge, MA, 1983).

Martin Ingram, 'Religion, Communities and Moral Discipline in Late Sixteenth- and Early Seventeenth-Century England', in Kaspar von Greyerz, ed., *Religion and Society in Early Modern Europe, 1500–1800* (London, 1984).

Norman L. Jones, *Faith by Statute: Parliament and the Settlement of Religion, 1559* (London, 1982).

R.T. Kendall, *Calvin and English Calvinism to 1649* (Oxford, 1979).

Peter Lake, 'The Significance of the Elizabethan Identification of the Pope as Antichrist', *Journal of Ecclesiastical History*, 31 (1980); *Moderate Puritans and the Elizabethan Church* (Cambridge, 1982); 'Calvinism and the English Church 1570–1635', *Past and Present*, 114 (1987); *Anglicans and Puritans? Presbyterianism and English Conformist Thought from Whitgift to Hooker* (London, 1988); 'Lancelot Andrewes, John Buckeridge, and Avant-garde Conformity at the Court of James I', in Linda Levy Peck, ed., *The Mental World of the Jacobean Court* (Cambridge, 1991); 'Defining Puritanism – again?', in Francis Bremer, ed., *Puritanism: Transatlantic Perspectives on a Seventeenth-Century Anglo-American Faith* (London, 1993); and with Michael Questier, *The Antichrist's Lewd Hat: Protestants, Papists and Players in Post-Reformation England* (New Haven and London, 2002).

Peter McCullough, *Sermons at Court: Politics and Religion in Elizabethan and Jacobean Preaching* (Cambridge, 1998).

Julia Merritt, 'The Cradle of Laudianism? Westminster Abbey, 1558–1630', *Journal of Ecclesiastical History*, 52 (2001).

Kenneth Parker, *The English Sabbath: A Study of Doctrine and Discipline from the Reformation to the Civil War* (Cambridge, 1988); and Eric Carlson, *'Practical Divinty': The Works and Life of Revd Richard Greenham* (Aldershot, 1998).

Paul Seaver, *Wallington's World: A Puritan Artisan in Seventeenth-Century London* (London, 1985).

Margaret Spufford, 'Puritanism and Social Control?', in Anthony Fletcher and John Stevenson, eds., *Order and Disorder in Early Modern England* (Cambridge, 1985).

John Spurr, *English Puritanism 1603–1689* (Basingstoke, 1998).

Nicholas Tyacke, 'Popular Puritan Mentality in Late Elizabethan England', in his *Aspects of English Protestantism c. 1530–1700* (Manchester, 2001).

David Underdown, *Fire from Heaven: Life in an English Town in the Seventeenth Century* (London, 1992).

Peter White, *Predestination, Policy and Polemic: Conflict and Consensus in the English Church from the Reformation to the Civil War* (Cambridge, 1992).

Keith Wrightson and David Levine, *Poverty and Piety in an English Village: Terling 1525–1700* (London, 1979).

6. Religions of the People

J.P. Boulton, 'The Limits of Formal Religion: The Administration of Holy Communion in Late Elizabethan and Early Stuart London', *London Journal*, 10 (1984).

Francis Bremer and Ellen Rydell, 'Performance Art? Puritans in the Pulpit', *History Today* (Sep. 1995).

Eric Carlson, 'The Origins, Function and Status of the Office of Churchwarden, with Particular Reference to the Diocese of Ely', in Margaret Spufford, ed., *The World of Rural Dissenters* (Cambridge, 1995); and 'The Boring of the Ear: Shaping the Pastoral Vision of

Preaching in England, 1540–1640', in Larissa Taylor, ed., *Preachers and People in the Reformations and Early Modern Period* (Brill, 2001).

Patrick Collinson, 'Shepherds, Sheepdogs, and Hirelings: The Pastoral Ministry in Post-Reformation England', *Studies in Church History*, 26 (1989).

John Craig, *Reformation, Politics and Polemics: The Growth of Protestantsism in East Anglian Market Towns, 1500–1610* (Aldershot, 2001).

David Cressy, *Bonfires and Bells: National Memory and the Protestant Calendar in Elizabethan and Stuart England* (London, 1989).

Andrew Foster, 'Churchwardens' Accounts of Early Modern England and Wales', in Katherine French, Gary Gibbs, and Beat Kümin, eds., *The Parish in English Life 1400–1600* (Manchester, 1997).

Adam Fox, *Oral and Literate Culture in England 1500–1700* (Oxford, 2000).

Ian Green, '"For Children in Yeeres and Children in Understanding": The Emergence of the English Catechism under Elizabeth and the Early Stuarts', *Journal of Ecclesiastical History*, 37 (1986); *The Christian's ABC: Catechisms and Catechizing in England, c. 1530–1740* (Oxford, 1996); *Print and Protestantism in Early Modern England* (Oxford, 2000); and 'All People that on Earth do Dwell, Sing to the Lord with Cheerful Voice': Protestantism and Music in Early Modern England', in Simon Ditchfield, ed., *Christianity and Community in the West: Essays for John Bossy* (Aldershot, 2001).

Christopher Haigh, 'Anticlericalism and Clericalism, 1580–1640', in Nigel Aston and Mathew Cragoe, eds., *Anticlericalism in Britain, c. 1500–1914* (Stroud, 2000); 'The Taming of Reformation: Preachers, Pastors and Parishioners in Elizabethan and Early Stuart England', *History*, 85 (2000); 'Communion and Community: Exclusion from Communion in Post-Reformation England', *Journal of Ecclesiastical History*, 51 (2000); and 'Success and Failure in the English Reformation', *Past and Present*, 173 (2001).

Ronald Hutton, 'The English Reformation and the Evidence of Folklore', *Past and Present*, 148 (1995).

Martin Ingram, *Church Courts, Sex and Marriage in England, 1570–1640* (Cambridge, 1987); 'From Reformation to Toleration: Popular Religious Cultures in England, 1540–1690', in Tim Harris, ed., *Popular Culture in England, c.1580–1850* (Basingstoke, 1995).

Peter Lake, 'Deeds Against Nature: Cheap Print, Protestantism and Murder in Early Seventeenth-Century England', in Kevin Sharpe and Peter Lake, eds., *Culture and Politics in Early Stuart England* (Basingstoke, 1994); 'Popular Form, Puritan Content? Two Puritan Appropriations of the Murder Pamphlet from Mid-Seventeenth-Century London', in Anthony Fletcher and Peter Roberts, eds., *Religion, Culture and Society in Early Modern Britain* (Cambridge, 1994); and Michael Questier, eds.,

Conformity and Orthodoxy in the English Church, c. 1560–1660 (Woodbridge, 2000).

Frank Luttmer, 'Persecutors, Tempters and Vassals of the Devil: The Unregenerate in Puritan Practical Divinity', *Journal of Ecclesiastical History*, 51 (2000).

Rosemary O'Day, *The English Clergy: The Emergence and Consolidation of a Profession 1558–1642* (Leicester, 1979).

Alan Macfarlane, 'A Tudor Anthropologist: George Gifford's Discourse and Dialogue', in Sidney Anglo, ed., *The Damned Art: Essays in the Literature of Witchcraft* (London, 1977).

Judith Maltby, *Prayer Book and People in Elizabethan and Early Stuart England* (Cambridge, 1998).

Ronald Marchant, *The Church under the Law: Justice, Administration and Discipline in the Diocese of York, 1560–1640* (Cambridge, 1969).

Christopher Marsh, '"Departing Well and Christianly": Will-Making and Popular Religion in Early Modern England', in Eric Carlson, ed., *Religion and the English People 1500–1640* (Kirksville, MO, 1998).

Peter Marshall, *The Face of the Pastoral Ministry in the East Riding, 1525–1595* (York, 1995); 'Discord and Stability in an Elizabethan Parish: John Otes and Carnaby, 1563–1600', *Yorkshire Archaeological Journal*, 71 (1999); 'Old Mother Leakey and the Golden Chain: Context and Meaning in an Early Stuart Haunting', in John Newton, ed., *Early Modern Ghosts* (Durham, 2002).

Julia Merritt, 'Puritans, Laudians, and the Phenomenon of Church-Building in Jacobean London', *Historical Journal*, 41 (1998).

Margaret Spufford, 'Can We Count the "Godly" and the "Conformable" in the Seventeenth Century?', *Journal of Ecclesiastical History*, 36 (1985).

Alexandra Walsham, '"The Fatall Vesper": Providentialism and Anti-Popery in Late Jacobean London', *Past and Present*, 144 (1994); *Providence in Early Modern England* (Oxford, 1999).

Tessa Watt, *Cheap Print and Popular Piety, 1550–1640* (Cambridge, 1991).

7. Catholics in Protestant England

J.C.H. Aveling, *The Handle and the Axe: The Catholic Recusants in England from Reformation to Emancipation* (London, 1976).

John Bossy, 'The Character of Elizabethan Catholicism', in Trevor Aston, ed., *Crisis in Europe 1560–1660* (London, 1965); 'The English Catholic Community 1603–1625', in Alan G.R. Smith, ed., *The Reign of James VI and I* (Basingstoke, 1973); *The English Catholic Community 1570–1850* (London, 1975).

Michael Carafiello, 'English Catholicism and the Jesuit Mission of 1580–81', *Historical Journal*, 37 (1994).

Anne Dillon, *The Construction of Martyrdom in the English Catholic Community 1535–1603 (*Aldershot, 2002).
Alan Dures, *English Catholicism 1558–1642* (Harlow, 1983).
Antonia Fraser, *The Gunpowder Plot: Terror and Faith in 1605* (London, 1996).
Christopher Haigh, 'From Monopoly to Minority: Catholicism in Early Modern England', *Transactions of the Royal Historical Society*, 5th ser. 31 (1981); 'Revisionism, the Reformation, and the History of English Catholicism', *Journal of Ecclesiastical History*, 36 (1985).
Caroline Hibbard, 'Early Stuart Catholicism: Revisions and Re-Revisions', *Journal of Modern History*, 52 (1980).
Peter Lake and Michael Questier, 'Agency, Appropriation and Rhetoric under the Gallows: Puritans, Romanists and the State in Early Modern England', *Past and Present*, 153 (1996); 'Prisons, Priests and People', in Nicholas Tyacke, ed., *England's Long Reformation 1500–1800* (London, 1998).
Roger Manning, *Religion and Society in Elizabethan Sussex* (Leicester, 1969).
David Marcombe, 'A Rude and Heady People: The Local Community and the Rebellion of the Northern Earls', in id., ed., *The Last Principality: Religion and Society in the Bishopric of Durham 1494–1660* (Nottingham, 1987).
Thomas McCoog, *The Society of Jesus in Ireland, Scotland, and England 1541–1588* (Leiden, 1996).
Patrick McGrath, *Papists and Puritans under Elizabeth I* (London, 1967); 'Elizabethan Catholicism: a Reconsideration', *Journal of Ecclesiastical History*, 35 (1984); and Joy Rowe, 'The Marian Priests under Elizabeth I', *Recusant History*, 17 (1984–5); 'The Imprisonment of Catholics for Religion under Elizabeth I', *Recusant History*, 20 (1991).
Anthony Milton, 'A Qualified Intolerance: the Limits and Ambiguities of Early Stuart Anti-Catholicism', in Arthur Marotti, *Catholicism and Anti-Catholicism in Early Modern English Texts* (Basingstoke, 1999).
Michael Mullett, *Catholics in Britain and Ireland 1558–1829* (Basingstoke, 1998).
Edward Norman, *Roman Catholicism in England from the Elizabethan Settlement to the Second Vatican Council* (Oxford, 1986).
Arnold Pritchard, *Catholic Loyalism in Elizabethan England* (London, 1979).
Michael Questier, *Conversion, Politics and Religion in England, 1580–1625* (Cambridge, 1996); 'The Politics of Religious Conformity and the Accession of James I', *Historical Research*, 71 (1998).
Marie Rowlands, 'Recusant Women 1560–1640', in Mary Prior, ed., *Women in English Society 1500–1800* (London, 1985); ed., *English Catholics of Parish and Town 1558–1778* (Catholic Record Society, 1999).

W.J. Sheils, 'Catholics and their Neighbours in a Rural Community: Egton Chapelry 1590–1780', *Northern History*, 25 (1998).
Alison Shell, *Catholicism, Controversy and the English Literary Imagination, 1558–1660* (Cambridge, 1999).
Alexandra Walsham, *Church Papists: Catholicism, Conformity and Confessional Polemic in Early Modern England* (Woodbridge, 1993).
Alexandra Walsham, '"Domme Preachers"? Post-Reformation English Catholicism and the Culture of Print', *Past and Present*, 168 (2000).

8. Charles I's Reformation

George Bernard, 'The Church of England, c. 1529–c. 1642', *History*, 75 (1990).
Robin Clifton, 'Fear of Popery', in Conrad Russell, ed., *The Origins of the English Civil War* (London, 1973).
David Cressy, 'Conflict, Consensus, and the Willingness to Wink: The Erosion of Community in Charles I's England', *Huntington Library Quarterly*, 61 (1998); *Travesties and Transgressions in Tudor and Stuart England* (Oxford, 2000); 'The Protestation Protested 1641 and 1642', *Historical Journal*, 45 (2002).
Julian Davies, *The Caroline Captivity of the Church: Charles I and the Remoulding of Anglicanism 1625–1641* (Oxford, 1992).
Kenneth Fincham, ed., *The Early Stuart Church, 1603–1642* (Basingstoke, 1993); 'William Laud and the Exercise of Caroline Ecclesiastical Patronage', *Journal of Ecclesiastical History*, 51 (2000); 'The Restoration of Altars in the 1630s', *Historical Journal*, 44 (2001).
Andrew Foster, 'Church Policies of the 1630s', in Richard Cust and Ann Hughes, eds., *Conflict in Early Stuart England* (London, 1989).
Ian Green, '"England's Wars of Religion?" Religious Conflict and the English Civil Wars', in J. van den Berg and P.G. Hoftijzer, eds., *Church, Change and Revolution* (Leiden, 1991).
Caroline Hibbard, *Charles I and the Popish Plot* (Chapel Hill, NC, 1983).
Ann Hughes, *The Causes of the English Civil War* (Basingstoke, 1991).
Peter Lake, 'Puritanism, Arminianism and a Shropshire Axe-Murder', *Midland History*, 15 (1990).
William Lamont, 'Richard Baxter, "Popery" and the Origins of the English Civil War', *History*, 87 (2002).
Christopher Marsh, 'Sacred Space in England, 1560–1640: The View from the Pew', *Journal of Ecclesiastical History*, 53 (2002).
Anthony Milton, *Catholic and Reformed: The Roman and Protestant Churches in English Protestant Thought 1600–1640* (Cambridge, 1995).
Conrad Russell, *The Causes of the English Civil War* (Oxford, 1990); 'The Reformation and the Creation of the Church of England 1500–1640', in John Morrill, ed., *The Oxford Illustrated History of Tudor and Stuart Britain* (Oxford, 1996).

Darren Oldridge, *Religion and Society in Early Stuart England* (Aldershot, 1998).

Jonathan Scott, *England's Troubles: Seventeenth-Century English Political Instability in European Context* (Cambridge, 2000).

Kevin Sharpe, *The Personal Rule of Charles I* (New Haven and London, 1992).

David L. Smith, 'Catholic, Anglican or Puritan? Edward Sackville, Fourth Earl of Dorset and the Ambiguities of Religion in Early Stuart England', *Transactions of the Royal Historical Society*, 6th ser., 2 (1992).

Margaret Stieg, *Laud's Laboratory: the Diocese of Bath and Wells in the Early Seventeenth Century* (East Brunswick, NJ, 1982).

Nicholas Tyacke, 'Puritanism, Arminianism and Counter-Revolution', in Conrad Russell, ed., *The Origins of the English Civil War* (London, 1973); *Anti-Calvinists: The Rise of English Arminianism c. 1590–1640* (Oxford, 1987); *Aspects of English Protestantism, c. 1530–1700* (Manchester, 2001).

David Underdown, *Revel, Riot and Rebellion: Popular Politics and Culture in England 1603–1660* (Oxford, 1985).

Alexandra Walsham, 'The Parochial Roots of Laudianism Revisited: Catholics, Anti-Calvinists and "Parish Anglicans" in Early Stuart England', *Journal of Ecclesiastical History*, 49 (1998).

John Walter, 'Anti-Popery and the Stour Valley Riots of 1642', in David Chadd, ed., *Religious Dissent in East Anglia* (Norwich, 1996); 'Confessional Politics in Pre-Civil War Essex: Prayer Books, Profanations, and Petitions', *Historical Journal*, 44 (2001).

Tom Webster, *Godly Clergy in Early Stuart England* (Cambridge, 1997).

Index